"Super."

—*The Biloxi Sun Herald*

"What Pistol Pete was to the no-look, 50-foot bounce pass Kriegel may be to the sports biography: transcendent."

—*Booklist*, starred review

"Terrifically well researched."

—*Deseret Morning News* (Salt Lake City)

"Kriegel gives voice to those moments of flight and daring, the high personal cost of devotion to a sport . . . energetic, fast-moving."

—*The Times Picayune* (New Orleans)

"Haunting."

—*Evansville Courier & Press*

"Kriegel captures the essence of Maravich . . . It's a tragic story, to be sure, but a compelling one that Kriegel tells so very well."

—John Perrotto, *The Times*
(Beaver County, Pennsylvania)

"A touching, incredibly sad portrait of Pete and his father, Press, and how attached they were at the heart . . . immaculate research."

—Jim Huber, HOFMAG.com

"Terrific . . . Just as Maravich's electrifying moves captivated millions on the basketball court, Kriegel's narrative will captivate readers."

—*The Vindicator* (Ohio)

"Kriegel's book will . . . lead you to places you would not otherwise find. It tells a story—some of it recorded and some of it forgotten, some of it exhilarating and some of it devastatingly sad. It is a story about a father and a son, about vanity, about commitment, about vision, about obsession.

—*American Srbobran*

"Kriegel's *Pistol* is different than the slew of other biographies aimed at the Pistol because all the stories in the perfectly chronological book are firsthand accounts from those who knew Pete Maravich best."
—*Tiger Weekly*

"*Pistol* is a classic American tale wonderfully told. With deep research and a vivid narrative style, Mark Kriegel brings us the joy and sorrow of Pete Maravich, an inimitable basketball player who was both timeless and before his time, an original talent haunted by demons—his father's and his own."
—David Maraniss, author of *Clemente: The Passion and Grace of Baseball's Last Hero*

"*Pistol* is not just a biography of a transcendent, doomed athlete; it is a mesmerizing tale of a striving, grasping American family as dramatic as myth, of a father and son as intertwined as Daedalus and Icarus. Kriegel has written the rarest of sports books: a fast-paced, through-the-night page-turner. This isn't a slam dunk, it's a tomahawk glass-shatterer. *Pistol* is nothing but sensational."
—Rick Telander, author of *Heaven Is a Playground* and senior sports columnist, *Chicago Sun-Times*

"Pistol Pete's moves on the basketball court defied the laws of physics. He did things you can't even film. He deserves a biographer with magic powers of his own, and he's found one in Mark Kriegel."
—Will Blythe, author of *To Hate Like This Is to Be Happy Forever*

fP

PISTOL

THE LIFE OF PETE MARAVICH

MARK KRIEGEL

FREE PRESS
New York London Toronto Sydney

FREE PRESS
A Division of Simon & Schuster, Inc.
1230 Avenue of the Americas
New York, NY 10020

First Free Press trade paperback edition February 2008.

FREE PRESS and colophon are trademarks of Simon & Schuster, Inc.

For information regarding special discounts for bulk purchases,
please contact Simon & Schuster Special Sales:
1-800-456-6798 or business@simonandschuster.com

Manufactured in the United States of America

1   3   5   7   9   10   8   6   4   2

The Library of Congress has cataloged the hardcover edition as follows:

Kriegel, Mark
Pistol : the life of Pete Maravich/Mark Kriegel.
p.   cm.
Includes bibliographical references and index.
1. Maravich, Pete, 1947–1988. 2. Basketball players—United States—Biography. I. Title.
GV884.M3K75 2007
796.357092—dc22
[B]
2006051526

ISBN-13: 978-0-7432-8497-4
ISBN-10:   0-7432-8497-6
ISBN-13: 978-0-7432-8498-1 (pbk)
ISBN-10:   0-7432-8498-4 (pbk)

Amid all this talk of fathers and sons,
it was a daughter who saved me:
This book is for Holiday Mia Kriegel

CONTENTS

CONTENTS

Listen to me, eyes of mine, guard that which is thine.
Father to son,
in a Serbian folk song

The radio was playing and the morning news was on. I was startled to hear that Pete Maravich, the basketball player, had collapsed on a basketball court in Pasadena, just fell over and never got up. I'd seen Maravich play in New Orleans, when the Utah Jazz were the New Orleans Jazz. He was something to see—mop of brown hair, floppy socks—the holy terror of the basketball world—high flyin'—magician of the court . . . He could have played blind.

Bob Dylan,
from the first volume
of his autobiography,
Chronicles

PISTOL

Previous pages: January 31, 1970: Pete Maravich moments after becoming college basketball's all-time leading scorer. At left, with the crewcut, is his father, Press. AP Wirephoto

PROLOGUE

January 5, 1988.

They cannot see him, this slouched, ashen-faced man in their midst. To their oblivious eyes, he remains what he had been, unblemished by the years, much as he appeared on his first bubblegum card: a Beatlesque halo of hair, the fresh-faced, sad-eyed wizard cradling a grainy, leather orb.

One of the regulars, a certified public accountant, had retrieved this very artifact the night before. He found it in a shoebox, tucked away with an old train set and a wooden fort in a crawlspace in his parents' basement. He brought it to the gym this morning to have it signed, or perhaps, in some way, sanctified. The 1970 rookie card of Pete Maravich, to whom the Atlanta Hawks had just awarded the richest contract in professional sport, notes the outstanding facts: that Maravich had been coached by his father, under whose tutelage he became "the most prolific scorer in the history of college basketball."

Other salient statistics are provided in agate type: an average of 44.2 points a game, a total of 3,667 (this when nobody had scored 3,000). The records will never be broken. Still, they are woefully inadequate in measuring the contours of the Maravich myth.

Even the CPA, for whom arithmetic is a vocation, understands the limitation in mere numbers. There is no integer denoting magic or memory. "He was important to us," the accountant would say.

Maravich wasn't an archetype; he was several: child prodigy, prodigal son, his father's ransom in a Faustian bargain. He was a creature of contradictions, ever alone: the white hope of a black sport, a virtuoso stuck in an ensemble, an exuberant showman who couldn't look you in the eye, a vegetarian boozer, the athlete who lived like a rock star, a profligate, suicidal genius saved by Jesus Christ.

Still, it's his caricature that evokes unqualified affection in men of a certain age. *Pistol Pete,* they called him. The Pistol is another relic of the seventies, not unlike bongs or Bruce Lee flicks: the skinny kid who mesmerized the basketball world with Globetrotter moves, floppy socks, and great hair.

Pistol Pete was, in fact, his father's vision, built to the old man's exacting specifications. Press Maravich was a Serb. Ideas and language occurred to him in the mother tongue, and so one imagines him speaking to Pistol (yes, that's what he called him, too) as a father addressing his son in an old Serbian song: *Cuj me sine oci moje, Cuvaj ono sto je tvoje . . . Listen to me, eyes of mine, guard that which is thine . . .*

The game in progress is a dance in deference to this patrimony. The Pistol is an inheritance, not just for the Maraviches, but for all the American sons who play this American game. The squeak of sneakers against the floor produces an oddly chirping melody. Then there's another rhythm, the respiration of men well past their prime, an assortment of white guys: the accountant, insurance salesmen, financial planners, even a preacher or two. "Just a bunch of duffers," recalls one. "Fat old men," smirks another.

But they play as if Pistol Pete, or what's left of him, could summon the boys they once were. They acknowledge him with a superfluous flourish, vestigial teenage vanity—an extra behind-the-back pass or an unnecessary between-the-legs dribble. The preacher, a gentle-voiced man of great renown in evangelical circles, reveals a feverishly competitive nature. After hitting a shot, he is heard to bellow, "You get that on camera?"

The Parker Gymnasium at Pasadena's First Church of the Nazarene could pass for a good high school gym—a clean, cavernous space with arching wooden rafters and large windows. At dawn, fully energized halogen lamps give off a glow to the outside world, a beacon to spirits searching for a game. As a boy, Maravich would have considered this a kind of heaven. Now, it's a way station of sorts.

Pete begins wearily. He hasn't played in a long time and moves at one-quarter speed, if that. He does not jump; he shuffles. The ball seems like a shotput in his hands, his second attempt at the basket barely touching the front of the rim.

But gradually, as the pace of his breath melds with the others' and he starts to sweat, Pete Maravich recovers something in himself. "The glimpse of greatness was in his ballhandling," recalls the accountant. "Every once in a while the hands would flicker. There would just be some kind of dribble or something. You could see a little of it in his hands, the greatness. Just the quickness of the beat."

There was genius in that odd beat, the unexpected cadence, a measure of music. The Pistol's talent, now as then, was musical. He was as fluent as Mozart—his game rising to the level of language—but he was sold like Elvis, the white guy performing in a black idiom. And for a time, he was mad like Elvis, too.

Once, in an attempt to establish contact with extraterrestrial life, he painted a message on his roof: "Take me."

Deliver me, he meant.

Now the accountant tries to blow past Pete with a nifty spin move. Pete tells him not to believe his own hype.

The Pistol wears an easy grin. The men in this game are avid readers of the Bible. But perhaps the truth of this morning is to be found in the Koran: "Remember that the life of this world is but a sport and a pastime."

Pete banks one in.

That smile again. What a goof.

The game ends. Guys trudge off to the water fountain. Pete continues to shoot around.

And now, you wonder what he sees. Was it as he used to imagine? "The space will open up," he once said. "Beyond that will be heaven and when you go inside, then the space closes again and you are there . . . definitely a wonderful place . . . everyone you ever knew will be there."

Back on earth, the preacher asks Pete Maravich how he feels.

"I feel great," he says.

●   ●   ●

Soon the phone will ring in Covington, Louisiana. A five-year-old boy hears the maid let out a sharp piercing howl. Then big old Irma quickly ushers the boy and his brother into another room. The boy closes the door behind him and considers himself in the mirror. He has his father's eyes. That's what everyone says. *Eyes of mine, guard that which is thine.* Guard that which fathers give to their sons to give to their sons.

The boy looks through himself, and he knows:

"My daddy's dead."

1. Special Opportunity

Press Maravich, then fourteen years old, can be seen in the 1929 *Condor*, yearbook of the Aliquippa, Pennsylvania, school district. He appears on page 48, on the far right, in a photograph of "Mrs. Thompson's Special Opportunity Group." One needs a mere glance to know that such opportunity was a euphemistic term as applied to the thirty-nine children in Catherine Thompson's custody. Most conspicuous is the large girl extending her arms downward, her hands in front of her dress, as if she were waiting to be handcuffed. Then there's the girl in the front row, her head tilted at an unnatural angle. And what of the odd sway through the torso of that boy in his ill-fitting suit? The faces are bewildered, quizzical, disconnected. There is, however, a notable exception.

His windbreaker is unbuttoned, his collar open, hands resting casually in his pockets. Chances are, the Maravich boy is hiding a wad of chew in his mouth. But his expression is striking—the unmistakable smirk of the luckless, as if he alone understands the inexorable course of what lies ahead, the Special Opportunity Group's manifest destiny.

The look is defiantly grim. The eyes announce what the mouth does not:

"I'm fucked."

He was the youngest child born to Sara and Vajo Maravich, of Pittsburgh's South Side by way of Dreznica, a fallow, rocky Serbian town in the Croatian province of Lika. The oldest, Milan, was seven months when he died on February 28, 1909. Twin girls, Marija and Marta, each died in April 1910. They were six months old. Velamir was only five days when he passed away, September 5, 1913. A year and a day later, Petar, the boy who'd be known as Press, was baptized at St. George, the Serbian Orthodox church on 25th Street.

Pittsburgh's industrial boroughs like the South Side were dominated by steel mills. It would be argued that "the soundest material measure of our potency as a nation . . . is our capacity to produce steel ingots." But the making of steel could also unmake a man's spirit. James Parton, writing for the *Atlantic*, famously described Pittsburgh as "hell with the lid taken off." "Six months residence here would justify suicide," Britain's eminent philosopher Herbert Spencer once told his host, Andrew Carnegie.

The production of steel consumed flesh and blood with the same regularity as it did iron ore and limestone. Typical was the night of March 11, 1918, when the driver of a Dinkey engine was killed in a collision with a railroad car near the No. 1 Open Hearth Mill at Jones & Laughlin's Southside Works. F. L. Thigpen, M.D., attending physician at South Side Hospital, listed the cause of death as "shock and hemorrhage as a result of partial amputation of Rt. Lower extremity and internal abdominal injury." The deceased was identified by his next-door neighbor, Theodore Tatalovich, his *seljac*, a friend for twenty years going back to their days in Dreznica. On March 28, a six-man coroner's jury ruled the death accidental. The coroner's report refers to the dead man by his Anglicized given name: Alex. He was thirty-nine, married, and father of a three-and-a-half-year-old son, Press Maravich.

There is no way to gauge the boy's emotional trauma, or if it had any bearing on his eventual designation as a member of Mrs. Thompson's Special Opportunity Group. Sara Maravich soon remarried, to a man named Djuro Kosanovich. He had arrived in the United States on December 4, 1913. Like Vajo Maravich, he, too, hailed from Dreznica and worked for Jones & Laughlin. Djuro went five-nine, 250 pounds, with a big jowly face and a flattop haircut. He was a gruff man, known to be an enthusiastic consumer of beer and whiskey following his mill shift. After drinking too much, he would make a whinnying noise, like a horse.

Sara Kosanovich, as she was now known, bore him two sons, Sam in 1919 and Marko two years later. In 1925, they moved to Aliquippa, about eighteen miles north of Pittsburgh on the west bank of the Ohio River. Named after a fabled Seneca Indian queen, Aliquippa was supposed to be a model for American industry, an answer for all that ailed Pittsburgh.

"We want to make it the best possible place for a steelworker to raise a family," William Larimer Jones, J&L's vice president and general manager, said on his company town's inception.

Little distinction, however, was drawn between the interests of these families and The Family, as the firm's ruling scions were called. Aliquippa was more than another company town; it was a massive social experiment, testing the limits of paternalism and conformity. As a condition of employment, J&L workers were expected to register and vote Republican. Unionization was forbidden. "In our town, they had a system of spying that made the KGB look like schoolchildren," recalled Joseph Perriello, who would help organize workers in the thirties. Informants were plentiful—on every block, in the churches and the bars and the social clubs. Unflattering reports could result in a visit from a local constable, typically skilled in the use of a billy club. The Aliquippa Police Department was, in effect, a subsidiary of J&L—not much different from wholly owned subsidiaries like the Woodlawn Water Company or the Woodlawn Land Company.

Woodlawn Land was The Family's agent in developing Aliquippa. The town was laid out per a series of twelve "Plans." The north end of town, Plans 1 and 2, included an area long known as Logstown, where Queen Aliquippa once waited impatiently for George Washington. Now it was for different settlers: Serbs, Croatians, and some Italians. Plan 3, for example, housed Germans, Irish, and English. Senior management, known as "cake eaters," lived in Plan 6. Plan 7 was Slovaks, Ukrainians, and Poles. Plan 8 had skilled workers from northern Europe. Plan 10 was midlevel supervisors. Plan 11 was home to Poles and blacks, known as colored. The company was beneficent enough to build a separate pool for the colored families.

The boss of the town was the company superintendent, Tom Girdler. "When I recall how well we realized the vision of The Family," he wrote, "I am proud to have had a part in the making of Aliquippa."

Girdler's pride in what he himself termed a "benevolent dictatorship" apparently blinded him to the town's less benevolent side; the thriving assortment of speakeasies, whorehouses, and gambling dens. In 1918, four years into Girdler's reign, a state supreme court justice wrote of Aliquippa, "It is said that the region is largely peopled by uneducated foreigners who invariably carry concealed weapons; that murders are common; and that when a quarrel ensues, the question as to who shall be the murderer and who is murdered is largely, if not wholly, determined by the ability to draw such a weapon quickly."

What's more, Aliquippa was a cruelty to behold. Leaving Pittsburgh by rail to the east, H. L. Mencken once declared the surrounding areas "the most loathsome towns and villages ever seen by mortal eye." And though Aliquippa was west of the big city, it would not have disappointed Mencken, as his assessment was based on "unbroken and agonizing ugliness."

J&L's Aliquippa Works stretched for seven and a half relentless miles, bordered on one side by the Ohio River and on the other by the Pennsylvania and Lake Erie Railroad. Deposits of raw materials by the rail yards formed mountain ranges of limestone, iron ore, and coal to go with the towering gray heaps of by-product called slag. As the engine picked up steam again, dishes and windows would rattle in nearby homes, such as the one on 117 Iron Street.

That's where the Kosanovich family, along with the Maravich boy, had settled. Their home, at the bottom of a hill overlooking the steel works, sat at the eastern edge of Plan 2, as close as one could live to the source of the "agonizing ugliness." From Iron Street, the assortment of furnaces—blast furnaces, open hearths, and Bessemers—looked close enough to touch.

"Plan 2 was the least desirable," recalls Milo Kosanovich, a nephew of Djuro. "It was closest to the railroads and the mill. The homes were just thrown in there, all duplexes and boarding houses. Everybody just stacked as close to the mill as possible."

Porches had to be swept, usually twice a day, to clear them of the "black sugar," a granular soot that blew in from the blast furnaces. To stroll down Iron Street was to feel the black sugar crunch under your feet. To look toward the heavens was to see a flaming orange sky. The Bessemer furnaces, pear-shaped vessels resembling squat cannons, would tilt and blow, a colossal bonfire.

People would come from all over to bear witness to this illumination. In neighboring villages, native Aliquippans would hear, "Hey, look, your town's on fire." The constant glow made it difficult to tell day from night.

Down on Hopewell Avenue, near the Logstown Elementary School, boys like Press would play past dusk bathed in the Bessemer light. The kids from Logstown were considered the most aggressive and competitive in all of Aliquippa. "I've often wondered," says former Aliquippan Sharon Danovich, "what that did to men like Press and my father. What was it like to grow up under an orange sky?"

"I will always remember the phrase: As the Bessemer glows, so will Aliquippa go," says Lazo Maravich, Press's close friend and next-door neighbor. "As long as the Bessemer was spouting flame and ash, you knew there would be jobs. It was a beacon. The course of life for most people was pretty well predetermined."

The furnace lit a route toward the inevitable, a destination for fathers and their sons and their sons' sons. Boys would ask each other, "Where you going after high school?" But it wasn't a question, as the answer was almost always the same: "Through the tunnel."

The tunnel was in fact a viaduct, an echo chamber separating Franklin Avenue and the mill. A young man trudging through for the first time could hear what the rest of his life would sound like.

In the meantime, boys like Lazo and Press amused themselves as best they could. They were the same age, of the same clan, their fathers being Maraviches of Dreznica. To the English speakers and cake eaters they described themselves as cousins. But in fact, Lazo was closer to a brother. Certainly, he was closer to Press than his step-brothers.

Mary Cribbs, formerly Mary Yovich of Iron Street, recalls Press as "the only one on the block who didn't have any brothers or sisters." When asked about the Kosanovich boys, Marko and Sam, she says, "No *real* brothers or sisters."

There was always a distance between Press and the Kosanoviches. Sara, mother to all the boys, was a fine cook. She could make beans and sauerkraut taste like manna. She could transform cabbage, potatoes, and just a little meat into big, hearty pots of soup. But she was not an assertive woman, and she could not bridge the gap between her past and present families.

Djuro Kosanovich had taken in her son, but did not embrace him. "I don't think the relationship was a very good one," says Helen Kosanovich, who would marry Marko.

"There was no relationship," according to a neighbor, Sarah Kostal. Asked if Press—the only one in that house with a different surname—ever thought of himself as a Kosanovich, she emphatically declared, "Never."

Apparently, the feeling was mutual. When he filed his petition for U.S. citizenship, Djuro Kosanovich declared two children, Marko and Sam, but made no mention of Press.

As first-generation Americans, Press and Lazo were caught between old customs and new ways. In search of Old World respectability, they were given music lessons: banjo for Press, the violin for Lazo. But the boys were ashamed of the instruments. They wanted to play *games*, a form of endeavor that men of the old country could never understand. They played football and mushball (like softball but with a bigger, spongier ball) and Buck Buck (also known as Johnny on a Pony). They played a makeshift version of basketball, nailing a bushel basket to a tree and wrapping rags around a rubber ball.

"No one had a real football or basketball," Lazo recalls. "No one ever bought a toy. Everything was homespun."

In winter, they'd warm themselves over a sewer. Or maybe they'd build a fire and loaf by the railroad tracks until the cops came to roust them. "We spent a lot of time on those damn tracks," says Lazo.

They'd sneak back from their music lessons along the tracks, lest any of their Logstown cronies see them carrying those sissified instruments. At night, they'd climb the rungs on the side of the railcars, throw down a ration of coal, and sprint home with it. "It wasn't like we were trying to beat the company out of a little coal," says Lazo. "It wasn't mischief. It was for our families. Men were making 33 cents an hour. When it came to the family's survival, everybody had a piece of the action."

They were chewing tobacco before they had passed through puberty. Most kids chewed Copenhagen snuff. Not Press, though. He chewed Mail Pouch, incessantly. Press had his own ideas—quite a lot of them, in fact. Nor was he shy about expressing them. It was alleged, facetiously, that the boy baptized Petar had more news than the *Pittsburgh Press*. That's how he got the name Press.

Unfortunately, the wisdom of his many passionately held opinions was lost on his teachers. "He was designated a slow learner, slow in reading," says Lazo, who, looking back, wonders if Press might have been dyslexic. Or, perhaps, a victim of neglect? All these years later, the recollection makes Lazo Maravich burn: "He was stigmatized. He was discarded. They threw him in the junk heap."

So much for the Special Opportunity he had been granted as a member of Catherine Thompson's class. Even his highest aspirations left nothing to the imagination. He was seen as a fatherless dimwit who passed the time under an orange sky. It would be his great good fortune to one day go through the tunnel and dodge beads of splashing molten metal. Of course, this wasn't news to Press. He knew that much by Picture Day 1929.

That same year Mr. and Mrs. Ernest Anderton came to run the Logstown Mission, a white-frame former Lutheran church at the corner of Iron and Phillips Streets. Mr. Anderton, an insurance agent from Beaver Falls by way of Great Britain, was a lay worker for the Presbytery of Beaver County.

"Anderton got to the youth," says Mary Cribbs. "He wanted them to know the Lord and keep off the streets."

"He was a lean guy with a good mop of hair and a gimpy arm—a good human being in every sense," says Lazo Maravich, a lifelong Aliquippan. "He didn't want us getting mixed up with the gambling or the drinking or any of that."

Logstown might have been poor, but it was rich with young souls to be saved. And Anderton's Mission, a beneficiary of the J&L Family's largesse, offered a range of inducements to bring young people closer to that end. With the Depression under way, there was a soup line for adults and graham crackers with milk for the kids. Sometimes, there was even ice cream.

"I was embarrassed," recalls Lazo, who was nevertheless too hungry to refuse.

Mrs. Anderton taught the girls how to sew. Boys would gather in the game room for Tiddly Winks and Ping-Pong, about which Mr. Anderton was a great enthusiast. Wednesday night was Christian Endeavor Night, with a slide show depicting biblical scenes.

But the single most powerful enticement was a basketball court in the Mission's main room. It was of modest dimension, perhaps 50 feet long and half as wide. The boys played where they prayed. The podium, the pews, and chairs were moved aside (in stark contrast to St. Elijah, the Serbian church, there were no icons or ornate gold Orthodox crosses). The floor underneath had been marked with foul lines and boundaries. It was a plane of good, level wood, not dirt or pocked pavement. You didn't have to worry about crashing into the metal rungs of a lightpole. The ball was made of leather, a proper basketball, not a bundle of rags. No need for a bushel basket, either.

"Real baskets with a net, rims, a wooden backboard, the whole thing," Press would recall. "And when we saw those baskets in the church it was like a professional hall to us. It was so exciting, a real thrill."

If the devil could barter for souls, then so could Ernest Anderton. Here was the deal: The boys could play all they wanted as long as they attended Sunday school.

And so did Press become suddenly devout. He sang psalms and

read his Bible and went to Sunday school. "He'd do anything to get a basketball in his hands, anything for another couple of hours playing ball in that Mission," says Lazo. "That drove him. Basketball became his life."

Why or how the game touched Press Maravich is another mystery of faith. But the effects were plain to see. The game—something about its rhythms and geometry—unleashed his body and unlocked his brain, his talent, his charisma. His devotion was obsessive, curative, and, finally, emancipating.

The beat of the game was a hymn in his ears, Press's *Ode to Joy*.

Unlike some of the other kids at the Mission, Press Maravich was never moved to utter a Confession of Faith, accepting Jesus Christ as his Lord and savior.

A savior he had found. But it wasn't Jesus Christ.

2. Mr. Basketball

Basket ball was invented in 1891 by James A. Naismith. Recently graduated from Montreal's Presbyterian Theological Seminary, Naismith was a physical education instructor at the International YMCA Training School in Springfield, Massachusetts, when he received a directive from the head of the department, Dr. Luther Gulick. It seemed that a class of eighteen, most of them football and rugby players, was bored to the point of distraction. "Those boys simply would not play drop the handkerchief," Naismith recalled.

He was given fourteen days to conceive of a diversion that could be played indoors, under artificial light, a game that required physical vigor but prohibited actual violence. On December 21, Naismith posted the thirteen original rules on two typewritten sheets before presiding over the game's inaugural scrimmage, an affair that witnessed a single score on a 25-foot toss.

"The game grew astonishingly quickly thereafter, thanks largely to the far-flung travels of Training School graduates and Naismith's genial willingness to share his rules with anyone showing interest," wrote Alexander Wolff, in a celebration of the game's first 100 years. "In addition, despite all Naismith's precautions, many Y's considered the sport to be too rough, and incipient teams banned from Y's found new homes in Masonic temples, dance halls and gymnasiums bounded by chicken wire that came to be known as cages. [Hence the term 'cagers.'] This introduced the game to even more people. Most fundamentally, however, basketball grew because there was a need for a simple, indoor wintertime game."

Naismith brought the new sport west when he accepted a faculty position at the University of Kansas. In the Midwest, companies devoted to the manufacture of rubber or ball bearings sponsored teams and leagues. Suddenly, gyms sprang up in barns in rural Indiana. Teeming urban slums, lacking anything resembling playing fields, proved to be especially fertile ground for the do-gooders who doubled as basketball's first messengers.

Still, by the time Ernest Anderton put a ball in Press's hands, the game remained in its infancy—a slow, almost static affair. The fixed plays did not allow for much improvisation. The ball moved from station to station. Then again, basketball was not so different from other facets of American life in that players knew their places. Guards remained in the backcourt, forwards on the wings, and the center in the middle. Every basket was followed by a tip-off back at center court.

Lazo and Press played their first organized ball for a Mission team, the Daniel Boys, so named for the biblical tamer of lions. And though the court was cramped, Mary Cribbs recalls that "the place was just jammed when they had the games."

That would have been the first time Press heard a chorus of praise. Such adoration made the game even more intoxicating. "Press was unique in his dedication and love for basketball," says Lazo. "He would eat, drink, speak, and sing basketball. He felt, innately, that this was the thing he could do well. It was *his* game and he played it with all his heart and soul. Oh, how he worked at it. He was always bouncing the ball, practicing his set shot. Once he got set and he got his eyes on the basket, you could start ringing them up."

The Daniel Boys played other church teams, winning more often than not. They were, after all, from Logstown. Press would call plays and bark orders in Serbian, leaving the cake eaters and others dumbfounded. He was then what he would always be. Even as a kid, Press could detect the physical tendency in an opponent. Was his weight on his heels? Was he leaning left or right?

He wasn't much for reading or writing, but he had an intuitive understanding of the game's geometry—lines charted against time—for the path that brought him closest and quickest to the basket. As the boys assembled for the tip-off, Press might notice that his man was ready to lunge. *"Napira,"* he would whisper at the center. *Forward,* tip the ball *forward.* As his man pounced, Press would take the tip and break toward the basket for an easy score. In tempo and vision, Press was ahead of the game. Basketball was still about fixed positions, but Press's instinct was to run.

There was, however, a downside to playing with him. "He always wanted something more," recalls Lazo. "If he felt you had any more to give, he wouldn't hesitate about telling you where to get off."

As they became teenagers, it became clear that Lazo didn't have Press's gift for the game. But that didn't ease the ferocity of Press's expectation. He already thought that the greatest component of talent was desire. The greedy bastard always wanted more. How many times had Lazo turned to him with a kind of exasperation that bordered on surrender?

"I can't give you anymore than I have," he would say.

Neither Djuro nor Sara Kosanovich shared Press's passion or aspirations. Then, again, why should they have? This bouncing ball didn't pay the bills. It wasn't a job, merely an indulgence the Kosanoviches could ill afford. For a time, Press would leave for games in just his street clothes. His stepbrother Sam would then toss his uniform and gym bag out the window, where Press could retrieve it, his secret intact.

There was, however, an adult who understood basketball in the way Press thought of it: as a calling. Nate Lippe was born in Cleveland in 1901 and played at Geneva College in Beaver Falls, where he was an all-star quarterback. Football wasn't even his best sport, though. In 1924–25, as a senior on the basketball team, Lippe—a quick, crafty guard—averaged an astronomical figure, better than 16 points on a team that scored fewer than 30 a game. Upon graduation, Lippe had hoped to enroll at the University of Pittsburgh Medical School. But that institution had already filled its quota of Jews. Instead, he began playing basketball for money. He played for the Enoch Rauh and A. P. Moore clubs in the Allegheny County League, setting a record with 14 baskets against Jones Motors. In Ohio, he served the

East Liverpool Elks as a player-coach. The pro and semipro leagues were regional confederations. But the great teams were barnstormers, and Lippe saw action against many of them: the Cleveland Rosenblums, the Washington Palisades, the Carlisle Indians (featuring Jim Thorpe), and the SPHAs (an acronym for South Philadelphia Hebrew Association). Word was, he even turned down a gig with the best of all barnstorming outfits, the Original Celtics.

In 1928, he became a full-time coach at Aliquippa High School. In his first full season, Lippe inherited a 4–8 team with only one returning letterman. Nevertheless, aided by what the *Condor* yearbook called "a world of basketball science as his background," his inaugural season—beginning with a 15–14 win over Freedom—proved triumphal. The only blemish on Lippe's record, a 17–14 defeat, came against Moe Rubenstein's Ambridge club. Lippe and Rubinstein had been teammates at Geneva, with Moe succeeding him as the team captain. Rubenstein had even played for Lippe with the East Liverpool Elks. But now, as coaches, they would embark on a fierce rivalry.

In Aliquippa, there circulated a story—never proven—that Lippe had married Rubenstein's girl. The Ambridge version, just as unproven, had Rubenstein stealing Lippe's girlfriend. The only sure bet was that these men detested each other, and that their sentiments had been passed on to their charges.

"It was always very heated between us and them," recalls Chuck Belas, who played for Lippe in the 1930s. "The gyms were always packed, and things were pretty tense. Everybody played a little rougher when it was Aliquippa and Ambridge."

Lippe, slightly built at five-nine, could play rough himself. A team manager can remember a gang of juvenile delinquents from Plan 11 horsing around in the gym. Lippe told them to knock it off—but only once. "One guy kept giving him shit," says Paul Piccirilli, the student-manager, "and before I knew it Lippe just nailed him."

"He was tough," says Pecky Suder, a gifted Aliquippa athlete who went on to play thirteen seasons of Major League Baseball. "He made you feel afraid of him."

He achieved this authority without many words. Lippe was a taciturn man. His feelings and affections remained mysteries—except one. "My father didn't talk too much," recalls his son, Dr. Richard Lippe. "But his first love was basketball." Such love was expressed as a kind of orthodoxy. Lippe had strict prohibitions against hotdogging or freelancing. One didn't take the game in vain. Set shots were released with two hands. Foul shots were taken underhanded. The ball was to be passed, not dribbled. He eschewed any attempt at the running game in favor of set plays, a methodical scheme that placed a premium on ball control. If you wanted to play for Lippe, you went by the book. He was, in basketball terms, a fundamentalist.

But if a boy believed in the game, Lippe would believe in that boy—and none more so than Press Maravich.

In the last week of February 1933, Ambridge beat Aliquippa by a score of 20–16, clinching the Section IV Championship of the Western Pennsylvania Interscholastic Athletic League. It was the second time that season that Rubenstein's team, with a perfect 10–0 sectional record, had beaten their cross-river rival, which finished at 8–2. Lippe promptly filed a protest, charging that two of the Ambridge stars had played in tournament games with professional players the previous year, and that one of them, the league's leading scorer, exceeded the high school age limit.

The Decisions Committee, meeting at the Fort Pitt Hotel, wasted little time rejecting Lippe's protest. What the coach lacked even more than a case was a sense of irony. Lippe's most promising player, one of the few underclassmen he ever used, was already a regular in games with professionals. What's more, he was perilously close to the age limit himself.

Press's high school record is a sketchy one, with several years unaccounted for. After Mrs. Thompson's Special Opportunity Group, he was placed in a vocational program, a lower scholastic caste intended to warehouse young men until they were old enough to work in the mill. By his own account, Press couldn't wait that long and phonied up his papers to get hired at J&L, where he worked a midnight shift as a pipe threader. When he wasn't threading pipe, chances were he could be found traveling western Pennsylvania and eastern Ohio playing under the name "Peter Munnell" for as much as ten bucks a game.

By 1932, this Maravich/Munnell character had become everything Lippe sought in a player, beginning with his fierce desire. The problem was that the school's vocational designation made him ineligible for varsity competition. "I can safely say that," says Lazo Maravich, who went on to become superintendent of the Aliquippa School District. "But you have to understand there was a lot of manipulation in those days. Hell, there were grown men working in the mill playing high school football. When Nate Lippe found out that Press was in the trade prep program, he got him out. He wanted Press to be eligible for as long as possible. Exactly how he did it, I'm not sure. But Lippe devised a way."

"P. Maravich," a forward, begins showing up in the box scores of the *Aliquippa Gazette* and the Beaver Falls *News-Tribune* in early 1933. He led the team in scoring on several occasions and was mentioned among the section leaders in field goals. But it wasn't until the following season, 1933–34, that Press came into his own, not just as a ballplayer, but as a local celebrity. He was now about 6 feet tall, with an outstanding set shot. Girls were crazy for him. Not only had his charisma grown with his prowess as an athlete, but he looked like a movie star.

"You ever hear of the actor, Victor Mature?" says Milo Kosanovich. "Press looked just like him: big, good-looking guy with coal black hair."

By now, Djuro Kosanovich had moved his family a short distance to 418 Hopewell Avenue, into an attached home that no longer faced the mill. But Press spent less time there than he did at the home of Olga Michalak in Plan 7. "One hell of a good-looking blonde," says Lazo. Press might have been smitten with Olga, whose brother was a high school teammate, but his heart remained with the game. He wasn't like other young men. "He didn't loaf," says Sarah Kostal, a neighbor. "He wasn't interested in taverns or beer gardens. He didn't play dice or cards. He just had basketball on his mind."

The "Lippemen," as the newspapers referred to Aliquippa's varsity, were undefeated in section play before again losing to Ambridge.

Rubinstein's squad had fewer injuries and more firepower, including the league's leading scorer, Johnny Michelosen. "He played the pivot like Dutch Dehnert of the New York Celtics," says Lazo. "Press couldn't match his size or muscle."

Press had other attributes, though, which he put on full display over the next several weeks. After the following game against Beaver High the *Daily Times* noted that Maravich "completely outclassed the other contestants for scoring honors by piling up twenty-eight points in one game by one man, more points than have been seen by county fans in a good while."

In fact, 28 points was more than most teams scored. Three nights later, for example, Aliquippa held Freedom to 13 points. Press had 20. Next up, Monaca. "Maravich again proved unstoppable when he functioned smoothly for fifteen points," wrote the *News-Tribune*'s correspondent.

"If I got the ball, I gave it to Press," recalls Pecky Suder. "You couldn't go wrong throwing it to him. He could shoot from anywhere." Press would have agreed. There was an imperiousness to his game. He expected the ball, as if it were his. "You didn't want to make him mad," says Suder.

As it happened, Press finished as the county's leading scorer, with what the *Aliquippa Gazette* called "the stupendous total of 76 field goals" (Michelosen and his Ambridge teammate, Mike Winne, tied for second place with 50). The scoring title invigorated his already burgeoning reputation.

Just weeks after season's end, 1,200 fans packed the high school gym to watch an amateur tournament with teams sponsored by local merchants. "Press Maravich, Eger Jeweler ace, totaled 30 points in three games to lead all individual scorers," noted the *Gazette*. The boy from Mrs. Thompson's Special Opportunity Class had become a source of pride for Aliquippa. And it wasn't just the girls who were attracted to the player with movie star looks. Boys like Wally Zernich, who'd go on to play at Pitt, studied his game and copied his moves. "He shot that two-hand set shot with his feet spread apart," says Zernich. "Nobody else did that. Everybody kept their feet together. But Press was a master. He was Mr. Basketball. He was our hero."

The following season, with Press the only returning letterman, Lippe's team went 16–5. Among the losses was an upset to Butler. "The biggest cause of the Aliquippa defeat was an injury to Maravich," wrote the *Gazette*'s Ralph Hobbs, Press's personal Boswell. "And anyone following the fortunes of the Orange and Black knows—'As Maravich goes so goes Aliquippa.' "

Still, the agony of this defeat was short-lived. This would be the year that Aliquippa finally beat Ambridge. Three quarters into their first meeting of the season, the score was 28–1. Hobbs rejoiced: "The worst defeat suffered on the basketball court by Ambridge in the last eight years!" The final, after Lippe emptied the bench, was 30–10. Press, with 14 himself, had been at his "most brilliant . . . as he collected five field goals, all long ones so beautiful that they never even touched the rim as they dropped through."

The rematch took place a month later in Ambridge. The capacity crowd was especially hostile. But that wouldn't deter Press on the occasion of his final varsity game.

Aliquippa won 32–25 "with Captain 'Press' Maravich closing out his high school career with one of the greatest individual performances seen in a long, long time," wrote Hobbs, who was to hyperbole what Press was to scoring baskets:

> The great Maravich struck rank, soul-filling terror into the hearts of the Bridgers. Press turned in the most sensational game of his life as he sank seven field goals from practically every position on the floor and added four out of five fouls for 18 points. But it didn't end there! He grabbed the tipoff consistently, made the Bridgers look downright foolish with his faking, clever dribbling, and when they massed to stop him, Press whipped unerring passes all over the floor. Hats off to a great boy who proved his greatness in a great game.

As the season ended, Press had gone from local celebrity to local legend. One referee who had watched his game mature called him "the nearest approach to Paul Birch that there is in high school circles." The comparison couldn't have been more flattering to Press. Just as kids like Wally Zernich idolized him, so did Press idolize Birch, considered the best player ever to don a uniform for Duquesne University. Press combed his dark hair, parted in the middle, just like Birch. He walked with a cocky strut, just like Birch. His room was adorned with photos of Birch he had clipped from the newspapers. Of course, he also shot like Birch, Duquesne's leading scorer, known for a time as "Pop 'Em In Paul."

The difference was that, unlike Birch, Press didn't figure on having a college career. The years he had lost to vocational training now seemed irredeemable. He was twenty years old, a D student with the academic standing of a high school sophomore. The end of his eligibility all but spelled the end of his formal education. Fame, as he would learn, was a fading commodity. Eventually, Press would trudge back through the tunnel. By December 1, 1936, his Social Security application indicates his employer as the Jones and Laughlin Steel Corporation. His was not a destiny to be evaded. In the meantime, though, he resolved to play as long as he could.

He played in all-star games. He played as a pro, still using the name Peter Munnell. He played in J&L's fiercely competitive intramural league, winning a championship for the blooming mill team. In 1936, he won another championship playing for Aliquippa in the Serb National Federation's first annual basketball tournament in Cleveland. He played for an outfit called the Ambridge Collegians. He played against everybody—even the Original Celtics.

Ballplayers of that era spread the game like gospel. They made believers in armories and county fairs, in ballrooms, barns, and bars—wherever two baskets could be affixed (backboards were not yet mandatory) and a crowd could be had. They'd play as many as three games a day. The best of these traveling troupes included the SPHAs, the Buffalo Germans, and a couple of all-black teams, the Harlem Globetrotters (begun as the Savoy Big Five out of Chicago) and the New York Rens (whose home court was the Renaissance Ballroom in Harlem). If the barnstormers were the game's itinerant preachers, the Celtics were its high priests.

"The Celtics have done more for basketball than any team in the world," said Paul Birch, who signed with them out of Duquesne in 1935, a year that saw the team lose just 7 of 125 games. "They revolutionized the game."

The Celtics, also known as the New York Celtics, established their first attendance record back on April 16, 1921, when 11,000 fans came to see them play the rival New York Whirlwinds at the 71st Regiment Armory in Manhattan. By middecade, they were guests of Calvin Coolidge at the White House. The Celtics were the first team to sign players to exclusive contracts, deals that inevitably attracted the best talent. The roster included future Hall of Famers Joe Lapchick, who, at six-five, was regarded as "the game's first true agile big man"; Nat Holman, who set the standard for shooting and floor leadership; and Dutch Dehnert, whose bruiser's build belied his grace. With Holman passing to Dehnert, whose broad back and big ass kept his defender at bay, the Celtics originated the pivot play. They are also credited with running the first zone defense and the first switching man-to-man defense. But the innovations didn't stop there. The Celtics were showmen. Celtics like Dave Banks, a five-five ballhandling wizard known as "Flash," were imbued with a sense of what might please the paying customer.

It was "Little Davey Banks" who won the crowd when the Celtics came to Aliquippa for a benefit game in 1935: "He dribbled like a demon . . . super-showmanship," wrote Ralph Hobbs. With three minutes to go, Press—just weeks removed from his last game for Nate Lippe—came in to guard Banks. "The thrill of a lifetime," wrote the *Gazette*'s correspondent.

The Celtics returned a couple of years later. This time, though, the paper would herald their arrival in a different fashion:

"PRESS" MARAVICH, CAPTAIN
AMBRIDGE COLLEGIANS, HOST,
N.Y. CELTICS TOMORROW NITE

The game proved to be a free-wheeling, high scoring affair, a 62–49 Celtics victory. Fans from all over the Beaver Valley packed the Ambridge gym. They came to see Davey Banks do "what every

player would like to do if only he dared 'show off' during a game."
They came to see Fritzie Zivic, the welterweight contender from
Pittsburgh who made an appearance for the Celtics. And they came
to see Paul Birch, now playing for New York, go up against the best
the locals had to offer. Nobody was disappointed, either. Birch scored
10. Press had 12.

Performances like this led Press to finally challenge his own sense
of fate, the belief that boys who grew up in Aliquippa were doomed to
die there. The idea of playing college ball wasn't exactly new to
Press. Back in '35, the *Gazette* reported that he would be attending
Geneva the following fall. Geneva wasn't the only school, either.
Duke University offered him a partial scholarship. Claire Bee, the legendary coach at Long Island University and inventor of the 1-3-1 zone
defense, wanted Press, too. And so did Chick Davies of Duquesne.

The scouts who made a habit of attending his games gave him a
sense of worth. They had come to tell him there was a better life
beyond Aliquippa. Press still needed more than two years of credits
for a high school diploma, but for the first time, he began to think he
might be able to hack it on a college campus. He had already spent
a couple of bleak years in the mill.

"He didn't want to spend the rest of his life going through the tunnel," says Lazo.

Of all people, Lazo understood. He was working nights at J&L
while attending Geneva. Perhaps that's why Press came to him that
day and told him about the little school in West Virginia. It was
called Davis and Elkins, D & E. The best of the Ambridge guys—Ed
Gutowski and Mike Winne—were already there. They liked it well
enough. Now the coach wanted him. It was a free ride, four more
years of playing ball. He had to get that diploma, though.

"Go," said Lazo. "Chase it."

His resolve became fierce. He attended night school in Pittsburgh and enlisted Lazo as his tutor. He took algebra and shorthand
and a class called "Problems in Democracy." Mostly, he got Ds,
though he did manage a C in senior English and an A in office practice. Press would never be much of a scholar. But on April 9, 1937,
at the age of twenty-two, he did become a high school graduate.

Soon he entered a new world, far from the acrid fumes and black sugar, set in the hills of Elkins, West Virginia. It would be difficult, almost impossible, to reconcile the bitter youth from Mrs. Thompson's class with his collegiate self. Against every expectation, Press became Big Man on Campus. There he is in yearbooks and archival photos in a shirt and tie, in letter sweaters and varsity jackets. Higher education had gentled his condition. Dates would arrive to pick him up in their fathers' automobiles. Press's natural charisma, which made girls want him, made young men want to follow him. By his senior year, the *Beaver County Times* announced that he would be featured in "Who's Who Among Students in American Universities and Colleges," an inclusion warranted by his status as president of the Student Body, president of the Student Council, president of the Junior Class, vice president of the Varsity Club, member of the Zeta Sigma fraternity and the Pan Hellenic Society. He was also a two-year varsity letterman in football (playing was a condition of his scholarship). Even his academic performance merited an "honorable mention."

The agent of this metamorphosis—nay, salvation—was what it had always been for Press Maravich. His development as a player paralleled the evolution of the game itself. He was now described as a "flashy" player. Though primarily a set shooter, he now could shoot on the run with either hand. Then there was his aptitude for the running game. The fast break might have been anathema to Coach Lippe. But it represented a tactical revolution in basketball, and it happened to be invented at Davis and Elkins. Coach Cam Henderson understood that the break, initiated with a quick pass from the rebounder to a middleman, could yield strategic advantages—three men against two, two men against one—and easy baskets. "Crafty Cam," as he was known, was coaching at Marshall University by the time Press arrived at D & E. But his successor, Bud Shelton, remained enamored with "the fast break style."

Basketball was beautiful. That much was evident in the arc of Nat Holman's set shot or the varying tempos with which Davey Banks dribbled the ball. But there were even more subtle splendors, movements that came naturally to Press, preceding even his ability to describe them. This was his instinct for the game. He did things on the court before he knew why.

As Marshall University was in Huntington, West Virginia, Press became friendly with Jules Rivlin, the great middleman who ran Cam Henderson's fast break. But unlike other players, who struggled to chase the middleman, Press knew instinctively how to defend against a running attack. You couldn't stop a guy like Julie Rivlin once he had the ball; the key was in preventing the middleman from getting it. Press did this by rushing the rebounder, to keep him from making the outlet pass. Cam Henderson, the story went, couldn't have been more impressed. He had never seen anyone do that before.

Henderson wasn't alone. Though Press lacked national attention, playing in the tiny West Virginia Inter-Collegiate Conference, he would impress the entire eastern basketball establishment. In January 1941, D & E played Claire Bee's Long Island University team in Brooklyn. Though the visitors would lose, Press tallied 27 of his team's 42 points. That was more than anyone had ever scored against the Blackbirds, who went on to win the national championship that season. There were times when Press would travel to some ecstatic region and couldn't be stopped. In one stretch against LIU, he made 9 in a row, an extraordinary streak for a set shooter who would let fly 25 to 30 feet from the basket.

"He left the court," wrote one reporter, "with the plaudits of the crowd ringing in his ears." Exaltation is addictive; a good crowd was a great high. This one stayed with him for a while. The next evening, in Philadelphia against a big-time LaSalle team, he scored 30. A few nights later, he went off for 36.

It is easy, perhaps too easy, to gauge a player's prowess in points alone. Still, by the time he graduated, Press had scored more of them—1,635 in four seasons—than even Stanford's legendary Hank Luisetti, who popularized the jump shot. The college paper predicted great things for the Big Man on Campus: "We'll bet that Maravich comes mighty close to equaling (Paul) Birch's fame."

As soon as the season ended, he signed with a pro team, the Clarksburg Pure Oilers. In fact, he had been playing for the Oilers under assumed names through most of his time at D & E. Athletic scholarships didn't cover room and board. His take from those barnstorming weekends went toward feeding himself and his varsity teammates. But he didn't have to lie anymore. He was what he was, by vocation and desire. On Tuesday night, March 11, 1941, Press Maravich made his official debut for the Clarksburg Pure Oilers against the Harlem Globetrotters in Sistersville, West Virginia. A full house was expected.

3. PRO BALL

In the fall of 1941, Press had a 30-point night against the Detroit Eagles. It so impressed Dutch Dehnert, now the Eagles' coach, that he promptly invited Press to join his roster. Dehnert's offer was no small honor. Just the previous March, at a four-day event held in the Chicago International Amphitheater and sponsored by the *Herald-American*, the Eagles had beaten the Indianapolis Kautskys (so named to honor their florist owner), the Harlem Globetrotters, the New York Rens, and, finally, the Oshkosh All-Stars to win the World Professional Basketball Tournament.

The salary, Press would recall, was "in the neighborhood of $3,000." The Eagles had been affiliated with the National Basketball League, a midwestern circuit, but now made their way as barnstormers, traveling from the heartland to the Deep South in a big black sedan. They played poker and slept in crummy hotels. Then it was on to the next town. They might drive all night and play all day, as many as three games. Despite the hardships, Press couldn't have been much happier. He was getting paid to play ball.

Then Japan had to go bomb Pearl Harbor. Press had enlisted in the Naval Reserve just months before, a designation that earned him $36 a month. On February 5, he reported to the naval base in Anacostia, D.C., for elimination flight training. This trial period rendered his spatial sense and leadership ability abundantly clear, as Press finished third in a group of eighteen prospects and earned a 3.5 of 4 in "officer aptitude."

On April 28, 1942, he accepted his appointment as an aviation cadet and reported to Pensacola, where his additional duties as athletic officer had him playing for and coaching the base basketball team. In qualifying as a patrol plane commander, Lieutenant Maravich was cited for "outstanding aptitude" as a prospective combat pilot.

As the commander of a Black Cat patrol bomber (PBY) based in the South Pacific, he would be responsible for a crew of eight, including three gunners. He presided over both bombing and rescue missions, his courage and composure remaining intact even under heavy fire. He was awarded the Air Medal, the commander of the Seventh Fleet citing his "distinguished" work in "seventeen combat missions, totaling 115 hours of flight, over enemy territory in the vicinity of operational enemy airfields." "Lieut. Maravich's performance of duty has been excellent," reads one evaluation. "On the night of 28 October, 1944, he was directly responsible for locating and directing the rescue of the crew of a PV [a twin engine monoplane used for bombing, reconnaissance, and rescue missions] that had crashed at sea."

Late in 1945, Press returned home. Wally Zernich recalls seeing him at his father's tavern on Hopewell Avenue, resplendent in his uniform: "No movie star could've looked better than Press in his Navy whites." The Srbobran, a Serbian American newspaper, covered his return under the heading: "A Hero Comes Home from the Wars." The article relates how Press managed to safely ground a bullet-ridden plane whose landing gear had been shot away and how "his gunners shot down nine Jap planes" in a single mission: "Press recalls the episode with the casual nonchalance of a typical athlete whose team has just pulled through in the dying seconds, but who hearkens back on the affair as just another game."

Of course, that's what he still wanted: another game, and another after that. Press was back in Pensacola, working as a flight instructor near the end of his Navy tour, when he heard from the man he idolized. Paul Birch, now player-coach for a new NBL team, the Youngstown Bears, was eager to sign him. On the eve of the season, the Youngstown Vindicator ran a two-page spread on Birch's boys, describing Press as "a Dick Dead-Eye with long shots. Substantially built, rough, fast and brimming with self assurance . . . He'll break the heart of opposition with his penchant for tossing them in from all angles."

Youngstown's inaugural effort against the Sheboygan Red Skins drew 2,700 fans to the South High gym. Otherwise, it proved to be a typical evening for the 1945–46 Bears. Birch, whose temper was legend, injected himself into a melee on the court and started throwing punches (two of Youngstown's finest were required to separate the combatants). The Bears, who couldn't match the height of Sheboygan's "skyscrapers," lost.

Less typical was the fact that Press came off the bench to score 13, tying Birch for high-scoring honors. Although the programs identified him as twenty-five, he was now thirty-one. He had spent the past several years in a cockpit flying over the South Pacific. As his knowledge of the game grew stronger, his legs had weakened.

"Press wasn't as quick as he had been before the war," says Pete Lalich, a Bears teammate who had been playing against him since 1936 in the annual Serbian tournament. "Age was catching up with him. He could still shoot, though."

He was always good with the ball, his dexterity still evident in his shot—he averaged a respectable 5.6 points a game—and even more in the way he ran the weave. Players would move in a semicircle above the foul line, passing the ball to the man approaching on the outside. But every once in a while, Press would change directions, flipping the ball back over his shoulder to Lalich.

"It was the first no-look pass—at least the first I can remember," says Lalich. "We knew exactly where we were on the court. It was all about rhythm. Nobody handled the ball better than Press."

He compensated with brains what he now lacked in body. Working off the weave, he would run his man into another and wait to hear "Switch!" As soon as his defender called for help, Press would break for the basket, an easy layup.

Not that any of this impressed the coach. "The tantrums," says Lalich. "It didn't take much to make Birch crazy. I remember his wife trying to calm him down, rubbing his neck at halftime. Even she had a hell of a time with him. I'm telling you, Paul Birch was a no-good SOB." The sentiment was by no means confined to the

Serbs on the team. Birch often punctuated his locker-room tirades by smacking one of his own players upside the head. Still, he seemed to take particular relish in riding the guy who had worshipped him. "He always took it out on me," recalled Press, "because I never talked back to him." Another player, Roger Jorgensen, sensed jealousy of the respect and affection Press had among his teammates: "He always had a smile. We always gathered around him, and I don't think Paul liked that."

One night Press took a vicious elbow in the mouth. The impact, as he told the writer Phil Berger, knocked him to the floor and split his lip. "I could put my finger right through my lip and touch my teeth," he recalled.

"Get up," said Birch. "You're okay."

Birch told the trainer to apply a bandage. This was nothing compared to what he had seen with the Celtics. "Hell," said Birch, "the Celtics played with broken hands, broken feet, broke noses, black eyes."

These past glories won Birch some fans among the sportswriters, who portrayed him as basketball's answer to Brooklyn Dodgers manager Leo Durocher. But they conferred no victories on the Bears. The Youngstown franchise was a hastily conceived expansion team in a regional league, far less established than the Kautskys or the Fort Wayne Zollners (Fred Zollner being a maker of automotive pistons). They lost their first nine games, finishing sixth in a league of eight teams, a record that did nothing to improve the coach's humor.

For the players, the season's sole consolation was all the poker they played while riding the rails between Rochester and Sheboygan and Oshkosh. Press and Pete Lalich would tip each other in Serbian, baiting the coach into raising or folding. The wagering was governed by one immutable law. "Birch lost," says Lalich, the mirth in his voice unmistakable six decades later. "He lost all the time."

It was during his season with the Bears that Press met Helen Gravor. On their first date, the story goes, he took her to Bill Green's nightclub in Pittsburgh. She was tall, slim, and Serbian, with dark hair and blue eyes. Helen, then employed as cab dispatcher, was somewhat less impressed with her date and the wounds he had so gladly sustained in the service of his alleged profession. He said he was a professional basketball player, but he looked like a boxer, what with the row of stitches above his eye. "He looked terrible," she said.

They danced, big band style. Then they embraced. "We should be married," said Press.

"You're crazy," said Helen.

The very next morning, he confessed his feelings to Lazo, who shrugged them off as a passing fancy. By now, they had spent enough nights on the town for Lazo to know Press's M.O. His most recent date was always the best, *the one*. "God, she was gorgeous," Press would say. "I could marry her tomorrow." Then tomorrow would come and Lazo would see him out with another hottie.

But after Helen there were no others. Lazo and the boys couldn't even get him to go out for a beer. "Press met her and that was it," he says. "It was love at first sight."

The anatomy of attraction is a curious composition of need. Helen was a knockout, sure. But, then, so were all of Press's girls. And now, looking back, one wonders if Press needed what she had even less than what she did not.

She was almost nine years his junior, born February 22, 1924, in Monroe, Michigan, but raised in Aliquippa. The exact fate of her parents remains unclear. Her father, Nick, is variously described as a town drunk, a fruit packer, and a man who joined the army to escape his family. "The father abandoned her," says Lazo. The desertion overwhelmed her mother. "The mother wasn't able to raise her," says Veda Milanovich, whose husband was an old buddy of Press. Whatever the case, or the cause, her mother died when Helen was still a girl.

Helen and her sister were sent to live with an aunt, Mildred Pevar, who ran a dress shop on Franklin Avenue in downtown Aliquippa. Though she was Serbian Orthodox, Helen attended services at the same Logstown Mission where Press played his first organized ball. On October 25, 1936, according to church records, she uttered a Confession of Faith. At that point, she couldn't have had much more than faith. Her real parents were gone, and her step-parents distant. "They had a business to run. They were just never there for her," says Lucy Biega, formerly Montini. "She had it very rough. But that's when she met my brother."

Elvidio Montini was strapping and handsome. The 1942 *Quippian*, the high school yearbook, describes him as a "he-man." As it happened, he also played ball for Nate Lippe. Helen, for her part, was a cheerleader. She can be seen in group photographs of the cheerleaders in the 1941 and '42 yearbooks. There is, however, no record of her graduation. No matter; by then she was in love. Not only did she love Veo, as he was called, but she loved his big, busy, affectionate Italian family. It was a lot easier, she found, staying with the Montinis in Plan 11 than with the Pevars near their downtown dress shop. "All my mother did was cook and clean and Helen enjoyed it," says Biega. "We were more of a family to her. She felt more comfortable with us. Helen never had that closeness. She needed family."

On October 11, 1942, Elvidio, a nineteen-year-old steelworker just four months removed from his graduation, and Helen Gravor, a beautiful high school dropout with no occupation to speak of, were married in Aliquippa. But their newlywed bliss was short-lived, as Veo soon went off to war, where he served as an infantryman in General Patton's Third Army.

Helen would peek through the window, sad-faced but expectant, as the mailman approached their home. She might be holding the baby. Ronnie Montini was more than a year old now. This was December 1944. The mailman's name was Paul Piccirilli, Nate Lippe's former manager. Everybody called him Pickles.

"Pickles," Helen would ask, "do you have a letter for me from Veo?"

"Not today, Helen."

This went on for a couple of weeks. Pickles felt like apologizing. "Maybe tomorrow, Helen."

And then, one gray day, the Western Union guy beat him to the Montini residence. Pickles knew what that meant. He didn't go near the house. For some reason, he went and told Coach Lippe. Then came the bulletin in the January 2 edition of the *Evening*

Times: "Staff Sgt. Elvidio Montini, 21, husband of Mrs. Helen Montini, of 147 Wilker St., was killed in action somewhere in Europe December 12, the War Department advised his relatives shortly after noon today."

"Helen was totally lost," says Veda Milanovich. "Her life was shattered."

"Helen went to pieces," says Lucy Biega. "I moved in with her so she wouldn't be alone. I tried to get her to go out." But it didn't do any good. Eventually, Biega recalls, "she left Ronnie for a while with my older sister, Violet. I can't even remember where she went."

There are gaps in Helen's history. Where did she go? When did she return? Or did she, as a matter of metaphor, ever fully return? Nothing is so certain as Press's intentions.

"It surprised me," Lucy says flatly. "There wasn't a girl in town who wouldn't have wanted to go with him. But he married her right away."

Of all the girls in the Beaver Valley, Press went for the widow with a fatherless boy.

"From day one, Press treated Ronnie like he was his own," says Lucy.

He would be for Helen and her boy what he and his mother never had.

They were wed, somewhat extravagantly, at St. Sava Serbian Orthodox Church on Pittsburgh's South Side. A great party followed, with Press's great mood setting the tone. "A big Serbian shindig," recalls Lazo, who served as the groom's "special sponsor." "Everybody got boozed up and let it all hang out." On a more decorous note, it was reported that Helen wore a "frock of aqua crepe, white accessories and a corsage of gardenias." The headline in the *Evening Times* read, "Helen Montini Is Bride of Former Naval Pilot."

The new husband was more accurately described in his application for a wedding license. Asked for his occupation, Press's novel answer was recorded as "Professional Basket Ball Player."

On June 6, 1946, the Arena Managers Association of America convened in the Commodore Hotel in New York City to establish a new league. The arena managers were not known to have an affinity for basketball, certainly not *pro* basketball. Most of them made their money on hockey and ice shows and rodeos. But now they sought to avoid those dark empty winter nights. The theory was to draft and develop college stars, exploiting their advance publicity. These clean-cut boys would play a faster brand of basketball than the crafty old men and war veterans now playing in the regional circuits. For ability and experience, the new league wouldn't be able to compete with the NBL. The NBL still had the best players. Then again, the new teams wouldn't be playing in Sheboygan and Oshkosh. They weren't named Zollners or Kautskys. They would be called Knickerbockers and Celtics and Warriors. Most important, though, the new league offered better venues in what would come to be known as better *markets*. You couldn't draw crowds if you had no place to put them. In New York, the Knickerbockers had occasional access to Madison Square Garden, firmly established as the capital of the college game. The new vintage Celtics had Boston Garden. Other games would be held in Chicago Stadium, Maple Leaf Gardens, and the Olympia in Detroit—a big step up from places like South High gym in Youngstown.

The Basketball Association of America, as it was christened, was also called (perhaps more accurately) the Arena Basketball League. The arena managers selected Maurice Podoloff, five-two, out of Yale Law School, as their first league president. Podoloff already had a day job, as president of the American Hockey League. "In whose office the BAA could be given some desk space," wrote sportswriter Leonard Koppett, noting that the new league's boss "knew as little about basketball as he did about hockey, and didn't pretend otherwise, but his knowledge of law and real estate and his familiarity with the club owners suited their needs." Podoloff understood, to paraphrase Calvin Coolidge, that the business of basketball was business.

Paul Birch promptly resigned from the Youngstown Bears to coach the BAA's new Pittsburgh franchise. The Ironmen, as the team was called, would play in Duquesne Gardens, where Birch still had great cachet. "It won't be long before basketball will be the winter counterpart of pro football and baseball loops," he said.

• • •

Birch's sentiments, however far-fetched they may have seemed, were shared by his whipping boy. Whatever his problem with Press, who himself had been unable to negotiate a new contract with Youngstown, Birch wasted little time in signing him.

The Ironmen included Coulby Gunther, a six-four New Yorker specializing in the hook shot; Hank Zeller, who was attending Pitt medical school at the time; and Brooms Abramovic, so named for his family's broom factory. The man who paid them, John H. Harris, was better known as the owner of the Pittsburgh Hornets, a minor league hockey franchise, and a promoter of ice shows. "The idea," recalled his former general manager, "was to keep the Gardens open."

Duquesne Gardens did not resemble the basketball meccas driving the new league. Built in 1890 as a trolley car barn, it was already considered a dump. To make matters worse, the Ironmen were to play most home games on Mondays, the worst night of the week, in deference to the Hornets' prior engagements.

The home opener came amid much fanfare. A crowd estimated at 3,000 saw the Ironmen lose, 71–56, to the Washington Capitols, coached by an ambitious young basketball impresario named Red Auerbach. Things only got worse for the Ironmen, who soon established a lock on last place. Forty-five hundred would show up at the Gardens if the Harlem Globetrotters were on the first bill of a doubleheader. The Globetrotters were developing a mesmerizing brand of basketball, melding sports and entertainment into a kind of performance art. But the Ironmen alone weren't much of a proposition, as sports or entertainment. They might get 1,000, 600, even 300 fans on a given night.

They traveled by rail and slept two to a room. Press would spread out a newspaper on his side and expectorate tobacco juice periodically throughout the night. Other than that, he was very popular with teammates. He was another year older, but still undiscouraged. Looking back, guys like Coulby Gunther cannot be overly impressed with themselves. As played in the BAA's inaugural season, the game was still relatively slow and stationary. It was another segregated league. "The black man hadn't come into the game yet," says Gun-

ther, the Ironmen's leading scorer. Desegregation would revolution-
ize basketball more than any other sport, changing the way it would
be played. But Press was already considering basketball's future. "I
remember that Press had a more radical approach," says Gunther, his
roommate. "He was already thinking about the running game."

Press was brimming with basketball strategy. What's more, his
desire was undiminished. He was most fierce where the game was
most physical: on defense and under the boards. "Tough guy," says
the Philadelphia Warriors' Jerry Fleishman. "He wouldn't hesitate to
take a taller man. And the way he would go for a rebound—he'd
drive into the boards, he'd go over you if he could. He wanted the
ball, and he had a gift for anticipating the bounce."

Still, Press could not please Paul Birch. By now, his reverence for
the man had devolved into a conflict that bordered on primal. After
an overtime loss, Birch threatened Press with a $100 fine if he so
much as came out of the shower. Press waited what seemed like an
eternity before rinsing off the soap. In Chicago, Birch threw him up
against a locker. The players broke it up before Birch could get off
any punches. That's not to say the coach didn't hurt him, though. As
the season wound down, and the Ironmen were left with just eight or
nine men, Birch would keep Press on the bench for entire games.

In a couple of years, the BAA would change its name, becoming
the National Basketball Association. But the Ironmen folded after
that first disastrous season. They didn't have the arena. They didn't
have the players.

The NBA wanted kids fresh out of college. There wasn't much of
a market for a thirty-three-year-old guard who had spent his best years
in the service. Press's preposterous idea that one could make a living
playing basketball had now run its course.

But in the death of his dream lay the genesis of another. Chuck
Mrazovich, a tall kid from Ambridge, recalls its proclamation. He
was playing in a semipro affair, "one of those games where you're
lucky to get a chipped ham sandwich and a fishbowl of beer," when
Press came in at halftime with a bottle of whiskey. He wanted to
make a toast.

"My wife had a boy," he said. "Pero."

"To Pero," said the players, before sipping from Press's bottle.

In Serbian culture, the son is a sun, around whom the family revolves. On June 22, 1947, with Helen in labor at Sewickley Hospital, Press met with the doctor. "If it's a girl, you pay the hospital bill," he said. "If it's a boy, I pay."

Some hours later, the doctor greeted him again. "You pay," he said.

Press would pay gladly. This boy would do what his father could no longer; his body language would articulate the old man's vanity, genius, ambition. Here was the boy who would surpass his father's imagination.

On June 24, 1947, an Orthodox priest from St. Elijah the Prophet came to the Maravich home on Beech Wood Avenue in Aliquippa. The baby was baptized Peter Press.

4. THE CULT OF PRESS

To provide for his new family, Press decided to embark on a career as a commercial pilot. But Helen, given her hard-earned fear of abandonment, didn't want a husband flying all over the country. She had already been scarred by familial separation. Now she wanted the man of her house to remain in the house. Why not, she proposed, become a coach?

So, as Press liked to recall, coaching was Helen's choice. At another level, though, the decision, if that's what it really was, seems inevitable. Press had a few interviews with the airlines. But circumstances hadn't changed the nature of his obsession. He was, as ever, "hypnotized with basketball," says Lazo, who, looking back, believes that Press was all but preordained to teach the game. Helen was quite encouraged, recalls Lazo, "but she didn't realize the implications."

To Helen, coaching was a job. To Press, it was a calling. He already had some experience in the annual Serbian-American tournament. He had played on the winning team in the inaugural series back in '36. In the years since, he had become Aliquippa's player-coach, winning championships in '47, '48, and '50. "We were the first team to win it four times," says Wally Zernich, who, like his brothers, played for Press's Serbian team when he wasn't playing at Pitt. "We had guys who were captains of their college teams. We had All-Americans. We had doctors and attorneys and educators on that team. But it didn't matter who you were. Press was the boss. You wouldn't dare say no to him. When we got into a huddle and Press told us what we were going to do, we did it without hesitation. We were thrilled to do it. We *believed* in him."

Authority was a function of charisma and reputation, and Press's had been burnished to a glow, particularly among the white ethnic sons of his hometown. The look in his eye might as well have been a call to arms. Not only had he kept himself in great shape, but his competitive streak was undiminished by the onset of middle age. Even as he pushed forty, Press still wanted the ball. He wanted the last shot. "That's how much he believed in himself," says Zernich. "That was his personality."

"He'd knock your head off playing three-on-three in a junior high school gym," says Chuck Mrazovich, who recalls himself as an "awkward, clumsy stringbean who had spent three years in the infantry." He was also Croatian, but at six-five, Press recognized his talent and recruited him as a ringer for his Serbian team. Press refined his game, instructing Mrazovich where to position himself for a rebound and encouraging him to actually dunk the ball, a rarity in those days. He got him thinking about the outlet pass. "Mraz," he would say, "get the ball and whip it out to the side. Let's run these guys into the ground." Press gave Mrazovich a good bit of what he needed to become an all-star at Eastern Kentucky and a draft pick of the NBA's Indianapolis franchise.

In 1947, Press became an assistant coach under Robert "Red" Brown at Davis and Elkins. In many ways, he was ideal for Brown, who had played his college ball for Cam Henderson. Not only was he developing a reputation as a great tactician, but Press could attract talent to a school like D & E. "I would have gone wherever he wanted me to go," says Joe Ceravolo, who arrived that fall from Aliquippa. "He was the Babe Ruth of our town."

Press resonated with a certain type of player: he wasn't necessarily from western Pennsylvania (though that helped), but chances were that he had already done time in the army of the mills; he had experienced enough of the real world to know how lucky he was to be playing the game. Press didn't recruit ability. He recruited desire. He wanted guys who loved the game as much as he did, who shared his confusion of basketball with salvation. Ceravolo had been a casualty of the Ambridge-Aliquippa wars, ruled ineligible when Moe Rubenstein discovered that he had played in a Serbian charity game with professionals. His senior year was ruined, his scholarship offers rescinded. But Press took him off the scrap heap.

His other recruits included Ted Chizmar, a navy vet who had been working as a crane hooker at J&L. Chizmar was exceptionally fast ("Could've played wide receiver on any goddamn football team," says Ceravolo) and ideally suited for what he called "racehorse basketball." But when asked of his qualifications for college ball, he says only that "Press saw a person who was devoted to the game."

"He was always talking about what the game could do for you," says Joe Pukach, another war veteran desperate to escape the seamless tube division at J&L, where his own father spent forty-seven numbing years. As it happened, Press saw Pukach play at the high school gym against the Pittsburgh Steelers basketball squad. "I just ran all over those guys," recalls Pukach. "They couldn't catch me."

In no time, Pukach found himself in front of an unimpressed Red Brown. "He can't play," the coach said disdainfully. "*Look* at him."

Look *down* at him, he meant. Pukach was five-four, about 125 pounds. "Who the hell was gonna look at me?" he says. "Only Press."

Pukach, Ceravolo, and Chizmar would all be named to the college's Hall of Fame and all go on to coach basketball themselves. They were known as the Ironmen — in deference to Press, but also, as Pukach says, "because Red Brown never took us out of the game." In 1947–48, they went 21–8, winning the league championship.

"It was very clear," says the former Gloria Marquette, then a student dating another of the team's stars, "that Press was changing a lot of people's lives."

He was only a first-year assistant (on the football team, too), but he is recalled as the dominant presence at practice and on the bench. He was more than a recruiter or a gymnasium preacher. He was a strategist. "One of the best game coaches I've ever seen in my life," says Bob Kent, who coached rival Beckley College. "We'd play each other, and after games we'd get together for coffee and he'd be sitting there till two, three, four in the morning doing X's and O's, talking about this theory and that theory."

"Press was one of basketball's great tacticians," says Ceravolo, who himself would go on to author a book on basketball offense. "Red Brown recognized that."

In the summer of 1948, he took a job as an assistant coach at West Virginia University in Morgantown, where he was studying for a master's in physical education. "My goodness, he must have been energetic," says Harold Forbes, associate curator at the West Virginia University Libraries, examining Press's transcript. "This is a pretty heavy academic load for somebody who's working." Press began in the fall of 1948 and completed requirements for his degree the following summer. From his coursework grew a primer called "Basketball Scouting," written with a friend, James Steele, soon to be a coach and teacher at McKeesport High School near Pittsburgh. The booklet, dedicated "to basketball coaches everywhere," advocates what has since become standard procedure: charting shots and noting each player's tendencies, "any weaknesses he may have . . . in ability or temperament." Press was particularly concerned with the playmaker, the guard with the ball. "Study carefully his eccentricities and methods," it reads. "For here we have the key to any team's success or failure."

By the time it was published, Press had become a head coach, accepting a job at D & E's archrival, West Virginia Wesleyan in Buckhannon. The immediate forecast for his Wesleyan Bobcats was not encouraging. Inheriting a dreadful team with little returning talent, he started four freshmen. But he transformed them by employing a tough man-to-man defense, the best in the conference. Defense is often dismissed as mere hustle, but in fact, it is an expression of desire, and the Bobcats had that in abundance.

Their coach had gone so far as to devise a system gauging their hunger for the game. The striking entry on Press's graduate school transcript is an A in Psychology of Coaching. Upon taking the Wesleyan job, he had begun to coach as if conducting an experiment in social engineering. Enlisting the help of a former colleague, Dr. Georgianna Stary, chair of the Psychology and Education Department at Davis and Elkins, he came up with a series of questions for his athletes. Their written responses, following a session with the doctor—an expatriate Czechoslovakian with a doctorate from the University of Prague—helped Press to determine their potential and mental fitness as ballplayers.

Once again, the player who best epitomized the virtues Press sought had grown up under the fiery orange skies of Logstown. George "Sudie" Danovich combined skillful shooting and ballhandling with tenacious defense. And though he only was five-six, his determination was such that Press would occasionally play him at forward against much bigger men.

Sudie had grown up without a father, in his grandmother's boarding house on 249 Calhoun Street, a stone's throw from J&L's No. 3 blast furnace, then the third largest in the world. As a child, he fell off a tricycle, tumbling down a flight of stairs and puncturing his right eardrum, an injury that left him partially deaf, especially to loud noises. His afterschool activities included cleaning the boarders' rooms, prepping their meals, flipping their mattresses, changing their spittoons, and bathing his invalid grandfather. Sudie's sole solace was basketball. He came off the bench for Aliquippa's 1948–49 state championship team. That was senior year, what figured to be the end of his career. But his mother called Press late the following summer. "Somebody's got to help Sudie," she said.

"Press emancipated a number of boys from the mill, and one of them was my father," says Sharon Danovich. "It was the best thing that ever happened to him. He would never have gone to college if it wasn't for Press Maravich."

"Press could do no wrong as far as Sudie was concerned," says Lazo.

The feeling wasn't reciprocal, or so it seemed to the other players, for Sudie was the coach's designated whipping boy. Press would scream at him all practice long, harping on every mistake. Then he'd ream him out some more in the locker room. "Okay, I got to talk to George alone now," Press would say. "Everyone out of here." The banished players would evacuate, feeling sorry for their point guard but lucky to escape the coach's wrath. Scapegoat Sudie provided a powerful incentive for them not to screw up.

What they didn't know was that Sudie couldn't hear most of what Press was bellowing at him. They didn't know that the coach positioned himself for his most vicious rebukes behind Sudie's right ear. What he did hear didn't hurt him much. After all, he was from Logstown. Meanwhile, as the players cowered outside the locker room, Press would be speaking softly to his point guard, telling George how well he was doing and how proud he was of him.

"He was more of a father type to George than anybody," says Hank Ellis, Press's assistant at Wesleyan.

As it happened, the team improved from 5–20 to 15–10 in Press's first year. Wesleyan would lose in the championship round of the conference tournament to D & E's Ironmen, although the game itself was something of an anticlimax, as Press's former charges were now seasoned and heavily favored upperclassmen. More interesting was the semifinal, in which the exhausted Bobcats squeaked by West Liberty. "Little George Danovich," as the college paper called him, "found the rough, hard-driving game to his liking and dropped in 16 points to top the Bobcat scoring." It was their second close victory in as many nights. The players then hoisted their coach on their shoulders and marched riotously into the locker room.

The season concluded some days later with Wesleyan playing Geneva College at the Aliquippa High School gym. The Bobcats' 2-point victory seemed less important than the halftime ceremony, in which their coach was honored by the St. Elijah Club. "Press Maravich Day," the *Buckhannon Record* called it.

The cult of Press was in full flourish. Unfortunately, it didn't pay the bills. Bob Kent, his one-time rival and long-time friend, remembers that they were both making about $2,800 a year. Press would be talking his X's and O's, until finally Kent would turn to him with a grin. "You dumb bastard," he'd say. "You should have taken that job with American Airlines."

Press's future had become the subject of debate even before the final game. "The only worries in the minds of Bobcat rooters are . . . holding on to Maravich for another season," noted the *Wesleyan Pharos*. "Many speculations are now being offered about Press's moving on especially since W.Va. University is without a basketball coach." On March 25, yet another "Press Maravich Day" was held in

Buckhannon, as local businesses were solicited to raise $400 "to give the popular Bobcat mentor as a token of their appreciation for his grueling work this past season."

It wasn't enough, though. Press took a job as assistant to Red Brown, the new coach at West Virginia. Then Davis and Elkins called, offering him Brown's old job plus a couple of sweeteners. He'd be making a $5,000 salary. He'd still have to double as an assistant football coach, as he had at both D & E and Wesleyan. But now he'd assume the title of athletic director, and with it a whopping $2,000 bonus. Press accepted the offer, apparently neglecting Brown's warning that the sum would not be forthcoming.

The move was a tacit admission that the wisdom of Maurice Podoloff, the NBA's business maven of a commissioner, had been lost on Press Maravich. He was now athletic director of a school without a home court; the Senators still played in the local high school. "We couldn't go on without a gym," he said, "and if no one else was going to do anything about it, I would."

He secured the services of assorted volunteers: carpenters, students, even the reporter who watched as he cleared a patch of land with a borrowed tractor. "Ground Cleared for Gymnasium," read the headline. His new star recruit, Mike Linkovich—almost thirty years old, straight out of the forging department at Colonna Steel—wheeled in the cement. And while the finished product bore no resemblance to Madison Square Garden, it stood as an unlikely shrine to one man's love for the game. "It wasn't much," Press would tell Phil Berger. "There was a tin roof that leaked. But we fixed that by stringing burlap sacks on the ceiling."

Over the next two seasons, his teams would go 57–19. But Press had begun to face obstacles that weren't reflected in the won-loss records. First, he was running out of eligible steelworkers. Not every high school star was dying to play at tin-roofed Memorial Gymnasium, as it was named. Take that kid from Clarksburg, for instance, Hot Rod Hundley. Press told him he'd be great at D & E.

"Coach," asked Hot Rod, "what's a D & E?"

Being the Babe Ruth of Aliquippa only got you so far. Even worse, Red Brown's warning had proven true. "I don't think he ever got the money they promised him," says Linkovich. "Press was making peanuts." It took him two years to realize that he was making less as D & E's athletic director than he would coaching Baldwin High School in Pittsburgh.

"As smart as Press was basketball-wise, that's how dumb he was financially," says Ceravolo. "He always needed money."

He spent two years at Baldwin before moving on, or back, to Aliquippa. The salary was about $6,500. With some summer hours at the mill, he could keep the family solvent. Again, Press would quickly alter the fortunes of a program that had fallen on hard times. The Quips were 9–13 his first year, and 16–6 the next. The coach himself had changed, though. To those now representing the old guard, he remained the conquering hero. But others saw him in a more ambiguous light.

Heir to a Dream, a famous son's idealized portrait of his father, depicts Press as a man who "hated the rebellion he saw" in disaffected teenagers. A new sheriff had come to the blackboard jungle, confiscating more than 300 switchblades. Then there was the kid who tried to taunt Press, calling him "big shot Navy man," as he explained his several nonnegotiable rules for phys. ed. class. The kid kept on until Press finally grabbed him from the bleachers and mercilessly paddled his ass in front of the other students.

"It was a piece of wood, three or four inches wide—he was pretty loose with that paddle," recalls Nick Lackovich, who incurred Press's wrath for a lesser transgression. "He was a military man. When he said he wanted your gym clothes white, he meant white." Lackovich's paddling came as a result of insufficient whiteness.

Press had become a hardass. The dashing pilot with movie star looks now wore his hair shorn to bristles, his flattop much like that of his stepfather, Djuro Kosanovich. Destesting the duck's ass haircut "and the dead-end world of apathy and troublemaking it represented," Press took it upon himself to form the Crewcut Club. "If you didn't belong, you couldn't play ball for him," says Pete Suder, the son of Press's old high school teammate, Pecky.

Suder recalls those seasons with wry bemusement. His high game was 28 points. But he was taken out before he could break the school record—30, as he remembers—which still belonged to Press Maravich. Perhaps Press wanted to preserve his standing as Aliquippa's best-ever scorer. Suder was never sure. It wasn't the kind of thing he felt comfortable asking his coach.

As an assistant, Press hired someone who had run his drills to perfection: Joe Pukach was an enthusiastic if undersized acolyte. He knew how to do things Press's way, right down to those underhand foul shots. "Press would run us like crazy, up and down the steps, around the gymnasium," said Mike Ditka, an underclassman who'd go on to fame as coach of the Super Bowl Champion Chicago Bears. "He'd put that steely look on you, and you knew he meant business."

Still, not every player saw Press as a mere authority figure. Joe Lee, his star point guard, recalls him with deep affection. Lee was black, as was half the Aliquippa team by now. His mother had passed away, and even by Aliquippa standards, Joe Lee was poor. Press would slip him free lunch tickets every chance he got. More than that, though, Press was governed by a level of concern Lee had not seen in other adults.

He took his team all the way to Madison Square Garden in New York City, as he wanted the boys to know, in some intimate sense, that their game had a capital, and within that, a cathedral. On Sundays during the season, he would drive them to the Duquesne University gym to watch varsity practice. On the way, he would listen to the Negro radio station. Press knew all the words to the spirituals.

"That's your heritage," he told Lee, who found Press to be a surprisingly good listener.

Once, Lee asked his coach why Aliquippa had no black cheerleaders.

Press thought about it for a while. "You're right," he said. "There should be."

Then there was the time he complained to Press about Mrs. Carver's physical education class, which included instruction in the rudiments of square dancing. Boys and girls would alternate partners as the music dictated—until a white girl found herself paired with a black boy. Then the music stopped, with Mrs. Carver instructing the black kid to remain on the side until a same-race partner became available.

"Don't go back to that class," said Press.

As per his coach's orders, Joe would report to the basketball office during Mrs. Carver's class. He brought a book with him to study. He got an A in gym.

Press's Aliquippa teams, it bears mention, also had their own mascot. He had sad, soft eyes and a big head mounted on a wispy frame, dense as a wafer. He was tiny, but ubiquitous. If you saw Press, you saw Pete. He attended practices. He'd wiggle his way into team huddles. At the home games, Suder recalls, "he'd sit on the bench right next to his dad."

Pete entered the second grade when Press took the Aliquippa job. But already, basketball felt like part of his being. For years, Press spoke of getting Pete "hooked," shooting in the backyard as the boy watched in awe. Pete would recall his early childhood in West Virginia with a clarity that makes no allowance for the subconscious: "I was so impressed as I watched him pump in shot after shot without missing. His plan worked very well. He knew almost any son would want to copy his father, and if his calculations were correct, I would be drawn into the sport he worshipped."

In Pete's version, Press brought him and Ronnie, then known as Ronnie Montini, to all the games and practices. But somehow, Ronnie escapes most people's recollections, all of which focus on the little boy. Ted Chizmar, who played for D & E when Pete was two, says, "Press always took Pete to practice and gave him a basketball to play around." Chuck Elkins, who played for him at Wesleyan, says, "I remember Pete being around three. Press would bring him to the gym and he'd be trying to dribble a little basketball." Hank Ellis recalls them in the basketball office, wadding up paper balls and shooting them into a trashcan. "Pete had to stay there until he made so many," says Ellis.

"He always wanted to be around Press," says Pukach. "But Press was always around basketball."

Woody Sauldsberry, who played with the Globetrotters from '55 through '57, remembers proud Papa Press bringing his son into their locker room when the team came to Pittsburgh. The Globetrotters were the biggest attraction in basketball. Abroad, they had drawn 75,000 to Olympic Stadium in Berlin. At home, their appearance before an NBA game, inevitably generating more interest than the main event, helped ensure the fledgling league's survival. The Globetrotters weren't mere minstrels or showmen. They could play the most advanced caliber of ball. In 1949, before 20,000 fans on a Monday night, they beat the defending NBL champion Minneapolis Lakers for a second time. George Mikan's Lakers, who'd go on to win the NBA title that year, would be humiliated by Marques Haynes, the world's most spectacular ball handler.

Now Press wanted his boy to have an audience with the Globetrotters. "His father knew some of the older players," recalls Sauldsberry. "He would bring him in the dressing room and the guys would take time with Pete. They would do some ballhandling tricks. Then he would do some. I remember he could dribble the ball down stairs. The kid was only seven or eight years old, but you could tell he was going to be good."

Press could tell, too, and he didn't mind sharing this bit of insight with his own players. Disgusted, he might call time during practice as Pete dribbled out on the floor and started shooting baskets.

"See how he is?" Press would bellow. "All basketball."

"He'd talk about how the kid listens and we don't," says Suder. "That's all he talked about: his son, his son, his son."

Theirs was an uncanny connection, blurring the boundaries of nature and nurture, a tremor that ran through the blood of both father and son. The impulse that led Press to literally chew through towels on the sidelines, led Pete, too. "Press pushed him like crazy," says Suder, who also recalls that the coach, unlike many steelworker fathers, "had his arms around him all the time." The game was an obsession, but also a kind of love, a shared desire. Press worshipped basketball. Pete worshipped Press.

On the afternoons of away games, the team would meet at four o'clock in the gym before riding out on a bus. Press would leave Pete there with the lights on and instructions: "Play." When the team returned to Aliquippa, usually between midnight and one in the morning, Pete would still be there, still shooting.

"Even then," says Suder, "I thought Press's whole goal in life was Pete."

5. Country Gentlemen

In accordance with the last will and testament of Thomas Green Clemson, South Carolina's Agricultural and Mechanical College opened in 1893, in the northwest corner of the state, not far from the Blue Ridge Mountains. Sixty years later, the university named for John C. Calhoun's son-in-law became a charter member of the Atlantic Coast Conference, the preeminent consortium of basketball schools in the United States. These included North Carolina, North Carolina State, Duke, and Wake Forest, the so-called Big Four.

That's not to say the Clemson Tigers didn't have a vital role in the league. The Country Gentlemen, as they were also called, played like country gentlemen. After three seasons, Clemson was 1–39 in conference play. Then again, that didn't bother too many people around the former Calhoun estate. Red Canup, sports editor of the *Anderson Independent*, would herald the season's arrival with something less than enthusiasm: "You've got to face it, men. Basketball arrives this week, and there are no bombshelters to hide in."

Clemson was a football school. As it pertained to athletic matters, the only man whose opinion mattered was Frank Howard, the football coach and athletic director known as the Baron. The Baron didn't much care for basketball, but by 1956 those several seasons in the ACC had forced him to reconsider the sport as an administrative matter. "I do think that being a basketball coach has become a full-time job," he said, somewhat grudgingly. "Most schools now not only have a full-time head coach, but an assistant as well." Until then, Clemson basketball had been the sole province of Banks McFadden, one of the school's most storied athletes. Howard relieved him of those duties following the 1955–56 season, though not, as he made clear, because he was unsatisfied with the state of Clemson basketball. Rather, given new rules that mandated the start of practice on October 15—right in the middle of football season—he had little choice. Banks's job as Howard's backfield coach trumped whatever responsibility he had to the basketball team.

The problem was finding his replacement. There weren't many candidates lining up to work in "the dark house," as North Carolina coach Frank McGuire called Clemson's Fike Field House.

The dimly lit gym sat about 4,500, as compared to North Carolina State's Reynolds Coliseum, the site of the annual conference tournament, with its capacity of 12,400. Fike wasn't much of a recruiting incentive, either. As one sportswriter put it, "A man who could sell anyone on that ancient shed could peddle bedwarmers in Hades." N.C. State assistant coach Vic Bubas, apparently miffed that the Baron wouldn't even let him hire an assistant of his own, turned down the job. So did Bones McKinney, a Wake Forest assistant who said that the Clemson gym was so dark "the referees had to use flashlights."

Even a high school coach from McKeesport, Pennsylvania, took a pass—but not before recommending someone who might actually be thankful for a thankless job.

It was Neenie Campbell who brought Press Maravich to Howard's attention. "He's sent me a mess of good boys," said Howard. "He knew Press and told me he's a good coach." In fact, the basketball fraternity (whose collective opinion wouldn't have mattered much to Howard, anyway) already considered him a coach's coach. His references included men who'd soon go down as legends: North Carolina's McGuire; West Virginia's Red Brown; Clair Bee, for whom Press ran a summer basketball camp at West Point; and North Carolina State's Everett Case, who held a clinic in Kokomo, Indiana, where Press had worked for the past eight summers. "All of 'em talked pretty good about this fellow," said Howard.

In typical Press fashion, he accepted the job without inquiring as to the salary, which, at about $5,600, was less than he was making at

Aliquippa. He was now running an ACC basketball program that lacked money, talent, and height. To make matters worse, places like Aliquippa would no longer serve as fertile recruiting ground. "Some fine high school players," Press said of his hometown, "but unfortunately, they're mostly Negroes . . . My own team last year [including the junior varsity] had 17 Negroes on a 25-man squad. Most of them will go to Duquesne, Michigan, Marquette, schools like that."

The Supreme Court decision *Brown v. Board of Education* was now two years old. Basketball figured to be one area of American life that shouldn't have required a court order. In most parts of the country, the game was moving forward—strategically, physically, and racially—without the benefit of politics or jurisprudence. But none of these changes seemed to register within the ACC, especially at Deep South colleges like Clemson, where the only one more popular than Frank Howard might have been Strom Thurmond.

Of course, Press wasn't brought down South to advance the cause of basketball or social justice. His mandate was a modest one. "Maravich took over," read Clemson's 1956–57 media guide, "with one thought in mind—bringing the Tigers out of the doldrums of the Atlantic Coast Conference cellar, a spot they have occupied for the past three years."

Soon a family of Yankees moved in, not far from campus. Press fell in love with a house on Rock Creek Road. It had a basement and green beans growing off the car port. That was enough for him to buy it on the spot. "Helen hadn't even seen the house until she got here," recalls Louise Bradley, a neighbor whose husband, Bob, was Clemson's sports information director. "But that was typical Press."

Helen made quite an impression on her new neighbors, the Bradleys and the Bagwells—Joyce, a science teacher at Daniel High School, and Howard, who just happened to be the school's basketball coach. "She just came over and introduced herself," remembers Joyce. "She was wearing slacks and a large man's shirt, and she said 'My son Ronnie will be playing on your husband's basketball team.'"

At the time, Joyce Bagwell had more pressing concerns, chief among them a newborn baby, Howie, with a terrible case of colic. She had been teaching chemistry and physics and, by her own admission, knew nothing about being a mother. But Helen helped her with the colic. She would put the baby on her shoulder just so and rub his back, and Howie would stop crying. Joyce Bagwell remains mystified, even more today than she was back then: "Helen was a very hyper person. But when she held that baby she had a patience and a calm you wouldn't believe. It was like she became a completely different person."

Helen looked like a model or a movie star playing a housewife. She was tall, with clear skin, a nice figure, a full mouth, and big greenish eyes. She wore her dark hair pulled straight back. She didn't even need makeup. Still, given an occasion, she'd avail herself of every cosmetic advantage to great effect. "If there was a ballgame or she was going somewhere with Press, she did nothing that day but prepare," says Joyce. "She did her hair, her nails, her makeup—all of it absolutely perfect. She used to tell me, 'When you go out you should look the very best you can.'"

She could cook, too. A variety of delicacies came out of her kitchen, from goulash to homemade coffee cakes to Jell-O with cherries. "I can still see her sitting in that kitchen with her apron," says Louise Bradley. "She would start in the afternoon cooking for Press and Pete and Ronnie. She thought it was really important that they eat well. She was very particular."

Such particularity extended to the housework as well. She washed and ironed with a sense of ardor. "I never saw anything like it: Pete's socks hanging on the clothesline," Joyce remembers. "They were beautiful. She would wash them until they were white, white, white. She worked so hard on those socks. And he had so many pairs."

Helen might flirt with the fifties ideal of domesticated perfection, but in other ways, she was undeniably different. There, in the heart of the Protestant Bible belt, Helen would relate the stories of her saints, the icons whose portraits she kept around the house. "She was always lighting a candle for one or another of those Serbian saints," says Joyce.

As Maraviches from Dreznica, the family's patron saint would have been Sveti Nikola, or Saint Nicholas. The Wonderworker, as he was sometimes called, was born in the third century A.D. and became the archbishop of Myra, in what is now Asia Minor. He was credited with rescuing mariners in a storm, restoring a murdered boy to life, and saving Myra from famine. And this was all long before he became what English-speaking people call Santa Claus.

"Helen was different from my other friends," says Louise Bradley. She was high-strung and louder, what with the way she would talk to Press and the boys. Press was the same way, only he cussed a storm. Yes, they were Yankees, but Louise could overlook that. "Sometimes you click with people, and me and Helen just hit it off," she says. Helen would come by just about every morning after dropping Ronnie and Pete off at school. She'd be wearing a nightgown under her raincoat and a scarf around her hair. Helen made it look very glamorous. She doted on Dorma, the Bradleys' baby daughter. "Maybe because they didn't have girls," says Louise.

They'd sip coffee, Helen would play with Dorma, and they'd talk. In Louise, Helen had a friend the likes of whom she hadn't had since Lucy Montini. She could talk to Louise about anything. And what she described was a kind of Cinderella fable set in Aliquippa, with her aunt cast as the stepmother. Her aunt didn't treat her as well as the other children, says Louise: "She had to do a lot of the work. She never blamed her aunt for it, though. She realized that they had taken her in, and that she wasn't her daughter."

To the outside world, Helen was a brunette beauty bearing parfait glasses of cherries suspended in Jell-O. But her interior life was haunted. Even those who had abandoned her returned as ghosts. There was nothing she could do, no spirit she could summon, not even Sveti Nikola.

The star of Press's first Clemson recruiting class was George Krajack, the sixth man on McKeesport's 1955 state championship team. Coming out of high school, no one figured him as an ACC player. But in retrospect, Krajack interprets his scholarship in demographic terms. First, even in the best of times, basketball talent was not abundant in South Carolina. Second, black athletes need not apply.

Still, the ballplayers had to come from somewhere. Pennsylvania seemed like a good enough place.

At six-three, Krajack was an improved version of the guys Press had been recruiting at D & E. Krajack didn't know a man in his family who didn't work in a mill. He loved the game, and he didn't care if Fike was the worst gym in the ACC, or that the cockroaches kept him company as he shot around at night. It was an opportunity.

Soon, he would be taking prospects around campus himself. He and Coach Maravich would show them the new science building and the new men's dorm. But they always tried to avoid "the dark house." Somehow, they always managed to lose the keys when new recruits arrived on campus. Of course, some kids were more insistent than others. They wanted to see where they'd be playing. "Many of them stood with their mouth wide open," Press would recall. "We had no alibis."

By his junior year, Krajack had become Press's best player. He led the team in scoring and rebounding. He understood the game and knew how good he was. But more impressive, at least for a young man in his position, he knew how good he was not. "I wasn't as talented as a lot of the guys I was playing against," acknowledges Krajack. "Press never had the same kind of talent that guys like McGuire and Everett Case had. He didn't have anybody who could break you down off the dribble. He didn't have anybody who could take over a game and win it by himself. None of us were good enough to freelance."

Meaningful improvisation—in athletics as in music—signals an artist. Clemson didn't have artists. Just ballplayers. "The only way for us to win," says Krajack, "was to give a good effort and run the plays." Press's plays, of course. In lieu of any virtuoso talent, Clemson had its coach's conceptual aptitude. He was forever designing schemes. Every meal became a strategy session. Ketchup and mustard bottles represented frontcourt men. Salt and pepper shakers became guards. "Press could move those salt and pepper shakers around until he figured out a way to beat anybody," says Krajack.

Such theoretical brilliance was difficult to measure at Clemson. The team's record remained, as expected, well below .500. But his squad was infinitely more prepared for conference play. The team with one conference victory in three seasons won three ACC games in Press's first season, the highlight of which was an overtime triumph against North Carolina State, the first time the Tigers had beaten the Wolfpack since 1941. He won four the second year, including yet another win over State and a sweep of Wake Forest. The following season, 1958–59, he won five, leading the *Independent*'s Red Canup to declare that, despite an 8–16 record, "This has been an exceptional year for Clemson in basketball." Such were the expectations for a school that earned only its third victory over Duke since the schools began playing in 1926.

Lost on aficionados like Canup were the defensive improvements Press had made. He was partial to a matchup zone he called *junto*, Spanish for "togetherness," a term he picked up while teaching summer clinics in Puerto Rico. In each of Press's first three seasons, Clemson allowed about 10 fewer points per game. The team Press inherited had barely bothered to play defense, allowing an average of 93.3 points a game. The team that finally beat Duke allowed 64.2.

Still, the stats couldn't measure the coach's aspirations. "I'm a fast break man," Press declared shortly after taking the job. "But first of all, we expect Clemson to play interesting basketball . . . They must play . . . basketball that the fans like to see." *Interesting* basketball. Here the old barnstormer and the newfangled conceptualist became one. The game, as imagined by Press with his salt and pepper shakers, had an aesthetic component, equal parts art and theory. At Wesleyan, he used the expatriate Czechoslovakian doctor. At Baldwin High School, he experimented with concave backboards, changing the angle of the rebound, and thus affecting the fast break. "I'll try anything which might help the game of basketball," said Press, who liked telling sportswriters that he had left instructions for a ball to be placed in his funeral casket. At Clemson, he predicted that basketball would "sweep the world" within a decade. A new breed of big, supremely athletic guards—the University of Cincinnati's Oscar Robertson and West Virginia's Jerry West first among them—would go down as the game's crusaders. "This West is the Billy Graham of basketball," said Press, who envisioned a not-so-distant future that included 3-point shots, 12-foot rims, and uniforms "so colorful, so resplendent in their shadings and combinations that people will come out to the game just to see them." Then again, he also went so far as to toy with the idea of outlawing the jump shot. "It's crazy," he said. "But it'd be interesting."

At a place like Clemson, Press's coaching acumen couldn't be judged in wins and losses. Lacking a player with the capacity for art, these experiments were his attempt at basketball science. Some were crazy, others brilliant. One was both. Perhaps it was a gift from St. Nick: the grand experiment, a supremely *interesting* player, a product of talent and desire, science and art, an expression of his father's imagination, a boy by which one could judge the man.

As a coach's coach, Press loved nothing more than entertaining other members of the fraternity. He was especially fond of Everett Case. "We'd go down there and beat his brains out and then Press would have us over for coffee and cake," says Bill Hensley, then the sports information director at N.C. State. They'd talk basketball as they sipped and nibbled. Then they'd adjourn for the main event.

"He was dying to show off little Pete," recalls Hensley. "We would go down in the basement and Pete would dribble for us on the concrete floor." The kid could dribble like the Celtics' Bob Cousy. "Then Press would put gloves on him so he couldn't feel the ball." The kid still dribbled like Cousy—and then some. Pete would be going between his legs, behind his legs, throwing it against the wall, catching it behind his back. He was a machine.

Finally, Hensley recalls Press producing a handkerchief: "He would blindfold Pete so he couldn't see the ball." Never saw Cousy do that. Never saw *anyone* do that. "Before or since," says Hensley. "We'd sit there for like half an hour, watching this little bitty kid dribbling everywhere. We felt then that Press might have something special on his hands."

That was during the 1956–57 season. Pete was nine.

Before long, he would be making the rounds with his father on the summer circuit. Their big stop was the Campbell College basketball camp in Buies Creek, North Carolina. For years, Press roomed with UCLA coach John Wooden. They were an odd couple, Wooden measured and modest while Press was loud and profane.

"Press was an enigma," Wooden says of his cussing colleague. "I came to understand that it was just his way. But he knew the Bible so well."

Not as well as he knew the game, of course. "One should never underestimate Press's knowledge of the game," says Wooden. "Over the years, he was the one I would go to for analysis on several aspects of the game." At UCLA, Wooden would become the most successful coach in basketball history. He'd win ten national championships and coach nineteen first-team All-Americans. Press never got to work with that kind of talent. He had only Pete.

Wooden first saw Pete when the kid was in junior high school, or maybe even grade school. It was around 1960, give a year or two. He was rooming with Press at Campbell, and Pete was performing the dribbling and ballhandling routines that would become so famous. "I saw him do things at Campbell I didn't think anybody could do," Wooden says flatly. In assessing the boy's talent and dexterity the coach compares him with some of the great black players he had known, going back to his days as an All-American at Purdue: "I had the great pleasure of playing against the New York Rens many times. They had some of the best ballplayers you could ever see. I watched the Globetrotters with Goose Tatum and Marques Haynes. None of them could do more than Pete. Pete Maravich could do more with a basketball than anybody I have ever seen."

Then again, as Wooden felt obligated to ask his enigmatic friend: To what end? All those tricks, what did they accomplish? "It's crazy," he said. "How many hours does it take to learn all that? Wouldn't he be better off learning proper footwork for defense?"

"You don't understand," said Press. "He's going to be the first million-dollar pro."

6. THE BASKETBALL GENE

The other sports, in Press's estimation, were evil temptations. Pete's adventure in baseball lasted until he was about nine. Unable to quench the boy's seasonal interest, Press took him out to shag some flies. "The sun was bright and directly over our heads," Press would recall. "I began hitting him some fungoes, trying to get the ball as high as I could. Well, he was running back and forth, catching the ball, a big smile on his face. Then it happened. He misjudged one or lost it in the sun. Anyhow, it hit him smack on the forehead. He started crying and by the time we got home had a welt on his head the size of an egg."

Press could scarcely believe his good fortune. He stayed up with the kid all night, icing the lump and discussing the perils of America's pastime. "Neither of us ever mentioned baseball again," said Press.

Ending Pete's football career required more thought. For a time, after the Maraviches arrived in South Carolina, Pete would hop a fence, beyond which was the famous Clemson field known as Death Valley. There the local boys would play four-on-four tackle. Slight as Pete was, he almost always played quarterback. Later, he played some for the Mighty Mites, organized ball for kids 90 pounds or less. Finally, by junior high, Press had to do something. "He had the eighth grade coach put me in a vulnerable quarterbacking situation," recalled Pete. "The secret orders were to cream the quarterback. After one pileup and several late hits, I retired my cleats."

In the father's mind, he was only saving the boy for what he was meant to do. Among Press's many theories was the one about "basketball genes." He loved to talk about who had them and who did not. Press needed only to see a kid run up and down the floor a few times to determine if he was genetically predisposed to the game. Of course, if ever a boy had basketball genes, it was Pete. And such a nature deserved to be nurtured in the most rigorous fashion.

The gloves and blindfolds were just the beginning. There were so many other drills. Pete learned the fundamentals, of course: dribbling with either hand, chest pass, bounce pass, foul shots, jump shots, and hook shots. But as the basics could become monotonous, Press invented a more elaborate regimen. Most of these moves were anathema to coaches of the day, but they kept Pete's interest captive. Often the ideas came to Press in his sleep, ladled to Pete from the stew of his subconscious. The sources of his inspiration included the Globetrotters (Press would light up at the sound of their theme music, noted one visitor, "Sweet Georgia Brown" making his "muscles twitch to the tune in basketball-time") and a five-foot-four-inch ballhandling wizard named Ah Chew Goo. Press had first seen Goo as a Navy man stationed in Hawaii.

"Press saw me play during the war, a lot of servicemen did," says Goo, who spent countless hours as a boy dribbling between chairs or throwing a ball against gym walls and telephone poles. He would fake three times before he passed with either hand. He could shovel pass. He would toss the ball behind his neck, or redirect its course with a seemingly unnatural spin. But his specialty was what he called a "90-degree, full-speed, cross-legged dribble" that left his man flat-footed and dumbfounded a couple of yards off the ball.

Before long, Pete would be able to do all that, too. In all, there were about forty forms and exercises—"Homework Basketball," as they would come to be known—to cultivate and harvest every bit of Pete's talent. Press and Pete gave them each names, like "Pretzel," "Ricochet," "Crab Catch," "Flap Jack," "Punching Bag." He would crouch, his arms moving in a figure-8 motion, between and around his legs, so rapidly that the ball looked as if it were suspended beneath his squatting self. He would bounce the ball two-handed between his splayed legs, catching it behind his back, then firing it forward, completing the pendulum motion. Not only would he avoid gonadal trauma, but his arms moved back and forth so rapidly they became a blur. Pete would wrap the ball around his body and neck with such velocity that he transformed into a kind of human gyroscope. The beat of the ball as he dribbled just inches from the ground approximated the staccato beat of a boxer on a speed bag. Perfected to Pete's pace, the drills had an almost hypnotic effect.

Press's old pupils were downright jealous. "The way Pete handled the ball—I wanted to be like him," says Joe Pukach.

"Where the hell did he get all those drills?" asks Chuck Mrazovich. "I would have liked for him to teach me some of that stuff when I was playing."

Jim Sutherland, two years older than Pete but already his closest basketball buddy, would work with the father-son team after Clemson's varsity practice. Press taught things that were then unheard of: looking one way while passing another, for instance. But more than that, Sutherland found himself immediately intoxicated by the rhythms of his exercises. "You'd keep doing them," he says, "because you just wanted to get better and better." Finally, there was the pull of Press himself: "You believed everything he said because he believed it. There was such intensity to his instruction. He was like a crouched tiger."

If he had that effect on a stranger, one can only imagine the power he had over his own son. Then again, as they shared the basketball gene, it was difficult to delineate between the father's will and the son's desire. Where did the man's obsession end and the boy's begin?

Already, varsity players at the local high school, Daniel, were taking note. "Pete was the first kid I ever saw who played one sport year-round," says Herbert Cooper, a forward. "The little fucker always had a basketball," says Jimmy Howard, the Baron's son, who played guard.

Pete would dribble the two miles between his home and College Avenue, the town's main drag. He'd dribble while riding the bicycle he found under his Christmas tree in 1956—alternating hands.

One day, Poppa Press told his son to get in the car and bring his ball. Pete did as he was told. Then Press instructed him to lie across the backseat with the passenger-side door open.

Finally, Pete balked. "What are people going to think?"

"Just do it," said Press.

Pete did it, dribbling as his father drove, learning to control the ball at different speeds.

Of course, he didn't have to be going anywhere to be dribbling. He'd dribble in the movie theater, keeping time on the carpeted aisle through a double feature. He'd dribble in Martin's Drugstore. It was in the drugstore that he took a famous bet: five bucks that he couldn't spin the ball on his finger for an hour. As Pete recalled in *Heir to a Dream*, "Several kids gathered around to watch. As the minutes passed, my friends began to see fatigue setting into my arm and hand. The boy who made the bet began to gloat, seeing that my index finger was bleeding. But, before he could start counting his money, I threw him a curve by switching fingers . . . I moved the spinning ball from each finger on my right hand to each finger on my left. When the tips of my fingers became tender, I spun the ball on my knuckles and thumbs."

Years later, Pete Maravich would famously declare his childhood self "a basketball android." But androids don't think or feel, and the ball wasn't merely an appendage of his body, but his psyche as well. He went to bed with it, lulling himself to sleep while practicing his shooting form. He would repeat the words—"fingertip control, backspin, follow-through"—like a mantra. For Pete, there was comfort in repetition. Still, he was a light sleeper, as was his father. Once, he woke in a driving rainstorm. "Lightning illuminated the puddles on our muddy basketball court," he said. "I forced open my bedroom window and crawled out into the downpour. In my bare feet I ran to the muddied ground and began to dribble . . . After several minutes, I stopped dribbling and lifted the ball toward the sky . . . A huge smile curled across my lips, for I knew if I could dribble under these conditions, I would have no problem on a basketball court."

His regular courts were the local Holtzendorff branch of the YMCA and the Fike field house, which included the "little" practice gym and the "big" gym, where Clemson played its home games. The midget Y team worked out Saturday afternoons in the little gym. Pete and some of the other boys would wait and watch as the dining room staff—black men in white kitchen tunics—finished running their full-court games.

Every once in a while, as their games wound down, Pete might insinuate himself into a game of horse or three-on-three. "Those guys were pretty good," says Leonard Keller, a friend of Pete's on that Y team. So was Pete. But he was a boy, and they were men. What's more, competition between the races, however casual, was prohibited. The few meaningful encounters young Pete had with black ballplayers came during the summer, when high school kids from Anderson would occasionally sneak into the little gym. Ed Coakley, one of Pete's closest friends, recalls that those games only endorsed the prevalent racial stereotypes: "The white kids were more fundamental. The black kids had the athleticism. We couldn't run with them. But Pete could."

Still, Fike held an even greater illicit thrill. While still in grade school, Pete and Jim Sutherland devised a way of breaking into the big gym. It was not without risk. They'd scale the wall and hug their way around the side of the building. There, on a ledge maybe eight feet above the ground, was an unlocked multipane window that tilted open just wide enough for them to squirm through. That left the boys in an enclosed area behind a stage at the north end of the gym. Now they had to climb a ladder and negotiate a series of planks about thirty-five feet over the gym floor. "Pretty spooky," says Sutherland. "Particularly up there in the dark." The boys would then let themselves down a ladder. It didn't take them long to locate and learn all about the electrical box.

Frank McGuire might have called it a dark house, but to Pete and Jimmy it was a big-time college gym, the Clemson Tiger emblazoned at center court. The golden oak was varnished to a high gloss. Your sneakers squeaked just so. Dark house? No. Not with the sun streaming through those big pane windows. The boys would pull the switch and play. They'd run Press's drills. They'd go one-on-one. They'd play until they lost all sense of time. "If you could pick anything you wanted to do, any place you wanted to be, that was it," says Sutherland. "It was heaven."

The game was full of untold ecstasies. Little Pete had a big smile — though never when he played. His expression belied the joy he derived from performing, pleasing, mesmerizing. He was energized by the awe of an audience, whether it be men watching him dribble blindfolded or the kids in the drugstore gaping as he spun the ball on his fingertips. But the effect was multiplied in front of a proper crowd. He first felt it as a seventh-grader, already playing for the junior varsity at Daniel. There were fewer than ninety people in the stands, but he was wired to them, each fan nourishing a strange, adrenalized sensation at his core. "Out in front of a crowd for the first time," he would recall, ". . . I just wanted to do everything and be everything . . . I wanted to put on a show."

Prodigies are peculiar, not just for their gifts, but for the prodigiousness of their practice regimens. Frail as he looked, Pete didn't acknowledge the usual boundaries of fatigue, age, or nerve. Nor did his routines distinguish between the athletic and the aesthetic, between the sport and the show. He had already begun challenging his father's players to games of horse for money. He would have to hoist the ball two-handed, off his hip. "He was like half our size, literally," remembers George Krajack. "But he took some of our guys' money."

At Campbell, Pete bet Wake Forest's All-American big man, Len Chappell, that he could make 24 of 25 free throws, with 20 of them hitting nothing but the net. He collected his winnings in Pepsis. In getting the better of Chappell, Pete had done something the rest of the ACC could not. It wasn't the only time, either. "I remember we played horse for an hour," says Chappell. "He shot me out of the gym."

Chappell, from a coal-mining town in central Pennsylvania, played his high school ball for a man named Tom Hess. Coach Hess, also a counselor at Campbell, would bring his son to camp, too. When they first arrived, Tommy Jr. roomed with his father in the janitor's quarters off the main gym. Campers were in bed, lights out by 10 P.M. But shortly before midnight, Tommy and his dad woke to a mysterious thumping sound. The elder Hess flung open the door. "Look," he said. There was Pete at the far end of the gym, shooting around. "I was eight," says Tommy. "Pete would've been eleven."

"I've never seen a basketball player like that," says Lefty Driesell, then the coach at Davidson. "He was the hardest-working athlete I've ever been around. It'd be 110 degrees, and he'd be dribbling or throwing the ball against a cement wall hours at a time."

"Pete," Driesell would say, "you're working too hard."

"I'm gonna be a millionaire, coach." The boy kept going, throwing all those fancy passes against the wall.

"I ain't never seen Oscar Robertson throw nothing but a plain old chest pass," said Driesell.

"They don't pay you a million to throw a plain old chest pass."

Even away from the court, Pete was never away from the game. He'd move his father's salt and pepper shakers as if they were his own chessmen. At night, as Press entertained his fellow coaches, Pete would sneak out of bed and eavesdrop, listening keenly to their amalgam of basketball strategy, basketball gossip, and basketball politics. His father's own aptitude, as Pete himself would learn, was lost on most fans. In this respect, it would be difficult to imagine a game more instructive than the one Clemson and intrastate rival Furman played at Fike in 1960.

It was January 7, the day Orthodox Serbians celebrate Christmas. Pete took his usual seat on the bench, to his father's immediate right. As Press, clutching his towel, gestured with increasing desperation, his son seemed to remain implacable. A series of time-lapse photographs appearing in the next day's paper reveal him as a study in study: chin resting on his hand, elbow on his knee, eyes on the action—Rodin's *Thinker* as a prepubescent boy. This game would give him much to think about.

"I tried every defense . . . nothing worked," Press told the reporters. "We used a 2-3 zone, a 1-3-1 zone, man-to-man, switching man-to-man, zone press, man-to-man press . . . what else is there? And they just kept pouring them through."

On the other end, recalls George Krajack, "It was one of those things. We had all the shots we wanted. They just didn't go down." Krajack led the Tigers with 20 points—"I should have had 40"—on 9 of 25 shooting, just about right for a team that made 31 of 98 on the night.

And though Clemson was now 5–7, its best start in years, the ignominy of losing to a team nicknamed the Purple Paladins was just too much for some to bear. That night, students hung Press Maravich in effigy. The dummy was outfitted with a striped tie, a vest, and a sign: "WANTED—ONE BASKETBALL COACH." Later, it was unstrung and burned. Merry Christmas, Press.

"I'm glad to see someone interested in basketball around here," said Press. "I was beginning to wonder."

Shortly thereafter, the university president released a statement condemning the students and saying he was "entirely satisfied" with the basketball coach selected by his football coach. Even the Anderson *Independent*'s Red Canup now understood what a thankless job Maravich had, toiling in an "out-dated fieldhouse which has sat idly by year after year while every possible move was taken to improve the status of football just next door." Press couldn't be fired for trying to make a run of it at Fike. Or could he? Suddenly, wisecracks no longer seemed appropriate. "This effigy business is embarrassing and hurts my family," Press would admit. "I feel sure it wasn't done by somebody who knows basketball and what I'm trying to do here."

Then again, who knew basketball? Who knew what he was trying to do? The fans? How could they? They weren't privy to his prized progeny or the opinions of his colleagues. Coaching wasn't a meritocracy. A basketball man's fate owed less to logic than luck. There was no amount of practice, no strategy to offset *one of those things*. Perhaps it was better for the kid to learn that now, while he was young. It would be a while yet before they could see this coach's life's work, years before they would begin to understand what he had been trying to do.

7. THE DEVIL IN RONNIE MONTINI

"You have another son," John Wooden once told Press. "But you never mention him."

Of all the facets to what Wooden so astutely understood as his friend's enigmatic life, none was more inscrutable than Press's relationship with Ronnie. In fact, Press would occasionally speak of Ronnie for the record. "He has all the weapons to be a good college player," he told the *State*'s Jake Penland. But he was quick to qualify these mentions. "Peter, my 12-year-old son, is an even better prospect."

By the time Ronnie was in high school, the disparity with which the coach regarded his sons was apparent. Certainly, his own players weren't blind to it. "Press did everything for Pete and all but ignored Ronnie," says Jim Brennan, the star McKeesport recruit who succeeded Krajack.

It is curious to think that Press, of all people, would ignore a boy as he had been ignored by Djuro Kosanovich. "I've heard people say that Ronnie was treated like a stepchild, but that's not true," says Louise Bradley, Helen's closest friend. "They had been here for months and months before we even knew that Ronnie was not Press's son." To be sure, Helen was only treating Pete in the same doting manner she had treated Ronnie. Ronnie was no stepson Cinderella—he'd be voted "best dressed" in his senior class—but rather, the first of her princes.

Still, the distance between Ronnie and Press was made more curious by the fact that the young man had what the coach treasured most: basketball genes. By his junior year at Daniel, he was six-four and a half. He had a rugged demeanor, which he put to great use under the boards, and a scorer's touch. As a junior, Ronnie set a Daniel scoring record with 37 points.

Then again, Ronnie had inclinations more potent than his basketball genes. "In some ways, he had a very attractive personality," remembers Ben Wagener, a friend of Pete's who went on to become a pastor. "But pretty dark."

"He was born," says Gail Garrison, one of Ronnie's high school girlfriends, "with that rebel gene." That alone made him and Press incompatible. It was not Ronnie's nature to submit.

"He did not adhere to training rules," says a grinning Jimmy Howard, who played football and basketball with Ronnie.

He did not adhere to *any* rules. He smoked. He drank. He fought. He screwed around. He skipped school. He smoke-bombed the girls' bathroom. He stole an Edsel. Only an administrator's sense of mercy kept him from being expelled the morning after Press's effigy was desecrated. ("It was just too much of a burden on one man in one day," said the principal.) Still, Ronnie seemed to spend less time at home than at Capri's, an Italian restaurant out near the Highway 123 bypass, where the drinking age was negotiable. "We drank there from the time we were 16," says Jimmy Lever, perhaps his closest friend.

Among the many endeavors that would've earned Press's enmity was football. Ronnie played both ways, as a center and a linebacker, a position that made great use of his talents. "He was a good one— mean as hell," says Dick Singleton, a head coach who understood the concept of training rules in relative terms. "We used to have 6 A.M. practice and Ronnie would be getting home at five-thirty."

Sometimes, he wouldn't come home at all. He'd run away periodically, the farthest he got being Roanoke, Virginia, where a cop busted him and Jimmy Lever as they ran a red light in a '49 Plymouth. The cop asked Ronnie for his name. "Montini," he said. It was the same name he had insisted on using in the yearbook his sophomore year. The cop wasn't impressed. They spent the night in jail.

Of course, none of this made him unattractive to the opposite sex. There was Gail Garrison, a cheerleader whose father tried to prohibit her from dating him. There was Rosie, the Episcopal minister's daughter. And there were a whole bunch in between. "He could have had any girl in high school," says Gail.

As the 1960–61 season began, Ronnie had firmly established himself as the biggest and best player on the Daniel varsity. He wouldn't be the only Maravich, though. Pete Carlisle, who had replaced Howard Bagwell as the coach, decided to put "li'l Pete," as he was sometimes known, on the roster—despite the fact that he was only in eighth grade. The move had already been the subject of much anticipation in the Maravich home. "Just you wait," Pete had told Ronnie after the latter's 37-point game. "I'll take care of that when I get up on the varsity."

The intrafamily rivalry made for some interesting moments, with Ronnie, the senior captain, warning Pete about hogging the ball. Once, in a game, he actually stole the ball from his kid brother to get a shot. Then there were those games of horse after practice. "If Pete got the better of Ronnie, Ronnie would have to remind him who's boss," says Carlisle. "He'd start pushing and hitting on him." No one else could touch him, though. Some of the kids used to tease Pete, call him "lightbulb head." But not around Ronnie. You didn't say anything bad about Pete when Ronnie was around—unless, of course, you wanted to get busted in the mouth.

Bagwell, now the coach of Boys High in Anderson, would recall a game in which little Pete's dribbling antics made the Anderson players look clownish. Finally, one of the Anderson boys hit Pete, knocking him into the stands. "Ronnie and Pete used to fuss all the time at each other," said Bagwell, "but Ronnie was mean as a snake if anyone ever messed with Pete. The next thing you know we had a free-for-all. Ronnie just knocked the devil out of the guy that hit Pete."

Ronnie went on to have a stunning senior season— "Best high school player I had ever seen," says Carlisle—culminating with a couple of memorable performances in the playoffs. He had 30 points and 31 rebounds in a win over Hillcrest. Two nights later, against favored Palmetto, he went off for 33 points and 26 rebounds, a game reported under the headline "Maravich Upsets Palmetto, 63–58." The papers carried news of his scholarship offers (as the season began, Georgia was a frontrunner, but Florida State was also very interested). But in all other ways, he found himself upstaged by an eighth-grader, charitably listed at 5-foot-6, 103 pounds.

"More like 85," says Jim Sutherland.

Based on size alone, it was difficult not to root for Pete, a coltish tangle of limbs.

"He was just a little thing," says Jimmy Lever, "but he could fake you out."

Already, Pete's play was conditioned by the crowd's reaction. "When I threw a behind-the-back pass the applause began," he said. So he kept throwing them. And he kept shooting. Pete still shot that two-hander off his hip; the slight lad still struggled to reach the rim.

But by late December Pete was starting and averaging 11 points a game. Press frequently attended practices. "We talked about Pete a lot," says Carlisle, who had played for Furman the previous season. "He was totally enthused about Pete. More so, I think, than Ronnie."

As it happened, the season ended with a defeat in the playoffs. Pete would recall a thrilling game with Daniel down a point as the overtime period was about to expire. Disregarding Ronnie's instructions to get him the ball, Pete dribbled out the clock. As the final seconds ticked off, the crowd began calling on Pete to shoot.

He shot. He missed. He wept.

"I took total responsibility for the loss," he would say.

Ronnie didn't take defeat nearly as hard. He graduated (barely) that June. Senior pictures in the 1961 *Summit* show Ronnie and his pal Jimmy Lever a row apart. The quote under Lever's photo reads, "The devil is afraid of music—sing, brother, sing." But under Ronnie's smiling face is this: "Wine, women and song are getting me down; I guess I'll have to give up singing."

He accepted a scholarship to play ball at Georgia Southern in Statesboro. But that didn't last long. He came home at Christmas with the bright idea of going to New York City and getting rich. This time, he couldn't talk Jimmy Lever into going. But Tommy McNeill was all for it. They got as far as D.C. this time. That's where they ran out of money. "I can remember standing outside the recruiting office flipping a coin," says McNeill.

Heads, they'd go to the navy. Tails, the Marines.

Something like that.

Next thing they knew they were maggots in a hellish place called Parris Island.

8. "PISTOL PETE"

From the Anderson *Independent*, December 3, 1961: "To look at the boxscore on the Daniel High basketball games you would hardly realize that Ronnie Maravich has graduated . . . Friday night, Pistol Pete Maravich, brother of Ronnie and son of Clemson Coach Press, popped in 33 against Pendelton."

Pistol Pete. The sportswriter came up with other names for him, including Little Mr. Big, Mighty Mite, and Poppin' Pete. But none of them fit as well. *Pistol Pete* worked just as a nickname should. Not only was it alliterative, but it identified a persona, an exaggerated, if somewhat comic reality. The ball came off his hip, like a gunslinger, and he was never, ever shy to shoot.

That confidence belied his stick-figure physique. That gangly, emaciated look, topped with a large head shorn to its bristles, suggested a victim of some sort. If not for the persistently wide grin, one could easily confuse him for a recently liberated ward of a stalag or a labor camp. America's hosiery manufacturers did not make a sock with enough elastic to stay up on those thin, underdeveloped calves.

But his nature was fully formed. He was then what he would become to the world, a scaled-down representation of *Pistol Pete.* "The talent, the moves, the floppy socks, all of that was there from the beginning," says Jerry McLeese, a twenty-one-year-old columnist for the *Independent* when he committed the nickname to print. "He had a long, thin neck, didn't look athletic at all. You would not suspect he could do the things he did—until he did them. He was doing stuff you had never seen before, things that mesmerized you."

77

The behind-the-neck pass comes first to McLeese's mind. "Other players would have to literally stop because they were so amazed. He turned players into spectators."

Daniel's pool of basketball talent and experience had been decimated by graduation. Pete Carlisle had gone to coach at a high school in Georgia and was replaced by Don Carver, one of Press's recently graduated Clemson players from Elkins, West Virginia. The only returning regulars were Pete—now a freshman wearing Ronnie's old number, 23—and Jim Sutherland, a junior.

The Lions weren't deep or experienced enough to be much of a team, but they were a hell of a show. When the Pistol was right, everybody in the house became a fan. His game had timing. It had wit. His were idioms never before uttered, at least not in competition. With the ball in his hands, he could speak in ecstatic tongues. Of his memories as an underclassman at Daniel, perhaps this is the most revealing: "I threw a behind-the-back bounce pass on the move through a guy's legs! . . . I was coming down on a three-on-one break, and my man was overplaying me to the left and giving me the open teammate on the right. But that was too easy a pass . . . As my man was sliding and I was dribbling, I noticed his legs moving in and out, in and out. Still on the move, I saw the right moment and threw the ball when his legs were out—behind my back, now, not a straight pass—and I put it right through him to a teammate on the left. He converted for the basket. The crowd, boy. The crowd, I want to tell you, they went beserk. I couldn't believe it. My man looked like somebody stepped on his head. I think right then, show time was born in Pete Maravich."

He turned them all into fans: the sportswriters, the other players, even the coaches, who found themselves watching, not coaching. But most of all, the Pistol charmed his creator. It was as if Press came under his own spell. Lazo Maravich could see the transformation Pete brought about in Press: "He was just taken away by what Pistol was capable of doing. He got to be as much a spectator as a father."

The rules Press held sacrosanct with other players did not apply to his own son. Press's guys were expected to play defense and hit the books—unless they were Pete. Back in the seventh grade, his math teacher asked why he wasn't turning in his homework assignments. "Sometimes I'm playing ball at six in the morning and nine at night," he told her. "When do I have time to do my work?"

"Well, talk to your father about it," said the teacher, Lola Hawkins.

Not long after that, Press came in for an audience with Mrs. Hawkins. He said that he intended for Pete to be a basketball player. "This," he said, referring to the missing homework, "was not very important."

"I think it is," said Mrs. Hawkins. "He's going to want to go to college."

"Don't worry about that," said Press. "I'll get him into college. He's going to do well with basketball. He'll probably make more money than you'll ever make teaching."

He was a maniacally driving father. But he was more than just that. To look closer was to see that this father needed the son more than the son needed his father. "When Pete came along everything went out the window," says Jim Brennan. "Press lived his life for Pete."

Jerry McLeese understood. "Pete is his first love," he wrote, "and to Press, Pete is basketball."

By the winter of 1961, the game, and the life it commanded Press to lead, was literally bleeding him. Choppy Patterson, his best player, had been lost for the season in an automobile wreck. Seven of his top eight players and four of his starters were sophomores with no varsity experience. As his nerves went, so went Press's stomach. The diagnosis was ulcers, for which his physician prescribed tranquilizers. The regimen included two before each game. The doctor wanted him to calm down and not take the game home with him.

"How can I do that?" Press asked. "All these years I've been waiting and searching for players that could compete in this league and the doctor wants me to forget about them? I tried to explain to him that the Maraviches live and breathe basketball." That included Helen, he said. "I've talked basketball so much my wife knows nearly as much about the game as I do. I worry about the game and she worries about me because I'm worrying. Soon after the doctor put me on pills for ulcers, my wife started having these terrible stomach pains.

So she went to the doctor and he put her on pills, too. He told her if she didn't stop worrying about me she was going to have a beautiful case of ulcers, too."

The real cure, at least to Press's way of thinking, was Pete. This Pistol had the magic bullet: a cure for all his regrets, immortality through basketball genes. Pete was his ticket to basketball heaven. Still, some couldn't help but wonder if Pete would become a kind of human sacrifice. John Wooden had warned him: "You're putting too much pressure on one boy."

The tardy or missing homework assignments were not a cause of much concern in the Maravich household. But the boy's lack of physical stature was regarded as a potential crisis. "Don't turn sideways when you're talking to me, Pete," the family physician, Dr. Billy Hunter, would tell him. "I can't see you."

Press had him hang from doorways to stretch some inches out of him. Helen would make him a concoction of raw eggs, Ovaltine, milk, and sugar in the hope of putting on pounds. But Pete's rebellion, if that's what it was, was dietary. "When he wasn't playing, he was eating candy, popcorn, and junk," says Ed Coakley, a frequent guest at the Maravich home, where he recalls a standoff over the dinner table.

"Eat that spaghetti," Press told him.

In fact, Helen made delicious spaghetti, the best Coakley had ever eaten. He'd already had several platefuls. But Pete had been stuffing his face with candy bars all day long. "I'm not hungry now, Daddy," he said.

"You eat your food," said Press. "Or I'm gonna beat your ass right now."

Coakley was scared to death. And that was before Press stood up. "You're gonna eat that food," he said.

The father was red in the face. He had the look that had intimidated many a college ballplayer. But it didn't scare Pete, who just looked at the plate of spaghetti.

"He never ate," says Coakley.

And there wasn't a damn thing Press could do about it.

•   •   •

By now, Pete wasn't playing quite as much horse. He had begun to play games of three-on-three and one-on-one with his father's players. They were four to eight years older, but he didn't defer—not with the basketball. Jim Brennan would give him some pretty bad noogies, but not bad enough to discourage the frequency with which he shot. Brennan would get on him all the time—until somebody whispered a warning: "Hey Jim, don't yell at Pete. Coach don't like that."

Sure enough, Press would be sitting in the corner of the gym, watching. Brennan was the toughest guy on that team, not to mention the leading scorer. But Press thought nothing of tearing into him. "You're the reason we're losing," Press would snarl in the locker room. "You're too damn selfish." God forbid, though, if anybody told Pete to stop chucking it up.

Two or three nights a week, Pete would practice with the Clemson freshman team. Freshman practice went from 6:30 to 9 P.M., at which time Press might appear and tell his prize recruit, Rudy Antoncic, to stay and play one-on-one with his son.

Antoncic was also from McKeesport. He went six-four, 195 pounds, and averaged better than 24 points a game for the freshman team, more than anyone, with the possible exception of Press, ever imagined he could score. Antoncic, with scholarship offers from places like C. W. Post and Waynesburg State, never thought of himself as an ACC player. Actually, he didn't think much of himself at all. A tenth-grade accident left him missing four or five teeth on the right side of his mouth. As his folks didn't have the money for a dentist, Rudy didn't do much smiling. The only respite from his self-consciousness came on the court. He took between 1,000 and 2,000 shots every afternoon in the schoolyard. In April of his senior year at McKeesport, he got a call from George Krajack, asking if he wanted to play some friendly one-on-one. Sure, said Rudy, it would be an honor.

Krajack won the first game 16–3 and all the while kept fouling Rudy harder and harder. "These aren't fouls in the ACC," he said.

"But we're not in the ACC," said Rudy. "We're in the playground."

"Get over it."

Krajack won the next game, 16–13. The normally timid Antoncic had begun to fight back, doing some grabbing and hitting of his own. The friendly outing had turned ferocious. "He beat the crap out of me," recalls Antoncic, who nevertheless won the last two games.

A few weeks later, Rudy got a call from Jim Brennan, who just happened to be passing through town. How about a friendly game of one-on-one, asked Brennan. The first time Rudy goes in for a layup, Brennan pushes him into the wire mesh behind the backboard. "Jim," says Rudy, "there's rules. You don't throw people into the damn wall."

"Next time, I'll push you through it."

One thing led to another, Antoncic remembers, until Brennan cracked him in the chest and then the face. Brennan was a fighter, and scary—too scary for Rudy to mess with. So he walked across the street and asked the lady in the grocery store for ice. He kept the ice on his face for ten, fifteen minutes. Then he went back to finish the game. This time, when Brennan went up for the ball Rudy knocked him into the wall and started throwing punches. He kept punching until Brennan was laughing. "What the hell's wrong with you, Rudy?"

Next, Brennan asked if he could come over to the house. "But you just beat me up," said Rudy.

"C'mon."

When they got there, Brennan asked Rudy's father if he could make a long-distance call. Rudy could hear him dialing and asking for the basketball office.

It took a while for Rudy to understand what had happened. He had just passed his audition for Press Maravich, for whom desire was the greatest talent. Two days later, Rudy had a full scholarship to Clemson. When he got to campus, Press went into his own pocket to get him the dental work he needed.

The least he could do was stay late after practice and play one-on-one with the coach's son. The twist was, the coach didn't want his son to be tested as he had tested Rudy. "Press had two rules for playing Pete," says Antoncic. "You couldn't hurt him and you couldn't block his shot. Press didn't want to discourage the kid. I mean, he was so skinny and weak."

Antoncic recognized bits of himself in Pete. They each had enormous love for the game and a belief in the sanctity of repetition. At the same time, Antoncic couldn't help but notice that Pete wasn't the typical western Pennsylvania ballplayer. "He had a certain arrogance and cockiness about him," says Antoncic. "His father was the head basketball coach. He had access to anything he wanted on campus. He was like the center of attention."

The boy wasn't trying to find a way out of the mill. He was a prince, and he knew it. Every once in a while, though, Antoncic would give him a little shove. Pistol Pete would only smile. "You can't stop me," he'd say.

The 1961–62 Clemson Tigers went into the ACC tournament with a record of 10–14. The conference tournament was a single-elimination affair, the winner of which advanced as the ACC's sole representative in the NCAA tournament. The three-day affair, the granddaddy of all conference tournaments, was played at Raleigh's Reynolds Coliseum, where it generated huge interest, culminating in the eventual coronation of a Big Four school. Clemson, among the league's charter members, had never won a tournament game, nor was it expected to anytime soon.

And then, without anything approximating fair warning, Press's team used a matchup zone—his junto defense—to dismantle North Carolina State 67–46. The Wolfpack, which had already beaten Clemson twice that season, was outrebounded, outhustled, and outshot on its home court. Coverage in the next day's *Charlotte Observer* began, "This one you'll never believe." The correspondent ranked the upset somewhere between David and Goliath and Jack and the Beanstalk.

"I'm ashamed of the whole mess," said a fatigued Everett Case, State's esteemed coach, drawing on a postgame cigarette.

Clemson's five sophomores then went against Duke, which, at 20–4, was the nation's sixth-ranked team, featuring Art Heyman, already established as an All-American, and Jeff Mullins, soon to be one. As it happened, neither of them could top Jim Brennan's 34 points. Clemson won its second tournament game in as many days,

77–72. Again, Press was carried off on his players' shoulders. "We can go all the way," he said. "We've got what it takes."

What it took, contrary to the prevalent opinions, was not the matchup zone. Victory wasn't a matter of strategy so much as psychology. A couple years later, Press would recall of that team: "I put up signs in the locker room, gave a million pep talks, and told them every time they lost that they were the better club. Belief. That's the important thing."

There were, however, limits to the power of belief. Maravich had nobody to match up with six-eight 240-pound Len Chappell, who scored 31 points as Clemson lost to Wake Forest in the final. Still, the larger point had been made. If Press could win with sophomores at a football school, what could he do at a basketball school with a basketball arena? Already, Syracuse was interested in his services. But the guy who was most impressed with Maravich was the coach he had just shamed.

Everett Case had been a coach since he was eighteen when he accepted the position at Connersville High School in his home state of Indiana. Over the next twenty-three years, he would win four state championships, posting 726 victories against only 75 losses. More than that, he is remembered for helping to make Indiana basketball a spectacle. He made a ceremony of cutting down the nets after championship victories. In the pregame, he had his players introduced under spotlights and to great fanfare. He thought to use a "noisemeter" to egg on the crowd. These were just some of the promotional innovations he would bring with him to North Carolina State. Like the old barnstormers, Case believed in selling the game.

"I remember the local Chamber of Commerce giving him an award as an outstanding salesman," says Vic Bubas, one of Case's assistants at State. "He was a great promoter, very much into the entertainment part of basketball."

In 1946, not long after arriving in Raleigh, Case inspected the construction project destined to become William Neil Reynolds Coliseum. It was to be a state-of-the-art arena, holding 9,000 fans. "Too small," said Case. "It needs to be bigger."

And so it was. When it opened in 1949, Reynolds could accommodate 12,400. "The basketball capital of the world," as one sportswriter put it, became the annual site of the Dixie Classic, another Case invention, matching the Big Four against some of the best basketball schools from up north.

The home team was more than worthy of its grand arena. Every season between 1947 and 1957 ended with 20 or more Wolfpack victories. Across the 1950s, State won more basketball games than any team in America. Case would earn ACC "Coach of the Year" honors three times.

But by the sixties, cracks in his empire had begun to show. The 1959–60 team went 11–15, Case's first losing season. The following year, which ended with a 16–9 record, turned out even worse. That was the season the coach finally realized that some of his guys had been shaving points and even dumping games for gamblers. Case reported his players to federal and state investigators.

"That killed him," says Les Robinson, a freshman guard when the scandal broke.

Case, a bachelor, liked to have a drink now and again. He dabbled in the stock market. But his consuming passion was basketball. "The basketball team was his family," says Frank Weedon, State's longtime sports information director. Turning in his players was like turning in his sons. The punishment included an abbreviated sixteen-game schedule for 1961–62. But Case, who announced that he would be retiring in '65, never really recovered. He was tired, heartbroken. His authority and trust had been irrevocably broken.

That's not to say the Old Gray Fox, as Case was known, didn't have a plan. In finding a successor, he sought a man to whom he could entrust what he most loved, someone to ensure his legacy. That was Press Maravich.

"He saw something in Press," says Weedon. "Coach Case would always say, 'He's a good basketball man.'"

Meaning: Case had found someone as obsessed as he was.

Case called Press in the summer of 1962, in Puerto Rico, where he was giving a coaching clinic. The understanding though not written into the deal, was for Press to succeed Case. The catch was that he would be an assistant again. Then again, being an assistant at State paid about $3,000 better than being the head coach at Clemson.

"Press asked my father for a raise," says Jimmy Howard. "He said they had offered him so much at N.C. State. My daddy said, 'You better get to N.C. State.'"

"I believe it is a step upwards in my chosen life's work," said Press, whose departing statement noted with pride that "basketball at Clemson is no longer a stepchild."

Everett Case wasn't called the Old Gray Fox for nothing. He had gotten his man. If the team was his family, then this move would go a long way toward determining his legacy, nay, his patrimony. Even on his way out, Case was figuring a way to bust the applause meter. Press was a fine coach, but Case had an ancillary motive as well. He had never forgotten the boy he saw perform blindfolded in the basement. The kid still had a few years to go, but it was never too early to plan for the future. North Carolina State had just become the odds-on favorite to sign Pistol Pete.

9. Changing the Game

As the North Carolina State job came up without much warning, Press moved to Raleigh while Helen stayed behind with Pete for her son to finish his sophomore year, or, as the Maraviches considered the calendar, his sophomore season. It was a good one, with the *Independent* noting that Duke's "scoring machine" of Art Heyman and Jeff Mullins was in fact less potent than Daniel's duo of Maravich and Jimmy Sutherland.

Gilly Simmons, coach at rival Anderson High, said, "I don't see how anybody is going to stop them."

Of course, someone did. Daniel was 17–3 headed into the semifinals of the conference tournament, but as Pete and Jimmy combined for a mere 44, they lost a close one to Greer.

Pete was known to weep or walk home alone after a loss. Press had never devised a drill for his son to deal with defeat. Pete took them all hard, as if grieving. To complicate matters, the stakes were only getting higher, with each game assuming more importance. The caliber of competition in Raleigh was a big step up from what it had been at Daniel. North Carolina was basketball country.

It was a Saturday morning in the summer of 1963 when Jimmy Broadway saw Pete shooting around at the Hillsborough Y in Raleigh. He figured this was probably the kid who'd just moved here from South Carolina, the one he'd been hearing about. Pete stood around 6 feet now, though there still wasn't much of him. "Couldn't have been more than 130 pounds, wringing wet," says

Broadway. Still, there was something about him that urged Jimmy to issue the challenge.

Jimmy's older brother, Olin, was the coach at Raleigh's Needham-Broughton High School. Olin had played at Wake Forest. And now big things were expected from Jimmy, who, at six-five, was the varsity's best returning player heading into his senior year. Of the dribbling waif who showed up at the Hillsborough Y, he recalls thinking, "I'm bigger, I'm stronger, I'm a year older. I shouldn't have any problem with him. I was quickly shocked, though, with his skills—his ability to control the ball, his accuracy in shooting. I thought I could push him and shove him, but he'd just scoot away from me. Now I can't tell you how our game ended up, but I feel like he beat me. I felt like he could have embarrassed me, but maybe he didn't use everything he had. I was just a straightforward-type basketball player, whereas Pete was already doing *abstract* things."

Perhaps it was this sense that inspired Jimmy to go one-on-one with him that morning at the Y. Pete, as Jimmy would soon learn, was not the least bit concerned with his classes at school. But as it pertained to basketball, one had the sense that he was privy to a higher knowledge. He approached the game like a martial artist. Practice was solitary, ritualistic, and almost without end. Jimmy would watch him as he flipped the ball behind his back, incessant target practice for an X he had marked on the wall.

"We were taught not to showboat," Jimmy remembers. "But now here comes Pete going behind the back."

Jimmy asked Pete to teach him the drills. They began to play and practice in tandem. It was not unusual for them to get in the gym when it opened at 7 A.M. and stay until 7:30 at night. "He practiced so much," says Jimmy. "But there were times—and I couldn't exactly tell you why—when he just had to stop. I mean, when you been at it ten hours straight, you got to slow down and stop some."

That gym could get awful hot. But Jimmy, so much bigger and stronger, would relent to the fatigue before Pete. Another Saturday morning stands out among Jimmy's recollections: the boys had been on the court so long Jimmy was about ready to throw up. Not Pete, though. Pete still wanted to shoot his free throws. "We'll go when I miss," he said.

It would be 178 free throws before he missed. Jimmy would always suspect the 179th was for his benefit.

That summer, Pete played a few games in the Y's summer basketball league. It was stocked with big-time talent, including a load of recent ACC stars. Olin Broadway and N.C. State's Bob MacGillivray played for the Rangers. Kenny Rohloff, State's recently graduated ace ball handler, played for the Comets. Rohloff's backcourt partner was Pete. His shot was developing now; he was using less hip and getting even more distance. A recitation of the league's "Tournament Highlights" notes a come-from-behind Comets victory in which Pete "caught fire and ran rampage through the bewildered Cardinals." Of his 12 second-half baskets, "most of them were canned from 30 feet out." The semifinal saw Rohloff foul out. In his absence, Pete went for 33. Though the Comets lost, their supporters were not all disappointed. "Seen in the crowd," wrote the Y's correspondent, "was Coach Press Maravich of State College who was scouting his son."

Press had been talking up Pete for a while, acting as his progeny's advance man. "Some people are born to paint and some people are born to write music," he once told Paul Phillips, then covering the high school beat for the *Raleigh Times*. "Pete was born to play basketball." "Press thought Pete was going to be one of the greatest players that had ever been seen," says Olin Broadway. "He would just say it in a matter-of-fact way."

Olin didn't yet know what to think. Now, going into his second season coaching the Broughton Caps, he had an experienced team with four seniors, including the two guards, penciled in as starters. Olin believed in a disciplined, physical game. You ran his plays; you never backed down. Occasionally, fights would break out in practice. But Olin was loath to blow his whistle. A little violence could be cathartic, bonding. Besides, he wanted his boys to hone their aggressiveness, to cultivate an intimidating edge.

Then there was Pete, the mere sight of whom inspired laughter. He wouldn't shower with the team. "It may alter what I've trained my muscles to do in the game," he said. This cockamamie excuse neglected the fact that he had yet to pass through puberty. "I think he was embarrassed," says Jimmy Broadway.

"He didn't have any meat on him at all," says Phillips, who fondly recalls the time Pete complained of a Charlie horse. Impossible, said one of the football coaches: "How can you get a Charlie horse on bone?"

Pete was listed at 145 pounds, about ten more than he actually weighed. "He looked so fragile," says Olin. "I was worried about his endurance." It didn't look as if he could last a season in the 4-A Conference, North Carolina's toughest. Pete might have been the only kid Olin ever told to rest more and play less. Pete didn't listen, of course. He'd stay on the court for hours after practice was over, then he'd go scrimmage against State players. Press would arrive to pick him up. "C'mon Pete," he'd say. "Gotta go."

But Pete would wave him off, telling him he still had to work on this shot or that move. He was always working on something. Press would look over at Olin, beaming with pride. "How about that kid?"

Olin had a difficult time reconciling the boy now on his team with the coach he remembered from Clemson. When Press first came to the ACC, he recalled, Clemson had a guy named Vince Yockel. Under the new coach, his scoring average fell from 21 to 14 points a game. That was the book on Press Maravich, who believed in subjugating the individual for the sake of the team. "The exception," says Broadway, "was his own son."

Then again, there was no way for any coach to obscure Pete's natural virtuosity. Certainly, Broadway didn't want to. In one game, senior forward Doug Bridges, the Caps' leading scorer the previous season, kept shooting on a play designed for Pete. But that ended just as soon as the coach called time and grabbed Bridges by the uniform straps.

Much to his relief, Olin's fear for Pete was unfounded. The kid never wore down, in body or spirit. Nor did his teammates try to intimidate him. "I think they were in awe of his talents," says Olin.

Pete had studied the great pros, guys like Elgin Baylor, and especially the guards, most notably Oscar Robertson and Jerry West. He took and adapted what he could. But unlike most kid ballplayers, he had no idol or model. When he imagined himself in the closing moments of the game, he wasn't Oscar or West. He wasn't black or white. He was Pete Maravich.

With the exception of his relatively modest leaping ability, Pete possessed every physical skill in abundance. He even surprised the coach with his enthusiasm for playing defense. Blessed with great anticipation, he enjoyed the challenge of checking the other team's high-scoring guard. Even more impressive was his strategic sense. His instinct was to freelance. Left on his own, there was no telling what he might try. But given a game plan, Pete would work it better than anybody Olin ever saw.

Against Wilmington, Olin devised a way to counter Claude Meares, the Wildcats' big rebounder. Jimmy ran off a screen to receive the ball in the high post. Pete was the only player capable of making the pass. He'd look right, pass left, and put the ball on Jimmy's right shoulder. Meares would get caught on the screen and foul. After running the play three times in a row, Meares had his third foul. He'd foul out in the fourth quarter. Then Wilmington started double-teaming Pete. "That's when I knew it was all over," says Olin. "No way you were going to press that kid. It was showtime."

Asked how his team had lost to Broughton, Burlington coach Twig Wiggins said, "We didn't have a Maravich. He's the smartest high school player I have ever seen. He controls their offense and he knows when to run and when to slow down."

The Caps were the 4-A regular season champs, with Pete, at 19.3 points a game, their leading scorer. They survived a scare in the conference tournament, as Pete, who had only 4 points, scored all 8 of Broughton's tally in the second overtime. The next night, Pete scored 29, including the last four foul shots, in a 63–60 win over Fayetteville to win the tourney. Going into the state championships at Greensboro Coliseum, Olin Broadway's squad was 19–3 and already considered a better team than Raleigh's five previous state champions. "With the way basketball in the area has been improving over the years, this 1964 club can claim to be Raleigh's best ever," wrote the *News and Observer*'s Grady Elmore.

Their bid for a state title began against Reynolds, the team from

Winston-Salem. With the score tied, Broughton held the ball for Pete to take the last shot in regulation time. He missed from 15 feet. The score was still tied with the first overtime about to end. Jimmy Broadway got the ball near midcourt. He fumbled for a split-second before heaving it. The shot was good. Or was it? One of the officials ruled Jimmy's basket was late. At the end of two overtimes, the Caps had lost, 64–63.

Some days later, Pete and Jimmy attended an ACC tournament game at Reynolds Coliseum. "We were still sick," says Jimmy.

By his senior year, Pete was six-three, 150 pounds. Just as he had run track to work on his speed and endurance at Daniel, he played tennis at Broughton. "He figured it would be good for his basketball game," says Olin. "Particularly the lateral movement." Whether the theory had merit was anyone's guess. The fact was, by the winter of 1964, there wasn't anybody in North Carolina—certainly not a white boy of high school age—who could stop Pete from scoring.

"A lot of schools would put football players on him," says the *Raleigh Times'* Paul Phillips. "They'd bang him and beat him, but he never took his eyes off the basket. Somebody could knock him upside down and his eyes would still be on that basket."

But one didn't have to stop Pete to beat Broughton. Excepting their star, the Caps returned only two lettermen, neither of them starters. Doug Bridges was at the Citadel. Jimmy Broadway was playing at Wake Forest. Olin, looking for a way to support a young family, had gone into the insurance business. The Caps' new coach—the fourth in Pete's five years of high school ball—was Ed McLean, who had played football, basketball, and baseball at Western Carolina University. "I was twenty-five," says McLean, recalling the manner in which the Maraviches would move their salt and pepper shakers. "Pete knew more basketball than I did."

Playing in such a strong league, without much talent or experience around their star, Broughton went 9–14. In many ways, though, the season set the tone for Pete's career. In lieu of winning was a fascination with his scoring. His numbers were staggering. Sportswriters love a natural underdog, and Pete did not disappoint. "I need 20 pounds badly, but I run and play so much I can't gain weight," he told the *Charlotte News* after a two-game road trip to the Queen City that saw him average 40 points. Even as bigger boys tried to beat him down, he stretched the limits of what could be reasonably expected in a brief, 32-minute contest with no 3-point shot.

He scored 22 on a severely sprained ankle that kept him out for long stretches against Fayetteville. Against Rocky Mount, he scored 31 in just the second half. He became headline fodder: "Garinger Wins; 43 for Maravich," "Maravich Scores 47 as Caps Trip Eagles," "Wilmington Beats Caps Despite 40 by Maravich."

Winning and losing was almost beside the point. It was as if tallying the points could somehow quantify his genius. His shot making created interest, an anticipation that Pete would soon be inhabiting another dimension. As one enthralled opponent put it after a game, "Guess we'll be seeing that boy on television."

Everybody liked watching the Pistol put the ball in the basket. Playing in the annual East-West All-Star Game, he set a never-to-be-broken record with 42 points.

When it was over, McLean asked the East's coach, "Why didn't you take him out of the game?"

"I didn't know I could."

In the summer of 1964, after eighteen years of marriage, Press and Helen took their first vacation together, a week in Myrtle Beach. "The pretty blue water rolled in and the palm trees swayed in the breeze," Press would recall. "Then I looked down and saw that I'd been diagramming basketball plays in the sand."

Helen might not have appreciated his obsession, but its value was never lost on Everett Case. He had been ill since the scandals, and his players could feel their standing slip with the inexorable decline in his health. "You could sense Coach Case was failing," says Hal Blondeau, a high-jumping forward from Maryland. The Wolf-pack finished 10–11 in '63 and 8–11 the following year, their first consecutive losing seasons in memory.

"We were sort of a dysfunctional family," recalls Les Robinson, a senior who began the 1964–65 season as a reserve guard.

Even their practices were bifurcated. For a couple of years now, they had been running two sets of plays in practice. Case's "center-opposite" scheme—initiated by the center going across the lane to screen for a forward—hadn't changed much since he was coaching Indiana high school ball in the thirties. "So archaic," says Blondeau. "Press's offense was totally different: lots of motion and double picks, one pick after another, stuff that not many people were doing in those days."

Traditionally, Case's offense worked because his plays had been executed by All-Americans. But the talent pool seemed to dry up with his increasingly desiccated state. The program's patriarch understood what was happening; Case was nothing if not concerned with his legacy. Center-opposite was for the time being. Press's sets and schemes—with their nutty names like Pogo, Pepsi, crossfire, and junto—were for the future. Whether dreaming up plays in the sand or diagramming them on a chalkboard, Press's conceptual focus was to compensate for a lack of talent. It is said, for example, that the four corners offense, later made famous by North Carolina's Dean Smith, was in fact begun by Press. He was still Case's assistant when he gave Kenny Rohloff instructions to dribble a very talented Duke team into a stupor. "Press did all the real coaching—he was highly, highly knowledgeable," says Rohloff, who recalls dribbling until fans threw pennies at him. But what looked like a stall was in fact an offense—an attempt for Rohloff to draw the double-team and hit a cutter going backdoor. Says Blondeau, "Press figured, 'If we can't match up with them offensively, then we have to do something different.' "

As it happened, the 1964–65 team, thought to be outmatched in every respect, was picked to finish near the very bottom of the ACC. "The motliest gang of backyard athletes ever assembled in the conference," wrote *Charlotte News* columnist Bill Ballenger.

At center was a veteran of the Korean Conflict. Larry Lakins matriculated in 1957, then spent three years with the Army Corps of Engineers. The joke was that he had been at State for three terms:

Eisenhower's, Kennedy's, and Johnson's. At twenty-five, he was already paunchy and balding. He smoked. Worse still, he was playing center at 6-foot-6. Then again, along with Blondeau, Lakins was one of only two Wolfpack players who could actually dunk.

Compared with previous State rosters, this one was full of unaccustomed athletic deficiencies. Blondeau could run and jump but couldn't shoot. Pete Coker, a transfer from Dartmouth, could shoot but not run. "Lungs so undersized he could play for only 10 minutes at a time," wrote Ballenger. Ray Hodgon, another shooter, was aptly nicknamed "Spaz." Larry Worsley, a junior forward, lacked jumping ability and basketball sense. "Needed three or four screens just to get him open," says Charlie Bryant, the freshman coach. Then there was Eddie Biedenbach, a hyper sophomore point guard. They called him "Wild Horse," as he was in need of a bridle. He was quick, a deft ball handler with a gift for picking his opponent's pocket. But otherwise, Biedenbach was bereft of basketball savvy. "I wasn't the smartest player," he says. "Running plays was difficult for me."

State opened with a ritual beating of Furman at home before losing to Wake Forest in Winston-Salem on Saturday, December 5. As usual, Everett Case road back alone with his driver. Only this time, the team bus happened to pass the coach's sedan, where he had had his driver pull over at the side of the road. Now his players watched as the Old Gray Fox hunched over in obvious pain, vomiting whatever the cancer had rendered of his guts.

What had only been whispered now became more explicit. "Everett was dying," says Frank Weedon.

Press, described as "Pete Maravich's father" in the preseason media guide, assumed the head coaching duties on Monday. The move came as no surprise. After the Wake game, Case had called him and Charlie Bryant into the still steaming shower, out of the players' earshot. "I can't take it anymore," he said.

On Tuesday, Press called the players together. He explained what had happened and had them watch film of their loss to Wake. The old center-opposite sets would remain in the playbook, he said, out of respect to Coach Case. But they would not be practicing them anymore. From here on, they would take the sport to the limits of its dimensions, both time and space. They would exploit every second of the 40 allotted minutes and every inch of the court's 94 feet.

"We are changing the game," said Press Maravich.

As the players ran out for the first scrimmage under their new coach, Press called after Les Robinson. "Get your ass back here," he said. "You're the new freshman coach."

Les was a senior, not expected to play much. But in Press's mind, he had some outstanding qualifications, attributes that would make for a fine coach, but also a confidant and an alter ego. Les was from West Virginia. His father was a purchasing agent for Union Carbide, but his passion was the promotion of a basketball game, the annual Sportsman Club tournament. Press himself had played in the Sportsman back in 1950, along with Ted Chizmar and Joe Pukach, on a team sponsored by Hawley's Snack Shoppe of Elkins. In the years since, the tournament had come to attract the biggest names in college and pro ball: Jerry West, Oscar Robertson, Elgin Baylor, Bill Russell, John Havlicek, Hot Rod Hundley. The games would sell out the Charleston Civic Center. "My father knew," says Robinson, "you had to sell the game."

Les had been steeped in basketball culture. As a kid, his father would leave him to watch Cam Henderson run practice at Marshall. The boy watched as the inventor of the fast break alternately cussed and charmed his charges. Henderson was charismatic; Les was taken in. "I became fascinated with coaches," he says.

His fifth-grade yearbook asked for a brief self-description. Les responded dutifully, writing in pencil. Red was his favorite color. Perry Como was his favorite singer. Asked what he would be when he grew up, he wrote, "College basketball coach." His mother had an idea that he should become an Episcopal minister. But the truth was, a coach was all Les ever really wanted to be. And he would have been quite happy if Press was the only boss he ever had. "There was no man in America," says Les, "I would rather have worked for, or been more loyal to, than Press Maravich."

Robinson—who, looking back, figures that Press "would have made a good preacher"—wasn't alone. Press inspired enormous allegiance and affection from that team. The other coaches and members of the athletic department considered him great company. They all wanted to play golf with him, though not as his partner. He was just as lousy a poker player. "When he got a good hand everybody at the table could tell," says Frank Weedon, referring to the big old smile that would spread across his face. "Nobody would raise his raises." What doomed Press as a gambler only endeared him to colleagues and players. He lacked any talent for duplicity.

What's more, he was a welcome departure from his predecessor. "Coach Case was the oldest coach you ever played for," says Robinson. He could be remote and downright mean. "Press yelled a lot, but he didn't yell mean," recalls Biedenbach, the unschooled point guard whom Press yelled at more than anyone. "I don't think he ever called me by my name. He always called me 'you little bastard.' But I loved that man."

Coach Maravich wouldn't hesitate to rip you a new one if you screwed up. But as one player recalls, "If you left your guts on the floor, he'd come by at the end of practice to say something nice." The players understood that their leader was, in his own way, as pure as he was profane. He wasn't like Case, who had interests off the court. Case loved to talk about and dabble in the financial markets. But not Press. There was no off-the-court with Press. He was all basketball.

And toward that end, he set about changing the game. For two years now, he had been watching these players up close. Everybody knew what they couldn't do. But only Press knew what they could.

Over the Christmas vacation, they practiced twice a day, two to three hours each session. Most of that time was devoted to a full-court zone press. The coach figured it would compensate for the team's lack of size and a dominant player. The defense would be unveiled against a very strong Yale team, the first game back from the break. Charlie Bryant called a coach who had just lost to Yale in the Sugar Bowl tournament. "They have two of the finest guards you'll ever see," he said. "You can't press 'em."

"But we've been working on a press."

"Good luck," he said. "Y'all are gonna need it."

Despite such prognostication, the Yale guards would dissolve under the pressure. "We could see it in their eyes," recalls Blondeau. "Whenever they turned around, there we were. We were in their jocks. We had such a focus."

State won, 91–66. More important, says Bryant, "the players were sold on the press." The press only strengthened their belief in their coach. It didn't end with defense, though. Rather, the coach had found an ideal cast to enact the old fast-break ideal: wingman to the middleman, then go. "The idea was that the team that's faster down the court wins," says Blondeau. "The secret was getting the ball out fast, but you also needed somebody who could push it, and that was Eddie Biedenbach. Eddie would push it and push it and push it."

Press broke his Wild Horse just enough. After taking over for Case, his team won 11 straight, including a come-from-behind victory over a North Carolina club that featured a future Hall of Famer in forward Billy Cunningham. Even down 14 in the second half, they never doubted themselves. Such was the rigor of their belief. "We beat teams we never should have beaten," says Pete Coker, also the son of a coach. "We were in our own little world, just living and breathing with Press." The Wolfpack would finish the regular season with a record of 17–4. The only team to beat them twice was Duke, which had a 7-footer in Hack Tison, and three future pros, including Jack Marin, who became an NBA All-Star.

The second of these losses came in overtime on the road, after a couple of calls State didn't appreciate, and inspired an angry locker-room vow. "They'll never beat us again," said Coker. "We'll get 'em in the tournament."

They would have the chance, of course, in the championship game. As none of Press's guys—with the exception of Biedenbach, who appeared in seven games with the Phoenix Suns—would go on to play in the pros, they tend to recall it as the defining contest of their careers. A charge ran through Reynolds Coliseum, as if a bolt of lightning could shoot from the cloud of tobacco haze above the arena floor. "It was electric," says Biedenbach, whose feeling for Duke remains just as vivid.

As a senior at a Pittsburgh high school, he was visited by a man from the university. His name was Slocum. "He picked me up at school," says Biedenbach. "Then he told me I wasn't good enough to play for Duke."

As it happened, State got 30 unexpected points from Larry Worsley. "Seemed like he was making them from half court," says Bubas. Still, the game was won with defense. Press bet that the six-six Lakins would be able to cover the 7-footer by himself. That enabled him to extend the zone, harassing Duke's perimeter shooters. Hack Tison and Jack Marin, who had burned State for 32 earlier in the season, combined for only three baskets. The Duke guards were having just as bad a time of it. "It got to the point where they didn't want to bring up the ball against Eddie," says Blondeau.

It was Biedenbach who hit the decisive basket. With 2:37 remaining, he drove the baseline and pulled up in a heavy traffic for a 5-footer. The shot was good, plus the foul on Duke. Unable to contain himself, Press ran out onto the floor and kissed the little bastard.

The victory qualified the Wolfpack as the conference's sole entry in the NCAA tournament and earned State a first-round bye. The next opponent would be Princeton, a team made famous by its star, Bill Bradley. The son of a banker from Crystal City, Missouri, Bradley was first team All-Ivy League, first team All-Academic, first team All-America. He had already won a Rhodes Scholarship to Oxford and a gold medal in Rome, where he was captain of the U.S. Olympic Basketball Team. The Associated Press, United Press International, and the Basketball Writers Association would all name him college basketball's Player of the Year for 1965. In three varsity seasons, he scored better than 30 a game.

But even more significant than the points was the manner in which he scored them. A new game was developing; segregation could no longer keep it secret. "We knew," recalls Pete Coker, "that a different style was being created in places like New York, Washington, and Philly." But Bradley represented a triumph, however perishable, of the old style. His "ancestral form," as the writer John McPhee called it, was celebrated in a lengthy profile in the *New Yorker*. "He dislikes flamboyance," wrote McPhee, "and, unlike some of basketball's greatest stars, has apparently never made a move merely to attract attention.

While some players are eccentric in their shooting, his shots, with only occasional exceptions, are straightforward and unexaggerated."

Here, then, was a Great White Hope. And more. Bradley, who turned down more than seventy scholarship offers to pay his own way at Princeton, personified the idealized collegiate athlete. His game was modest, practiced, even Protestant. Not only did he belong to the Fellowship of Christian Athletes, but he taught Sunday school (even after road games) at the First Presbyterian Church in Princeton. Through no fault of his own, Bradley, for whom khakis and white shirts were a standard-issue uniform, had made an art of conformity.

"We were mesmerized by Bradley," says Les Robinson, recalling a deflating, unexpected rout, losing by a score of 66–48 to the Ivy Leaguers. "Press showed me film of the game the next day . . . We weren't guarding him like we guarded other guys. That's what killed Press, that we were in awe of him."

Even Bradley was astonished by State's passivity, the way Press's players—some of the most ferocious defenders in the ACC—would congratulate the Princetonians after a score. By halftime the Wolfpack had just 16 points. Bradley himself would finish with 27, shooting six for seven in the second half.

"We basically stood around and watched him," says Blondeau, still dumbfounded as to why.

The consolation game of the Eastern Regionals saw State play a St. Joseph's team that had come into the tournament ranked third in the nation with a record of 25–1. State won by 22. As it ended, some of the shell-shocked losers asked, "How did you guys ever lose to Princeton?"

With the exception of that loss, it had been a wonderful season, proof of what Press could do at a basketball school. He was voted the ACC's Coach of the Year, beating Duke's Vic Bubas by a vote of 82 to 9. "Seldom has there ever been such a stampede in favor of one coach," noted the Charlotte *News and Observer.* But the most convincing evidence of Press's coaching aptitude—and his outrageous aspirations for changing the game—wasn't an award, but a performance. It had happened earlier that season, over the Christmas break at Reynolds Coliseum. Only a half dozen or so guys were there, but Bill Bradley himself could inspire only a fraction of the awe they felt that day.

They were playing three-on-three. There were four starters: Coker, Lakins, Worsley, and Tommy Mattocks. There was Les. Pete made six.

"We loved to play against Pete," Lakins would recall. "He was the coach's son. Coach worked our tails off. That was our only retaliation."

They bellied him. They pushed him. They shoved him. They hit him. "We were beating the shit out of him that day," says Coker.

Then again, none of the corporeal punishment made any difference. Whatever Pete threw up came down through the net. There were jump shots, hook shots, set shots, bank shots, left- and right-handed shots, driving shots, and shots that seemed to come all the way from Guilford County. The game went on for hours, as each player took his turn trying to guard Pete. None of them could.

By now, Les had an idea of how good the kid was. They would play one-on-one most Saturdays. The games were to 21, best of three. Of maybe 100 games they played, Les won two of three only once. Still, he had never seen the kid like this: the way he was taunting starters on an ACC championship team, teasing them with that high yo-yo dribble. And then, as soon as you lean or lunge, you're embarrassed, he's gone.

Bill Bradley might reach a state that was hypnotically economical, but Pete was already his stylistic antithesis. Everything about this boy's game was funky and flagrant. He went behind the back, over the back, between his legs, between *your* legs. Then there was that pass with English on it, the one that bounced off the floor at an absurd angle. Years later a basketball writer would liken the ball's movement to something that came off a pool hustler's cue stick. But the sense of timing suggested the work of an accomplished comedian.

As the game wound down, toward the end of its third hour, Pete invented a shot. He was fading to the deepest corner. The stairs to the dressing room, just beyond the court, led down from the court level. "Going down," Pete called, as he threw up a high, arcing hook shot. He didn't stop to watch it swish though the net. He didn't even break his stride. He just kept going, right on down to the locker room.

Coker and Les ambled over to the bench and sat, speechless, shaking their heads, wondering if the show they had just seen—the finale of which they would call the *going down shot*—had really happened. Finally, Coker spoke: "Les, you ever see anything like that?"

Les shook his head no. "I think that was the best performance I've ever seen."

Coker wasn't arguing. "I think he might be . . ."

Les was nodding now.

"Might be the best who ever was."

10. THE DEEP END

In 1965, anticipating the arrival of his star recruit, a 7-foot-2-inch New Yorker named Lew Alcindor, John Wooden placed a call to Press. Wooden's resume already included a couple of national championships, his UCLA Bruins having won the NCAA tournament in '64 and '65. Still, when in need of basketball advice, Press was the sage he sought.

"I'd go to him first," says Wooden.

This time, his query concerned the efficacy of the high-low post offense—Wooden had never used it before—and how the scheme might exploit Alcindor's rather formidable talents. Press explained the offense in both form and function, giving his wholehearted endorsement. That was enough for Wooden. UCLA would win the NCAA tournament in each of Alcindor's three varsity seasons, beginning a streak of seven consecutive national championships, from 1967 to 1973.

Press's contribution to college basketball's greatest run, perhaps the most perfect dynasty in all of sports, comes as no surprise to Les Robinson. As a graduate assistant, Les loved nothing better than to listen to Press's prognostications as he told his acolyte where the game was headed.

"I remember him saying that the black man was physiologically equipped better than whites," says Robinson. " 'They're quicker and they jump better,' he said. 'They will dominate the game.' "

Press's understanding of genetics and physiology might have been suspect, but the hegemony of blacks in basketball—a taboo topic in the South in the sixties—has since become incontrovertible. It is worth noting that 1966, the year Alcindor played on UCLA's fresh-man team, was the only time in eleven seasons that the Bruins would not win the championship. In their absence, Texas Western made history by starting five blacks and beating Kentucky, coached by an arch segregationist named Adolph Rupp.

Unlike Rupp and his ilk, race didn't matter to Press. Rather, it was recruiting that he considered the bane of his existence. By all accounts, Press had become a terrible recruiter. "Kissing a sixteen-, seventeen-year-old kid's ass is not proper," he would tell Les. "A boy should be *dying* to play basketball."

Auditioning a kid from McKeesport with a series of street fights, then paying for his dental work, was fine by Press. He would do just about anything for the player who had proven his love for the game. But he wouldn't grant any illicit inducements. Nor would he swell a teenager's head with false promises.

He was working with a higher level of talent than he had at Clem-son, but he had yet to land that big recruit, a blue-chip talent, the kind of player who would ensure a program's good fortune. Then again, he never tried to. "I never thought Coach Maravich's goals were to get to the Final Four or to coach a national champion," says Robinson. "His goal was not to recruit the best players. His goal was to maximize the talent on every team and outcoach other coaches."

In a peculiar way, recruiting well would have defeated Press's purpose. One might even argue that he felt more comfortable being outmanned. Less talent meant more coaching. By that measure, 1965–66 would prove another successful season. "Maravich," wrote *Charlotte News* columnist Ronald Green, "got every ounce that could be gotten out of his material. It was not unusual for him to stay awake until five or six o'clock in the morning, diagramming plays, dreaming up defenses, figuring ways to beat teams that were sup-posed to beat [State]."

As Larry Lakins had finally graduated, the team wasn't quite as good. At one point, Press benched Tommy Mattocks—one of three players averaging better than 15 points a game—to send a message about his "sluggish play." Still, the Wolfpack had a record of 18–8, earning another date in the conference finals with Duke, then the second-ranked team in the country. This time, State was leading by 4 with three and a half minutes to go when Biedenbach stole the ball from Jack Marin, sped downcourt, and passed to Mattocks. But Mattocks was already thinking about shooting, not catching, and the ball went out of bounds. That mishap marked a change in the game. Suddenly, State was being called for a walking violation, and then a carry. Duke kept hitting its shots. The final: Duke by five, 71–66. Press studied the game film the next morning. "I was real sick," he said.

This particular agony proved fleeting, though. By then, Press had other worries.

Diana Maravich, daughter of Ronnie and wife Ramona, was six months old when State won the ACC championship. That afternoon, before Press left the house—so wound up he had barely eaten in three days—he took time to play with the little girl. "She's his good luck charm," explained Helen. "He adores that child."

Photographs of baby Diana, bow in her hair, had already been featured twice in newspaper profiles of the coach's dutiful wife, or, as one sportswriter put it, "one of America's most beautiful grandmothers." The pieces, generously spaced spreads in the women's pages of the *Charlotte News* and the *Raleigh News and Observer*, show Helen in idealized feminine poses: adorned with pearls, her hair swept back, beaming at the baby she cradles or delighted to be wielding a wooden spoon over the stove.

The façade itself was a remarkable achievement. Indeed, Helen almost hinted at her condition. "I'm a very sensitive, emotional person," she told the reporter. "I was born that way." Helen's was a veiled admission of what Pete's boyhood friend recognized by the occasional tremor in her hands. "The most nervous woman I've ever been around," says Ed Coakley.

Even back in South Carolina, Helen could barely contain herself during the basketball games. She would get up and yell—far more animated than the southern code of conduct would deem appropriate—particularly if she thought Pete was getting a bad deal from the refs or the other players. "She just loved him so intensely," says Coakley.

Sometimes, though, the action was just too much for her. Back in the '62 ACC tournament, she had to leave her seat and pace the corridor, as Clemson upset Duke. The former Helen Gravor had internalized the Maravich malady. "Basketball has just been our life in this family," she explained. "I guess that's why we're all nervous wrecks."

"She was always a depressive," recalls Dr. Billy Hunter, the family physician in Clemson.

Being a coach's wife only exacerbated her separation anxiety. Press would be gone for frequent and occasionally long stretches—recruiting trips, scouting missions, basketball camps, and road games. It seemed as if she never saw her husband. "The lonesomeness was just terrible," she once said.

And it only got worse. When she left Clemson, she also left her best friend in Louise Bradley. She began to drink. She began to withdraw. "Helen was a delightful, beautiful girl," says Lou Pucillo, State's 1959 ACC Player of the Year, now coaching the freshman team. "Then all of a sudden, we didn't see her anymore. It was some kind of hidden thing. Press wouldn't talk about it."

Press would greet him outside the door. "Helen's sleeping," he would say apologetically.

The State players heard stories but saw little. It was accepted that their coach's wife did not attend games or, with rare exceptions, team functions. She didn't even come to the door. Pete's friends came to understand that the house at 508 Northglen Drive, and what went on inside, were out of bounds. "I never set foot in there," says Jimmy Broadway, who recalls seeing Helen only twice. The first occasion was Spirit Night, a kind of pep rally for the parents. The other time, Pete answered Jimmy's knock at the door. Jimmy could see her in the background: shuffling slowly across the den, ghostlike, in her bathrobe.

Among the few people allowed in the house were Charlie Bryant and his wife, Helen, the Maraviches' neighbors on Northglen Drive. Press's assistant was shocked by what he saw: furniture and furnishings left as they had arrived the day of the move to Raleigh, in boxes piled up in the living and dining rooms. "They never, to my knowledge, uncrated the stuff," says Bryant.

Perhaps she was tired of moving. Or maybe she was just tired. Her lonesomeness was a fertile swamp from which poltergeists of the past would rise and rot her mind. Helen's spirit had begun to cave in. It was hoped that the granddaughter might help. "She was thrilled to death to have Diana," says Louise Bradley, who visited regularly from Clemson.

In addition to the photos of Helen, the *News and Observer* profile also featured a shot of the baby in the arms of a light-haired woman, "Mrs. Ronald Maravich," who was visiting from South Carolina. Ronnie had met Ramona in the Marines. In October 1964, Diana came to stay with her grandparents while her mother finished what was described as a secretarial course.

In fact, the union of Ronnie and Ramona was already doomed. "Ramona wanted to give the baby up for adoption," Louise remembers. "Helen and Press tried the best they could to talk her out of it. They even went to the place of adoption. But when they realized that she was actually going to sign the papers, they knew they couldn't let that happen. They said, 'We'll take her.' And that's what they did. They took Diana and raised her as their own. I remember Helen telling me that Ramona would not lay any claim to Diana."

She was their daughter. That's what they told everybody. That's what they told Diana.

Unfortunately, having a daughter had no salutary effect on Helen. "She was so afraid that the kid was going to get sick," says Charlie Bryant, who recalls Helen's fear of germs becoming so pronounced that she would follow him around the house with paper towels and cleaning solution, wiping anything he might have touched.

When Diana first arrived, Press couldn't so much as change a diaper. He proved a quick study, though. The same maternal muscles that deteriorated in Helen began to develop in Press. This was the best part of him, maybe the only part untethered to basketball, an undiscovered capacity for love. Now he would excuse himself from the games of cards and golf that had been his sole diversion. "Gotta go," he'd say. "There's a sweet little girl I got to look after."

Now, as he pushed fifty, Press acquired the skills to care for a baby girl. In Helen's increasingly frequent absences, he did everything for

Diana: the bathing, the feeding, the wiping, and the holding. "He was the best mother he could be," says Louise.

What's more, he was freer with his affections than he had been with the boys. He doted on Diana in a way he never had before. "Almost," says Louise, "like he worshipped her."

These good works were lost on Helen, however, who periodically checked into the psychiatric ward at Duke University Hospital. Sometimes, Press would be on the road. When that happened, Les—and only Les—would get a call: "Why don't you go over and see Helen."

Sometimes he went alone. Other times he went with his wife, Barbara, whose own mother was an alcoholic. She was like a "coach," as Les puts it. As a ballplayer, he was accustomed to orthopedic problems. What he now saw was new to him. He remembers a pregnant teenager sharing a room with Helen, and he remembers Helen's face. She always had cold cream on her face. "I could see where she was a beautiful lady in her day," he says. "But she looked wiped out. She looked like one of those old movie stars who've fallen on hard times in their late forties."

Most of all, though, he remembers the way Helen held his hand, and how it took some getting used to. "I'm not a real touchy person," says Les. "That was a little uncomfortable for me. I couldn't get up and leave."

She would reach for his hand as he arrived at her bedside. And, unlike other people, she would not let go.

As Helen went off to one nuthouse, Ronnie went to another, a place called Vietnam. Perhaps nuttier still was Coach Maravich cast in the role of Mr. Mom. But there was, at least to Press's way of thinking, a solution. The worse it became at home, the more he looked at Pete to set things right. The balance of power between father and son now shifted, irrevocably. Press needed Pete more than Pete needed Press.

And as the father-coach became even more of a stage mother, his teenage player-son began talking back. "They loved each other with an undying passion, but they would fight like cats and dogs," says Charlie Bryant, who noticed yet another contradiction in the relationship: "You couldn't be around Press for five minutes and not have him talk about Pete." On the other hand, Press would sing Pete's praises to everyone but Pete. Alone with his son, he would dwell on the few flaws in his game—not the magnificent moves, but the misses and the mistakes. Family nights became, as Pete himself would recall, "entire evenings of strategy sessions and chalk talks . . . I could score thirty points in a crucial game, but Dad would point out all the mistakes I made hoping I would not repeat them again. Perhaps the mistake had been a turnover or a poorly timed shot; whatever it was, it seemed to override any of the positive points."

Where Pete was concerned, the goal was always within his grasp, but never attained. The burden did not ease up, as if Press believed that only perfection brought salvation. Indeed, Press's very conception of Pete, and what the boy would do for the game, kept him going. "I don't know whether he thought of Pete as a basketball player or a son," says Frank Weedon. "But if Pete was just a *person*, not a basketball player, Press might have fallen off the deep end, too."

"It wouldn't be fair," Press once said. "I am going to send my boys away to play for somebody else."

That was back in Clemson, when Ronnie was a rising junior with Pete headed into the eighth grade. But as Pete closed out his high school career, Press ceased such pronouncements. Rather, he let it be known that his boy would not be playing for a rival ACC school. "I can't afford to let him play for anyone else in the conference," he said. Then again, with just the slightest twist of that logic, he really couldn't afford to let Pete play for anyone else at all.

Lou Pucillo recalls a conversation as they prepared to tee off at Wildwood Country Club. "Press, you can go all over the country, and you won't find a player better than Pete."

"Yeah, I know."

"You gotta coach him."

"I don't know if I want to coach my son."

Lou looked up from the tee. Press was bluffing again. Or trying to, at least. Who did he think he was fooling with that big old shit-eating grin?

• • •

Ed McLean, Pete's coach during his senior year at Broughton, told the college recruiters they had to go through Press. "Every one of them I talked to said his father was going to make the call," says McLean. "I never thought he'd go anywhere but with his dad."

"He *had* to coach Pete," says Les. "That was given. In Press's mind, that was the ultimate."

By December of Pete's senior year, Press had decided that Pete would attend prep school, Edwards Military Institute, instead of going directly to college. His reasoning was twofold: first, Pete needed to gain some weight; second, he needed to raise his board scores. The ACC had a strict rule disqualifying anyone with less than 800 on the Scholastic Aptitude Test.

In the meantime, Press began offering the most promising prep stars an unusual incentive to join the Wolfpack. It wasn't for everybody. In fact, one might argue that Press had come up with a whole new way to muck up his recruiting efforts. Charlie Scott, a high-scoring guard who'd go on to become an All-Star in the pros, might have become State's first black player if not for the coach's unusual sales pitch. "When you're in high school and somebody's recruiting you, you always think they're going to tell you how great you are," Scott said. "But I'll never forget Press Maravich telling me that the biggest privilege I would have would be to play with his son, Petey."

In December 1966, Edwards Military Institute played the N.C. State freshmen. Press insisted on riding out to the game with Les, now in his second season as the freshman coach. Knowing how much Press had invested in Pete, Les had grave misgivings about coaching against his boss's son. He knew Pete's game as well as anyone. They had played all those one-on-ones. Then there were Saturday mornings, when they tested prospective recruits by playing two-on-two, Les and Pete versus a couple of high school seniors. "Who we got coming in today?" Pete would ask. God, how he loved to embarrass those boys. Les would never forget the guys they beat 21–3.

"What do you think?" asked Press.

"Not ACC caliber," said Les.

Press took a pass. Of course, one of those kids, Chad Calabria, went on to have a storied career in the Big Ten. With that in mind, Les warned his freshmen as best he could: Don't go for Pete's fakes, don't lean when he teases you with that high dribble, try to keep him from getting the ball. "Pete wasn't going against your average high school all-stars," says Les. "These were ACC scholarship players." Didn't make much difference, as Pete led all scorers and dominated the State frosh.

That put Press in a fine mood for the drive home. He'd look up from his cup of tobacco spit, and shake his head with wonder. "He's gonna be a great one, isn't he, Les?"

Les agreed, happy for the man who had made him a coach, and feeling much relieved for himself. "That was the only game I was ever glad I lost," he says.

Les recalls Pete as having scored "40-something" that night at Edwards. In fact, he scored only 26, and 33 in the rematch at Raleigh, another blowout win for Edwards. Still, it's easy to understand Robinson's recollection, as Pete's 40-point efforts were becoming almost common. He even hit 50 against Charleston Southern.

The problem was, his board scores weren't rising with his line in the box scores. Pete never liked school, but he disliked Edwards most of all. Perhaps that's why Press had Les drive Pete back after spending weekends in Raleigh. Press had warned him, "He's going to fight you, Les. He won't get out of the car."

Sure enough, Pete didn't want to get out. Finally, Les had to grab him. "You're going in," he said.

"You don't know how bad it is," said Pete, who prevailed on Les to see for himself. Pete's room was up on the third floor of the dorm. Even Les had to admit it was a shit hole. He'd want to escape, too. That's what he thought when he saw the rope. It was thick, attached to the bed post leading out the window.

"What's this?" he asked. "You ain't slipping out on me."

"My dad put that there."

"Your dad?"

"In case there's a fire."

When he got back to Raleigh, Les asked Coach Maravich if he knew anything about a rope. "Hell yeah," said Press. "That place is a damn firetrap."

When it came to Pete, Press would leave nothing to chance. Just as he took precaution against fire, so did he guard against any natural disasters brought on by adolescence. He would not lose this boy to the temptations that took hold of Ronnie. Pete would recall his first flirtations with vice at the age of twelve. These included a kiss from a pretty brown-haired girl — "I almost fell off the porch," he said — and a beer on the steps of the Methodist Church in Clemson. That first sip required more than a little peer pressure to overcome his father's warning. As Pete told his pal, "He said if I ever drank beer, he'd take me out and shoot me with a .45."

Such threats had their intended effect on the boy's social life. "No sweethearts. As far as I know, senior prom was his first date," says Ed McLean, who asked the next morning if Pete had taken her out to breakfast.

"Nah," he answered glumly. "I took her home around midnight."

There were two Petes. With the ball in his hands, he had supreme confidence. Off the court, he became shy and awkward. Bob Sandford, two years older than Pete, recalls, "We would go places and you could see him tagging along, looking around. Asking a thousand questions, all about girls."

Sandford, a fine athlete from Cary High School, played small college basketball in Virginia. After his freshman year, he got a job at the Hillsborough Y, where he recognized Pete as the little, starved-looking boy he had played with at the Campbell College camp. Now, in the summer of '64, with Pete going into his senior year, they became fast friends. Bob was sharing an apartment with three other guys, all ballplayers, and was well-known at places like the Jolly Knave, a local watering hole. Pete saw in Bob what he had been looking for in Ronnie: a protector and a guide. They played ball just about every night and all day on the weekends.

On one such occasion, as they headed off to the gym, Pete discovered that he had forgotten his socks. As basketball hosiery was of utmost concern to him—he wore two pairs and liked to push the outer pair down around his ankles—he wouldn't play without them. Bob told him to get some out of his drawer, from which Pete selected the oldest, droopiest, most abused of gray wool socks he could find.

He might not have missed a shot that day.

"It's the socks, Pete."

"What do you mean?" he said.

"Clearly," said Bob, "it's the socks."

Next day, Pete wore them again. And again, he could not miss. Droopy haberdashery, melding adolescent vanity and superstition with a basketball aesthetic, became a mandatory part of his wardrobe. He cared for his socks—the more worn out, the better—with as much concern as his mother had, hanging them out to dry on the line. "They were his good luck charm," says an old friend. "You didn't mess with Pete and his socks."

Three or four nights a week, Pete would call Press and tell him he was staying over at Bob's. There was one caveat. "I had to promise he wouldn't drink," says Sandford.

At the age of seventeen, Pete had already seen enough drinking. That's one of the reasons he liked staying at Bob's. It was getting to the point where he couldn't stand being home. "His dad would be off trying to recruit," says Sandford. "Ronnie and his wife were busted up. Diana was just a little bitty thing. And that was bothering Pete, because Diana was there while his mother was drinking."

Some nights, Bob would pick him up in his '52 Chevrolet. Helen would come to the door, "drunk as a skunk," he remembers.

"She's messed up, man," Pete would mumble disgustedly. "C'mon. Let's get out of here."

Their nights out began as a comic adventure, with Bob trying to get Pete to overcome his shyness. "Pete," he'd say, "if you want to meet girls, you got to learn how to dance. And let me tell you, if you can play basketball, you can dance."

Next thing he knew, Bob had him practicing the Shag, which was all the rage in Carolina. Regrettably, all the shagging in the world couldn't transform the teenage Pete into a ladies' man. But he became addicted to beach music. Every chance he got he'd be putting the Drifters or the Tams on Bob's stereo.

"Pete could never do anything in moderation," says Sandford.

At the age of eighteen, Pete started drinking beer with the guys. The problem, again, was one of excess. If Bob had two or three, Pete had to have eight. "At a hundred and fifty pounds, he's wasted," says Sandford. "And when he's wasted, he starts running his damn mouth."

On more than a couple of occasions, Sandford had to step between Pete and the offended party. Of course, there were times when Bob just couldn't help the boy. One morning during his Christmas break from Edwards, Pete showed up at Reynolds for varsity practice with a big black eye and a swollen cheek.

"What the hell happened to you?" asked Hal Blondeau.

He had come home with beer on his breath, he explained, and the old man just popped him one.

On the bright side, at least Press didn't use the .45.

To make matters worse, Pete did not meet the minimum 800 board score required to qualify for the ACC. "We kept thinking he was going to make it," recalls Charlie Bryant. "And he would get, like, 796. He took the test several times, but it was always the same thing. Pete never applied himself."

The scores might not have surprised Mrs. Lola Hawkins, his seventh-grade math teacher, but they came as a great disappointment to Press. Pete, on the other hand, seemed to take it in stride. "I think initially Pete wanted to get away from his daddy—which would have been a real good thing for Pete, but not for Press," says Bryant.

Pete would have been happy to attend West Virginia. Not only was it Jerry West's alma mater, but George Krajack had just been hired as an assistant to Coach Bucky Waters. Waters, who had played under Everett Case and coached under Vic Bubas at Duke, saw Pete as West's successor. "You're in that league," he assured him.

Waters wasn't blowing smoke. "In my lifetime," he says, "I have not seen a better offensive player than Pete Maravich."

West Virginia was a basketball school, but, unlike State, it required no minimum SAT score. Pete also liked the wide-open style of play. But most attractive for him, there was no Press. "He did not want to play for his dad," says Waters. "It looked like a lock."

But then, without any warning, Press heard from Lousiana State University in Baton Rouge. Founded in 1860 as the Louisiana State Seminary of Learning and Military Academy, its first president was William Tecumseh Sherman, best known as a Union general for his famously brutal March to the Sea. LSU had grown from nineteen students and four professors to an enrollment of approximately 17,000, but still required able-bodied male students to take two years of Reserve Officers Training Corps courses. LSU was regarded as a fine football school, having won the national championship in 1958. But as it concerned basketball, LSU made Clemson look good. At least Clemson played in a basketball conference. LSU played in the Southeastern Conference, which consisted of one national power-house, Kentucky, and a couple of traditionally respectable teams in Tennessee and Vanderbilt. The other eight were strictly football schools.

The basketball program had experienced some success with the matriculation of Robert E. Lee Pettit Jr. A six-nine forward from Baton Rouge, Pettit later admitted that he chose LSU only "because I doubted I could measure up to expectations on a fancier scholarship." In fact, he would score better than 27 points a game in college and be inducted in the NBA Hall of Fame. But with his graduation in 1954, the expectations for Tigers basketball returned to normal, which was to say, relentlessly dismal. Teaching basketball at the "Old War Skule," as it was known, was nobody's idea of a glamour job. In the early 1960s, Coach Jay McCreary's duties included taping his players' ankles before practice. It got so bad that by April 1966, McCreary's successor, Frank Truitt, quit after only one season to go to Kent State. Truitt had gone 6 wins against 20 losses. Only the standards of LSU basketball would qualify such a campaign as a success. "A good start," wrote the *Morning Advocate*'s Bud Montet. "A lot of fans will hate to see Truitt leave."

So thankless was the coaching job that Athletic Director Jim Corbett soon placed a call to Press. Corbett, who had served as chairman of the NCAA Television Committee, understood his business and how it was evolving. He needed to sell the game in the Deep South. He needed to change the culture of LSU basketball. He needed an attraction that could finally push forward a much talked of plan for a new arena on campus.

"Someone told him that the best basketball prospect in the country was Pete Maravich and that Press wasn't a bad coach himself," says Bud Johnson, LSU's sports information director and a Corbett protégé.

Corbett called Press and, following a brief introduction, asked two questions. First: "Would you be interested in becoming the basketball coach here at LSU?" Then: "Would you bring your son with you?"

To hear Press explain the situation, it was all about the money. He was still in debt and had already been negotiating with the NBA's Baltimore Bullets. Thinking he had nothing to lose, he would soon ask for what he thought to be an absurdly rich contract: five years guaranteed at $15,000 per. Still, Corbett knew a bargain when he saw it and shook hands with Press on the spot.

There were other factors. Everett Case, now on his deathbed, was said to have given the deal his wholehearted blessing. Press himself cited the lure of the "$5 million" field house LSU had on the drawing board. But the primary motive was supposedly financial. Reporters estimated that Press would be getting a $5,000 raise over his salary at State. The deal, said Press, was "one I just couldn't afford to turn down."

"Press wanted you to believe the overriding concern was money," says Hal Blondeau. "But I think we all saw through it."

"He was going to coach Pete," says Les, "and I don't care where it was." Baton Rouge, where the university required no minimum board score, was no obstacle. "He would have coached Pete in Alaska," says Lou Pucillo.

The problem was, Pete didn't want to go to Baton Rouge any more than he wanted to go to Alaska. He did not want to be part of what Bucky Waters called "a package deal." He wanted to go to Morgantown, West Virginia.

Waters understood the pressure on Pete and the case for him to attend LSU: *You've got to do this for the family.* But there was a flip side to that argument. It was said, with ample justification, that there were only two sports at LSU: football and spring football. What's more, the gym smelled like a barn, which is pretty much what it was. "You're going to need a frontal lobotomy," said Waters, who likened the task of bringing basketball to the bayou to "a lot of missionary work."

"Press was having a fit," says Bob Sandford, who was home when he took the coach's call and handed the receiver to Pete. Bob could hear Press yelling as if he were there in the room.

"You're going with me," said Press.

"The hell I am," said Pete. "I'm going to West Virginia. I already talked to Bucky Waters."

"The hell *you* are," said Press.

"LSU, that's a doggone football school," said Pete. "They probably don't even have a gym down there."

"You go to West Virginia, you don't ever bring your ass back into my house again."

Finally, Pete came up with a deal of his own: "If I'm going to LSU, you got to buy me a car."

Pete would repeat his demand in a later conversation, this one in front of Les Robinson. "Car my ass," said Press, before storming out.

Les was taken aback. Ordinarily, if a recruit had asked him for a car, Press would've probably smacked the kid. But this wasn't an ordinary recruit. This was a blue-chipper. "The only one he ever signed," says Les.

There were still other discussions between father and son, coach and player. But the negotiations finally ended with Press reiterating his position: *Don't ever come home again.*

"Pete caved in," says Waters.

But the West Virginia coach could not hear the violent urgency in Press's voice. It was unlike anything Pete had heard since he'd come home drunk. This time, Press left little doubt. He would've used the .45.

•   •   •

Soon, Bud Johnson called a big press conference at a hotel in New Orleans. Press wasted little time at the podium before informing everybody that his son would be "a superstar." The sportswriters, most of them, did a double take. They glanced over at each other. No one quite knew what to make of this. Coaches didn't brag on their players, much less their sons. Some of the guys chuckled along, figuring Press was kidding.

Press was dead serious, though. When he said superstar, he meant it. "Just wait," he said. "Wait'll you see my boy."

11. King of the Cow Palace

As a condition of his employment, Press had agreed to take on the previous regime's assistants: Jay Mc-Creary, who had remained with the program since being relieved of his duties as head coach, and Greg Bernbrock, the freshman coach. This meant that Les Robinson had to get a new job, which he found as coach of Cedar Key High School in Florida. "Don't expect miracles the first couple of years," Press advised him. "Just work the youngsters on fundamentals and defense."

While Les waited for an assistant's job to open up, Press kept him on the LSU payroll as a scout, for $25 to $30 a game plus meals and gas. "He padded the mileage," says Les. "Those checks were huge for me."

In the meantime, they kept in touch by mail. Press was an assiduous correspondent, though his protégé was not at all encouraged by the first round of dispatches from Baton Rouge.

September 6, 1966: "Helen worries pretty much about hurricanes."
September 23, 1966: "I cancelled seven [coaching clinics] because of Helen's condition. When I mention hurricanes to my wife, she goes all to pieces."
October 18, 1966: "The coming season scares the hell out of me . . . This is the worst basketball situation I have ever faced—ever, ever!!! . . .
"Need players badly. Lots of 'em. Trying to break color line. Am

after one but I doubt if I can get him. He doesn't want to be the
first one."

January 17, 1967: "My wife has been pretty sick Les. Geez, I'll get
drunk when she gets well. Can't do anything with her being
sick. Must do home chores, feed, clean, clothe the baby, do
dishes, coach, etc. Even doing a poor coaching job because of
the situation . . .

"We are 3–11. Didn't expect to win 3. Have the dumbest club in
America."

February 21, 1967: "It isn't funny, Les. Last nite Mississippi State beat
us 66–64. We had them 64–60 with 27 seconds to go. Both
times our *damn stupid seniors* thru the ball out of bounds to M.
State . . . dumb bastards . . ."

Press would recall his inaugural season at LSU as "the roughest
year I have ever had in basketball." There was additional indignity in
having to play home games at the John M. Parker Agricultural Coliseum, an arena that smelled like his team played. "Cow manure and
horse manure," said Russ Bergman, a sophomore guard who grew up
on a farm in Illinois. The Cow Palace, as it was known, not only
stank, it was cold. Bud Johnson would recall a cold February in
1958 when he had to wear a topcoat on press row. Heat was achieved
only by the aggregate body warmth derived from densely attended
events. Not for basketball, though. The Cow Palace did not even
come under the aegis of the athletic department. Rather, as it
belonged to the School of Agriculture, basketball season had to be
sandwiched between the annual horse show in the fall and the rodeo
in the spring. That made for an abbreviated home schedule, with the
Tigers forced to begin each season with a month of practice at a local
high school. They didn't get into the agriculture building until late
November. Even worse, when the rodeo came to town in February,
they had to vacate the premises and go on the road.

By then, of course, the season was long gone. The 1966–67 Tigers
would finish 3 wins against 23 losses. "I don't have one damn guy
with a single basketball gene," fumed Press, who all but gave up on
the varsity.

"Toward the end of the year, Press was more interested in the freshman team," says Ralph Jukkola, who, as a six-three sophomore, was the team's best rebounder.

Press wasn't alone. In fact, all anyone seemed to care about was the freshman team, which is to say: Pete. After all, this was the coach's design. The cult of Press was modest compared to what came now: the cult of Pete.

The fascination began with his arrival on campus. It was July or August when a puzzled Pete asked Bud Johnson, "How come I don't see anyone playing ball?"

"Pete, it's 95 degrees outside."

The next day, with the Louisiana sun beating down at high noon, Johnson drove by the University High School basketball courts. There he was, on the gooey hot asphalt, doing his basketball homework. Johnson would recognize these oddly mesmerizing drills when he saw them later that summer, as Pete demonstrated in time with Press's lecture for a summer school coaching seminar.

However, for some of Pete's new teammates, it was easier to watch him than to play with him. For male freshmen, the year began with a series of humiliating rituals. They were issued yellow and gold beanies to place atop their freshly shaved heads. They marched every morning. They had to wear pajamas to the first football game. Such was indoctrination at the Ole War Skule.

Still, by contrast, acclimating to Pete could result in even more embarrassment. "In high school, every pass was a chest pass or a bounce pass," recalls Randy Lamont, a six-eight center. "Now the balls were coming from behind his back and between his legs. You were getting hit in the chest with perfect passes, but you had no idea where they were coming from. They were from angles we had never seen before. It took a lot of getting used to."

Players accumulated bruises, fading tattoos to remind them where and when they had missed one of Pete's passes. They used to say that the only time you didn't have to worry about Pete throwing you the ball was when he was looking right at you.

He was now listed as six-five, 180, a figure that was probably 20 pounds too generous. "There had been some publicity about how great the coach's kid was supposed to be," says Jukkola. "But my first impression of Pete was: Look at this skinny, bald-headed thing. Then you played against him. He could do some stuff."

On the eve of the season, a local guy named Boots Garland showed up to ref an intrasquad game between the varsity and freshman teams. "Where's the Maravich kid?" he asked.

"There in the corner," said one of the assistant coaches. "The one sitting down."

"No, really," said Garland. "Where is he?"

About two minutes into the scrimmage, Garland faked a cramp and called an official's time out. He hobbled over to his officiating partner and whispered, "Are you seeing what I'm seeing?" Pete had already performed several amazing basketball acts Boots had never before seen. He would finish the afternoon with 49 points, a fact duly noted in the press release drafted to alert the media of his debut for the freshman team. The Baby Bengals were to open the season against Southeastern Louisiana College, Thursday, December 1, 1966, 5:45 P.M. at the Cow Palace.

That day saw Pete tally an even 50 points, 16 assists, and one standing ovation as the team left the floor following a victory by the absurd score of 119–70. "From this day hence," wrote *Advocate* sportswriter Joe Planas, ". . . a lot of people are going to start going to a lot of LSU basketball games—a lot earlier."

Press's theory—selling his son to sell his team—worked to a fault. As varsity players made their way into the locker room, with the freshman game still in progress, the Cow Palace would be packed in a way not seen since the days of Bob Pettit. But a short while later, as they emerged in their uniforms, ready to warm up, they found a crowd that had already undergone severe atrophy. What was measured in the thousands might become a gathering of hundreds. Players would joke among themselves that everybody must be getting popcorn. But soon enough, reality set in. "We came to realize," says Jukkola, "that they ain't coming to watch *us* play."

The frosh team's 5:45 P.M. starting time altered the rhythms of college life. Cheryl Talbot Macaluso, a freshman in 1966, recalls students who'd "schedule classes just to make sure they had enough time to get to the 'Cow Palace' to stand in line for three hours just to have the chance to see a skinny kid play basketball."

The kids in those lines gladly endured cold or rain. The lines themselves became a party. And with Pete, so did the Ag Center. The Cow Palace became a place to be seen. More than that, one had the sense that Pete was helping them mark time in their lives. Amid the stink of horse shit rose the perfume of possibility.

"As soon as he touched the ball, people would be on the edge of their seat," said James Carville, a future presidential advisor who also arrived that fall. Carville takes special delight in recalling a "great rumor that was circulating": that Pete would literally bounce the ball into the basket.

The cult of Pete wasn't limited to students. Governor John Mc-Keithen became a fixture in the front row at the Ag Center. "A great basketball fan," said Press, who kept tabs on the governor's attendance. For years, an artist's rendering of the proposed Assembly Center had been featured in the LSU basketball media guide—but ground had never been broken on the project. That was about to change, though. "Because Pete was so hot as a player, the governor personally moved it up on the priority list," says Bud Johnson. Athletic Director John Corbett died suddenly of a heart attack during the season, but his business model was already taking shape. Press wasn't the only one with a vested interest in his son. Anyone with a stake in LSU or the new arena could recognize the economic imperative for the Maravich boy to play as Pistol Pete.

The configuration of the freshman team only accentuated his talents. When Press took the job back in May, the recruiting period was all but finished. Still, he tried to acquire some real talents. Harold Sylvester was a forward from St. Augustine, an all-black Catholic school in New Orleans. It wasn't long after he arrived in Louisiana that Press started visiting Sylvester. "The governor is coming to our games," said Press. "But the big thing is, you'll get an opportunity to play with my son."

Sylvester liked the guy; Press seemed ahead of the curve on racial issues. But he found himself thinking, *Your son? Who the hell is your son?*

He found out when Pete started showing up for games at St. Augustine. "Aside from the priest," Sylvester remembers, "he was the only white guy in the gym." They got to talking and struck up a kind of friendship, though it wasn't enough for Sylvester to become LSU's first black athlete. Tulane, in New Orleans, was a better school with a better basketball program. More than that, though, Sylvester felt more comfortable in his hometown. "It was safer than being in Baton Rouge, which I considered to be the backwoods at the time," he says.

Then there was Herb White, the most sought-after ballplayer in the state of Georgia. Kentucky wanted him. Tennessee wanted him. Georgia's governor made a personal appeal, telling Herbie how much the local folks wanted him to attend the state university. Under normal circumstances, guys like Herbie White would never consider playing for LSU. Still, Press figured it was worth a shot. Not long after he took the job, an envelope arrived at White's house in Decatur. Inside was an autographed publicity photo of Pete:

> Hi Herbie
> Hope you are a future LSU "fighting Tiger"
> > Best always,
> > "Pistol Pete" Maravich

Herbie studied the shot, shaking his head with astonishment, thinking, "Who the fuck is this guy?"

In terms of recruiting, Press found himself in his customary position. Most of the incoming freshmen had been signed by the previous regime, including Lamont and Jeff Tribbett. A 6-foot guard from Lebanon, Indiana, Tribbett had played alongside Rick Mount, a prodigious scorer who had been the first team sport athlete featured on the cover of *Sports Illustrated* while still in high school. Tribbett, a quarterback in football, was a reliable ball handler and a good shooter, with a sober sense of his talent and its limitations. Feeding Mount had trained him to caddy for Pete.

As Coach McCreary found guys like Tribbett and Lamont in the Midwest, Press returned to the territory he knew best, quickly signing two players from Aliquippa High School. Paul Milanovich was a six-three forward whose father had played on the Serbian teams and helped Press land his job at the high school. Rich Hickman, another 6-foot guard, had aroused only mild interest from places like Indiana State, University of Pennsylvania, and Ball State. But in Press's estimation, Hickman had outstanding qualifications: his father had worked forty years at J&L Steel, he had been recommended by Joe Pukach, and he could shoot. And like Tribbett, he understood exactly what his role would be at LSU. "I'd bust my ass and not complain," says Hickman. "Press made no bones about it; he was there to make Pete the high scorer and he was looking for guys who didn't mind."

Given what he had to work with, and what he wanted to accomplish, Press drew up a three-guard offense for the freshmen. Pete, Tribbett, and Hick became a triumvirate. On campus, they were known to golf and party. On the court, they'd run and gun. It was just freshman ball, but the scheme functioned as designed: to antagonize any reasonable quantitative expectation of college basketball. Pete seemed to set a new record with every game.

He averaged 43.6 points on a team that averaged 98.8. He scored 66 on 51 shots against a club team, the Baton Rouge Hawks. He led the team in assists, with a one-game high of 18. He took 604 shots and 234 foul shots. Pistol Pete—the moniker was now ubiquitous—was impossible to discourage, much less contain.

"I don't think those southern boys appreciated the way we played," says Paul Milanovich. "Pete was always getting roughed up."

He took a boxer's shot above the eye against Southern Mississippi in Hattiesburg. The cut opened like a baby's mouth, and he was taken to a local emergency room to be sewn up. LSU was losing in the second half when student trainer Billy Simmons saw the gym doors fling open: Pete. "Didn't even say hello to Coach Bernbrock," says Simmons. Instead, he proceeded directly to the scorer's table, reported for duty, and shot the Baby Bengals to victory. He went 12 for 12 from the line, finishing with 42 points and nine stitches. What's more, he had kept a perfect season alive.

The frosh were 17–0 going to Knoxville for the season finale with Tennessee. Pete had an off game—12 for 36 for a mere 31 points—but had sparked a late rally. Still, with seven seconds left, Tennessee was ahead, 75–73. Three seconds later, in violation of all probability, he managed what the *Advocate* circumspectly described as "a clever move" to draw a foul. Pete was an 83 percent free-throw shooter. He hit the first, but missed the second. So went the perfect season.

"He couldn't believe he missed that shot," says Simmons. "He talked about that his whole college career. But you've got to understand what he did to get those free throws. He got the ball off the inbounds and cut in front of a guy from Tennessee who was trailing the play. Nobody else even had the savvy to even think about that kind of thing."

Pete went AWOL after the game. His teammates became worried. Even his dad was worried—until it was learned that he walked the two miles back to the hotel. Not to be outdone, Press recalled his own high school career, the time he lost in Rochester and walked the twelve miles back to Aliquippa.

One wonders, then, if the solitary, sleepless funk that defeat engendered was part of the basketball gene. Whatever the case, the missed foul shot kept Pete from appreciating what he had already accomplished. His achievements were reflected in the numbers, of course—thirty-nine LSU freshman records had been set that season—not to mention the attendance figures. In the recent past, it would have been impossible to imagine the scene for LSU's final home date: fans actually being turned away before the freshman game. A building with the capacity for 8,000 fans was packed with 9,200. Famous Tiger fans now included the governor and Al Hirt, the trumpeter from New Orleans. Pete was a weekly guest on his father's television show, but his exploits were a daily topic of conversation in the coffee shops and barber shops. The Maraviches spread the game as preachers spread the gospel. As Bud Johnson noted in one of his many press releases devoted to Pete's glories, suddenly sporting goods stores couldn't stock enough basketballs, hoops, and nets. What Press had built for Pete all those years ago now became a common sight in football country. "Fathers," wrote Johnson, "were called upon to construct backyard goals."

Shooting baskets in the backyard—good training for all God-fearing white boys—evoked the most idyllic images. That's not to say anyone in Baton Rouge would argue that all ballplayers were created equal, or even God-fearing. Press's program observed two standards: one for Pete and one for everyone else.

Press didn't enforce strict training rules; rather, based on his own experience, he incorrectly assumed that college boys would be men. Nevertheless, there came a point in the season when he became outraged at reports of flagrant carousing and curfew breaking by some of the varsity players. Press wanted to kick them off the team.

"If you kick them off," said Coach McCreary, "you've got to kick Pete off, too."

"Why?" asked Press.

"Because he was with them."

The offense drew no sanction. Players quickly learned that the best way to avoid any trouble was to party with Pete. "If Pete was with you, usually nothing would happen," says Jukkola.

Then again, there were times when Pete—who couldn't hold his booze any better in college than he had in prep school—couldn't get out of his own way. The coaches kept it quiet, but he was suspended for a game in January. "Flu, that's what I was told," says Tribbett, who scored 37 in Pete's absence.

Still, Pete's punishments were exceedingly rare. The program, and Press, depended on keeping him happy. Les Robinson would recall a phone conversation with Press not long after he arrived in Baton Rouge. The payments, he said, were killing him.

Les didn't understand. The coach was making $15,000 a year, a huge score.

"I got the house payment," Press explained, "and the two car payments."

"Two?"

"Yeah," said Press. "I got Pete a car."

12. SHOWTIME

For father and son, working at the edge of art and science produced a kind of vaudeville. "Showtime," as they called it, toured the state, hitting towns like Shreveport and Alexandria, enticing the people, provoking their gossip, selling them on Tiger basketball. Each LSU player had his own Homework Basketball drill to display as a specialty. But the main attraction—nay, the only attraction—was Pete. His skills were more than a mere draw. "Pete was an advertising campaign," says Bud Johnson, the athletic department's publicity man. As for Press, he was barnstorming again, a basketball Barnum like Jim Furey of the Original Celtics or Abe Saperstein of the Globetrotters.

"Press would do the talking; Pete would do the dribbling, the passing, and the spinning," says Russ Bergman. "They would experiment. They had to keep coming up with new stuff, like a circus act. If they were going into a new town, they'd say, 'Showtime's got to get better.' Then Pete would start adding to his bag of tricks."

They were already a big hit on the summer circuit. Lou Pucillo recalls being at Campbell with Dolph Schayes, the Hall of Fame forward for the Syracuse Nationals. They were playing golf on a Thursday when Schayes asked, "You going tonight?"

Every Thursday night Pete took the stage. "Can't miss Showtime," said Schayes. "I bring the family."

More than the old pros, though, Pete had a hold on the kids. Campers looked forward to his ballhandling exhibitions as the highlight of their week. Teenagers like M. L. Carr, from Charlotte, idolized him, rehearsing the Homework Basketball routines until they could do them in their sleep. "I knew I couldn't be like Pete," says Carr. "But I did every drill religiously."

Carr attended the camp with a buddy from home, among the first blacks to attend the summer sessions at Buies Creek. Pete wasn't like anyone they had ever met. "He didn't see black or white—he picked us as his guys," says Carr, who followed him around like a puppy all week long.

At sixteen, Carr had a sense of the game and its stylistic antecedents, the most current being black. He knew about Earl "the Pearl" Monroe from Winston-Salem State Teachers College, author of the spin dribble. He knew of Providence's Jimmy Walker and his famous crossover, a change of hands dribble that made the quickest defenders look slow. Then there was Archie Clark, who had perfected the stutter step, a hesitation move. "But Pete," says Carr, "was the best I'd ever seen. Once he started doing all that stuff with the ball I was in awe. He did things the Globetrotters couldn't do yet."

In fact, Pete was already being called "a bleached Globetrotter." But unlike the Globetrotters, for whom antics now overwhelmed athletics, Pete made his moves in authentic game conditions. The competition was high level, high stakes, the expectations increasing at an exponential rate.

With the droopy socks and a head of hair that was now vaguely Beatle-esque, there was a growing sense that Pistol Pete would morph into something more iconic than just a basketball player. In anticipation of his varsity debut, Press saw to it that LSU had a new pep band and a squadron of pom-pom girls. He arranged to videotape Pete's games and the Homework Basketball drills. Left to Press, there would be a fully documented record of exactly how he and his son had conspired to change the game.

Press was not alone in forecasting Pete's greatness. "He's as good as any basketball player I've ever seen," said Doug Moe, a two-time All-American at North Carolina. Moe, who was six-six, 220 pounds, based this opinion on a series of spirited one-on-ones that summer at Campbell. Then a rookie with the New Orleans Buccaneers of the upstart American Basketball Association, Moe bet a teammate that the kid would average 35 points a game as a sophomore.

In fact, Pete came out of the gate averaging 45 points on 42 percent shooting. "I'm in a slump," he said.

As Press's design never accounted for a slumping Pete, LSU had little margin for error. The Tigers were woefully short, not to mention woefully short on experience. There wasn't a senior on the roster. The recruits included a couple of junior college transfers: a six-seven All-American from Iowa, Steve Shumaker, and Rich Lupcho, an otherwise unwanted guard from Coffeyville (Kansas) Junior College by way of Aliquippa. Of the two, Press was partial to the undersized Lupcho—"five eight in elevator shoes," as he was described—who just happened to be Joe Pukach's nephew. There were never enough guards to please Press, who continued to start Hickman and Tribbett. "Just dumb luck," says Tribbett, still chuckling over his good fortune to have started as a sophomore. "It just so happened that we walked into such a horseshit basketball program."

By Press's calculation, Pete would have to shoot 40 times a game for LSU to have a chance of winning. Not only did the theory violate every strategic principle of the game, it had never been done. Shooting at such an absurdly rapid rate—better than a shot a minute—would prove physically and psychologically grueling. Pete's number 23 might as well have been replaced with a bull's eye. As a coach, Press understood the burden this would place on his son; as a father, he could live with it. "He's got more pressure on him than any kid in America," he said.

As Pete's varsity career began, signs of this stress were less than apparent. Early in the season, after LSU beat Texas handily on the road, veteran Southeastern Conference referee Charles McCarthy went out for a bite and a couple of beers. He was walking back to his hotel in the wee hours when he heard the most goddawful attempt at singing. McCarthy turned to gaze on the happy, if melodically challenged crooner. He had a coed on each arm.

"Hey, Mr. Charlie," exclaimed Pete, "how you doing?"

By now, Pete's game had become the subject of some discussion among league officials. Coming down full stride on the break, he had a move whereby he would wave his hand over the ball, then tip it with the other hand in the opposite direction. It looked, in the most literal sense, like a magic trick. Such apparent impossibility moved a ref to blow his whistle, signaling a traveling violation.

"How can you make that call?" said an outraged Pete. "You've never even *seen* that move."

In fact, the call became the subject of an SEC officials' meeting. The refs examined the tape until, at long last, they had to shake their heads in grudging agreement with the kid: *He might be right.*

Suddenly, calling LSU games had become a complicated proposition. Guys like McCarthy wanted to work only with experienced partners. If you were teamed with a guy who hadn't been around, he might go into shock seeing Pete for the first time.

Officials had to rethink the game as it pertained to the league's new sensation. "One thing you didn't want to do is foul him out of the game," says Charlie Bloodworth, another veteran SEC official. "Pete put more people in the seats than anybody."

To whistle Pete for a foul was to incur the wrath of Press. "You son of a bitch," he would holler, "you foul him out and these people are gonna go crazy. They didn't come to see you call the game, they came to see him play."

Everybody wanted to see the Pistol. Fan mail arrived at the LSU athletic department by the sackful. Practices became targets of opportunity for groupies and autograph seekers. His prized practice socks were pilfered from the trainer's laundry bags. That's when Pete started washing them himself, a ritual cleansing with Woolite over a slopsink in the trainer's room. Those socks were talismans; teenage boys began to abuse their own white hosiery until they were acceptably gray and droopy. And this was in *football* country.

Reporters from Georgia and Mississippi who had never even been to a basketball game started making themselves seen. Suddenly, games in places like Oxford and Athens and Tuscaloosa were selling out. Visiting Georgia's Stegeman Coliseum, a venue that held fewer than 11,000, Pete drew 14,200, described as the biggest basketball crowd in the state's history. Down in Tuscaloosa, at Alabama—a shrine to Bear Bryant's gridiron glories—15,014 turned out for LSU, the most people ever at an SEC basketball game.

With Pete in the house, big gyms seemed like stadiums, and mere bandboxes felt as if they had been transformed into great arenas. Many of these evenings concluded with fans standing to cheer in appreciation of the road team.

Among the first of these occasions was the night of January 11, 1968, at Tulane's home court in New Orleans. A gym that held about 4,400 had been packed well beyond capacity. LSU's pregame routine included layup lines with Pete going through his repertoire of tricks as he fed each player cutting to the basket. It wasn't only the audience that found itself enthralled; opposing players couldn't take their eyes off him. "You were never supposed to look at your opponent during warm-ups," says Johnny Arthurs, a high-scoring forward for Tulane. "But there we were: watching Pete put on a show."

In preparation for the game, Tulane coach Tom Nissalke had spent a great deal of time studying films. His shot charts indicated that Pete went right 90 percent of the time. The best way to play him, Nissalke concluded, was to force him the other way. "Make him go left," Nissalke kept hollering from the sidelines. "He can't go left."

Pete went left for 52 points and 8 assists that night. But his line doesn't begin to tell the story. "I've never seen a righthanded player throw a lefthanded behind-the-back bounce pass going full speed on a two-on-one fast break—and hit the outside man in stride for a layup," wrote the *States-Item*'s Peter Finney.

Then there was this, from George Sweeney's lead in the next day's *Times-Picayune*:

It had a revival atmosphere.

The 6,000 partisan Tulane fans who took up all the available space—sitting and standing—left the Wave Freret St. gym believers last night.

Those who didn't express themselves verbally, just mumbled in amazement.

That's the way Pete Maravich has left 'em this season . . .

Pistol Pete's worksheet for the evening was worth a two-minute standing ovation by everyone in the house except the Tulane bench.

The story appeared under the headline "Greenies Are Believers," though some of the Tulane players remained unconvinced. "I remember looking at the films after the game," says Arthurs. "Pete had a move where he got out on the break and dribbled between his legs and then behind his back. We made the coach replay it again and again and again because no one believed he actually did it."

It was the kind of move that prompted Bud Johnson to wonder. Every so often, Pete would do something he had never done before. On those occasions, Bud would ask, "Hey Pete, how come I never saw you practice *that* one."

"Oh yes I have," Pete would say. "Many times."

"When?"

"In my head."

In my head.

In a flash, as anticipation met circumstance, Pete produced a collective gasp, a beguiling instant widely interpreted as improvisational wit. And no one was more vulnerable to the seductive power of these moments than the man who had made it possible. To Press, these were the sacred seconds, a synthesis of conceptual art and performance art. Here was the payoff, the ecstasy, the high, the justification for his addiction to Pete. Finally, he could lose himself. As he told *Time* magazine that season, "I get to the point where I don't coach him. I just watch."

Typically, Rich Lupcho sat on the bench next to the coach. Press would slap him on the knee when Pete did something extraordinary. "Did you *see* that?" Press would holler.

He had become as much a spectator as a coach.

"He lived in awe of what Pete created," says Bud Johnson.

Which is to say, what *he* had created.

Les Robinson joined the team in Gainesville just after New Year's when the Tigers were playing Florida. Press assigned Les a seat on the bench and had him keep track of Pete's assists and steals, which he thought were being deliberately undercounted by opposing teams' statisticians. "They're screwing him everywhere he goes, Les."

Certainly, Press was more concerned with stats than with Florida's six-ten All-American center, Neal Walk. LSU had no answer for

Walk, nor did Press even attempt to devise one. The result, a 97–90 LSU defeat, was reported in the *Advocate* under a headline that read: "Maravich 'Held' to 32 Points."

The defeat was less troubling to Les than what he now saw in his mentor. "He wasn't the same coach I knew at N.C. State," says Robinson. "He had already become obsessed with Pete's numbers. He had gone from being one of the greatest coaches in the game to the coach of the greatest player in the game. That's the only criticism I have of Coach Maravich: he loved his son too much."

Others, including some of Press's oldest coaching cronies, were less diplomatic. They saw Pete's shot selection as an endorsement of selfish play. Not that Press would be deterred by mere criticism. "I wish he'd shoot a thousand times a game," he said.

In Pete's first season of varsity ball, LSU improved from 3–23 to 14–12, while violating the game's every orthodoxy, not to mention the very principles that made Press—proponent of ensemble basketball, erstwhile creator of the junto defense—a great coach in the first place. Though he had long arms and great anticipation—the physical tools to be a great defender—Pete couldn't be bothered with defense. "Pete had to work so damn hard on offense," says Rich Hickman, "he used defense to rest."

Once again, John Wooden chalked it up to the enigma of Press. "If any of my players made a behind-the-back pass," says John Wooden, "they'd be sitting on the bench. Same thing with the dunk. I didn't permit any of that."

It's worth noting that the NCAA voted to outlaw the dunk in 1967. The move was considered a preemptive sanction against Lew Alcindor. In a larger sense, it was a sanction against a still-emerging black style of basketball. Literally and metaphorically, the NCAA had found a way to keep the black man down. And yet, this wasn't solely a racial matter. The issue concerned propriety, modesty, and the limits of athletic expression. How much would be tolerated in America's student athletes? (Very little, in the case of Alcindor, as Wooden didn't allow his players to be interviewed.) These weren't hippies or yippies, after all. These were good kids, maybe the last kind of good kids. These were ballplayers.

For the dons of the NCAA, the prototype was still Bill Bradley, whose greatness had been, in part, a rebuke of flamboyance. On the eve of his first varsity season, Pete held out the spectacularly naïve hope that he, too, might actually blend in. "Just another fish in the pond," he said, explaining that he wanted to be known as a winner, not a scorer.

But that wasn't Press's plan. Nor was it Pete's nature. So now here came the Pistol, whose game was immodest, flagrantly attention seeking, irresistible. He commanded the attention of all eyes in the house. Another fish in the pond? He'd have a better chance of growing gills. The crowd nourished a rapturous urge in him. "The louder it got, the more pumped up he became," says Billy Simmons. "The crowd was like a drug to him. You could see it in his eyes."

Opposing teams devised any number of ways to deal with Pete. Unable to force him left or right, recalls one former Tulane player, "the only real option was to hit him. And let me tell you, he got roughed up a lot."

The arduousness of Pete's undertaking seemed to register on his face. Those same soft pop star features contorted to form a pained mask as he dodged defenders on his way to the basket. Physical abuse may have raised the degree of difficulty, but it would not detract from his game. Despite his reedlike body, Pete had the heart to take it.

As far as sanctioned strategies, the most common were the box and one or the triangle and two, zone defenses with one or two defenders shadowing Pete wherever he went on the court. Kentucky's Adolph Rupp had another idea. Knowing that Pete could get his points even if double- and triple-teamed, Rupp decided to cover Pete with a single defender and make sure no one else did any real damage. Of course, with so much more talent at every other position, Kentucky could afford to let Pete get his points.

The coach who had the most success against Pete was Tennessee's Ray Mears. Press had disliked Mears since his days at State, when the Vols' coach had the bad form to call time-out in the closing moments of a Tennessee victory. Press had vowed to get even, though it was beginning to look as if that would not happen in his natural lifetime.

"Press wanted Pete to be his glory boy, so I studied Pete," says Mears. "I put in a lot of time figuring out how to give him trouble." Not only did Mears have excellent talent at his disposal, but he decided to keep a minimum of two very physical defenders on Pete at all times. If that wasn't working, he used three. When playing LSU, he says, "you didn't have to worry about the other guys."

Tennessee disrupted Pete's path in a half-court set, pushing him toward the middle as he tried to run the baseline. Still, Pete did his best work on the break. And here, Mears identified the weakness in Press's design, just as Press had noticed it in Cam Henderson's attack all those years before in West Virginia.

He deployed his players to prevent the first pass. As the ball was being inbounded, the Vols were already swarming around Pete. "We cut off the pass to him," says Mears. "That stopped him from running. His father was highly upset with me."

As a sophomore Pete averaged 19 points against Tennessee—but 45.8 against everyone else.

For a time, the national media tried to make the collegiate scoring title a three-horse race between Niagara's Calvin Murphy, Purdue's Rick Mount, and Pete. But the numbers couldn't sustain much suspense, as Pete won going away. He scored more points (1,138) than any sophomore in history. He set records for most field goals (432) and most field goal attempts (1,022) and the highest single-season scoring average (43.8). He was named to five different All-America teams and voted the SEC's Most Valuable Player. On December 22, 1967—seven games into his varsity career—he eclipsed Bob Pettit's single-game SEC scoring record against Mississippi State. On January 29—a day after sitting out practice with a 104-degree fever—he went for 54 against Vanderbilt. On February 17, he scored 59 against Alabama, setting, for the second time that season, the single-game SEC record. In all, he hit the 50-point mark nine times that season.

The fascination with Pete's scoring might not have made for sound team basketball, but it was great box office. Press went so far as to float the idea of putting a floor down in LSU's 68,000-seat football stadium. Why not? he figured: "The Globetrotters do it all the time."

Like the Globetrotters, Pistol Pete had become an attraction that transcended the game. After a while, wins and losses almost seemed beside the point. There were other kinds of victories, ones measured in fame and fortune. A country songwriter named Woody Jenkins would compose "The Ballad of Pistol Pete":

> . . . .
> *Maravich, oh Maravich*
> *Talk of you in years to come*
> *How you could pass, how you could run*
> . . .

The Pistol was featured in *Time* and *Newsweek*. There would be a photo spread in *Life*. But the piece that codified the emerging Maravich myth was a cover story in *Sports Illustrated*, "The Coed Boppers' Top Cat." Written by Curry Kirkpatrick, it served as a chorus of *auld lang syne* for Bill Bradley and all he represented. (Forget Oxford. No one would remember Pete so much as cracking a book.) The Prince was dead; long live the Pistol. Kirkpatrick bore witness to the creation of a celebrity. He noticed the "coeds with long brown hair and pussycat eyes" as they all but purred, *"Pistol Pete is so cute. Sure is, sure is."* At the same time, Kirkpatrick saw the end game for Showtime: "Everybody in the world, the world that really counts, will know Pistol Pete Maravich," he wrote. "He will make a million dollars playing the game of basketball."

The ambition, stated so explicitly, did nothing to repair Pete's reputation with the basketball establishment. In April, shortly after the season, Pete was invited to try out for the Olympic team, coached by Oklahoma State's Hank Iba. It is difficult to imagine a coach who would be less enamored with Showtime. Iba, then in his mid-sixties, still believed that good basketball was methodical and low-scoring.

Pete played sparingly during the Olympic trials in Albuquerque. John Bach, an Iba assistant who coached his scrimmage squad, was none too pleased with the Pistol act. Pete responded by thumbing his nose at Iba, Bach, and the entire basketball establishment, putting on a Showtime clinic during warm-ups and tossing in an impossibly long hook shot in his final game. The guards eventually selected to represent the United States in the Mexico City Olympics were Glynn Saulters, Charlie Scott, Jo Jo White, Michael Barrett, John Clawson, and Calvin Fowler. "You're going to tell me Pete didn't belong on *that* team?" says Dan Issel, an All-American at Kentucky who also failed to make the cut. "He got jobbed."

"A big joke" was how Press put it in a letter to Les Robinson. "Politics played a big part. But Pete learned the hard way."

Better to be among those who appreciated you. Such appreciation, Pete had learned, endowed him with a certain economic leverage. He had come to recognize that his talent was worth more than a VW Bug. By the summer of '68, Pete was making a killing at the camps. Florida State's Dave Cowens, a counselor at Lefty Driesell's camp, would recall getting paid about "$35 a week" (plus room and board) while Pete received $100 for each of his nightly Showtime clinics.

"The kids loved him," says Driesell. "But he used to hold me up a little bit."

Typically, Pete might call from Atlanta just days before camp was set to begin. "Coach," he'd say, "I ran out of money."

"All right then," said Lefty. "I'll get you an extra hundred."

The next day, Pete would call from Charlotte. "Coach," he'd say. "Think I'm going to need another hundred."

"You know I'll take care of you, Pete. Just get your butt in here."

Pete was always flush in the summertime. "Let's go to Daytona," he'd say.

"But Pete," said Bob Sandford. "I got $45 to my name."

No matter, Pete had just done a camp. He pointed to his pocket. "Nine hundred," he said.

So they went to Daytona, where Bob won a dance contest and they met some honeys from Tennessee. They were walking down the boardwalk when they heard an old carny barker start calling after them. He ran a basketball stand, an undersized rim mounted on a creaky wooden frame. It shook with the swirling winds coming in off the ocean. In front of the old carny was a rack of big, bouncy rubber basketballs, some less than spherical, most of them worn smooth.

Behind him were six stuffed bears. "So big a kid could hardly carry one," says Sandford.

"Fifty cents a shot," said the carny. "Two in a row wins a bear."

"Bob," Pete said theatrically, "I believe I'm gonna try this. Give the man a dollar."

He missed the first shot, hit the second.

"I won," said Pete, raising his arms in mock triumph.

"No, young man," said the carny. "You got to hit two in a row."

"Bob," said Pete. "Give the man another dollar."

Pete made quick work, two in a row. "Did I win now?" he asked.

"Let me see that," said the carny, as he inspected Pete's ball and handed him another one.

Didn't matter. Pete hit two more and Bob slid forth another dollar.

"Okay," said the barker. "You shot enough."

By now, though, a crowd had gathered, and their protests became vociferous: "Hey man, you took *our* money." "Let this guy shoot!" "Yeah, let 'im shoot!"

Pete hit his next four shots, eight in a row. Bob lined up four giant bears in a nice neat row.

"That's it," said the carny. "You are not shooting again."

Then Pete, still holding a ball, waded back into the crowd, which had grown to seventy, maybe eighty people. He was 30 to 35 feet from the basket, maybe more. They were far enough out on the boardwalk that Bob could hear the waves crashing. The wind was howling a fierce tune.

"How 'bout if I shoot from here?" asked Pete.

"Well, hell yeah," said the carny. "We can do *that*."

Pete hit the first shot. People in the crowd were beside themselves. The carny tossed the ball back disgustedly. Only then did basketball's superhero reveal his true identity, launching into his Showtime routine: spinning the ball like a gyroscopically powered top, under his arms and behind his back, off his knees, his head. He ended with the bullet drill before finally putting up the shot. Swish.

That was ten in a row, five bears.

Someone called to the carny from the crowd, "You just been had by Pistol Pete."

"You can walk back out there into the ocean," says the carny. "You ain't shooting again."

Pete and Bob handed the bears to some kids. Then they walked off with the honeys from Tennessee.

Chances are, they celebrated with a few beers. And a few more after that. For every night that ended like that one in Daytona, there was another that concluded less blissfully, with Pete urinating at frat parties, putting his fist through a cheap bathroom wall, or picking a fight.

To be sure, he drank because he was a college kid who liked to get high on beer. But he also drank for his father; Press's hopes and expectations formed a cruel yoke around his thin neck. He drank for his mother, too, as they shared a burden in their blood. He drank because no matter how many points he scored, it would never be enough. Amid all his record-setting triumph, all that apparent joy, there was an undertow of grief. To watch Pete hoist a beer was to see a college kid having a good time. But to look in his eyes was to see the sadness in his soul.

How much he drank is open to question. Pete is described variously as having a hollow leg and being a lightweight. Less debatable than his tolerance, though, was the gusto with which he drank. Everything was a competition. He tried to drink as he shot the ball. He kept score. What's more, he lacked an off switch.

Typical was a summer's eve when Bob interceded on Pete's behalf with two very angry U.S. Marines.

"He called me a son of a bitch," said the first Marine.

"My friend here just had too much to drink," said Bob, "so why don't y'all just go on home and we'll call it a night."

"I ain't leaving till I whup his ass," said the first Marine.

"You ain't whupping no one's ass."

The first Marine kept on talking until Bob punched him in the mouth, knocking him out cold. Then the second Marine issued a warning, saying he knew karate, only before the word "karate" came out of his mouth, he was splayed across the hood of his car. By the time Bob came back with a golf club, the two Marines were burning rubber.

Suddenly, Pete became very animated again. "That'll teach you to mess with us," he hollered after them. "You sons a bitches."

This kind of trouble only became more difficult to avoid after Ronnie returned from Vietnam. For years, Helen and Press would weep while listening to his voice on the taped messages he sent home. Finally, after two tours with Force Recon, Ronnie showed up in Baton Rouge with horror stories of hand-to-hand combat and mutilated bodies. "The only thing he wanted to talk about was Vietnam and how many people he killed," says Bob Sandford.

The Marines hadn't mellowed him. Still, the family turmoil had become so intense that life with the Maraviches now seemed more disorienting than the jungles of Southeast Asia. "Between the basketball and media and my mother's drinking," says Ronnie, "it felt like I was the only one who had his feet on the ground."

The night of Ronnie's homecoming began as Pete picked him up at the airport in a brand new muscle car, a blue Plymouth GTX. It ended with his kid brother loaded and plowing into a stalled automobile. Pete was charged with driving while intoxicated and taken to police headquarters, where he was given a contempt of court citation for a previous charge and finally released after posting a $300 bond.

The court was infinitely merciful compared to Press, who found the wreckage of the GTX in his driveway the next morning. Still, Press's wrath had no deterrent effect, as Pete and Ronnie kept on partying.

The darkest and saddest parts of Pete—those places hardwired to a mother's angst and a father's obsession—were stirred when Ronnie was around. He was carrying a pain that ran deeper than anyone knew. There was that odd night when Ronnie left the bar early and Pete took a booth, where a girl asked if she could join him. She had a friend, though, a biker type: big, burly, bearded. It took Pete a couple of extra beats to figure out that this might not be a healthy situation. Not long after that epiphany, he was jumped in the parking lot. There were two of them. The guy who came from behind put a blackjack on his skull. Then they beat him down. Pete was on his back, bleeding and nearly unconscious when the blur came into focus.

"Suddenly, the girl from the bar kneeled down beside me and started laughing," he would recall. "Without warning, she pointed a handgun at my face and stuck the barrel to my mouth."

"Pistol Pete," she said. "You're dead."

Pete, for his part, had his mind on that trigger. "Pull it," he was thinking. "Pull it."

The Maravich family dynamic was in fact a form of dynamic tension. Showtime was created like diamonds from coal, born of incalculable pressure, increasing across the generations. Press's ambition, the expression of his deepest need, only exacerbated Helen's sense of isolation. The more alone she felt, the more she drank. But her dependence on alcohol only increased Press's dependence on Pete. The burden Pete carried incited an instinct to escape. For years, he could lose himself in the game. Repetition was therapy. But now, as the stakes of this game had become outrageously overt, he sought other forms of refuge. He drank. And when drinking did not bring relief, he suffered moments like those spent longing for that floozy to pull the trigger.

At some level, father and son might have understood their mutual dependence, but they were blind to Helen. It would be years before Pete could admit that "a beautiful woman was crumbling before our eyes."

There were more hospitalizations. There were shock treatments. But there was no remedy. She would sneak out with a cigarette and a drink, only to be met by a phantom. Mildred Pevar, the dead aunt who had taken her in, now appeared with regularity on her patio in Baton Rouge.

Helen confided in Louise Bradley, swearing her old friend to secrecy one summer afternoon when she was visiting from Clemson.

"Couldn't you attend meetings?" asked Louise.

"Oh no," said Helen. "Press would find out."

That night, the Bradleys and the Maraviches broke bread like old times. Then Press insisted on taking out the film projector and showing highlight reels of Pete. Pete was his answer for everything.

"The only positive thing in Press's life was Pete's performance," says Bud Johnson. "He was existing on three hours sleep a night. He did the cooking. He did the cleaning. He had a sick wife, a son who was the focus of national media attention, and a program that was suffering from about 100 years of neglect."

Then there was Diana. In a letter to Nick Lalich, his teammate from the Youngtown Bears, Press described her as "the center of our life." But in fact, Press was basically a single father. What stands out in Johnson's recollection is Diana sitting on Press's lap as he read her bedtime stories. He also remembers that Diana—she just turned four as Pete began his junior year—would fall ill just before the team went on the road. "A cough, a fever, whatever," says Johnson. "It was psychosomatic. Diana would get sick because she knew that Press was going to leave and that she would have to be with Helen for a few days."

Usually, the team would fly home the day after a game. But on at least one occasion, after playing Vanderbilt, Press took a call that left him visibly shaken. He spoke to both Helen and Diana. Then he told the managers and the coaches to get everyone together, they would be flying home that night.

His ability to coach was suffering. For the first time in his career, Press wasn't making the correct tactical and personnel decisions. Then again, a sleep-deprived coach of Pistol Pete could cut corners on strategy. "Press had a kid who could get off his shot against any three guys," says Johnson.

Game plan? Who needed a game plan?

Going into the 1968–69 season, Press had already lost two big men, Randy Lamont to injury and Steve Shumaker to disillusionment. Shumaker, the junior college All-American who had arrived amid such high hopes, never understood why he played so sparingly on a team sorely lacking for height and size. Then again, the first practice didn't augur well for his LSU career, as he got into a little scrap with Pete under the boards.

The following month, LSU played Florida State in the Milwaukee Classic. Shumaker's family drove all the way from Iowa to see him play. Instead, what they saw was Pete shoot 17 for 41 as the

Tigers were blown out by 30. Though LSU was severely outrebounded, Steve barely got off the bench. He never forgot that. "I had dreams, too," he says.

After the season, Shumaker returned to the family farm and made a solemn vow. "I will never," he said, "coach my kids."

In Shumaker's absence Press signed Danny Hester, another junior college All-American. He was six-eight, 220—big and strong, with enough talent to have been invited to try out for the Olympic team. Hester was a marked departure from the role players Press had been recruiting to complement his son. In fact, in Hester's case, it was Pete who did most of the recruiting. They had met during the Olympic trials and Pete followed up with a handwritten note, telling him how much the team would benefit from Hester's considerable ability. The Pistol wanted a big man to ride shotgun with him. Hester was flattered by Pete's attentions and the opportunity to showcase his talents. Playing alongside Pete would mean Christmas tournaments in Hawaii and appearances on national television. Danny was already thinking of his own pro career. On his recruiting trip to Baton Rouge, he shared his plans to do some scoring of his own. Some of the older players, like Jukkola, just shook their heads.

They knew that Press didn't believe in sharing the burden, or the glory, at least not in relation to his son. Soon, Press would be instructing Pete not to pass the ball if he came within 15 feet of the basket. "You shoot it," he said. When a reporter from *Life* inquired about the double standard that permeated the LSU program, Press shot back, "If he gets special treatment, it's because he is special."

As the season began, it would have been difficult to argue with Press. Pete, who had naïvely declared that the quest for scoring championships was "all in the past," found himself averaging a mere 47 points eight games into his junior year. He was shooting a higher percentage and passing for more assists, the most outrageous of which—a 40-foot behind-the-back toss—came opening night against Loyola. Over Christmas, LSU traveled to Oklahoma City for the All-College tournament where the Tigers beat two undefeated teams in Wyoming and Duquesne, then ranked ninth in the country. Duquesne's vaunted defense was allowing an average of 52 points a game. Pete scored 53. The Tigers were 7–1 before New Year's 1969, their only loss coming in a brawl-marred double-overtime against Tulane.

The Green Wave's victory was in large measure due to the efforts of Harold Sylvester, maybe the only black person in the arena, now a sophomore. Sylvester had 32 points and 22 rebounds, but recalls the game as the beginning of a ritual, the first of his regular engagements with Pete. "You would start developing an ulcer the night before," he says. "You just knew he was going to do something that would make you look silly. I considered myself something of a defensive specialist, but in all the time I played him, I never blocked his shot, never stole the ball. All I did was try not to be embarrassed." On the other hand, Sylvester would remain unimpressed with the quality of Pete's supporting cast. "Pete *had* to shoot," he says. "There was nobody else."

Danny Hester would have begged to differ. But whatever the case, one-man shows did not make for winning basketball teams. A slump was inevitable. Pete kept scoring, of course. Again, he would finish the season as a first team All-American and the NCAA's leading scorer. There was a slew of new records. He scored more in two seasons than Mississippi State's Bailey Howell—previously the SEC's leading career scorer—had in three. He broke the two-season scoring mark of Houston's great Elvin Hayes. He also set a new personal best with 66 points in the rematch with Tulane.

Then again, LSU lost that one, too. After the great start, the Tigers went 5–12. "Press's agenda was to promote Pete, not necessarily to win games," says Danny Hester, who had become disenchanted.

Pete himself was disheartened, as the expectations rendered every victory an ephemeral one. "This year I think I've played only about three good games," he said after being voted the SEC's Player of the Year. The high scores no longer got him very high, nor did they guard against his lows. The strain had begun to show.

He played with a bone spur in his heel and a bad left knee that finally buckled against Auburn. It was thought that the torn cartilage would require surgery in the off-season. By now, a good bit of him seemed permanently black and blue, as defenders who couldn't stop him left him thoroughly bruised. Nevertheless, among officials, he had acquired a reputation as a crybaby. Pete was thrown out of a game against Vanderbilt, after momentarily squaring off with a ref who turned a blind eye as he was knocked out of bounds.

The stress became most manifest in his relationship with Press. An often told story has Press and Pete bickering during a time-out late in a game. Apparently, Pete didn't agree with his father's choice of plays. Press responded with a closed fist, upside the head. "I'm the coach," he said. "You're the player."

"They were both so much alike," says Dexter Bott, the team manager, who more vividly recalls another incident at the end of a practice. Most of the players were down at one end of the floor when they heard Pete begin to scream. "Something just lit him up," says Bott. "He went past the point of arguing about basketball to where he got nasty, as angry as I'd ever saw him." He kept screaming and cursing in Press's face until, finally, he just ran out of steam. The team waited for Press to return fire with his own barrage of obscenities, or maybe worse. But that never happened.

Instead, as if to acknowledge that an irrevocable line had been crossed, Press modulated his response. "Are you finished?" he asked.

Pete, still heaving with anger, said nothing.

"You might be a hero today," said Press. "But you can be a bum tomorrow."

A bum? He already felt like one, at least most of the time. The respites were spent with Jackie Elliser, a stunning redhead from Baton Rouge. To behold her—as Pete first did on September 21, 1968—was to believe that syrup coursed through her veins. This was at Southdowns, a bar near the campus. Guys would shoot pool and drink beer while the girls would dance to the house band, which just happened to be John Fred and his Playboys, best known for their hit "Judy in Disguise":

> Judy in disguise well, that's what you are,
> Lemonade pie with a brand new car.

It might well have been playing when Pete looked up from his beer and saw her reflection in the mirror behind the bar. "I saw her laugh and push her long hair away from her face and onto her shoulder," he remembered.

Pete got her name and number from a mutual friend. Jackie might have been the only girl in Louisiana who hadn't heard of Pete Maravich. "I don't go on blind dates," she said.

Finally, she relented. He came to pick her up in the Volkswagen, which made her laugh, as she'd never be able to understand how he fit into that thing. His face was a little broken out, his hair had just been cut too short, and he wore strange spongy shoes that suggested an orthopedic purpose. "Like they should've given him a cane to go with those shoes," she says.

They went to an LSU football game with Russ Bergman and his girlfriend, and though Pete drank a little too much, it didn't seem to bother Jackie. She thought he was cute. But more than that, he was endearingly goofy. "I laughed at him the whole night," she says. "I thought he had the greatest sense of humor."

He invited her to a Dionne Warwick concert. They saw *Winnie the Pooh*. They went out for pizza. Then, being the romantic that he was, Pete invited her to practice. That's where she met Press, who was unlike anyone else she had ever come across. First, there was the matter of his language, everything was *sonofabitch* and *you bastard*. Then that gaze: "He had these piercing black eyes and he would just stare a hole through you. I thought he would think of me as an intrusion, a distraction to his son."

It was not an unfounded fear. "Women and basketball don't mix," Press was fond of saying. When Rich Hickman, for instance, married his longtime girlfriend, Press reacted somewhat less than effusively: "Congratulations, you dumb son of a bitch. Don't let it fuck up your game." In lieu of a wedding gift, Press made the whole team run the stadium steps—backward.

"I was scared to death," says Jackie, who needed only a couple of months to learn just how enigmatic Press could be. To begin with, the coach was a great housekeeper. He would scrub an item of cookware for fifteen minutes straight. Jackie could see her reflection in his pots and pans. And for all the cussing, she says, "he was really a teddy bear." Pete might have stirred Press's raw need and ambition, but it was Diana who brought out the tender part of a gruff man. He'd take her to dinner at the Piccadilly, a buffet restaurant. He'd read her stories. He'd do her hair.

As for Helen, Jackie found her to be exceedingly warm and ever in need of an embrace. "Starved for affection," says Jackie. "She was the same way with Pete. She used to hug him so much, always loving on him."

Jackie put a lot of loving on Pete, too. Taken together, the pairing made as much sense as any play Press had diagrammed. Jackie was ample where Pete was angular, soft where he was bony, light in all those places where he was dark. Jackie was comfort food for the famished belly of his soul. And best of all, she didn't care a damn for basketball.

Yes, she had a vague notion that it had something to do with putting the ball in the basket. Beyond that, she did not know, or care to know, anything about the game. What she comprehended most clearly came from the crowd. "The reaction of the people," she says, "the way they would jump up and down when Pete had the ball."

The last game of Pete's junior year—Saturday, March 8, 1969—saw the Tigers travel to Athens, Georgia. As the Cow Palace was hosting legitimately important business—the Quarter Horse phase of the Spring Livestock Show—most Louisiana papers didn't even bother to send their writers. Besides, LSU had long since been eliminated from the SEC race. The team needed a win just to break even on the season.

With ten minutes to play, the Tigers were down 59–44. Then, without warning, a mere game became something "seldom matched in SEC basketball." Pete scored 13 straight and 24 of his team's last 29 points, most of them on outrageously distanced jumpers.

The game went into overtime. "The crowd starts cheering," says

Les Robinson, who was watching from a seat near the LSU bench. "They don't care who wins. They came to see a show."

As the extra period ended, it looked as if the Maravich magic had finally run its course. Georgia's Jerry Epling had the ball with a 2-point lead, trying to run out the clock. "The Georgia players were doing the right thing," says Robinson. "Then I heard something I never heard before or since. The crowd started booing the home team. The players didn't understand. It discombobulated them."

With twelve seconds remaining, Epling, who had managed to put the game into overtime on a long jumper, took an ill-advised shot. This one missed. Six ticks later, Maravich had tied the game again.

The second overtime proved less competitive, but even more memorable, with Pete scoring 11 of LSU's 12 points as the Tigers took an insurmountable lead. The performance was nearing its finale now. "Our place sat, like, 11,000, but there must have been 13,000 in there," says Georgia's Herb White, who had already fouled out trying to guard Pete. "The fans were going nuts. You could not hear anything." Pete might as well have been conducting the dribbling portion of his clinic. "Our guys are running around after him, falling down on the floor. He's going into his whole Marques Haynes Globetrotter act and we can't even catch the sumbitch to foul him."

"They had fire in their eyes," Pete would remember. ". . . I thought they were going to kill me. I started dribbling to midcourt, then to my bench."

There were just seconds left. Pete never even broke stride as he threw up a shot for his 57th and 58th points on the night. "A 30-foot hook shot over his head," as it was described in Monday's editions of the State-Times. "The ball hit the bottom of the net without touching the rim of the basket."

"Our cheerleaders started dancing," says Herb White, "then the fans came pouring out of the stands and carried him off the floor."

"They were going after him like Elvis Presley," Les Robinson remembers. "They just wanted to touch him."

Of course, Les had seen it before, the outrageously nonchalant parabola of his final shot: *the going down shot*. Les caught up with

Pete in the dressing room after the game. Middle of winter, and the kid came out in sunglasses.

He hugged Les. For once, if only briefly, Pete was in awe of himself. "Les," he whispered, "I think it's the greatest game I've ever played."

All of Pete's tricks and his vast repertoire of shots have been made into a movie, Homework Basketball, which never fails to amaze its viewers, including Carl Stewart, the coach of all-Negro McKinley High in Baton Rouge, who, after one showing, exclaimed, "My God, he's one of us!"

"The Coed Boppers' Top Cat," Curry Kirkpatrick,
Sports Illustrated, *March 4, 1968*

13. ONE OF US

By the mid-1960s, basketball was a stylistic hybrid, evolving in parallel worlds. There were two distinct games, born of two Americas: black and white, urban and rural. One was learned in an asphalt schoolyard enclosed by a chain-link fence. The other was practiced under a hoop mounted in the driveway alongside a picket fence. Rarely did they meet, especially in the South.

Consider the case of Billy Packer, Wake Forest's All-ACC guard, who, in late 1959, walked into Whitaker gymnasium on the campus of Winston-Salem Teachers College, a charter member of the Colored Intercollegiate Athletic Association. The only white kid among a couple thousand fans, Packer had come to get a look at the Rams' guard, Cleo Hill. From Newark, New Jersey, Hill—the *amazing* Cleo Hill, as he was often called—had an assortment of hook shots, set shots, and jump shots and extraordinary leaping ability.

At the insistence of the Winston-Salem coach, Clarence "Big House" Gaines, Packer took a seat by the home team's bench. Before long, the ACC's reigning ballhandling whiz was in awe. "Billy didn't say much to me, but I knew exactly what he was thinking," Gaines would write in his autobiography. "He was thinking that the black kids in a tiny girls' college in the tiny CIAA played better basketball than mighty North Carolina, North Carolina State, Duke and Wake Forest in the mighty Atlantic Coast Conference."

On a Sunday morning a few days later, Coach Gaines happened by his office on his way to church when he heard a game in progress. Who could be playing *now?* he wondered, as he peered through the gym door. There was Packer and a couple of the Wake players versus Hill and a couple of his teammates. "I watched for a few seconds, then closed the door before anyone noticed me," Gaines would recall. "What I had witnessed was probably illegal."

Despite the sanctions against such race mixing, those Sunday morning games at Whitaker gym became a surreptitious custom. The players from either side of town weren't crusading integrationists. They just wanted the best game they could find. But Packer, like Pete, was a basketball-obsessed son of a coach, and soon he would be able to catalogue undeniable differences in style. As for ballhandling ability, the black players weren't much different. Certainly, Packer, who himself used a disappearing ball move that confused even ACC refs, was difficult to rival as a dribbling trickster. Rather, in Packer's recollection what distinguished the black players was a matter of athleticism. "Cleo could pin your shot above the backboard," says Packer. "To play above the rim was not something that was done back then. I mean, who could dunk?"

Hill, on the other hand, recalls the white guys as being more accomplished shooters. "They could shoot," says Hill. "They worked the ball and ran a lot of picks. But we were more physical than they were, and that's how we beat them."

By the midsixties places like Winston Salem Teachers College had become veritable basketball laboratories. Gaines understood his place in the game's history even if basketball's white mandarins did not. His coaching mentor had been John McLendon, of North Carolina College for Negroes (later, North Carolina Central University). It was McLendon, Gaines insisted, who transformed "a mild passing game into a running game."

One may argue the relative contributions of McLendon, who learned at the side of John Naismith himself, and Cam Henderson to the evolution of the fast break. But the style that McLendon bequeathed to Coach Gaines, among others, was at worst distinct. At best, it was a more advanced form of basketball.

"A free-flowing, wide open game," recalls Packer.

Of course, it entertained as well. Jerry McLeese, then a columnist for the *Winston-Salem Journal*, would take his six-year-old son to watch Big House's team play. The boy was captivated by what he called "the players who pass the ball behind their backs."

There was, of course, more to the style than mere trickery. As talent can be measured against time—in the midst of adrenalized pandemonium, great athletes tend to experience the game in slow motion—this uptempo brand of basketball was ideally suited for great, if unorthodox players. After Cleo Hill, Gaines found an ex-shipping clerk from Philadelphia, Earl Monroe, whose offensive skills seemed so supernatural as to warrant the nickname "Black Jesus."

All these years later, McLeese, who had covered Daniel High School for the Anderson *Independent*, can't help but compare Monroe and Maravich. Just as the moniker "Pistol Pete" appeared under his byline in 1961, when the kid was in ninth grade, McLeese also coined the rhyming handle for Monroe: "Earl the Pearl." The Pearl and the Pistol were much alike as prodigious scorers (in 1966, Monroe broke Cleo Hill's CIAA single-game scoring record with 68) who fed off the crowd. To the naked eye, it seemed as if each man could violate the laws of physics. Monroe's signature move, for example, involved a split-second, full-speed, 360-degree counterclockwise rotation—with the ball. Still, when considering Monroe and Maravich, one substantial difference stands out. As pleasing and improbable as the Pearl could be, says McLeese, "Pete was flashier."

One wonders, then: Was his game black or white? Neither or both? The answer depended on whom you asked. Either side could stake its claim.

But there was no denying Pete's basic attraction, or the fact that it cut across the racial divide. Danny Hester liked to recall a night that saw Pete (after a few beers, no doubt) walk into a black gin mill in

Scotlandville, Louisiana, and start to dribble. He went through the whole Showtime routine, much to the delight of the establishment's patrons. "They were going crazy," said Hester.

One's father might have appreciated the virtues of, say, Bill Bradley. But fans, at some level, are all teenage boys. And the vestigial adolescent in men of either race could not help but cheer. What Pete did—the idiom in which he performed—was cool.

The White Negro, as Norman Mailer christened the hipster, had already become a stock character in American culture. The most popular example was Elvis Presley, the white boy performing in what had begun as a black form, rock and roll. Perhaps it was no accident that Elvis was southern. Pete, despite his Aliquippa birthright, considered himself southern, too. Unlike his father, he had grown up in a strictly segregated society. He could play to applause in every black bar south of the Mason-Dixon line. That's not to say that a mere sport endowed him with a special understanding or empathy on the subject of race. He did not know, nor could he have known, what it was like to be, as Coach Stewart put it, *one of us*. As a ballplayer, Pete took for granted his inalienable right to perform, whether his venue was the Cow Palace, the joint in Scotlandville, or the court at the Blundon Home, an orphanage in the heart of a black Baton Rouge neighborhood known as "the Bottom."

Some of the best ballplayers ever to come out of Louisiana were fatherless sons of Blundon, which, at 650 West McKinley Street, was just blocks from the LSU campus. First among these players was Leslie Scott, a six-three guard who averaged almost 40 points a game for a McKinley team that won the 1962 championship of the Negro high school league, the Louisiana Interscholastic Athletic and Literary Organization. It was said that Scott could shoot like Jerry West and, later, that he could handle the ball with the flair of Earl the Pearl. Scott would average about 27 points a game as a freshman for Loyola of Chicago and finish his career among the final cuts from the Los Angeles Lakers roster. By then, though, he had long since ruined his knee, an injury that doomed him to obscurity. He remained famous only in the memories of the kids who had grown up imitating him at Blundon Park. Two of them, Marvin Turner and

Freddy Hilton, formed the starting backcourt on McKinley's 1967 championship team.

As it happens, Turner, the point guard, has a distinct recollection of Pete showing up at Blundon in the off-season. "There had never been a white guy who played like that—he had a soul game," says Turner. "He reminded us of Leslie Scott."

Hilton has another, equally distinct recollection: the night that Pete and Press showed up at the McKinley gym. The crowd began to buzz. *The coach is here. And there goes his son, Pistol.* This was Hilton's senior year. There had been a hopeful murmur that he might break the color line and be the first black player to go to LSU. Perhaps Hilton himself had dared to hope, as he and his step-father had done the landscaping on Coach Maravich's house. Then again, there had also been talk that the Tigers would need two basketballs for Pete and Freddy. "I think he saw me shoot 58 that night," says Hilton, referring to Press. But the coach never knocked on the McKinley locker-room door, never came calling on Freddy Hilton.

"Maybe the time wasn't right," he says, wistfully.

Or maybe two shooters was one too many.

The first black basketball player to receive a grant-in-aid scholarship to play at an SEC institution was Perry Wallace, who matriculated at Vanderbilt in 1966. Compared to LSU, Vanderbilt, a private liberal arts university in Nashville, was a bastion of enlightenment.

"When Press came to Baton Rouge in 1966, he told the media, 'I'm going to recruit blacks,'" recalls Bud Johnson, then the sports information director. "And no less an authority than the president of the university said, 'My coach was misquoted.'"

As a native Louisianan, Harold Sylvester couldn't have been overly encouraged by the prospects for meaningful integration. Back when he was a sophomore in high school, just days after the assassination of Malcolm X, a New Orleans–style experiment in progressive race relations—a game pitting all-white Jesuit against his all-black St. Augustine team—had to be held in secret, behind locked doors. Still, Sylvester found the Cow Palace to be especially inhospitable. "Not a friendly place," he says.

In his first varsity game there, Sylvester was thrown to the floor in the midst of a brawl, where a white man was quickly on top of him. Sylvester started swinging. Several desperate moments passed before he would realize that this man wasn't there to kill him.

In fact, he was trying to save him. Knowing the incendiary nature of the situation, one of the LSU coaches—either Press or Jay McCreary, Sylvester is uncertain—dove on him like a live grenade. The brawl was the culminating event of a tense day in the Ag Center. It began with a display of placards asking, "Why No Black Athletes?"

The question wasn't lost on SEC players, especially those who had competed against blacks in high school. "I knew the deal back then," says Herbie White, who played at a black rec center in his hometown of Decatur, Georgia. "After playing against these black guys all summer, going back to the white varsity was like going to the B team."

Tommy Hess, an undersized Pennsylvania point guard whose father had coached in many a camp with Press, was shocked when practices began at LSU in the fall of '68. "All white guys," he says. "Guys I could actually guard."

Most SEC schools were still willfully oblivious to Kentucky's defeat at the hands of Texas Western. The Civil Rights Act of 1964 and the Voting Rights Act of 1965 did not yet apply in places like Baton Rouge. One man's opportunity was the basis for another man's resentment. "We used to always say, 'Boy, if we could play against them guys we'd show them who could play some ball,'" says Fred Hilton, who refuses to consider Pete Maravich in anything but qualified terms. "He was a great player against the guys he was playing against. But I don't know how you can compare greatness unless you're playing against the best."

Rejected by Press and the SEC, Hilton's argument all but calls for an asterisk to be placed by the names of anyone who had ever played in the all-white league. Perhaps he is right. But Pete's career was never about mere SEC records. His purpose—certainly as Press saw it—was to make history. There was one surefire way to do that, one record that would immortalize the Maraviches and forever preserve their standing in the game. Becoming the leading scorer in the history of college basketball would be a singular accomplishment. It could not be claimed by any race. It could not be shared. *One of us?* No. Never. Pete belonged to no tribe.

Even as he'd make his history, he was alone.

Before his senior season had begun, his likeness was again featured on the cover of *Sports Illustrated*: "Pistol Pete Maravich: Hotshot of a Super Crop." The *Sporting News,* in its preseason forecast, declared, "The most amazing scorer in college basketball history has only himself as a genuine challenger . . . In the Southeastern Conference nobody asks how the LSU Tigers will do this season. The assumption is Pete will be terrific and the team so-so again."

Actually, they would be better than so-so, as the supporting cast had become considerably more talented with the addition of two sophomores. Al "Apple" Sanders was a big, exceptionally rugged rebounder—he'd average 15 boards a game in his first varsity season—the best white boy to come out of Baton Rouge since Bob Pettit. Then there was Bill "Fig" Newton, who, at six-nine, had finesse and a soft touch, averaging 20 points a game on the freshman team. From Rockville, Indiana, Newton had wanted to play with Pete since seeing him become the first sophomore to win the Star of Stars award in the annual East-West All-Star game in Indianapolis. "Going into college," he says, "I didn't know if I could play. But I figured the worst thing that could happen was I'd have the best seat to watch the greatest who ever was."

The Tigers were already 5–1 when they left for the West Coast. The first game of their road trip was a rematch with Oregon State, which, having lost the first time, now opted to stall with point guard Freddie Boyd given custody of the basketball.

"Shoot the ball, Freddie," said Pete. "Nobody wants to see this."

Freddie held the ball.

Pete dared him to drive to the basket.

But Freddie still held the ball.

Finally, Pete sat down on the court and crossed his legs. Then he called to the crowd, "Tell Freddie to shoot the ball."

Pete knew what he was doing. The fans had paid good money to see the Pistol. Now they started booing the home team. The booing got louder and louder until Oregon State relented. The new strategy was, literally, to beat down Pete. He took 31 foul shots that night, hitting 30, a new NCAA record. LSU won 76–68.

Next stop was Los Angeles, where the Tigers would play John Wooden's perennial champs, UCLA. The arrival of Pete—"this gangly kid with the Age of Aquarius look and the Ringling Brothers sideshow," as the *Los Angeles Times* called him—led the sports section, complete with a photo layout. The Maravich saga was more compelling than ever. Soon, barring injury, Pete would replace Oscar Robertson as college basketball's all-time leading scorer. Then there was the idea—more interesting, perhaps, than the pursuit of the Record—that seemed so perfect at the tail end of the sixties. Pete and Press had become archetypes: the rebellious son and his authoritarian father, the longhair and the crewcut. What sweetened this story, though (at least for public consumption), was their common purpose. Of course, Pete liked to *do his own thing*. And yes, he had a Joe Namath poster in his dorm room. But that didn't make him a hippie or a bum. "What I want to do more than anything else is to win for my Dad," he told the *Times*. "He's taught me everything I know about this game—everything. And he's taken such a terrible beating down here for what he lets me do. I've seen what it's done to him, how it's changed him."

The UCLA game would not improve matters. Press was a notoriously bad scheduler. He didn't book patsies, nor did the old barnstormer believe in breaks. UCLA would be his team's fourth game in six nights, an itinerary that had taken the Tigers from Baton Rouge to Charlotte to Corvallis, Oregon, and now Los Angeles.

"A definite advantage," said UCLA's Wooden, whom Press liked to call "Padre." "We felt we could put pressure on them and then really run."

In fact, as each of his five starters would go on to play in the NBA, Wooden's team could run on anyone. By halftime, the score was 69–40. "Then we go in the locker room," recalls Tommy Hess, "and Press jumps all over Danny Hester."

But Hester, who would finish with 27 points, was the only LSU player having a good game. Pete, on the other hand, was horseshit.

Coming in with an average of almost 49 points, he shot 14 for 42, with 18 turnovers. Press didn't say a thing to his son, though. Instead, he told the media, "You didn't see the real Pete out there tonight. He's a damned tired boy."

The game would end with two new records. UCLA's 133 points was a new team mark. The crowd of 12,961—"Most of them," the *Times* acknowledged, "had come to see Pete"—set the standard for attendance at Pauley Pavilion, a record that would last many years longer than Wooden's championship run.

In another respect, the game represented divergent paths taken by old friends. Wooden could not argue with Pete's skills. Press had created the greatest ball handler he had ever seen. Even with Pete at his worst, it was no longer difficult to imagine him making good on Press's vow to become basketball's first million-dollar player. Then again, Wooden's prescience bears mention as well. He had warned Press all those years ago at Campbell. A million dollars? "Yes," said Wooden, "But he'll never win a championship."

Padre might have suspended judgment had he traveled on with Press and Pete to Honolulu, where LSU played St. John's in the Rainbow Classic. St. John's scored 39 points in the second half. Pete scored 40, a stretch that included what Redmen coach Lou Carnesecca called "the best 15 minute performance in basketball I had ever seen."

The passes were more memorable than the shots, as they were thrown in ways the city-slick Carnesecca had never even considered: blind, behind the head, off the wrist. Upon his return to the mainland, Carnesecca alerted the New York basketball establishment. "You talk of Jerry West or Oscar Robertson or any of those great ones," he said. "Maravich is better."

It took only fifteen minutes for Carnesecca to come under the same spell as Press. "I'm supposed to be the coach and I'm supposed to be watching the whole game. I wind up just watching him," said Carnesecca, who would be leaving St. John's after the season to run the Nets, New York's franchise in the upstart American Basketball Association. "They say his father wants to coach him in the pros. I'd let him coach. I'd just be the general manager and count the money."

For every coach who knew better there was another who couldn't resist. For every John Wooden, there was a Lou Carnesecca or a Red Rocha, the Hawaii coach who, like Press, still recalled the great Ah Chew Goo making fools of servicemen from the mainland. Rocha would always recall a sequence that began with Pete taking an outlet pass near midcourt. As he pivoted to face his basket, he found a defender already up in his jersey. Pete quickly put the ball behind his back and flipped it two-handed over his head. The ball met a streaking LSU player in full stride for a layup. "Never saw Goo make *that* pass," says Rocha. "Never saw anyone do that."

Lost amid the celebration of Pete's game was the fact that LSU, suffering from overconfidence and sunburn, somehow managed to lose to Yale in the tournament's championship round. Then again, by now, championships seemed almost pedestrian in relation to this real-life myth. All anyone would remember was the Pistol, a boy who transformed mere headlines into encomiums. Consider the January 6, 1970, edition of America's newspaper of record, the *New York Times:* "Maravich Is Hailed as Basketball Artist."

By now, even Kentucky fans understood. The crowd for his final game in Lexington, then home to the nation's second-ranked team, was well beyond the capacity of Memorial Coliseum. As the available standing room was occupied, people took to sitting in the aisles. "It was obvious," recalled one Kentuckian, ". . . that the fire marshal was a basketball fan." More astonishing was the reaction as Pete was introduced: the notoriously hostile Wildcat partisans suddenly tamed, then grateful, on their feet cheering for at least five minutes.

LSU even got a game off Tennessee. The Tigers had a healthy lead when Pete went into his Showtime bit dribbling out the clock. With about a minute to go, Les Robinson, who was listening to the game on radio, turned to his wife. "Pete's gonna call time out," he said.

Barbara Robinson, pretty knowledgeable about basketball herself, didn't understand.

"Just listen," said Les.

Les hadn't forgotten what Mears had done against State all those years ago. He knew Press hadn't forgotten, either.

The LSU fans were counting down the seconds as Pete dribbled right over to the Tennessee bench. He might as well have been in Mears's face when he signaled for the ref to cut the clock and prolong Tennessee's agony.

Mears's payback had been a long time coming, though not as long as Pete's appointment with the Record, which came at last on January 31, 1970, at home against Ole Miss. With official attendance at 11,856, the Ag Center was absurdly beyond capacity. Still, with more than 1,000 students turned away at the gates, the game was broadcast on closed-circuit television in the Student Union. Pete needed a mere 39 points to pass Oscar Robertson's career total of 2,973 and become the leading scorer in the history of college basketball. With 7:50 remaining and LSU comfortably ahead, Pete tied Robertson with a fifteen-footer. Then he started missing, each shot igniting a battery of flash pops from the photographers assembled at courtside. He failed to connect on his next seven chances. "I don't think he missed that many in a row since he was seven years old," says Jeff Tribett, who went up to Pete during a break in the action and asked if he planned on scoring another basket.

"Eventually," he shrugged.

With 4:41 remaining, Pete put up a fading twenty-three-footer from the right-hand side, one of his trademark shots. "We just stopped and watched the ball, hoping it would go in," says Rich Hickman. "We wanted him to get that record so bad."

Swish.

"He was relieved to get it over with," says Fig Newton, who sees the moment more clearly in retrospect than when it happened. "I think about it lots of times—the *pressure* Pete had on him."

The plan was for Fig and Apple Sanders to hoist him on their shoulders. But Fig had fouled out, so the task went to Apple and Bob Lang, who raised this suddenly bewildered boy in herky-jerky stages. Tribbett shook his roommate's hand and winked before excusing himself from the epicenter of a gathering storm. "Other people wanted to be part of it," says Tribbett. "I just wanted to sit and watch."

There was an understanding that Pete had just passed, in an excruciatingly public way, from one phase of his life to another. In doing so, he had shed a protective layer. What Pete had shared with guys like Tribbett and Hick was now being claimed as public property. The court was awash in people—players and fans and hangers-on and children who had snuck into the ecstatic scrum just to touch the Pistol. Pete smiled, but with something less than full joy. He looked up at the scoreboard. "Please," he told the newsmen who had hit the floor in a wave-like assault, "let us finish the game."

But the reporters were unable to stop themselves. They had to know what it felt like to have broken Oscar Robertson's record.

"I think I'm very fortunate," said Pete. "I followed him ever since I was a young boy and I always felt he was the greatest."

It was the answer he had rehearsed. He seemed dazed and distracted. But there, in the background, some rows back, was Press. Even in that crowd, he stood out, needing no flash, illuminated with pride.

The president, hoping to improve his standing with America's young people, sent congratulations, assuring Pete, "The Nixons are among your fans." The missive from the White House was just one of many tributes bestowed on Pete that season, the grandest of which was the Naismith Award, given to college basketball's outstanding player.

In setting the record, he had passed into a higher, more permanent rung of eminence. But fame of this magnitude exacted a price. He couldn't go anywhere without being recognized and, in some way, accosted. Even Broussard Hall, where the athletes lived, was no longer a safe haven. Football players came banging on his door at all hours of the night. They'd want to shoot the shit. Or shoot some pool. Or wrestle with an honest-to-goodness celebrity. Mostly, though, they wanted autographs—for their brothers, their kid sisters, for themselves.

"The pressure just kept building," says Rusty Bergman, now a graduate assistant coach. "It got to the point where Pete was like

Elvis. He had to move out of the jock dorm senior year just to get some peace and quiet."

Privacy, perhaps. Peace and quiet? Never.

Pete came home one day during his senior year and found his mother as he'd never quite seen her, or rather, as he'd never bothered to see her. Her face was deeply lined. There were circles under her eyes. She seemed to be in a trance, a cigarette smoldering between her fingers, its ashes forming a pile on the floor.

"Oh, hi, Pete. So, you decided to come home, huh?"

"Look at you," he said

Look. Even Pete couldn't be blind anymore. Soon, he and Press would discover the bottles hidden in the couch cushion, in an old pair of shoes, in the chandelier. Then there was a vinegar bottle filled with booze.

Confronted, Helen finally lashed out. She was another human sacrifice to the Game. This obsession shared by her husband and her son had shut her out and shut her down. Helen was almost a ghost herself now.

It was more than Pete could handle. He propped her up. He shook her. Then he cocked his fist. "With all the strength I could muster," he recalled, "I drove my fist past her head and into the plaster wall."

Then he stormed out.

So this was life at the top of the mountain. You were alone. Nixon could have told him that. Elvis, too.

14. MARKED MAN

Pete exceeded the 60-point mark three times that season. He had 61 against Vanderbilt. His career high of 69 came at Alabama, a game that LSU managed to lose, 104–106. Pete had 47 points in the second half of an eventful evening, which began with Danny Hester being ejected and ended with Pete chasing a heckler as the teams walked off the court. "One of those Alabama football players," says Hester. "They were riding us pretty hard the whole game." But the most memorable of these 60-point outings, the harbinger of what was hoped for, even expected, came in a shootout against Kentucky.

The game was broadcast on national television, picked up by 206 stations, more than had carried the famous UCLA-Houston game two years before. That contest, held in Houston's Astrodome before a crowd of 52,693, was cast as a battle of behemoths—Lew Alcindor versus Elvin Hayes—and considered a dress rehearsal for the eventual national championship. Kentucky-LSU, on the other hand, had no real championship implications. The Tigers, who'd finish the regular season 20–8, were having a fine year, but they were no real match for Kentucky, which had been ranked 1 or 2 through most of the season. Besides, the idea of nationally televised SEC basketball was still a mildly preposterous concept. Eddie Einhorn, whose Television Sports Network specialized in airing regional games, held the Conference's broadcast rights. When he started airing the games back in 1965, attendance was so sparse that he had to move all the people to one side of the gym so the camera could see them.

The Pistol changed all that. As his presence all but guaranteed standing-room crowds, Einhorn no longer had to double as a stage manager. More important, though, was Pete's effect on ratings. "Much higher when he was on," says Einhorn. "We tried to do LSU games as often as we could."

The problem was that college basketball, particularly in the Deep South, remained at best a provincial concern. Typically, a nationally televised game featured teams from big markets with large fan bases, like UCLA or Notre Dame. An SEC game, no matter how promising the individual matchups, was deemed a losing proposition, until Einhorn gambled on LSU-Kentucky. Einhorn had no rooting interest. He didn't care who won. But as there was a direct correlation between Pete's points and the ratings, he just wanted the Pistol to keep firing.

Einhorn placed his bet on Pete's final game at the Ag Center, a 2:30 P.M. start, February 21, 1970. For most of the afternoon, Pete had been at his best and the game unexpectedly close. But with 9:17 left and LSU down a basket, 80–78, Pete cooled—just long enough for Kentucky to run off with the game.

"He's human." So read the lead in the next day's *Louisville Courier Journal*. The final was 121–105. Dan Issel finished with 51 points to Pete's 64. Not only had Pete again failed to beat the Kentucky varsity, but he was now out of chances. That's not to say this was anything but a happy ending for Eddie Einhorn. What had been dismissed as regional filler was in fact a ratings bonanza.

And despite Pete's momentary displeasure—he didn't come out for the postgame interview—nothing could bode better for his impending fortune. There was nothing new in the idea of Pete's game as a touchstone for basketball and commerce. It should have been fully apparent since sophomore year, when he appeared on the cover of *Sports Illustrated*. The magazine's black ink had a distinctly plummy hue. As a result, Converse was deluged with calls for its standard low-cut "Chuck Taylor" sneakers—in purple.

Season tickets sales, about forty when he arrived in Baton Rouge, now hovered around 4,000. An $11.5 million arena with accommodations for more than 14,000 fans was scheduled for completion in the spring of 1971. A concrete dome suggesting a giant flying saucer that had landed on campus, the LSU Assembly Center, as the state legislature proclaimed it, was already known by another name: "The House That Pete Built."

But attendance was no longer the most important economic barometer in the sporting world. The engine that drove the business was television. And as fate would have it, the National Basketball Association had just announced a $17 million deal with ABC, worth nearly four times the current contract. The average crowd at an NBA game had more than doubled in the past five years. Ratings were up 12 percent over the season before. More than 20 million viewers had seen the Christmas Day contest between the Boston Celtics and the Phoenix Suns. "Our growth," concluded league commissioner Walter Kennedy, ". . . was directly related to the telecasting of games."

With this in mind, executives saw Showtime as a pilot for Pete's pro career. The *New York Post*'s Larry Merchant looked to Pete as basketball's version of Joe Namath. Pistol Pete's rookie contract, like Broadway Joe's, would reflect the cutthroat competition between established and upstart pro leagues. And, as was the case with Joe, Pete's individualistic flair would make for great television. As an agent told Press, "I don't want a penny from the first million."

There was one best place for Pete to showcase his wares: not only the nation's media capital, but the basketball capital. The networks and the pro leagues were headquartered there as well. It was only appropriate that Pete's first visit to New York coincided with LSU's appearance in the National Invitational Tournament, a venerable event held every March at Madison Square Garden.

The bid was made possible by SEC champion Kentucky, which would be representing the Conference in the NCAA tournament. The NCAA, a single-elimination playoff then limited to thirty-two teams, took only one entrant from each conference. This left a lot of very good clubs to compete in the NIT. At 20–8, LSU was one of them. But so were such perennial powerhouses as North Carolina, Duke, Cincinnati, and Marquette, which, at 22–3, was the eighth-ranked team in the nation.

Though the NCAA would produce college basketball's national

champion, the NIT still conferred plenty of prestige. It was considered the venerable tournament, tethered to the game's history and its most famous arena. With the Knicks on their way to the 1970 NBA title, New York was more than ever the center of the basketball universe. "The City Game," memorialized later that year in a book of the same title, linked the schoolyard scene with the Garden itself. Pete Axthelm's account gave narrative form to the Knicks' championship run while excavating fallen or obscured playground legends, urban versions of Leslie Scott. In addition to great players, the city game had also produced a culture of aficionados, all of whom felt eminently qualified and very eager to inspect this unfathomably young, white, and seemingly instant legend, the Pistol.

As Press had been talking up New York since playing against Clair Bee and LIU back in the thirties, Pete knew all about the city's basketball supremacy. "It has always been a dream of mine to play in New York," he said. "New York has the kind of basketball fans I like to play for."

That was back in January, when the possibility of playing at the Garden first became real. In the months since, however, Pete had come to understand more about the role being scripted for him. For the Pistol—and those who would profit from his presence—the NIT wasn't a tournament so much as a rite of passage. It was the ideal venue for Pete to take his place in the pantheon of the game's greatest players.

"Pete Maravich and the Garden and the NIT are made for each other," wrote Merchant. "He comes to the Garden in the best tradition of Luisetti, Mikan, Gola, Robertson and Bradley, to show the big town his stuff. He comes to the NIT, which is less a tournament than a Broadway musical these days, to do his number."

The hype had already achieved critical mass. "A staggeringly over-publicized situation," wrote the *Times*' Leonard Koppett. As observed by a *Daily News* reporter, Pete's arrival warranted encirclement by "the city's full publicity paraphernalia, including the bright lights and TV cameras of the three major networks, a face full of radio microphones and enough of a press corps to remind you of the days when there were still eight newspapers in this town."

Into this mix, the majordomo himself came forth. "Did anyone ever tell you," asked Howard Cosell, "that you remind them of Joe Namath?"

That famous nasal twang served notice: the hype machine was now operating in an irreversible gear. The Garden concession stands had been stocked with books and magazines and phonograph records celebrating the Pistol. If Pete had become a promotional vehicle, Press was driving the bus.

The New York writers had been enticed by the St. John's game in Hawaii and Coach Carnesecca's favorable comparisons of Pete with some of the greatest names in the game: West, Robertson, Alcindor, Jerry Lucas, and John Havlicek. But even better copy, they learned, was Press. Earlier that season, during an interview with a New York columnist, the old man declared Pete "the best damned basketball player I've ever seen."

He wasn't touting his kid to courtside gossips in Clemson or Raleigh or Baton Rouge anymore. Rather, he had begun to refer to his son's professional prospects. There had already been talk (all true) of a million-dollar offer to make Pete a white Globetrotter. Press might have loved the Trotters, but his kid wasn't a novelty. He had raised Pete to raise the game. With the right big man, said Press, a guy who could feed him the outlet pass on the break, "He'd make it as big as anyone ever did."

Coaches and fathers are expected to employ false modesty when speaking of players and sons. But Press, willfully oblivious to these conventions, had actually amped up the level of expectation once he arrived in town. To hear Press for the first time was to hear a man claiming to know more about basketball than 8 million New Yorkers combined. This was Pete's moment, but it also belonged to Press. As one reporter noted, "The coach maintains that he and Pete are 10 to 15 years ahead of their time."

Unfortunately, all the deification and commercialization and son-worship lost sight of one point. Even at his best, it was plain to see: Pete was human. When asked of his motivation, the son spoke of his father: "He's given his life to basketball . . . We really want to win this one for him."

He might as well have said, *I'm here to save the family name.*
No pressure there.

LSU's first opponent was Georgetown, a team that assigned a five-eleven defensive ace, Mike Laska, to shadow Pete everywhere he went. It wasn't a bad strategy. After the game, Georgetown coach Jack Magee would brag that Maravich "never met a kid as tough as that little [bastard]."

In fact, Laska had help, at least another man or two at all times. But the larger point was well taken, as the Pistol's Garden debut was considerably less than had been hoped for. "His worst game," said Press. With Pete looking strangely tentative, LSU never established its trademark fast break. The truth was he had hurt his knee, an injury he wanted to remain secret. But the knee wasn't the reason. "He was emotionally wiped out," said Press. "He had the Garden jitters."

As it ended, LSU won, 83–82, the margin of victory supplied by the two free throws Pete hit with nine seconds left. He would finish with 20 points—ten fewer than high scorer Danny Hester—on 16 shots. He also had 5 assists in a game that saw both teams combine for only 18.

That's not to say, however, that he failed to impress. Larry Merchant's review of opening night—citing an assortment of spectacularly unorthodox passes—ran under the headline, "Merely Brilliant." The pros in the audience were even more enthused. "Pete has made a fan of me," said Jim Gardner, owner of the Carolina Cougars. "He's exciting, he moves, he represents youth and the youth movement. I think he's going to turn out to be the greatest sports personality since Arnold Palmer."

"Tremendous talent," said Pete Newell, the San Diego Rockets general manager. "I think he can help any franchise."

For Pete, though, the game remained nothing but a source of regret. "I had a slap pass I wanted to use," he said. "I had a few passes that I wanted to throw that I didn't. It was a pitiful game on my part."

Neither the win nor the winning free throws gave him much, if any, solace. Not only was he almost 27 points shy of his average, but the curtains hadn't opened on the Broadway production of Show-time. In every sense, he had failed.

Unfortunately, he couldn't pretend that basketball was merely a game. The familial burdens, the business, and the hype (part of the business, actually) now overwhelmed a sport that had once offered him refuge. What, then, to do? He could, as was his habit, drink or drive recklessly at an excessive rate of speed. But as this was New York City, his incredible, indestructible Volkswagen was unavailable.

"Pete and I went out and got shitfaced that night," says Hester. "Apple had to carry him through the hotel lobby to the elevator."

The next day, practice was interrupted by a stranger. "Is there a Pete Maravich here?" he asked.

The man drove a cab. Pete, in a high state of inebriation, had left his wallet in the backseat the night before.

Practice resumed, though by that point, one wonders if Press's charges were paying much attention. Press had warned them that the games would be physical. They wouldn't be getting many calls this far north. And though Press was usually tolerant of nocturnal distractions, he had issued words of caution for this particular occasion. "I told the little bastards before they came here, 'Look, this is New York, the NIT . . . It's not a little Podunk tournament . . . This thing has history behind it.'"

And now his players, his own flesh and blood first among them, were taking a chance at ruining that history. Two days after slipping past Georgetown, the Tigers beat Oklahoma, 97–94. Again, Pete hit a pair of free throws to clinch the game. He had played better, drawing any number of "oohs" and "aahs" from the full-house crowd. Still, it wasn't the game the fans were expecting. Pete had 37 points, 8 rebounds, and 9 assists, but Oklahoma, down 17 with just six minutes left, made the game close. Perhaps that had something to do with Pete's 14 turnovers.

"Felt like I made 35," he said.

Failure, again. The crushing weight of expectation had become apparent even to some in the media scrum. "A perfectionist who will never attain perfection," wrote the *News*' Gene Ward. "He sets too severe a standard for himself, one which neither he nor any man could possibly live up to because he is, first of all, an innovator."

Press blamed television, saying the kids had been up all night watching the tube. Then again, who did Press think he was fooling? Even he had to know that the problem was much as it appeared: "I can tell when they get up in the morning," he said. "They look like they'd been on a three-day drunk."

The partying—especially Pete's—had continued unabated. "I used to think he was just a guy who couldn't hold his booze and didn't know when to quit," says Rich Hickman. "Now I think he drank to get away from real life."

By contrast, the Tigers' next opponents were basically sequestered. "We're staying in a place I call the Convent," said Marquette coach Al McGuire. "Nobody can escape."

McGuire—of Milwaukee, Wisconsin, by way of Far Rockaway, Queens—was the kid brother in a great New York basketball fraternity. His oldest brother, John, was by turns a uniformed patrolman, a nightclub owner, and a gambler. The middle brother, Dick, with the most basketball talent, was a star for St. John's and the Knicks, a team he now served as general manager. Al, with John's glib charm and a fraction of Dick's talent, became a coach. He specialized in harvesting talent from the fertile New York playgrounds. His best players were typically black kids from Harlem or Bedford-Stuyvesant whom he had taught to play in the style of the old New York basketball establishment. McGuire believed in a crafty brand of ball control and aggressive team defense, a style Press likened to "watching grass grow."

The approach, however, paid great dividends. Not only was Marquette a clear favorite to win the NIT, but it had spurned an NCAA bid in order to finish the season in the Garden. McGuire's rationale, as Axthelm recounted in *The City Game*, was rooted in a vendetta pitting the New York wiseguy against the Kentucky Baron.

Adolph Rupp of Kentucky hated Al so fiercely that he helped arrange for Marquette to be bracketed in a division far away from Kentucky in the 1970 NCAA regional playoffs. McGuire responded by snubbing the NCAA altogether and bringing his team to New York . . . Amid the resulting furor, he also commented that Rupp had good reason to avoid Marquette: a year earlier, Pat Smith, the six-foot-three-inch center from Harlem, so thoroughly outplayed Kentucky's six-foot-nine-inch All-American Dan Issel that Issel had managed only seven shots in the game as Marquette scored a smashing upset. "Naturally we stopped Issel," added Al. "We stop all stars. Our kids respond to that sort of challenge."

In this context, a denouement featuring Pete and Marquette at the Garden seemed a foregone conclusion. Certainly Pete prepared as if it were a fait accompli. He was physically and psychologically drained. His body was covered with bruises. His legs felt rubbery, and his knee was in bad shape. The night before the semifinal game, he cancelled an appearance on *The Dick Cavett Show*, retired to his room at the New Yorker Hotel, and told the front desk to hold his calls.

Then there was a knock at his door. Someone had a six-pack. What began as a nostalgic evening, with friends recounting the hilarities of their college years, quickly devolved into a drunken bash. "The party continued into the night and I got totally wasted," Pete would recall. "I drank to feel good and forget."

Also, to escape. Already fearing the worst, Pete medicated accordingly. The court might have become a savagely unforgiving place, but a sufficient quantity of alcohol provided temporary amnesty from guilt and responsibility. "His eyes," recalls Rich Hickman, "looked like two piss holes in a snow pile."

Dreadfully hungover, he managed 9 assists on 4 of 13 shooting against Marquette. His 20 points were less than the margin of LSU's 101–79 defeat in the semifinal round. Watching grass grow?

"We mowed his lawn tonight," said the Marquette players.

"He's good," McGuire said of Pete, "but I'd take Dean Meminger against him one-on-one up in Harlem any day."

Meminger, who checked Pete part of the night, would of course concur, implying that the hype had been less than color-blind. "There are a lot of cats in the parks that are just as tough as Maravich," he said.

If Pete felt bad before, his sense of guilt was now profound. Certainly, it would trail him more closely than Meminger ever did. He didn't understand his behavior as an act of self-inflicted sabotage, but he knew full well that he had failed in the worst way, dashing his daddy's dreams. "My stupidity not only contributed to a loss," he later wrote, "but humiliated my dad, and that was unbearable."

He had suffered a hip pointer in the game, as the condition of his bad knee continued to worsen. "By the time we played Marquette," says Bud Johnson, "he had no lateral movement." So instead of practicing for the consolation game with Army, Johnson arranged for him to receive whirlpool treatment in the Knicks' training room, where he was accompanied by student-trainer Billy Simmons. There, they struck up a conversation with none other than Knicks forward Bill Bradley. Earlier that morning, Pete had been captivated by the precision of Bradley's own solitary drills. Pete's teammates would recall it as the only time they saw him in awe of another player.

But now, as they spoke in the training room, they were interrupted by a flamboyantly attired black man in a leather coat and big brimmed hat. Walt Frazier, known as "Clyde," was already an All-Star with a burgeoning reputation for shutting down the opposing team's big gun.

"Pistol Pete," he said with a sly grin. "I got something for you when you come in the league."

"Yeah," said Pete, "what's that?"

"Defense," said Frazier, who quickly turned to leave after delivering his punchline.

Billy Simmons would always be struck by what Bradley said next, one white hope to another. "You've got no idea," said Bradley. "You're a marked man. Everybody wants to shut you down."

Pete didn't look so upset, but you never could tell. He internalized everything. After Bradley walked off, Billy asked him, "What do you think?"

Pete tried to play it off by nodding after Bradley. "I think he got a fat ass."

• • •

Mrs. Thompson's Special Opportunity Group, 1929. Press is the glum-faced boy in the third row, far right.

The St. Elijah's team that won the 1936 Serbian-American tournament, the first of four championships Press would bring home for Aliquippa. Pecky Suder, number 3, is far left, first row. Lazo Maravich is far right, wearing number 9. Press is third from the left, number 12. "Press was the boss," recalls one teammate. "You didn't dare say no to him."

Barnstorming with the World Champion Detroit Eagles, 1941. Press, now wearing number 10, stands next to coach Dutch Dehnert, the former Celtic great.

As a Naval cadet,
Press showed all the right stuff.

The Cult of Press, West Virginia Wesleyan University,
Autumn 1949. George Danovich is far right.

Back in Aliquippa, James Naismith's game was changing. By 1954–55, almost half
of Press's team was African American.

Pride and Joy: Press with toddler Pete.

Helen, baby Pete, and the boy
formerly known as Ronnie Montini.

The family before it went nuclear.
Clemson, South Carolina.

Off the court, little Pete
had a big smile.

Ronnie Maravich
Center

From the 1961 *Summit*, the Daniel High School yearbook:
An eighth-grade prodigy who played varsity ball, and his hell-raising brother,
Ronnie, a senior who played linebacker and center on the football team.

A not-so-happy home: Diana as an
infant with her biological mother
and her adoptive one. Raleigh,
North Carolina, December 1964.

The bony basketball wizard of Needham-Broughton High School.

"Pistol Pete is so cute."
LSU sophomore year.

Fan mail arrived by the sackful.

Press sending his boy into battle.

Showtime: No one had ever seen these moves before.

Eyes of mine: The proud papa
embracing his son,
who had just become
the most prolific scorer
in NCAA history.

After losing for the last time
to Kentucky.

College Basketball's Player of the Year,
picking up yet another award at
the LSU Basketball Banquet, 1970.

Richie Guerin explaining the facts of NBA life as Pete
gets ready to make his pro debut with the Hawks.

Pete took his lumps as a rookie.

But as the sponsors would tell you,
he still had great hair.

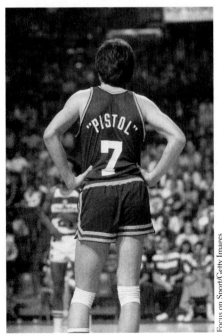

With the Jazz, 1975, an expansion team's
marketing plan stitched on the back
of his jersey.

Jackie could cut through the sadness. [ABOVE] The happy couple dressed up for a drink, and [LEFT] dressed down on their wedding day, January 11, 1976.

That Seventies Show: [RIGHT] The resplendent superstar in shades and polyester at the press conference announcing what would be his final contract with the Jazz, August 1977. [BELOW] Partying with Rich Kelley (left) and Aaron James at Studio 54, December 1977.

Finally, he achieved harmony with the pro game. For a time, says Rich Kelley, he was the best player in the league.

Then his knee went out. He would never be the same.

Focus on Sport/Getty Images

That's not to say there was nothing left. Flashes of Showtime with the Celtics, 1980.

Courtesy Jackie Maravich

The grief in his eyes was never more evident than after he quit the game.

Courtesy Jackie Maravich

God told him, "Be strong and lift thine own heart."

He found peace as a husband and as a father of Jaeson (left) and Josh.

For the first time, he also found peace as a son: with Press at their camp in Clearwater, Florida.

In the name of the father: [ABOVE] Jaeson, who became an NAIA All-American at William Carey College, displays his tattoos. [RIGHT] Despite the warnings of his mother and brother, Josh insisted on walking on at LSU.

Jackie with Josh (left) and Jaeson, as the boys sign *Homework Basketball* DVDs, 2005.

For four years now, Pete had played without ever acknowledging an assortment of orthopedic maladies, ankles, knees, and feet being the most common. Earlier that season he had shot down Vanderbilt while concussed with blurred vision. "Tough guy," says Simmons. "It was hard to keep him off the floor."

But on the eve of the consolation game with Army, Pete and Press decided to hold him out of the game. Coached by a fiery young disciplinarian named Bobby Knight, Army's methodical and physical style made it the last team Press wanted to play. Why risk further injury? There was too much at stake The *News*' Dick Young reported that Maravich had "okayed" a Carolina Cougars deal worth $2 million plus fringe benefits. The big benefit was to have been a coaching job for Press with another ABA franchise, the Pittsburgh Pipers. The *Post*'s Larry Merchant chimed in, knowing full well what the Pistol could do for the upstart league: "His presence would guarantee a television contract for the ABA."

Army was a losing proposition, a consolation game without the prospect of consolation. Still, the idea of sitting out added to Pete's despondency. He had come to New York to take his rightful place as the son of a basketball god, but now this expedition for glory would conclude with him on the bench in street clothes. As the crowds had nourished him this long, he knew what was coming. He deserved it, like a penance.

In the locker room, as LSU prepared to take the floor, Pete turned to Rusty Bergman, now a graduate assistant. Pete asked Rusty to walk out with him for the player introductions. He didn't want to go out there alone.

"What are you talking about?" asked Rusty.

"They paid good money to see me play," he said. "Now these people from New York are gonna boo the hell out of me."

15. THE BLACKHAWKS

The expiration of Pete Maravich's basketball eligibility also marked an end to his academic studies, such as they were, twenty-nine hours shy of a degree at LSU's College of Business Administration. Mrs. Lola Hawkins, his math teacher back in Clemson, might have been perplexed to learn that little Pete was now on the verge of a fortune he would have found all but incalculable in her seventh-grade class. Still, even Pete's professors found his logic unassailable. "What's more important," asked one, "twenty-nine hours or $2 million?"

The enterprise named Pistol Pete now stood at the precipice of the richest contract in sports history. The NIT hadn't gone well, but it hadn't discouraged his suitors in any number of business ventures. The most dedicatedly fervent of these seemed to be the Carolina Cougars of the American Basketball Association. Cougars' owner Jim Gardner, who had made a fortune in Hardee's hamburger franchises, had been courting both father and son Maravich since Pete's junior year. At thirty-five, Gardner had abandoned his political ambitions (already an ex-congressman and, almost, the governor of North Carolina) to embark on a career as a basketball impresario. In keeping with the Broadway Joe theory of economics, it was reasoned that Pistol Pete could go a long way toward ensuring the viability of a first-year team in what was then a three-year-old league. The Cougars were designed as a regional franchise for a basketball hotbed, the heart of ACC country. After it became clear that Press would not become the team's inaugural coach, Gardner hired Press's old pal, Bones McKinney. The Cougars played in the Greensboro

Coliseum, an arena that just happened to be managed by another of Press's old basketball buddies. Bob Kent, a rival coach in their West Virginia college days, had remained in touch through the years, rooming with Press at various basketball tournaments and NCAA conventions. In the spring of 1969, he was dispatched to make the initial contact with Press on the Cougars' behalf.

The figures being thrown around were a measure of how much the world had changed since 1965, when Namath's rookie contract with an upstart league, widely reported at $400,000, changed the business of sport. Pete's prospective agreement—predicted to be three to five times what Namath's had been—would also include a wider range of ancillary goodies. Gardner and his people were talking about percentages of the gate, even a movie deal with MGM. Of course, there would be a Maravich hamburger franchise, Pistol Pete's Hamburger Courts.

Perhaps the most powerful incentive to sign with the Cougars was the ABA itself, whose owners agreed among themselves that Carolina should be the team to draft Pete. As the new league encouraged an innovative, wide-open, fast-breaking style, Pete had been put on its "most wanted" list of college prospects before his senior year. With an emphasis on entertainment, the ABA—with its red, white, and blue basketball—went out of its way to offend the sport's orthodoxy. Unlike the NBA, ABA rules mandated a three-point shot line, something that, by one sportswriter's meticulous calculations, would have brought Pete's college scoring average to over 52 points a game. An entirely reasonable consensus held that Pete couldn't miss in the ABA. The style of play was, in many respects, the very game Press had been preaching the past four years.

Through most of Pete's senior season, the Cougars remained the heavy favorite to secure his services. But the situation became more fluid in December 1969, three months before the NIT, when Bob Kent was hired by Tom Cousins, a developer who had moved the St. Louis Hawks to Atlanta the year before. Cousins was no basketball man. "In the four years I went to the University of Georgia," he says, "I probably went to one game."

The area of his avid expertise—his sole concern in buying the team—was real estate. With large holdings of air and land rights in downtown Atlanta, he envisioned a new skyline for the city, the heart of which was then vacant after dark. Cousins commissioned a study concluding that the most efficacious way to correct this condition (and therefore keep his parking lots full) was to build an arena. At the time, all Atlanta had was a decrepit municipal auditorium built in 1906 and Georgia Tech's Alexander Memorial Coliseum, an aging fieldhouse with a seating capacity of 7,192.

With the land-use study in mind, Cousins purchased the Hawks. The franchise began in 1946 as an entry in the old National Basketball League. Representing a triumvirate of clustered metropolises— Moline and Rock City, Illinois, and Davenport, Iowa—that saw much action in the Black Hawk War of 1831, the team was christened the Tri-Cities Blackhawks. Five years after their inception, they moved to Milwaukee, where their name was shortened to Hawks. In 1955, they relocated to St. Louis. Finally, in 1968, Cousins moved them to the Peachtree City.

From the beginning, Cousins planned on leaving basketball decisions to the basketball people—with one exception. In January 1968, before buying the team, he accepted a colleague's invitation to attend a game at their alma mater in Athens, Georgia. It was Pete's sophomore year, and as it happened, he hit the free throws to ice LSU's victory. More memorable, though, was the show he put on prior to that. One didn't have to know basketball to appreciate magic. "I was fascinated by what he did that night," says Cousins, who recalls the crowd's awe as Pete flipped in a looping hook, a version of the famous *going down shot*, as he walked off the court before half-time.

Months later, after buying the team, he met with his coach, Richie Guerin, and the general manager, Marty Blake. "I don't know anything about basketball," Cousins told them. "But if we ever have a shot at this guy Maravich, I want him."

Guerin voiced concern: "I don't know if he'll ever make it in the NBA."

But Cousins didn't care about the NBA: "He'll make the sport in Atlanta, Georgia."

Making the sport in Atlanta would make the new arena, which would markedly enhance the downtown property values, not to mention all those parking spaces. And who better to start up a new arena than the man who had done wonders managing the Greensboro Coliseum, "generally acknowledged as the best man in his field," according to *Sports Illustrated*: Bob Kent.

In the first official meeting with his new employee, Cousins revealed that the Hawks had obtained a "secret" draft pick from the San Francisco Warriors. This bit of good fortune had come as compensation for the NBA rights to Zelmo Beaty, an All-Star center who had earlier left the Hawks for the ABA. The pick wasn't supposed to amount to much, as the Warriors were forecast as a strong team. But with San Francisco starting to plummet in the standings, the Hawks had begun to contemplate a greater advantage.

"I wish there was a way to get next to this Maravich kid," said Cousins.

"I think I know how," said Kent, who began explaining his decades-long relationship with Press. Upon hearing this story, Cousins became one very happy real estate man.

In short time, Bob made a trip to Baton Rouge. "You need to be with us in Atlanta," he told Press.

Press told him about all the extras Carolina was dangling, the movie deal especially.

"Let me tell you about that movie deal," said Bob. "You ever see one of those movies with a lot of extras, say, a guy on an ambulance stretcher with his arm hanging out?"

"Yeah," said Press. "So?"

"So that's your big movie role."

Kent had another idea. He wanted Press to come work for the Hawks. The job would come with a nice title—vice president of player development—and considerably more money than he had ever made. It wasn't just a negotiating ploy, either. Having known Press all these years, Kent figured he would be an asset on the basketball side of the operation.

But Press surprised him. "I really appreciate it, Bob," he said. "But I'm not riding on the kid's coattails."

• • •

As dictated by San Francisco's precipitous drop in the standings, Atlanta obtained the third pick in the draft behind the Detroit Pistons and the San Diego Rockets, each of whom opted for far less pricey big men. Detroit, a cold northern city Pete would not play for, selected Bob Lanier, six-eleven, 260 out of St. Bonaventure; the Rockets, reluctant to shell out Maravich money, opted for Rudy Tomjanovich, a six-eight forward out of Michigan. Then Atlanta cast its bet on Pete.

"Drafting Pete Maravich is good business," said Richie Guerin.

Jim Gardner hadn't even known how much trouble he was in for until Bob Kent was seen at the NIT. His response was to issue a threat, telling the *Atlanta Constitution*, "Tom Cousins will think Quantrill's Raiders [a band of Confederate guerrillas] were a bunch of amateurs if Atlanta lucks out and signs Pete Maravich." The money he didn't spend on Pistol Pete would go toward stealing away Lou Hudson, Atlanta's All-Star swingman, and Walt Hazzard, Atlanta's starting point guard.

Cousins was unmoved. "With everything else equal," he said, "I think Pete would rather play against the better competition in the NBA."

The owner's argument required no basketball knowledge. Rather, Cousins's point was steeped in an understanding of people's natures, especially the ego forces that had conspired to create an attraction like Pistol Pete. The Pistol wasn't conceived as a side show for the *other* league. He was always intended to be the main event. Anyone who had seen the prepubescent Pete perform in front of the fraternal order of coaches knew that Press had developed his game expressly *for* the basketball establishment. Press wanted his creation measured against those already recognized as the best, players like Oscar Robertson and Jerry West. "You won't find them in the ABA," he warned Pete. Playing in the ABA would be like preaching to the choir. Press, whose modest statistical line from his season with the Pittsburgh Ironmen was now included in the NBA record books, wanted converts, souls of the old school. Pete's skills, after all, were a demonstration for their benefit, a way of saying: Behold my glory, my life's work. Earlier that season, in response to a question about coaching his son the star, Press had said quite emphatically, "Pete will do what I tell him." Now it became clear that Press's power extended to career matters as well.

Toward this end, he declined the entreaties of all prospective sports agents. Instead, Press determined that the negotiations would be handled by an old friend, Art Herskovitz, Aliquippa High School, class of '42. Herskovitz, whose parents ran a grocery store in Plan 11, enlisted the help of another lawyer, Les Zittrain. It was Zittrain who had the pleasure of making the formal announcement, on March 26, 1970, at a banquet at the Atlanta Tipoff Club, where Pete had arrived to collect and display the James Naismith Trophy. "Gentlemen," he began, "Pete Maravich will play next season with the Atlanta Hawks."

Zittrain declined to specify a dollar figure but characterized the contract as "one that compensates the greatest basketball player in the world." Dated March 23, 1970—three days before the banquet—it provided for $1.5 million over five years, personally guaranteed by Cousins. Pete could not be cut or traded. If the team were to move from Atlanta, he would become a free agent. In addition to salary and bonus payments, he was to receive a personal secretary, an apartment, and before each new season, a new car with a telephone. He'd also get $50 a month for gasoline—this at a time when a gallon cost 36 cents.

The value of the contract was widely reported (and somewhat inflated) as being worth $1.9 million, making it the richest in sports history. That was $400,000 more than Bob Lanier received as the top pick, and half a million more than the previous year's top pick, Lew Alcindor.

"I can't understand his decision," said Cougars general manager Don Dejardin. Carolina's offer was $2.5 million with a $250,000 life insurance policy and a $20,000 annual annuity that kicked in at age forty.

"I think time will show that Pete has made a mistake," said the Cougars coach, Bones McKinney, who didn't think the Hawks ran enough to exploit the talents of their new acquisition.

Then again, McKinney's was not a widely held view in Atlanta, where it was estimated that the local NBA team had increased its roll of season ticket-holders by one-third in the twenty-four hours after Pete's signing.

Over the years, the franchise had undergone a metamorphosis, from the Tri-Cities Blackhawks to the predominantly black Atlanta Hawks. Nothing too unusual there, as pro rosters only reflected the sport's changing demographics. Yet there were special ironies in the case of the black Hawks, and to appreciate them one should begin with the amazing Cleo Hill, of Winston-Salem Teachers College.

Hill was St. Louis's first-round pick in 1961, the eighth player selected in the draft. With "the Big Three"—a front line of Bob Pettit, Cliff Hagan, and Clyde Lovellette—the Hawks had the best record in the Western Conference for three years running and had been to the Finals the prior two. But they could not beat Boston. Such a fate abounded in irony, as the Celtics' dynasty was born in 1956 when St. Louis traded to Boston the draft rights to one black player, Bill Russell, for two white ones, Ed Macauley and Hagan. Russell would become the game's greatest defensive center, retiring with an average of 22.5 rebounds a game and 11 championship rings. Macauley, a Hall of Famer, would retire three years after the trade. Hagan, also a Hall of Famer, would play ten seasons for the Hawks. Still, as the 1960s began, it was understood that the Big Three would not be around forever. The game was changing.

Drafting Hill was coach Paul Seymour's attempt to help the team evolve. Seymour, who had played thirteen seasons with the Syracuse Nationals before moving to the front office and drafting All-Star shooting guards Hal Greer and Dick Barnett, figured he knew something about the position. "Cleo," said Seymour, "was the answer." The coach wasn't exactly going out on a limb in making this assessment. "The most complete player I've had," said Big House Gaines. "He had the greatest assortment of shots of anyone I've ever seen." He was also an excellent defender.

These skills were put on full display through the early part of the season. In his first appearance, in an exhibition game against Oscar

Robertson and the Cincinnati Royals, Hill scored 26 and fouled out with seven minutes to go. Against the Lakers, his line was 20 points, 12 rebounds, 7 assists. In North Carolina, where the Hawks traveled for a series of exhibitions with the Philadelphia Warriors, he found himself a big crowd favorite, especially in places like Winston-Salem.

However, his efforts were not appreciated by the Big Three. Perhaps in Hill they saw a harbinger of the game that would eventually render them an extinct species. The flair and exuberance with which he played seemed to offend members of the triumvirate, who would groan or smirk or roll their eyes as he made a move. They complained to Seymour about his one-handed passes. Occasionally they would admonish Hill directly: "Can't you give up the ball without a show?" But most of the abuse was parceled out as subtle ostracism. "The cold shoulder," said Hill.

It's worth noting that the Big Three were all white. Pettit, from LSU, and Hagan, from Kentucky, had played at staunch segregationist schools. Also worth mention is St. Louis's reputation among black players in the early sixties. "The Mississippi of the league," says Woody Sauldsberry, who became a Hawk after stints with the Globetrotters and the Warriors. And though Hill himself is careful not to charge racism ("It wasn't about prejudice, it was about points," he says), the racial element is impossible to ignore. Hill's pal Billy Packer had watched the exhibition in Winston-Salem closely. "It was obvious what was going on," he says. "If Cleo had been white he would have been accepted by that team."

The prospects for team harmony became even more dismal as the Hawks prepared to play the Celtics in another exhibition game in Lexington, Kentucky. Refused service at local dining establishments, five members of the Celtics refused to play. After hearing of the boycott, Hill and Sauldsberry, also denied service, decided to sit out as well. Some sportswriters saw the move, not as a protest, but as an embarrassment for two former Kentucky greats—Hagan and the Celtics' Frank Ramsey—and called for the boycotters to be punished.

By the time the regular season arrived, Hill began to think that the Big Three were trying to sabotage him and Coach Seymour. "I'm not saying they lost games deliberately," Hill told the *Winston Salem Journal-Sentinel*, "but they knew a slump would bring a change. They played harder when other backcourt men were in there. They wouldn't give me the ball. It was so obvious that we were blowing points."

"I wouldn't treat a dog the way they treated him," said Seymour.

In the second game of the season, Seymour called time and lit into his veterans. "Next guy who passes up the rookie gets fined," he said.

In issuing his ultimatum, the coach was willfully disobeying the orders of his own owner, Ben Kerner, to keep Hill on the bench. Sauldsberry recalls the owner's reaction as Seymour put Hill in the game: "Kerner, who was sitting straight across from me with his mother, says, 'Get him out of there.' "

"Screw you," said the coach.

After 14 games, nine of which the Hawks lost, Seymour was fired. "I felt Hill had the most potential," Seymour told the Associated Press, "and my battle for the kid cost me my job."

"Paul is entitled to his opinion," said Pettit, who made it clear that he was speaking for the other two-thirds of the Big Three. "There's nothing we want more than for Cleo Hill to be the greatest ballplayer in the world. We don't care who plays or who scores as long as we win."

As it happened, Pettit became the Hawks' interim player coach. Cleo Hill was sent to the bench. He played unevenly, appearing in 58 games, averaging about five points and 18 minutes a night. At 34 percent from the field, the great shooter he had been was no longer in evidence. Under Coach Pettit (whose coaching career lasted just six games) and Fuzzy Levane, who finished the season, the Hawks shunned the fast break to walk the ball up the floor. But the old formula didn't work. The reigning Western Conference champions finished the season 29–51.

Perhaps the Big Three had it coming. More severe was the price Hill paid for playing what he calls "the wrong game for the wrong team at the wrong time." It didn't matter how good he was, or what he might have been. No one can play with guys who don't want to play with him. That kind of ostracism could destroy any player. Certainly, it destroyed Cleo Hill. Sauldsberry, who was soon traded to the Chicago Zephyrs, no longer recognized what he saw in his friend on the Hawks. "Cleo looked like he forgot how to play," he says.

Not playing had cost him the athlete's one irreplaceable commodity, something he had always taken for granted. "My confidence," says Hill. "I lost my confidence."

The course of change—too late to be of much comfort to Cleo Hill—was nonetheless inexorable. Lovellette left the Hawks after the season. Robert E. Lee Pettit retired in 1965. Hagan went to the ABA a year later. In their places, the Hawks had stockpiled an assortment of All-Star-caliber players, all of them black, through the draft: point guard Lenny Wilkens, Zelmo Beaty at center, Bill Bridges at forward, and Lou Hudson, a dead-eye shooter. Joe Caldwell, another six-five swingman who might have been the game's most underrated player, had been acquired in a trade.

By 1968, the Hawks were again the best team in the West, with a record of 56–26. Unfortunately, the standings had no effect on attendance. They just couldn't draw. "When we lost Pettit and Hagan the fan support just wasn't there," says Gene Tormohlen, the team's backup center. "Ben Kerner couldn't make any money, so he sold to Tom Cousins."

The relocation proceeded without Lenny Wilkens, a future Hall of Famer. Wilkens, who grew up in Brooklyn, didn't like the idea of moving his family to the Deep South. But there was also a financial side to his decision. Marty Blake, then the general manager, recalls that the new owner "didn't want to spend any money to sign Lenny."

Wilkens wasn't the last player the Hawks would lose over money. Beaty, the team's reigning Most Valuable Player, would jump to the ABA the following year. Still, the 1969–70 Hawks managed to turn in another solid season before eventually losing in the conference finals to the Lakers, a team featuring Wilt Chamberlain, Elgin Baylor, and Jerry West.

The Hawks couldn't match that kind of talent. But they were an authentic ensemble, worthy of admiration. Six players had double-digit scoring averages. At season's end, when it came time to name an individual as team MVP, Richie Guerin had the words "HAWK TEAM" inscribed on the trophy. The coach had been in the league since 1956 when he was drafted out of Iona. And in all that time, he said, "I've never seen a more close-knit team."

The cast, which made little distinction between supporting and starring roles, included Walt Hazzard, Wilkens's replacement at point guard, and Walt Bellamy, who had filled the spot left vacant by Beaty's departure. Bridges, the team captain, had become the best rebounding forward in the league. Then there was Hudson, scoring better than 25 points a game.

But the dominant personalities on that team—and the most liked—were Guerin and Caldwell. By speech and temperament, Guerin was immediately identifiable as a New Yorker of the profane variety. To Atlanta's ruling class, the distinction made him almost as much of an outsider as his black players. To be sure, in his mod clothes and tinted glasses, Guerin could be one of the guys. But he could just as easily be a kick-ass drill sergeant. A former Marine, Guerin administered tongue lashings as needed, but without favoritism or hard feelings. Just because Richie might get in a guy's face didn't mean they wouldn't be drinking side by side at the bar a few hours later.

Not only could the coach outdrink his players, but he could still outplay a few of them. In 1962, Guerin had averaged 29.5 points a game for the Knicks, making him the first guard to score 2,000 points in a season. But greater than his scoring ability was the ferocity with which he competed. Guerin believed there was a right way to play the game. On the night of March 2, 1962, in Hershey, Pennsylvania, he scored 39 as Wilt Chamberlain set an astonishing record with 100 points. But while fans and fellow players saw Chamberlain's performance as a source of wonderment, Guerin was offended. The Warriors, he would recall, "began fouling us in the backcourt to kill the clock and give Wilt more time to operate. To me it was embarrassing to play the game that way—a mockery of the sport. I just didn't want any part of it, so I began intentionally fouling, looking to get my six personal fouls and leave the court."

Now, more than eight years later, Guerin offered one final example of how to play the game, occasioned by Atlanta's playoff series with the Lakers. Not only was Georgia Tech's fieldhouse the smallest arena in the league, but its gym floor, laid over cement, was the hardest. The eighty-two-game regular season left many of his players with aching, deadened legs. To make matters worse, the Hawks emerged from their impressive first-round defeat of the Chicago Bulls with a severely depleted backcourt. Hazzard had broken his wrist. His backup, Don Ohl, had the flu. So Guerin suited up, to the disbelief of Frank Hyland, an *Atlanta Journal* writer who had shared "a couple of pops with him the night before."

He scored 31 points that night, including a hook shot over Chamberlain that tied the score at halftime. The Hawks would eventually lose the game ("I ran out of gas," said Guerin) and the series, but not before the outgunned team had proven a larger point. The Hawks played the right way.

They also played against type. Not only were they a black team— seven of Guerin's first eight players were of African descent—but they were partial to a slow, methodical game, as that was the style that happened to blend best with their talents. Bellamy had never been one to run up the floor, and Hudson was a set-up shooter. The exception was Joe Caldwell, or Pogo, a nickname derived from his seemingly supernatural vaulting ability. While at Arizona State, Jumping Joe cleared the hood of a '55 Mercury.

Caldwell had been an All-American and a member of the 1964 Olympic team. Detroit selected him with the second pick in the 1964 draft and paid him $11,500 as a rookie. "Gotta wait your turn and learn how to play this game before you ask for the money," he says.

By 1970, Caldwell figured his wait was over. The year before, he had held out in training camp, turning down a multiyear contract with the Hawks to sign a one-year deal. A good season, he believed, would put him in an advantageous bargaining position. It was sound reasoning, as the playoff series with the Bulls solidified Caldwell's place among the most versatile and valuable players in the game.

"That guy jumps so well he inspires the whole Atlanta team," said

Jerry Sloan, a Chicago guard and noted defensive specialist, after Caldwell scored 39 on him in the opening game of the series.

On the other end of the floor, Bulls coach Dick Motta noted that "Caldwell is the best defensive player in the league."

His teammates would agree. "By far," says team statistician Hank Kalb, "the most popular player was Joe Caldwell."

"I loved playing with Joe," says Bill Bridges.

At six-five, Caldwell usually guarded the opposing team's top scorer while averaging 21 points a game. What's more, he added another dimension to the offense. The typical Hawks possession ended after a succession of passes, with a Hudson jump shot. But every once in a while, recalls Hank Kalb, "Caldwell would get loose on the break and forget about it."

"Bridges used to throw him that long pass," says Tormohlen, "and he was gone."

"It was a thing of beauty," says Bridges.

Unfortunately, such beauty went largely unrecognized in the Alexander Memorial Coliseum, where attendance was fewer than 5,000 a night. Atlanta was college football territory and didn't care much for basketball, especially the pro variety. But there was another problem as far as the gate was concerned. As one white player put it, "They had a 7,100-seat arena they had to fill every night, and they weren't going to do it by having a black team in the heart of the South. They had to have Pete and they had to have him be the star."

And no one else but the Pistol, the missionary who brought basketball to much of the Deep South. The players understood, or at least claimed to. "Let's face it," Bridges said the day after the draft, "a white player of his ability is what Atlanta and the NBA need. He may be the greatest gate attraction to come in the league, and that doesn't hurt. It could mean a couple of hundred thousand dollars to all of us Hawks . . . I like playing before a crowd . . . More people, more money."

As the sixties began, the Hawks were a white team unwilling to accommodate a black virtuoso's talent. But now, at the dawn of a new decade, the Hawks were a black team forced to accept a white sensation. At least one old Hawk was all for this experiment in compulsory integration. For Cleo Hill, the Pistol Pete experiment wasn't about race or regret, or even money. It was just basketball, and Hill couldn't help but root for the kid.

"Pete was entertaining," he says, "and the NBA was getting kind of boring."

16. The Unbearable Whiteness of Being Pete

On May 25, 1970, Press wrote to Les Robinson, catching him up in the aftermath of the season. For a change, Press was optimistic about his incoming freshmen, particularly Collis Temple Jr., a six-eight center out of Kentwood, Louisiana. "This damn Yankee finally broke a 100 yr. old tradition by recruiting a negro athlete," he wrote, admitting his surprise. "I've received only a handful of derogatory mail."

On the family front, Diana was now six, "real grown up for her age." Helen's condition, meanwhile, remained the same, which was to say not good at all. All in all, it had been a trying season for Press. "If I didn't have the Pistol," he wrote, "then it would have been disasterous [*sic*]."

As for Pete, he explained, the famous contract had been backloaded, with a lot of the money kicking in after his fortieth birthday. It might have been difficult, if not impossible, to imagine Pete as an adult, but that was the idea, to provide for him through middle age. "He'll live a pretty good life," wrote Press. "He deserves it."

Father and son had recently returned from New York, where they had filmed a commercial for Uniroyal, the manufacturer of Pro Keds basketball shoes. Pro Keds—like Seamless, makers of an official "Pistol Pete" basketball—was one of several major endorsements. But the big deal, certainly the most symbolically potent, was Vitalis. Before even playing a game for the Hawks, Pete had appeared in a national campaign for the new Dry Control hairspray. Sneakers and balls were one thing, but this was another entirely, unheard of for a mere basketball star. Vitalis would pay him $100 grand for a series of commercials. "An exorbitant amount to pay an athlete," Mel Ciociola, the Madison Avenue hotshot who signed him, said proudly. In one of the spots, Pete ends up with the foxy girl, the ice cream cone, and admiring glances from children. In another, he manages to hit the game-winning shot despite interference from his abundant sandy brown locks. In a league dominated by the Afro, Pete's coiffure made sponsors drool. It was enough to believe that Vitalis's voice-over man had spoken in all seriousness when he said, "That's just got to be the best hair in the league."

Finally, the business of basketball had found its fair-haired boy. The problem was, business and basketball did not necessarily mix. Even Richie Guerin's endorsement of Pete as "good business" pointedly neglected his virtues as a player. It's not that Guerin was blind to them. In fact, he thought Pete had as much talent as any player he'd ever seen—but not yet close to what Guerin considered a state of competent professionalism. Pete's shot selection would have to be modified. He'd have to play defense. And he'd have to learn to play for a coach other than his father. Pete would be a delicate, time-consuming project.

The most sensitive task, however, would be in navigating the intramural politics of the locker room. Guerin hadn't earned his players' respect for nothing. But now he had to integrate a great white rookie with a veteran black team. Not an easy sell.

Just the day after Pete's signing, the coach got snippy with a reporter who inquired about a behind-the-back pass Hazzard had thrown.

"Walt didn't look like Maravich," Guerin stressed. "Maravich looks like Walt." For the record, the coach would entertain no comparison between the rookie and his veterans. "Maravich has to prove himself as a pro," he said. "They already have."

There would be no affirmative action on Richie Guerin's team. Pete would have to earn his spot like everyone else. But all the talk of an equal opportunity roster ignored the impending reality. Soon

Pete would arrive in Atlanta with his record-breaking contract, driving a new Plymouth GTX (equipped with telephone and a soft top made of real alligator) and living in an apartment complex where his black teammates would not be welcome. In anticipation of the Pistol, the team was already redesigning its logo and jersey in Day-Glo colors. With Lou Hudson already wearing number 23, Pete chose 44. Though the number was intended to further memorialize his college scoring average, it had also been made famous by Jerry West. Certainly, no one in the team's executive offices would have objected if the number suggested a succession of white hopes. The team had already commissioned an advertising campaign heralding the "New Hawks"—leaving the old Hawks to wonder just what had happened to the defending Western Conference champions.

Bridges, who had been Guerin's deputy in the locker room, was the first to make his displeasure known. He was upset that Walt Bellamy, who had been a midseason acquisition, was making $80,000. But more than that, his concern was Pete's deal. Going into his ninth season with the Hawks, Bridges was not only the team's captain and the peacemaker, but its leader in rebounds and minutes played. He had seen action in all eighty-two games, averaging 40 minutes a night, and was making $50,000.

"I'm not asking for a million," he said, "but I do expect some compensation for what I've meant to the Hawks."

Bridges spoke with both Tom Cousins and the new general manager, his brother Bob. He was told how much he had meant to the franchise, and that his departure would be a great loss. But based on the limited seating capacity at Alexander Memorial Coliseum, his request for a raise was denied.

What the owners considered an explanation, however, Bridges considered an excuse. He didn't hold out, or ask to be traded. But his relationship with management and ownership would never be the same. He thought of basketball as a calling. He loved the game, thought it capable of producing sublime moments, like those when Caldwell took his outlet pass without breaking stride. But the real estate man he now played for didn't know about that. Bridges found himself wanting to tell Cousins: *You're fucking with my life's work.*

Instead, the erstwhile good soldier began to catalogue his assorted resentments. He had gone along with a request not to go public with players' complaints about the state of segregated housing in Atlanta. He had lost good friends, and for no good reason. With Lenny Wilkens and Zelmo Beaty, they had been poised to win a championship. Now he had to stand by—on legs made to ache by Georgia Tech's concrete floor—while the Western Division champions were dismissed in favor of the *New Hawks*.

However antiquated the notion, Bridges had been drafted as a Hawk and thought he would die as one. But these *New Hawks* were not the team he had signed to serve. Then again, maybe he should have seen it coming. Just a year before, he had to tell the all-white band to stop playing "Dixie" during warm-ups at the Georgia Tech fieldhouse. To Bridges, *New Hawks* became a cruel misnomer. "We were nothing but pawns," he says. "Black pawns."

The next old Hawk to take his shot with Cousins was Caldwell, who installed carpet in the off-season and was none too pleased that management hadn't procured his services for their new corporate offices. Caldwell, who made between $40,000 and $50,000 the previous season, had planned for just this moment. Pete's windfall, he figured, would augment his own. Over a steak dinner, Caldwell informed Cousins that he wanted a new deal worth exactly one dollar more than the rookie. The asking price, he argued, wasn't personal. Rather, he had waited his turn, during which time he had solidified a reputation as the league's most underrated performer. What's more, as much as the owners thought they needed Pete, Pete would need him. Caldwell might have been the only guy on that team whose game was compatible with Pete's.

Outside of Bridges, he was the best friend Pete could have in that locker room. On defense, Caldwell could cover for Pete's mistakes and lapses. On offense, he was the guy who could catch the funky stuff Pete would throw. And unlike anyone else on the roster, he says, "I could have run with him. Running was my game."

Caldwell might have persuaded Cousins that he was the more accomplished player. His basketball argument was unassailable. But to Cousins, the issue wasn't about basketball so much as the economic exigencies of show business.

"John Barrymore is a better actor than John Wayne," he said, "but the people come out to see John Wayne."

"John Wayne?" Caldwell sneered. "What's that got to do with me?"

On September 17, 1970, as the Hawks convened in Jacksonville, Florida, for training camp, their best player began his holdout. Over the next six weeks, the negotiations became increasingly bitter. Finally, on the night of October 30, the Carolina Cougars general manager made an announcement at Greensboro Coliseum: "Joe Caldwell has just received the best contract in basketball."

At $175,000 a year, it was $50,000 sweeter than the salary the Hawks were said to have offered. The signing initiated a legal battle between the Hawks and the Cougars while temporarily scuttling the merger talks between the rival leagues. But the legal machinations, dealing in the concepts of image and harm, solved nothing. "We're telling Joe we can't afford to pay, that we're playing at Georgia Tech, but we can afford to pay this white superstar college player," says Guerin, imagining himself in the place of his veterans. "I would be totally offended myself."

The coach didn't try to justify the team's position with his players. "You can't make it right," he says. The damage was done. Joe Caldwell was gone.

"And who gets blamed for that?" asks Hank Kalb, the statistician. "Pete. It was always Pete's fault."

The Hawks had lost their most popular player, only to gain a scapegoat, a collecting vessel for the team's resentments.

Of all people, Caldwell understood what Pete would now face, a pincerlike pressure, trapped between the expectations of his public and the bitterness of his teammates. Says Caldwell, "It had to make him crazy."

Pete didn't make it any easier on himself, what with the way he played in training camp. Bill Bridges would get him the ball on the break, the court aligned in anticipation of what the big man calls "pure perfection." "That's the high you play for," says Bridges. "And all of sudden, something would short-circuit in his brain."

An errant pass. A foolish move. A bad shot. Moves that worked in the SEC didn't necessarily work in the NBA. "There was," says Bridges, "a time for showtime and a time to play ball." At the dawn of his pro career, Pete seemed incapable of making that distinction.

"Training camp, that's when things started bubbling to the surface," says Herb White, whom the Hawks drafted out of Georgia. "Pete came in and he's trying to force his style of play. He's taking off and hitting guys in the back of the head with passes and taking bad shots. Let's face it: Pete took a lot of shots, and some of them were bad. I thought Richie Guerin was going to hang himself."

White, from nearby Decatur—where his high school teammates included Hank Kalb—would himself become a subplot in camp. An eighth-round draft pick without big college stats, he made the team over a black guy from a small college.

"Not because he was white," says Guerin. "Herbie had some talent." The coach, who would start White five games that season, was more easily convinced than some of the players. The least welcoming of them was Walt Hazzard, a classically trained point guard from UCLA. From the beginning, Hazzard didn't like Herbie.

"You know why you made the team," he said.

As Hazzard had little cause to be concerned with the eleventh man on the team, one can't help but think the real target of his remark was Pete. Of all the Hawks, Hazzard was the one with the most to lose. Like Pete, he was a mediocre defensive player who couldn't play without the ball. Eventually, Hazzard and Maravich would become mutually exclusive propositions. Hazzard understood that, just as he understood that management wasn't going with a black point guard over a white hope.

If Hazzard's feelings were personal, other old Hawks disliked only what the Pistol represented. But the anticipatory media glare surrounding Pete, as he struggled to adapt to his new team and a new game, only intensified the bitter sentiments. A typical exhibition game might end with Pete scoring a dozen or so points and Lou

Hudson about 30. But afterward, dozens of reporters would be gathered in front of the Pistol's locker with only one or two chatting up Sweet Lou. "I don't care how good a guy you are," says White, "that kind of stuff gets to you after a while."

It's only human nature, and it divided the team along racial lines. But again, the Hawks went against type. The black game was advertised as vertical, the province of great leapers. But as it turned out, at six-two, Herbie White was easily the best dunker on a team that was now without the services of Joe Caldwell. Long before the dunk became a commercialized exercise in basketball braggadocio, Herbie would put on his own show in pregame warm-ups: windmills, 360s, two-handed 360s, even a maneuver designed to demonstrate his "elbow hang." A packed house at the Garden would rise in unison to cheer his pregame performance. To see Herbie's bit was to remember him. Years later, the great Wilt Chamberlain would speak of "a white boy who played for Atlanta around 1970. Never got off the bench, but in warm-ups he could dunk better than anyone I've ever seen." *Sports Illustrated* would name him as the most underrated dunker in NBA history.

Still, Herbie's high-flying act didn't win him any friends in his own locker room. Nor did it help that Herbie and Pete, already pretty good pals, became roommates on the road. "I caught some heat for that," he recalls. "I guess they thought I was on Pete's side all the time." Pete's *side*. After a while, you had to declare: you were with Pete or the brothers. It was, in the most literal sense, black or white.

The Hawks opened the regular season at home against Lew Alcindor and the Milwaukee Bucks, which, having traded for Oscar Robertson, were favored to win the championship. But neither the Big O nor the Big A, as they were then called, were the reason that ABC's *Wide World of Sports* paid $75,000 to broadcast the game. The network had to equip Alexander Memorial Coliseum with extra lighting banks in anticipation of the Pistol, who checked into his debut game at the beginning of the second quarter.

From *Sports Illustrated*: "The loudest cheer of the afternoon erupted when Pete broke up a Milwaukee fast break with an interception, dribbled full court to his own foul line and shot a jumper that jiggled around the top of the basket before dropping through for his first professional field goal. Maravich again looked good two minutes later when he scored on a showy fast break engineered by Hazzard, but that was all. As the lead changed hands in the third period, it was Pete's desperation cross-court pass that was snatched away by the Bucks' Bob Dandridge. The interception led to a breakaway basket that, more than any other play, shifted the momentum to Milwaukee."

Pete scored all of 7 points in a 107–98 loss and castigated himself in the postgame media gathering. The world had been hoping for an exhibition from Press's boy. Instead, closer inspection would have revealed a confused creature with Helen's haunted eyes.

"I felt," said Pete, "like a ghost was sitting on me."

Before the season started, he had been offered the lead in a Hollywood movie. "It was going to be the story of a college star who hits the skids," explained Pete, who turned it down for fear that the story's darker elements would harm his image. By midseason, however, he might have questioned his decision, as his real life seemed infinitely more perverse than anything that could have been imagined in Hollywood. The defending Western Division champions started out 7–21. Pete spent more time on the bench than he had since eighth grade, tending to sit there with his arms folded in an almost fetal position. "I was so frustrated . . . I couldn't see straight," he said. "It seemed like I'd go crazy."

On the court, his worst habits—including his tendency to dribble into the corner—were magnified. In his first game against Boston, for example, he logged 13 turnovers. The best guards, like the Knicks' Clyde Frazier, soon came to understand that Pete was his own worst enemy. "You try to get him angry at himself," Frazier later explained. "If he makes a bad pass or you steal it from him you might be able to break downcourt for an easy layup because he's at the other end talking to himself." Clyde found that the best hair in the league could be exploited: "You sort of wait for him to stop dribbling. Then for a second all the hair that's been flying in the wind comes down over his face and he can't see. That's when you steal the ball."

Once, at the Garden, Pete turned to the timekeeper in a tortured aside. "What's wrong with me?" he asked.

As the losses mounted, the team embarked on a course of team meetings that took on the worst aspects of political discourse and group therapy. The old Hawks would rail at The System and storm out, while the new Hawks withdrew even further. The tension remained constant, the problem unresolved.

What went on behind closed doors wasn't much different from what happened on the court. Guys who remembered the joy with which Pete had played as a teenager were dismayed at what they now saw. Hal Blondeau, who had played for Press's championship team at State, saw the Hawks at the Garden that season: "It was four black guys and Pete. It was like he wasn't there. They just wouldn't give him the ball."

"I saw a lonely guy," says Pete Coker, another member of that State team. "He was separate and he knew it."

"As welcome as George Wallace at a Rockefeller house party," wrote the *Constitution*'s Jesse Outlar.

Harold Sylvester, now finishing his degree at Tulane, watched on television. Sylvester still recalled Pete trying to recruit him, the only white face in the St. Augustine gym: "Race was never an issue with us. It was all about the game." Now he saw Pete paying for the sins of the South. Says Sylvester: "He was the wrong guy to ask to pay."

Meanwhile, the crowds kept urging on the Pistol: "Shoot, shoot, shoot!"

Shoot what, though? Maravich would quip bitterly about buying a pair of gloves to keep his hands warm. "They get cold without the ball," he said.

Pete's talent made a permanent freeze-out impossible; eventually, he would get his shots, though nothing he did seemed to impress the right people. Just a few weeks into the season, he went 9 for 13 with 8 assists against the Buffalo Braves. He did this despite sustaining a five-stitch gash over his left eye. But George Cunningham, the *Constitution*'s beat writer, chose to dwell on his turnovers as evidence that "the rookie is far from ready for starting duty in the National Basketball Association."

His first experience with criticism was proving an unforgiving one. Against the 76ers, he was greeted with a sign that read: "Hey, Pistol Pete, why do hot dogs cost two million in Atlanta and only 35 cents in Philadelphia?" Pete failed to see the humor, though. He saw humor in nothing that rookie year. "Pete would take it all personal," says Hank Kalb, who had become a close friend. "Remember: this was a kid who had played for his dad his whole life."

And there was nothing Daddy could do for him now. On November 24, Pete personally erased a 20-point Knick lead at the Garden. Maravich, wrote the *Post*'s Leonard Lewin, "made a close game of a near rout by pouring 18 points in the last period from every conceivable angle." He scored 40 that night—to the amazement of everyone but his own teammates, who were upset that Hudson, an All-Star, had been moved from his guard position to small forward to make room for Pete in the starting lineup. "Why should we change for him?" asked Bridges. "He should change for us."

Jerry West, who tallied 36 points and 11 assists in his first meeting with Pete, said there was "probably more pressure on Maravich"— none of it alleviated by wearing number 44—"than on any rookie in the history of professional sports." If an opponent could see as much, then those who worked alongside him—teammates and the press, in particular—shouldn't have been so willfully blind. The signs were difficult to ignore: the way his eyes darted around in conversations, the way he gnawed at his fingernails, the way he drank. Yet the depiction of his persona remained carefree. Even the boozing— Pete had been arrested in Knoxville on charges of public drunkenness and disorderly conduct before the season even started—didn't seem much cause of concern. "The incident has been checked out thoroughly," wrote one Atlanta columnist, "and he comes out clean."

Besides, if Broadway Joe could drink like a fish, then why not Pistol Pete? Even his apartment was made to seem vaguely reminiscent of Namath's famous bachelor pad on the East Side of Manhattan. "Atlanta's most eligible bachelor," as Pete was proclaimed, resided in a two-bedroom townhouse with a pool table and a bar that sat seven. Like the phone in his car, the trimmings were fashionably loud, with shag carpeting and beaded entranceways. His sheets, bedspreads, shower curtains, dishes, even his soap were all monogrammed "Pistol."

"I think he paid someone to decorate the place," says White.

The décor might not have been Pete's taste, but it revealed him, nonetheless. Haywood Hale Broun, who visited on assignment from CBS News, would recall an apartment that "looked like a decorator's showroom. It was the most un-personal kind of place, full of stainless steel furniture and non-objective paintings. It depressed me just to look around." But the journalist, who interviewed Pete on a couch protected with plastic slipcovers, was less troubled by the condo's aesthetic than by the sense that it reflected the Pistol's problems. "He was so much the instrument of his father's desire that there wasn't much to Pete himself," Broun told an interviewer years later. "I think it emptied him of personality."

Broun's conclusion may be extreme. On the other hand, Pete's wasn't the domicile of a man who could make his own decisions, or even get out of his own way. He was damned to play a role scripted by the wants and needs of others. The Pistol was a product of repetition, but also perception. "Maravich-style hairdos are springing up all over Atlanta, and it is said that area high school coaches are being driven crazy by kids trying to play Maravich-styled basketball," George Cunningham wrote in the *Constitution*. "Is this an indication that he may be a leader of the new generation?"

The writers tried desperately to endow him with Meaning. But they also pried like gossips. What do you use in your hair? Who's your girl? And by the way, who's your girl? Nothing doing there. He refused to talk about Jackie, identifying her only as "someone I really love."

She had taken an apartment of her own in Atlanta. Part of what had enthralled Jackie—the awe Pete inspired in his fans—now became a cause for concern. She didn't like her man being advertised as a bachelor, nor was she comfortable with celebrity life. "People were always after him," she says. "He felt like he was always being watched or judged."

"I understand what happened to Elvis Presley," says Hank Kalb. "Being with Pete was like having an appointment with royalty. You were in the presence of greatness, fame, power. You think I didn't glow when I told my buddies that I was hanging out with Pistol Pete?"

Unlike the rest of his teammates, who left the Coliseum through a side door, Pete had to sneak out a secret back exit to avoid the fans who stalked him after games. It got to the point where he couldn't even go out to dinner, what with all the autograph seekers. Pete's request for them to wait until he finished eating proved futile. The guys would return to their seats, but all the while keep staring at him. "Before long I'm so nervous I can't eat and the whole evening is ruined," he said.

Actually, the guys were better than the girls. In Philly, they attacked in unison as he came out for warm-ups. "Peeeeeeeete," they shrieked. Pete ran. He knew the drill by now. They wanted to pull on the best hair in the league. Finally, the cops were called in to keep the nubile mob at bay while Pete warmed up with the team.

Older women were, if nothing else, easier than the teenyboppers. Atlanta was a hub for southern cuties: stewardesses, secretaries, receptionists, country music queens. And they all wanted to be with Pete. After a game or a practice, he'd walk out to his GTX to find their phone numbers under his windshield wipers.

The nights were full of surprises, like the time Herbie woke to a phone call. "My husband," the woman explained. "I'm separated."

Pete was in the other room with her friend. The friend, she said, was separated, too.

Herbie called to Pete, "We got to get out of here."

They scrambled to get their clothes on. But as they did, watching from an upstairs window, they saw a pickup truck pulling up, two guys in the cab. Pete and Herbie didn't bother with the stairs. They took the window, maybe a ten- to twelve-foot drop. "We didn't have any choice," said Herbie.

Life on the road was even crazier. The phone in their room never stopped ringing, even if the Pistol was already out and about.

"Pete there?" they would coo.

"Sure, darling," said Herbie. "C'mon up."

Most of the women didn't know any better. All they knew is they were looking for a tall white guy with brown hair and a wispy moustache, which, in keeping with the style, the roommates had each grown.

Finally, after the Hawks had been around the league a few times, they were sitting at a bar when Pete turned to Herbie and shook his head. "Man, I keep running into all these chicks and I tell them I'm Pete Maravich, and they say, 'No you're not. I already met Pete Maravich.' "

It was all part of the pro game: the broads and the booze. Who was going to tell them to stop? Certainly not the coach. Once Herbie and Pete took Guerin up on his challenge to down a vodka martini for every round of beers they ordered. Soon enough, the rookies found themselves under the table.

Unfortunately, none of these late nights made Pete feel any better. His mental state was one of high misery, worse than ever before. Compounding the problem was a lack of what may be called people skills. He had led, or, rather, had been led through a curiously sheltered life, never learning how to make friends. Now he tried picking up everyone's tabs at restaurants and bars. But that only made him seem like a show-off, able to burn the bread that management wouldn't spend on his teammates. An even worse offense was *not* grabbing the check. Then he was just a cheap sonofabitch.

"He was trying so hard to be one of the guys, but it was a 'damned if you do, damned if you don't' situation," says White. "He just could not figure out what he had to do to fit in with those guys, and it drove him fucking nuts."

They talked about it incessantly. "Herbie," Pete would ask, "why do they hate me?"

"Maybe they don't hate you," said White. "Maybe they just don't like your game."

But Pete couldn't separate himself from his game. To his way of thinking, they were indivisible. He tried to change, both himself and the way he played. He just didn't know how.

At various points in the season, he sought out the team captain. Bill Bridges was going through his own turmoil: his resentment against ownership and the breakup of his marriage. Bridges didn't drink, but he would watch as Pete threw them down. Then Pete would open up, becoming an oddly animated jumble of sensitivity and hostility. Though Bridges considered Pete the personification of all that had gone wrong with the team, he couldn't help but feel for the kid. His pain was as obvious as his reddened cuticles. "He just mutilated his fingernails," says Bridges. "My heart went out to him."

Then one night on the road, Pete came knocking at Bridges's door. He had been drinking. "Captain," he said, "I saw this and I wanted you to have it."

Pete presented him with a painting of an ambiguous figure. It was male, a man or a boy of indeterminate race. He was tan enough to be white, brown enough to be black. He was sitting in a chair, a rope around his neck. His legs and arms were strapped down, as if awaiting electrocution. The representation was sufficiently morbid for Bridges to feel insulted, though he did accept Pete's invitation to join him at the bar, where Pete explained about his father and how Press had made him dribble until his fingers were raw and bloody. His eyes had welled up with tears.

"I felt deep pain for Pete," recalls Bridges, who nevertheless excused himself. "Somehow I had gotten caught up in Pete's unconscious. I had to get out of there."

Bridges studied the painting for a few days, maybe even a few weeks. Was *he* the man in the chair? Or was it Pete? It was Pete, he concluded, it had to be. Just to be sure, though, he showed it to the guys in the locker room, soliciting their opinions. They didn't have much to say, mostly just shook their heads as if to say, *That's Pete, crazy motherfucker.*

Still, as bad as Bridges might have felt for the kid, Pete still pissed him off. Bridges did what he was obliged to do for a teammate. There was that night when Pete was getting roughed up by the Suns' Dick Van Arsdale. During a time-out, Guerin told Pete to let Van Arsdale go right on through the next time he had the ball. "Billy and Jim," he said, addressing his burly forwards, Bridges and Jim Davis, "you guys take care of business."

Next time Van Arsdale got the ball, the lane parted like the Red

Sea. Van Arsdale proceeds directly to the hoop, where he was met most painfully by Bridges and Davis, who took him to the floor. At the next time-out, Guerin tells his gifted rookie, "Okay, Pete, you're on your own now."

That's how it should have been, but not how it was. Management coddled Pete. Guerin had asked his captain to take Pete under his wing. Under his wing? As far as Bridges was concerned, a championship team had been broken up to make room for a white hope. They could pay Pete damn near $2 million, but wouldn't pay him near what he was worth. And Guerin wanted *him* to hold the kid's hand?

Still, nothing offended the captain's sense of basketball propriety more than Pete's incomprehensible inconsistency in running the fast break. The irony was that Press, who bred Pete to run the break, would have considered Bridges the ideal outlet man. He lived to throw that first pass to the guard and watch him go. Of all the facets to the game, says Bridges, "that's where I got my biggest thrill."

Equal and opposite to the thrill, however, were those moments when he would look up to see Pete going between his legs, or something equally unnecessary and harebrained. "The team would freeze for just a second," recalls Bridges. "But that's all it takes to break the rhythm. And you don't get that rhythm back again."

The captain would stop to stare and glare, as if to say, *Why would you mess that up?*

Pete puzzled him. He had more talent than any rookie Bridges had ever seen. But after a while, the captain stopped trying to figure the kid out. His rebound became less consequential than the decision that followed. Pete would be waiting for the ball, just as he had been trained to do. But then Hazzard would come into Bridges's line of sight, and it was Hazzard who got the ball.

"I stopped passing to Pete," says Bridges, who thought of the freeze-out as "a protest move."

Such uncivil disobedience went unremarked, though not unnoticed. Guerin knew what was going on. Bridges, for his part, felt something that approximated guilt. Cutting Pete out of the break, the break he was born to run? There was nothing more he could have done to drive Pete mad.

• • •

That raving maniac made an appearance at the Playboy Towers in Chicago, between 3 and 4 A.M., the morning of February 16, 1971. As he and Herbie arrived back at the team's hotel, Pete became embroiled in an argument outside, flinging his wallet at the cabbie who had dropped them off. Herbie was left to retrieve the billfold as Pete, impossibly loud and drunk, staggered toward the elevator. Herb figured the worst was over as the elevator doors opened on their floor, revealing Walt Bellamy, all 6 feet 11 inches of him.

"Pete just snapped," White recalls. He jumped on Bellamy's back and started to rant. At first, it sounded as if Pete were speaking in tongues. But then some of his words became decipherable. At first, Herb couldn't understand why he was saying what he was saying, as Bells was about the most laid-back guy on the team. And as crazy as Pete could be, the one craziness he didn't suffer from was racism. White's insight has arrived only over decades. He now understands that Pete had finally broken. The raving lunatic was strangely sane: his slurs were an incantation, a desperate, profane prayer for release. He wanted out.

"I hate you," he screamed. "I hate all of you niggers."

Bellamy could've broke him in half. Instead, he just shook his head. The big man wore a look of recognition, resignation, and finally pity. *Pete.*

"Take this crazy motherfucker back to his room," he said.

The following night, Atlanta lost to the Bulls, 102–118. Pete scored 8, shooting only once in the second half. Whether this was a twisted act of contrition or his own equally twisted attempt at protest is not known. But the Chicago episode warranted an intervention from Guerin, who finally explained the facts of this basketball life. Basically, it came down to this: Guerin wasn't his daddy, and he wasn't ever going to be his daddy. Pete was on his own now.

At that point, the Hawks seemed a lost cause, the reigning division champions doomed to finish out of the playoffs. But then, without much warning, as if in answer to another prayer, there appeared a new, reformed Pete, a glimpse of what might have been and what yet could be. He even played a little defense, recording 5 steals (along with 37 points and 9 rebounds) in a win over the Suns. Over the last seventeen games, he averaged 29 points. In seven of those, he went over 30. In three, he exceeded the 40-point mark. More important, the Hawks went 12–5 in that stretch. Even his teammates had begun calling him "the new Jerry West." He gave the team hope, white or otherwise.

As it happened, the Hawks would make the playoffs, where they were matched against the Knicks, defending NBA champs who had finished with the best record in what was now the eight-team Eastern Conference. The games were close, with New York having to come from behind in two of their victories. Still, to no one's surprise, the Hawks lost 4 games to 1, but not before Pete had demonstrated a larger point.

The final game included a stretch that saw him go 8 for 10 with Clyde Frazier trying to cover him. "Some of the shots," wrote the *Post*'s Larry Merchant, "were out of Earl Monroe's advanced course on one-on-one circus layups."

Frazier would have to add to the scouting book on Maravich: "He can make the most incredible shots. When he's hot, you just have to wait until the hurricane lets up."

Even Walt Hazzard, his fiercest critic, had to agree. "He can beat any man in the league."

"He's proved himself to us," Bridges said after the game. "He's going to be much greater than Jerry West."

But Pete, for his part, was more concerned with a misplay in the first half. A collision with Knicks center Willis Reed had knocked the wind out of him, and seven-one Greg Fillmore caught him with an elbow. Not long after that elbow, which made him see double, he lost the ball on the break. "If I make that one," he said, "20,000 tongues are sitting on chairs and it might have taken the fire out of them."

The game, like the season, left him with nothing but regret. Even more perplexing were his postgame remarks, as he began speaking of his great desire to win a championship. But unlike most championship fantasies, Pete's ended with him walking away from basketball, and the pressure. "I'd be satisfied with my career," he said. "I'd quit." Reporters didn't know what to make of that, this rookie who sounded so old and weary. Accolades no longer nourished him. Already he was planning his escape. He couldn't endure another season like this.

"You don't know what I've been through," he said. "It's not worth it."

Pete's worth was a relative concept. But the man best qualified to measure it employed the standards of business, not basketball. To Tom Cousins, Pete had already proven himself—and then some. The windfall had begun with ABC writing a $75,000 check, good only if Maravich appeared in the season opener on *Wide World of Sports*. The loss to the Bucks was almost immaterial, as Atlanta would appear on national television five times during the regular season. The year before, the Hawks couldn't even get a buyer for their local broadcast rights. But now Cousins turned "a substantial profit," as a team spokesman called it, by auctioning the rights to several bidders. With Maravich, the Hawks sold out thirteen home games, up from only three when Joe Caldwell had them in first place. The team had dropped 12 games in the standings only to see attendance rise by more than 20 percent. The Hawks, who had lost more than $250,000 the year before, had seen gross revenues jump by 50 percent, according to the *Wall Street Journal*. On the road, Atlanta even outdrew the defending champions, New York's Knickerbockers.

More important—considering the owner's theory of Pistol Pete as the bait in transforming his real estate deal—was the midseason announcement that the city of Atlanta, Fulton County, and the City-County Recreation Authority had approved a new $17 million arena to be built and operated by Cousins Properties, Inc.

"Without question," says Cousins, who went on to earn a reputation for philanthropy in Atlanta's black neighborhoods, "I don't think there would be a new arena if we hadn't gotten Pete Maravich."

Officially, that arena would be christened the Omni, but again, as was the case with LSU's Assembly Center, people were calling it "the house that Pete built."

17. TAKE ME

Among the slights that continued to plague Pete through the off-season was the Rookie of the Year award. The balloting for 1971 resulted in a tie between Dave Cowens, Boston's ferociously mobile center, and Geoff Petrie, a high-scoring marksman on the Portland Trail Blazers, an expansion team. That didn't bother Pete, who was the first to admit that his own rookie season had fallen short of expectations. Rather, as the honor was bestowed by fellow players, it was the vote itself that hurt. For all his adjustment problems, Pete finished with an average of 23 points a game, 33 over the last month of the season. Still, he received only four of 192 votes.

In Pete's mind, it was proof of the league-wide jealousy that ruined his first pro season. "I want to forget it," he said. "I'll be regarded as a second-year man, but I feel like a 10-year man." The season might have aged him, but not his fans. The most dedicated were the youngest, their esteem and affection undeterred by the envy of his contemporaries or his own bouts of self-loathing.

Bob Kent would always recall how he transformed the country club in Sarasota, where Pete would stay at his condo. Somehow, word would spread that the Pistol was around. The private club was soon invaded, a makeshift spectators' gallery forming before they had even left the practice range. "About 50 of them," recalls Kent. "Young kids, just showed up out of nowhere."

It was also in Sarasota that Pete was arrested after the season. He would plead no contest to drunk driving, a charge that earned him a $150 fine, one year probation, and stern words from Court of Record Judge Marvin E. Silverman. "You can forget about alcohol," he

211

warned, "or if you continue you will probably end your career around a telephone pole or become debilitated."

The judge's admonition, carried as wire service briefs in the Atlanta papers, didn't receive much coverage. Having ended the season by shooting the Hawks into the playoffs, things were looking up for Pete. In July, the first annual Pete Maravich Basketball Camp would open on the grounds of a state college in California, Pennsylvania. The $125 tuition entitled campers to a week's worth of instruction from Pete, Press, and Joe Pukach, plus a T-shirt and an official Pistol Pete basketball.

On July 23, the next to last day of the first session, word came that the Hawks had traded Walt Hazzard for Herm Gilliam. An excellent defender who could substitute for either guard, Gilliam would shore up a glaring weakness in the Hawks' backcourt. What's more, the move would allow Lou Hudson to return to his natural position, where he and Pete seemed a lock to become the league's highest-scoring guard tandem. But most of all, the trade was the inevitable confirmation of what Hazzard had feared when Pete first signed. "I had two players in the same role. Both needed the ball to be effective," says Guerin. "I had to move one or the other. Obviously, I'm not going to trade Pete."

A player could divine his future from the numbers on his pay stub. In Hazzard's case, the numbers translated into a one-way ticket to Buffalo. Pete's check, on the other hand, said it was his ball, his team. The Hawks would adopt a fast-break offense. No longer would Pete apologize for the way he played. The game's self-appointed ortho-dox—among them, a newsman from Detroit who wrote that he should never throw another behind-the-back pass—were in for a show. "Wait'll he sees what I've been working on this summer at my clinics. I've got some new things ready," said Pete, whose concern was not the decrepit critics, but the fans who conveyed their blessings with a roar. "I just get chills when I get a good cheer."

Given the way his team had finished the season before, such talk from Pete was now considered an encouraging sign. No less an authority than *Sports Illustrated* picked the reconstituted Hawks to win the NBA's newly created Central Division.

Though Pete could not have been happy about the absence of Herb White, who had torn up his ankle, camp convened in Jacksonville with cause for real optimism. Even the *Constitution*'s George Cunningham, whom Pete considered an enemy, would write that the second-year pro had "established himself in full control of the Hawk attack."

And then came Picture Day, September 20, 1971. Pete showed up "shaking uncontrollably," reported the *Journal*'s Jim Huber. He had a fever of 103 and a severely infected throat. The first diagnosis was viral tonsillitis. Then it seemed more like strep throat. But as penicillin had no effect, Pete was soon hospitalized. He couldn't talk, much less swallow, and had to write messages on a clipboard for the nurses. Nothing worked. Not even the flowers people sent cheered him up. Rather, they reminded him of death. "I feel like I'm in cold storage when they're around," he said.

Five days into his hospitalization, Pete broke out in a rash covering most of his body. Now the attending physician figured it might be a case of scarlet fever. Pete didn't care anymore, he was flying out the next morning.

That's when the doctor confronted him: "You know you die from scarlet fever."

"If I am going to die," said Pete, "I want to die in Atlanta."

Finally, in Atlanta, the Hawks' team physician announced that Pete had mononucleosis. The diagnosis was made even though, as one correspondent put it, "every test for mono proved negative." Still, for all the unexplainable symptoms, there wasn't much for him to do but rest and read his fan mail. There was a lot of it, as many as fifty pieces arriving each day, about 80 percent of the team's mail. Not only did Pete get more than his teammates, but his mail was qualitatively different. There were get-well cards and autograph requests, of course. But also well represented were the crackpots and would-be sweethearts requesting his presence at the prom or a lock of hair.

Meanwhile, it had been several weeks since he had been able to eat any solid food. His weight dropped from 205 to 168. Predictions that he would return in time for the season opener soon passed. A month after Picture Day, his attempt to shoot baskets and run up and down the court left him exhausted. "I thought I was going to black out," he said.

The team that had complained about Pete a year before now lost 10 of its first 14 games without him. Finally, he returned to the lineup on November 17 in a loss to the Seattle Supersonics. The game was notable, not just for Pete's 12 turnovers but for Lou Hudson's absence. Just as one star came back, another was gone, a victim of back spasms. By himself, in his depleted state, Pete was not nearly enough. "He tried to keep us coming back in the fourth quarter, but he just couldn't do it," Guerin noted afterward. "He was too tired."

Unfortunately for Guerin—whose team captain, Bill Bridges, was traded to Philadelphia two days later—Pete's endurance was not about to improve anytime soon. Within a week of his comeback, while playing up in Buffalo, Pete went just 3 for 9. In obvious pain, he was having trouble reaching the rim on free throws. "I was dead before I stepped on the court," said Pete, who found the sensation alarmingly similar to what he had experienced in his pro debut. In other words, the ghost was back, sitting on him.

The Buffalo game continued to haunt him. That ghost inflicted a form of panic that made his pulse race. "My heart, man, I just couldn't take any more," he said a week later. ". . . I love basketball but it's not worth my life."

Before long, Pete was wondering aloud if it would be better to sit out the entire season. That wasn't like him; he played through pain. Even as he came back from illness, he faced his usual litany of orthopedic problems: a bone spur in his big toe, tendonitis, and chronically aching feet. "You could just look at them and tell they were sore," says Gene Tormohlen, Guerin's assistant. "Pete played when a lot of guys wouldn't have dressed out." Then again, in his emaciated state, there wasn't that much of a season left anyway.

By mid-January, the Hawks were 16–30, preparing to entertain the 76ers, their third game in as many nights. But the ghost could disappear with as little warning as it had arrived. Against Philadelphia, Pete exploded with a 50-point game, the first of two he would have that season. His range made him a threat from almost anywhere on the court. What's more, at six-five, with his assortment of moves, other guards couldn't do much more than foul him around the basket. Asked to rate the Hawks' guards, going back to Lenny Wilkens, Guerin said flatly, "Pete has lots more than any of them in natural ability." This wasn't just the opinion of a coach trying to flatter his key guy. "There wasn't a player in this league who could play him," said Pat Riley, a Lakers substitute who'd go on to become a championship coach. "He was just that unique."

On January 23, as the Hawks prepared for their game with the Milwaukee Bucks, Herm Gilliam took Pete aside. "Thrill me," he said. Of Pete's 35 points, 14 came in the last four and a half minutes. He also had 14 assists, controlling the game's tempo as the Hawks beat the defending champs on the road, 118–113. Not bad for a guy still eighteen pounds under his playing weight.

The team paradigm had been immutably set, reflected in a headline that ran above George Cunningham's byline: "As the Pistol Goes, So Goes [sic] the Hawks." The problem was, even as the season progressed, one never knew who would show up for the game— the Pistol or the ghost?

In keeping with the unexplainable nature of his malady, his weight never returned. By season's end, he still looked undernourished at 179 pounds—this despite forcing himself to eat four meals a day, the last of which was a supercaloric, postgame feast. "If I didn't do that," he said, "I'd probably be 150."

The pounds were an accurate barometer of his strength, or lack thereof. As it happened, the Hawks would finish the season with the same lackluster record they had the year before, 36–46. Then they would lose their playoff series, 4–2, to the Celtics. No surprise there. Rather, what had to trouble the Hawks was Pete's anemic play through a crucial stretch in March. In contrast to his strong finish the season before, Pete was now barely shooting the ball. On March 8, he went 0 for 4 in a loss to Chicago. On the 12th, he managed only 11 against the Cavaliers. Then it was 13 at New York. Finally, on the 15th, he went scoreless on one shot in twenty-two minutes against Seattle. Being overworked and underweight had left him chronically fatigued. But one also had to wonder, as Richie Guerin did, "Maybe it's something within him."

As Pete went, so went the Hawks. But Pete went as Press went, and the past two seasons had not gone well for the elder Maravich, either. Press never approved of the way Guerin handled his boy, and Press's was the opinion that still mattered most to Pete. He was still trying to coach his son, watching as many Hawks games as he could, keeping in constant phone contact, offering opinions and advice, solicited and otherwise. It was enough to make some folks back in Baton Rouge question his priorities, especially as LSU basketball fell back on hard times. The Tigers had been hit hard by injuries. To make matters worse, one guard expected to start had left school. The backcourt situation was so desperate that Bill "Fig" Newton was forced to become a six-nine guard, perhaps the first. But an even bigger problem, as Newton recalls, was the "power vacuum" left in Pete's wake. Press wanted to be the coach he had been before LSU. There were no more double screens or clear-outs for Pete. "He started using all five players," says Tommy Hess, who became an undersized starting point guard. "Molding us into a group."

Unfortunately, that didn't sit well with his best player, Apple Sanders, a favorite son in his hometown of Baton Rouge. Sanders, who didn't help matters by breaking his ankle before the season, had waited his turn. He had been there for Pete's glory years, and now he wanted some glory for himself, not to mention the kind of college stats that would make for a fat pro contract. A coach who had recruited so many Yankees at the expense of local boys, Press wouldn't win any popularity contests in Baton Rouge. The sentiment against him became more strident—in the newspapers and behind closed doors. "Press's critics had access to the athletic director," says Bud Johnson, the sports information director. The problem had become a political one. And Press, who had never bothered to cultivate many allies in the bayou, was one lousy politician.

With 14,164 seats, the LSU Assembly Center—an edifice owing its very existence to the Maraviches—finally opened in January 1972. But it was already too late to secure any home court advantage. By then, the season was a lost cause. The Tigers would finish 10–16.

The following Monday morning, Tommy Hess walked into the basketball office, wanting to talk to Press about becoming a graduate assistant. He knew something was very wrong when he saw the coach smoking one of those skinny stogies, a habit he thought Press had given up months before. Jay McCreary, the assistant coach, was already welling up.

But Press was on fire: *"Those motherfuckingsonsofbitches fired my ass!"*

All the lousy jobs he had taken, and he had never before been fired. But Apple Sanders's envy—and the poison that came from it—was a symptom, not a cause. In a larger sense, Press was still paying for the ambition he had used his son to serve. By embracing the star system, he had forsaken what he did best, which was teaching team basketball. But in Pete's wake, Press found it impossible to be the coach he had once been, as other guys were now demanding to be stars.

Word of the firing caused less grief in Louisiana than it did in basketball country, North Carolina, where people still remembered Press's ACC championship team. Under the headline "Love Was Not Enough," the *Charlotte News*'s Bill Ballenger wrote, "Nobody knows the game of basketball better than Press Maravich . . . Expulsion from the game he loves is a great tragedy."

It's worth noting that Pete's mysterious March slump came just after his father's firing. He observed no distinction, literal or metaphorical, between blows he suffered and those directed at his father. It was as if they inhabited the same body. Speaking of his jersey, now displayed in a trophy case on campus, Pete would say, "It's got a big hole in the back of it . . . right where they stuck the knife."

He vowed never to return to LSU, but that didn't assuage his anger. Boots Garland, one of Press's pals, recalls visiting the Maravich Basketball Camp over the summer. As Pete couldn't go into town for fear of being bothered, they just sat in Boots's car, with a case of Iron City beer, as Pete railed against LSU and its athletic director.

"Chickenshit," said Pete. "They didn't give him a chance."

Still, that's not what Garland best recalls of Pete in that off-season. Rather, what comes first to mind is a wedding reception in the New Orleans French Quarter. Pete was drinking. Boots was drinking. Nothing unusual there. But then Pete pulled him off into a side room. Once they were alone, Pete began to tear up and break down.

"He wanted to tell me something," says Boots, recalling the way Pete had begun to heave and sob. It was as if Pete wanted to confess something. But that chance was lost when revelers barged into the room, muffling his cry.

Boots didn't know exactly what the problem was, but something was sure enough killing the kid. Pete was walking around in a world of trouble, a world of his own, in fact—just him and the ghost.

"The gift was not enough," says Bud Johnson. "He kept searching."

The answers, Pete came to think, were to be found in new methods, physical practices that evolved into systems of belief. The first of these was karate, an undertaking that began as a way to supplement his game. For three seasons now, Pete had been a target. Every player in the league shared a determination to, as Pat Riley put it, "knock him down every time he put the ball between his legs or did something that was flamboyant." For two seasons now, Pete had borne the abuse—aside from some whining to the refs—with an admirable stoicism. But now he had reached his limit. These guys who kept roughing him up, putting their hands on him, they were in for a surprise next season.

"Wait till they try to handcheck me," he told a friend. "I'm gonna put something on their ass."

Then he would unveil his knuckle rap, a swift, subtle move, but painful enough to make his antagonists cease and desist. In short order, however, karate became an end in itself. At first, Pete's enthusiasm for martial arts seemed Elvis-like, a celebrity's colorful eccentricity, not unlike the boots and brimmed hats he had taken to wearing. But at least one newsman saw Pete's endeavor for what it was. "He needs constant reassurance," the *Journal*'s Jim Huber wrote. ". . . Needs it like a heart patient needs oxygen."

By reputation—not undeserved—he was brash and arrogant. But

he'd also pull people aside and ask questions designed to elicit the awe he had inspired in the crowd.

"How'd you like that one, huh?" he'd ask. "It okay? People like it?" Translation: *Do they still love me?*

He was twenty-five. He had managed to grow a full, bushy mustache to go with his long locks. But Pistol, a moniker that management occasionally had him wear on the back of his game jersey, remained every bit a child star. His natural insecurity had been exacerbated by the past two seasons.

Karate was a way to retrain and restore his self-confidence. Years of study with Grandmaster Press left him ideally suited to the practice of martial arts. He was accustomed to hours of rigorous, devotional, solitary practice, and to the idea of movement perfected, that a physical form could rise to the level of beauty. Bob Sandford, who stayed with Pete for a week or so that summer, remembers, "I'd get up at eight, eight-thirty in the morning, and he's already down the street at that damn karate center. And he'd stay there until nine o'clock at night. He was obsessed."

"He loves the damn stuff," Press wrote in a letter to old friends. Such love was unchanged by the lumps he took that summer, injuring his leg, his hip, and his jaw. More often than not, though, Pete gave better than he got. He seemed to have a reservoir of anger from which to draw.

There was that night he punched a hole in the wall at Hank Kalb's apartment. Then there were his fellow students at Tracy's International Karate Studio. "I always dreaded sparring with him because his arms and legs were so long," says Greg Smith, an instructor working toward his black belt at the time.

Smith recalls that Pete was not always controlled in a combat situation. "Once he hit me on the side of the head," he says. "All I remember is stars." Out cold.

I'm gonna put something on their ass.

Elvis couldn't have said it better.

The Omni, a 16,000-seat arena that Tom Cousins managed to build without any public monies, opened that fall. Described as state of the art, it was in fact nondescript, save for a roof that looked like a giant waffle iron. On October 15, the Hawks' first regular season game in their new home, Pete scored 28 as the Hawks beat the Knicks, 109–101. "Easily his best all-around game and his best defense since he came into the pros," chirped Cotton Fitzsimmons, who had replaced Richie Guerin as the coach. "Great, just great."

"The New Pete," as he was being called, wasn't nearly so impressed with himself. He had affected a less engaged, seemingly serene outlook. If he didn't have to be a basketball performer, he said, he'd be perfectly content as a bartender on the beach in Fort Lauderdale. He claimed to be unburdened by expectation, all those hopeful forecasts for himself and the team. "I'm not at all optimistic about the future," he had said before the season. "I'll just take things as they come now."

This ostensible nonchalance extended to his new coach as well. After two frustrating seasons with Pete, Guerin had been kicked upstairs, assuming the general manager's duties. Fitzsimmons, on the other hand, was coming off two very encouraging seasons coaching the Phoenix Suns. But when asked how he felt about the change, Pete was noncommittal. "I don't feel anything," he said. "It happens."

Fitzsimmons's task wasn't nearly as difficult as Guerin's had been trying to integrate Pete. He faced no internal racial rebellion. The Hawks were finally accustomed to their star attraction, as he was to them. Even Lou Hudson, the sole holdover from St. Louis and someone who had grave misgivings about the Pistol phenomenon, could not deny that his game had prospered statistically. That Hudson was the first teammate to outscore Pete since the tenth grade was, in large measure, Pete's doing. Going into their third season together, Pete knew how and where to find Lou on the court. "He knows that I don't have to see him to get him the ball," said Pete.

And then, the ghost started sitting on him again.

On Saturday, November 4, after scoring 44 in a win over hapless Philadelphia, it was reported that Pete had been suffering from "excruciating head pain" for the past few days (during which time he had 31 in a win at Houston). "I'm going to the doctor on Monday," said Pete. "I hope my problem is a migraine."

Of all people, Pete should have known that such optimism would prove unfounded. Despite assurances from the same team physician who had diagnosed him with mono, the headache did not go away in a couple of days. Rather, it continued unabated, until November 8, when the Hawks traveled to New York. Pete was in the hotel when a strange numbness spread across his face. In a panic, he called the team trainer.

"I can't blink my eye," he said.

The headache had morphed into something worse. Not only could he not blink, but the entire right side of his face was suddenly paralyzed, limp and drooping at the eyelids and the mouth. The image in his mirror was that of a melting man. Pete had never been so frightened.

The next morning, the day of the game, he saw a specialist who diagnosed the condition as a temporary facial paralysis called Bell's palsy. There was no cure, he said. Pete would have to wait it out— could be two weeks or two years. In the meantime, his speech would remain slurry. He'd have to tape his right eye shut just to sleep.

He tried to play in protective goggles, but lasted only six minutes against the Bucks. Rather than risk "the same embarrassment," as the *Journal* called it, he sat out the next game, a loss to Golden State. His slack-faced symptoms remained painfully plain to see, but the new coach had begun to ask the same questions as his predecessor. "I think it is more of a mental thing," said Cotton Fitzsimmons. "Pete's got it in the back of his mind the fact that something physical seems to have happened to him ever since coming into the pros."

Pete wouldn't disagree. What he needed wasn't a trainer or a doctor so much as a physician for the spirit, someone who could purge his poltergeist. "A witch doctor or something," he said.

But then, with the same swift stealth that marked its arrival, the ghost was gone.

Meanwhile, as if to serve the terms of his banishment, Press had moved with Helen and Diana to Boone, North Carolina. The town of 8,000 was home to Appalachian State University, where he had accepted a job as the new men's basketball coach. Press, who by now was extolling the virtues of vitamin C and protein, was sleeping less than ever. Up there in the Appalachians, the TV signal went off at 1 A.M. Press would then read his Bible before finally, inevitably, drawing up plays. He would conceptualize new schemes until three, four, five in the morning. Then he'd roll into the office between nine and ten, where he was joined by Russ Bergman, the assistant he had brought from LSU.

Every morning was the same. "Rusty," he would say, "let me show you this new offense I drew up last night."

Unfortunately, what the mountains had in lumber and coal, they lacked in basketball genes. Appalachian State was not only the doormat of the Southern Conference, but thought to be the very worst team in the nation. Upon Press's arrival, the roll of Mountaineer season ticket holders was estimated at a grand total of eight. As for the players, the elder Maravich described them as "small, thin and inexperienced." His starting center was six-six. By contrast, North Carolina State, whom his team would play in late November, had a seven-four center, Tom Burleson. Though Burleson had already played on the U.S. Olympic team, he wasn't even the best player at State, which would go undefeated that season. That honor went to a six-four phenomenon named David Thompson. Standing still, Thompson had a 42-inch vertical leap. It was said, even among Press's old friends at State, that Thompson was as good as Pete.

"Good as Pete?" Press asked incredulously. "Impossible."

One imagines even Press had cause to doubt himself after the game, which the Wolfpack won 130–53 in Reynolds Coliseum. In some sense, the score was a measure of how much Press had fallen. Back in Raleigh, the old guard still delighted in recalling as good a coaching job as there was, the unlikely run to the ACC championship. But those who could remember Press's coaching glories were dwindling in number. More people now recognized him as a crewcut novelty. He could see it in the kids he tried to recruit. Press Maravich meant nothing to them. In their eyes, his standing was derived solely from being Pistol Pete's father.

He drove home alone that night, almost two hundred miles from Raleigh to Boone. Unable to sleep, he turned on the radio, helped himself to a big chaw of tobacco, and replayed the game in his mind. At some point, Helen appeared in the den.

"Eighty points," she said.

Press corrected her: "Seventy-seven."

Before long, it would feel as if the mountains were closing in on him. Helen would feel the same way: smothered.

At least Diana, now eight, seemed to like her new life. She would see her first snow that winter. There was a December morning that made the town seem like a winter wonderland as Press drove her to school. "If you ever get fired up here," she told her daddy, "let's not leave Boone."

The Hawks would go 12–4 that month, becoming a winning team for the first time since Pete's arrival in Atlanta. Despite the Bell's palsy and a severely sprained foot, by Christmas he was the league's fourth leading scorer and seventh in assists. Still, none of it made him happy.

Carl Braun, the former Knick coach and a friend of Richie Guerin's, was puzzled by what he observed. "As hard as he tries, I don't believe Pete has learned to enjoy playing the pro game," said Braun, who, like Press, had played in the old BAA. "Watch his expression . . . never changes when he makes a great play."

Pete was unable to partake in the exuberance he created. Even his selection as a starter on his first All-Star team became twisted in his own conspiratorial lens. "I've always been a target," he told the *Journal*'s Mike McKenzie. "This just means that many more guys will be beating on me now."

The only honor Pete claimed to covet was a championship. He would win the ring and retire. That was his planned escape. Unfortunately, this would not be the year. He scored 26 a game that season, his average a point less than Lou Hudson's (a statistical tandem that, by itself, should have damaged Pete's reputation for selfishness). The Hawks finished 10 games over .500 in 1973. But again, they proved no match for the Celtics, who had won 68 regular season games, best in the league.

Atlanta lost its opening-round playoff series 4 games to 2. Pete went into his usual funk. Press tried to explain: "He never learned to lose." Then again, losing wasn't a skill Press had taught him.

In its formative stages, the 1973–74 season, Pete's third in the pros, seemed to bear out yet another *Sports Illustrated* forecast, again picking the Hawks to win the Central Division. With Walt Bellamy now thirty-four and heading into his thirteenth NBA season, Atlanta didn't have nearly enough up front to be an authentic contender. But the team could provide real basketball fans with moments worthy of awe and admiration. Pete and Herm Gilliam were coming off a season that saw them tally more assists than any starting backcourt in the league. Hudson, back at forward, had a genius for filling the lanes and moving without the ball. In many ways, Sweet Lou, as he was called, was the perfect player to complement Pistol. His seasons with Pete would coincide with the best scoring years of his career. His game combined Bill Bradley's virtues with superstar numbers.

Interestingly enough, in his memoir of that season, *Life on the Run*, Bradley would refer to Pete as "the white darling of Atlanta." The description ignored a new consensus that had emerged among their peers. Not only had Pete's starting berth on the All-Star team been determined by a vote of his fellow players, but so was his selection to the ten-member All-NBA team. Some of Pete's biggest fans were the guys trying to check him. They knew that, when all else failed, he was still Pistol. Like that night in Houston when he was a perfect 8 for 8 in the fourth quarter, scoring 15 points in a little more than two minutes to win the game.

On nights like these, Pete would say plainly, "There was no reason to hold back. I would have shot from 40 feet and it would've gone in."

He was averaging almost 30 a game, but again, his real accomplishment defied quantification. He was doing in the pros what he had done in high school and college. As Dave Anderson wrote in the *New York Times*, "He's playing basketball as nobody ever quite did before."

Richie Guerin was gone by now, pushed out of the front office in favor of thirty-three-year-old Pat Williams, whom *Sports Illustrated* described as "a promotional wizard fresh from crowd building stints in Philadelphia and Chicago where he staged such halftime acts as Victor the Wrestling Bear and Little Arlene." A devout, churchgoing man, Williams had been blessed with a flair for shameless hype. At 105 pounds, Little Arlene earned her measure of notoriety by ingesting 77 hot dogs, 21 pizzas, and 19 Cokes during halftime of a 76ers game.

What's more, Williams was absolutely enthralled with Pete, whom he had first seen in the winter of 1968. He was general manager of the Spartanburg Phillies, a minor league baseball team, the night he lit out with a couple of local sportswriters to catch the Pistol in one of his vintage performances in Athens. "We were overwhelmed," says Williams, recalling an effort that exceeded even his promoter's imagination: "You couldn't make that stuff up."

Meeting Pete in person, though, proved somewhat underwhelming. Williams was wearing a sports jacket when they were introduced. Pete quickly called attention to the brown lapels. "Dandruff," chuckled Pete, who acted as if it were the funniest line he had ever heard.

With a mandate to raise attendance at the Omni—typically half full for Hawks games—Williams knew he had to sell Pete. "But the novelty wore off," he says, noting that he wasn't alone in his misgivings about Maravich. "He was a confused, troubled guy. You rooted for him, but it was hard to like him with that fire he had raging inside."

After all the controversy and the first two lousy seasons, there were limits to how many tickets Pete could sell, particularly in what was still college football country. Williams even solicited suggestions from his players. The only one he received, though, was from Pete, who proposed screening *Deep Throat* at halftime.

Williams's burden wasn't relieved when the Hawks, after their too-brief run in first place, went into their typical tailspin. Before the season was over, there were losing streaks of four, five, and five games again. By early February the team was eight games under .500, and its star was pissed and paranoid, feeling scapegoated for all that had gone wrong. He often seemed absent—to the media, with whom his feud was now out in the open, and to his coach, whom he appeared to ignore during time-outs.

Then, one night in Houston, referee Jim Capers whistled Pete for a technical foul. Pete was so incensed he had to be restrained, a task that fell to teammates Gilliam and Hudson, who suffered a bloody nose for his efforts. Maravich would return to the game, but only in body, not in spirit. Finally, Fitzsimmons sent him to the bench for good with nine and a half minutes left before the Hawks' eventual loss.

The two would meet upon the team's return to Atlanta. Later that same morning, the Hawks issued a press release announcing "the indefinite suspension of guard Pete Maravich for disciplinary reasons." Though the coach refused to divulge specifics, his action had little to do with the game—Fitzsimmons had been called for seven technicals by the same ref. Rather, it owed to Maravich's postgame performance: getting drunk on beer before he even left the arena, causing a scene at the hotel, and babbling without pause on the flight home.

Fitzsimmons intended the suspension as a demonstration of tough love and hoped that Pete would return in a couple of days. He even went out of his way to plead Pete's case with the media. "When we lose," said the coach, "it's always his fault."

But these considerations were all for naught. Though the suspension would last only two games, Fitzsimmons had already lost Pete. He was learning what Guerin had before him: that for Pete, Press was an impossible act to follow. "You could tell," he said, "that there would never be another coach like Press for him."

Of course, Maravich couldn't have been too happy when the Hawks recorded their first consecutive wins in six weeks without him. First they beat the division-leading Capitol Bullets. Then they beat the Lakers. Each of these victories was earned by slowing down the tempo. Under a headline that read "A Tarnished White Hope," the *Constitution*'s Furman Bisher quoted Fitzsimmons as saying, "I went against my own game these two years trying to make it work with Pete . . . It won't work. I'm going back to my old game."

Pete would never have another conversation with Cotton Fitzsimmons; in fact, he wouldn't so much as acknowledge the man. After returning to the lineup in Philadelphia, he scored a measly 8 points (20 fewer than his average) on 9 shots as the Hawks lost by 20. "I can play any way they want me to," he said defiantly.

The Hawks finished the month with another 2 wins and 7 losses. There would be injuries to Hudson, Gilliam, and Bellamy. But the blame all went to the Pistol. "When I shoot; we lose; when I don't shoot, we lose," he said. "What's the difference?"

By now, he had begun talking, mostly to the out-of-town writers, about retirement and death as either/or propositions. The stress, he seemed to be saying, was killing him.

"I don't want to play 10 years in the NBA and die of a heart attack at 40," he told Andy Nuzzo of the *Beaver County* (Pennsylvania) *Times*.

"Everyone thinks I'm just talking, but I'm serious," he told the *New York Post*'s Peter Vecsey, who wondered how a twenty-six-year-old prematurely retired ballplayer would spend his time. "Go to Hollywood," said Pete, a movie buff. ". . . I've been the villain around here for so long, I figure I'd be a natural."

Meanwhile, Cotton had already gone to Pat Williams, telling him to trade Pete. "This isn't going to work," he told the GM. "See what you can get for him."

Much to his amazement, Williams couldn't find any takers.

No one wanted to pay the kind of money required to secure Pete's services. But more than that, no existing franchise wanted to take the risk, even on a white boy. Word around the league had the kid cracking up. He might have been the NBA's second leading scorer, but he was still the object of snickers and eye-rolling. Often mentioned was his famous halftime interview with Skip Caray, the Hawks' play-by-play man. Pete was dead serious when he confessed a devout belief in UFOs and extraterrestrial life forms. He had even painted a message for them on the roof of his condo:

"Take me."

Take me. You wonder which of Pete's ghosts it was intended for.

18. Smothered

The off-season was a month old when Pat Williams paid a visit to the condo. He told Pete how much he liked the décor. Then he got down to business. "We'd like to trade you to New Orleans," he said, referring to a yet unnamed expansion team. "We got a great deal."

Said deal—soon to become famous as "the Louisiana Purchase"—was widely reputed to be a steal for the Hawks. It included four first-round picks, two second-round picks, and a couple players from the expansion draft.

"Is that all?" asked Pete, whose contract gave him the right to veto any trade.

He was furious about an April 15 meeting he attended with his lawyers, Williams, and one of Tom Cousins's men. Pete had come away with the feeling that they had actually resolved some of their differences. Certainly, the prospect of a trade was never broached, though it had already been in the works at least a month. "I really can't tolerate any more deceit and deception on the part of the coach and the present administration," said Pete, sounding very much as if he had a speaking part in the unfolding Watergate saga.

By now there was enough bad blood to form a poisonous moat dividing Pete from the press and management. Twelve days would pass before he approved the trade, eventually acknowledging that it was no longer practical to remain with an organization that didn't want him. Playing for an expansion team doomed to occupy the lowest rung in the standings, his oft-proclaimed desire for a ring would not be fulfilled in New Orleans. But even more than a championship, the erstwhile child star wanted to feel loved again.

Curiously enough, news of his impending departure struck some oddly affectionate notes, as certain parties were now free to admit what it was they really wanted to see on a basketball court.

"If imitation is the most sincere form of flattery, then the Pistol was the most flattered player in the NBA," wrote the *Constitution*'s Al Thomy, fretting over the fate of the Hawks. "I can't think of anything duller than a disciplined offense."

"The trading of Maravich," predicted the *Journal*'s Ron Hudspeth, "will turn a mediocre team into a dull, mediocre team."

Even Cotton Fitzsimmons, the object of his star's ire, felt obliged to remark, "Without a doubt, Pete is the most exciting player I've ever coached."

But the most interestingly mournful tribute belonged to a feature writer named Keith Coulbourn, a self-confessed "hero worshipper" who had celebrated Pete's arrival in Atlanta four years prior. Coulbourn dwelled on what had become perhaps the most spectacular move in Pete's arsenal: whipping the ball through his legs full speed on a fast break to find his man upcourt for an easy basket. To appreciate that pass was to abandon, if only for a moment, any sense of fate or consequence. "That incredible pass between his legs while in midair is simply unforgettable," he wrote, "though I couldn't care less whether they won or lost the game."

New Orleans was a curious choice for a professional basketball team, as the city didn't even qualify among America's top thirty-five television markets. An ABA franchise had to abandon the town after three seasons, the last of which, 1969–70, saw the Buccaneers average only 2,599 fans at Tulane's gymnasium. This new team, it was decided, would split its home dates between the Municipal Auditorium, an old opera house where the Mardi Gras balls were held, and the Loyola fieldhouse, with a leaky roof, a single dressing room (visiting teams would disrobe behind a makeshift curtain), and an elevated floor that required a shrimper's net to prevent players from falling. Both venues sat fewer than 7,000. Also, as of the day Pete was introduced, the franchise still lacked a name.

That's not to say the enterprise—whose primary backer was Sam Battistone, owner of the Sambo's fast-food chain—lacked a reason for being. The Superdome, like the LSU Assembly Center, had already been pushed through the legislature by Governor John McKeithen, one of Pete's greatest fans. Another spaceship-like dome, this one with a diameter of 680 feet, it would require 20,000 tons of structural steel and 169,000 cubic yards of concrete. Expected to open in 1975, the Superdome would be home to the NFL's New Orleans Saints. It would be the site for Super Bowls and industrial-strength rock concerts. But it would also become the first multiuse stadium to house a professional basketball team. The details and the configuration were still to be determined, but it was clear that the Superdome would have a considerably greater capacity than any other NBA arena, with as many as 40,000 seats.

Those seats needed to be filled. And that need was commensurate with the need for Pete. New Orleans may not have thought of itself as a basketball town. But everybody loved the Pistol. For months now, ever since the franchise had come into existence, team officials found themselves harassed by people in the streets, asking, "When are we getting Pete?"

"We didn't have the population base that could support forty-one home games—unless we had something special," says Barry Mendelson, the team's first vice president of business operations. "Pete Maravich was that specialness. We were bringing home the favorite son. He became a promotional and marketing imperative."

Same old, same old. The difference was that, for once, the burden of expectation would be eased somewhat. Nobody expected an expansion team—soon to be christened the "Jazz"—to actually win. Rather, the citizens of New Orleans wanted another excuse to party, a show. Down in Louisiana, people had come to consider the Pistol as an indigenous form of entertainment, kind of like jazz.

For Pete, locker-room life with this new team was exactly unlike his experience with the Hawks. He had more than mere respect; he was regarded with awe. Aaron James, a Louisianan who played his college ball at a black school, Grambling, idolized the Pistol as a kid. Though a six-eight forward, he says, "I grew up wanting to score like Peter."

"Because of the ragtag nature of an expansion team, there were no jealousies," says Rich Kelley, who played on those early Jazz teams. "We were all clearly playing in Pete's wake. He didn't have a Bill Bridges or a Lou Hudson or anybody sniping at him. We were mostly rejects, and it made for a more convivial locker room."

There might not have been any championship rings to be had in New Orleans, but at least there was a kind of support system in place. Bud Johnson, the new team's PR man, was an old friend of the Maraviches who understood the business of Pete—what he had to sell, and what he had to protect—from his years at LSU. Brother Ronnie was now bartending at Moran's in the French Quarter. "The Mayor," people called him. For friends, he knew to pour with a heavy hand. He knew how to have a good time, and where they were to be had. But the years hadn't gentled him much. You didn't want to push Ronnie—"a big brooding presence," says Rich Kelley—especially after he had a couple of pops.

As for the players, Pete already had a good friend in Neal Walk, the former All-American center from Florida. Walk was also the product of a hard-driving father, the basis for what he calls "my simpatico with Pete." And though he didn't share his pal's fascination with UFOs, Walk was already looking for a new way. He had begun experimenting with meditation, kung fu, and vegetarianism. Soon Pete would be, too. Their preworkout stretching sessions proved fertile for the exchange of ideas.

Unfortunately, Walk understood all too well how their world had changed from college, where the idle hours were passed "drinking beer, chasing chicks, and hanging out." These past years misspent as a great white hope had clearly exhausted his friend.

"I hated to look across the table at him and see the sadness in those brown eyes of his," says Walk. "Pete was manic, but he wasn't unaware. He understood that some other life might be better than this one."

Sometimes, though, one had to wonder if Pete wanted to do anything with this life at all. The question became most apparent when he was behind the wheel of his brand-new Porsche. It was nothing for him to jack up the speedometer well over 100 mph—on city streets. Walk would recall how New Orleans became a blur, "everything flying by" as he gazed in horror out the passenger window: "Pete slow down, you're going to kill us!"

Pete would just laugh, as he pressed the accelerator ever closer to the floorboard. The guys had a name for him: Speed Racer, abbreviated to "Speed."

Speed would brag about making the seven-hour trip from Atlanta to New Orleans in less than five. Aaron James never doubted him. James, who had a red VW convertible, recalls Pete giving him a 10-minute head start on the 15-minute ride home from the practice gym at Tulane to the suburb of Metairie, where they both lived. James would floor the VW the whole way, but he never once beat Speed to Metairie.

Press and Russ Bergman spent the afternoon of October 9, 1974, playing golf at the Grandfather Country Club on Highway 105 in Linville, North Carolina. On the eve of what would be another trying season, it was good to see Press relax, or at least to try. With their round concluded, the coach drove Russ home, dropping him off at the Mountaineer apartments right off campus.

Strange, thought Russ: his wife wasn't home. Usually, Ann would be cooking supper about this time. Russ waited for her. He waited a little more. Finally, he dialed the coach's number, figuring Ann might've gone over to visit with Helen and Diana.

A policeman answered the phone.

"Is Ann Bergman there?"

In fact, Ann had been there. She had received a call when Russ and Press were still out playing golf. The policeman had asked for Coach Maravich. That's when Ann raced over in the car. Upon arrival, her worst fear was confirmed. Diana had been home when it happened. Helen had shot herself with a .22 caliber pistol. The way the story would be told, she was on the phone with Ronnie when she pulled the trigger.

Soon, Press arrived to find his home transformed into a crime scene. The gun was his, for protection, he explained. He kept the pistol in one place and the bullets in another. "I didn't think she would find it." He kept saying that. *I didn't think she would find it.*

Then he asked about Diana, who had already been taken to a neighbor's house. As the coach's presence was needed immediately at the hospital, Ann checked on Diana.

"I'm going back to your house and get your things," she told the child. "Is there anything special you want?"

Diana, now ten, explained that tomorrow was class picture day at school. Her mother had put aside a special dress for the occasion. She told Ann exactly where it would be hanging.

"Okay, sweetie," said Ann, not knowing what else to say.

Before Helen was pronounced dead at approximately 9 P.M. at Catawba Memorial Hospital, Ronnie called Pete, telling him to get the next flight to North Carolina. Pete told Jackie he would call from Atlanta, where he would be changing planes, and that she was to inform him of any change in Helen's condition.

"The same," Jackie told him, lying.

She was only trying to save him a little pain, a finite amount, minutes, perhaps hours. Pete would find out soon enough; he had the rest of his life to be haunted by his mother's death.

Helen Maravich was buried in Aliquippa, at St. Elijah's Serbian Cemetery. Just days later, the Jazz had an exhibition game in Chicago, after which it was discovered that their star had gone AWOL.

"Where's Speed?" asked Neal Walk. "Anyone seen Speed?"

In fact, no one could remember him getting on the team bus. Guys split up and began to search. It was Walk who found him in a bar on Rush Street, where Pete was already destroyed with liquor. Walk would speak, with something other than humor, of having to stuff Pete into a suitcase to get him home. Once back in New Orleans, he transferred custody of his friend to Jackie.

"He was way, way fortunate with Jackie. No telling what would have happened to Pete without her," says Walk. "She always saw the beauty in him."

• • •

On November 10, the Jazz found themselves down a point to the Portland Trail Blazers in the final seconds when Pete put up a fadeaway jumper from deep in the corner. "I went out of bounds, the shot went through and the game was over," he said, recalling the great glee that followed. "You'd have thought we'd won the world championship that night."

In fact, there were only 5,465 on hand that night to see the Jazz's inaugural victory at Municipal Auditorium. The team's record now stood at 1–11. A week later, following three more losses, management fired its coach, Scotty Robertson, formerly the coach at Louisiana Tech. Robertson was succeeded by a hard-drinking, cigar-chomping ex-Marine, Butch Van Breda Kolff, who had been Bill Bradley's coach at Princeton. Van Breda Kolff's appointment seemed to only change marginally the Jazz's fortunes. Another two months would pass before the team won its fourth game. At 4–34, the Jazz were arguably the world's worst basketball team outside of Appalachian State.

Press had not recovered from Helen's suicide. "He was totally, mentally blown away," says Russ Bergman. "I didn't realize how much he loved her until he had lost her. He was like a zombie."

On January 12, the Mountaineers lost on a last-second shot to the Citadel, a military college now coached by Press's protégé, Les Robinson, whom he had told to drop by for a visit after the game. They shook hands. Les recalls having misgivings about beating his mentor. He also recalls Press being more official than usual. If so, such formality was only in accordance with the terms of his surrender.

"This is the last game I'll ever coach, Les."

In a matter of months, his permanent replacement showed up in Boone. Bobby Cremins had played at South Carolina for Frank McGuire, and at twenty-seven, would become the youngest head coach in Division I history. Cremins remained deferential as he approached what was to be his new office, not wanting to bother Press. Still, Press insisted.

"Sit down," he said. It was time for an old coach to impart his wisdom to a young coach. But for once Press had nothing to say about the game—no X's and O's, nothing that could be diagrammed or considered in logical terms. Rather, he issued a warning. "After a while," he said, "these mountains will start coming in on you. They'll smother you."

19. ALL THAT JAZZ

Through the first two months of the 1974–75 season, Pete's scoring average—about 17 a game—was off 10 points from the previous year. He suffered through a severe case of tendonitis in his right ankle, a pulled hamstring, and an infinitely more debilitating case of depression, which began to lift only in January.

The reemergence occurred, curiously enough, around the time of his father's firing. In his fifth pro season, Pete had developed a scraggly tuft of hair protruding from his chin and a tendency to pontificate. "I'm not like Muhammad Ali, who's a real controversial figure," he told the *Los Angeles Times*. "I'm a manufactured one."

The numbers were more compelling than anything he said. Suddenly, Pete seemed capable of producing a masterpiece whenever he took the court. In leading the Jazz to their first consecutive wins, he went for 38 points, 11 rebounds, and 8 assists against Houston, followed by 42 points, 10 rebounds, and 17 assists versus Seattle. Next it was 40, 14, and 13 in a close loss to Buffalo.

Pete was beginning to articulate a case for himself to be considered with the best guards ever to play the pro game. After all, neither Jerry West nor Oscar Robertson had won a championship until he was paired with a great big man. West had Wilt Chamberlain. Oscar had Alcindor, or as he was now known, Kareem Abdul-Jabbar. Could Pete be blamed for having to play with Mel Counts, Otto Moore, and Neal Walk, whose muscular frame had shrunk twenty pounds since he gave up meat?

Even former antagonists found it difficult to ignore his genius.

There was that well-dressed fan in Atlanta, the only team the Jazz seemed to beat with regularity, who came charging down from the stands to yell at Van Breda Kolff. "Hey coach, put Pete in. We came to see Pete."

His own teammates would've paid to see him. "If there were five fast breaks, he'd throw five different passes—some with topspin, some with backspin, sidespin," recalled Jimmy McElroy, a guard who played on the early Jazz teams. "My favorite was his pass between the legs, where he'd jump up and whip it through the legs to you."

Unfortunately for Pete, not everyone was so impressed. His own coach considered such a pass an abomination. Butch Van Breda Kolff, like Press, had played in the old BAA. Like Press, he had severe notions about how the game was to be played. Of course, Press detested him from the beginning. Not long after Van Breda Kolff's hiring, Press wrote Bob and Louise Bradley, complaining that Pete's talents were being squandered in the new coach's scheme. "Doesn't shoot or even handle the ball," noted Press, who warned that the Jazz were "only cutting their own throats."

For Van Breda Kolff, who himself flunked out of Princeton, the ideal was Bill Bradley, whose ability was an almost cerebral commodity. He felt differently about virtuoso performers, dominant physical talents like Wilt Chamberlain. As coach of the Los Angeles Lakers, Van Breda Kolff went all the way to the seventh game of the NBA Finals against the Celtics. But in the closing minutes of the ultimate game, Chamberlain found himself watching from the bench. Wilt was not only the game's greatest center, but by every statistical measure, the most dominant player in basketball history. Butch didn't care. In his own way, he was as monumentally stubborn as Press. The Lakers would lose the championship, 108–106, as Chamberlain remained on the bench.

Van Breda Kolff didn't want players thinking they were bigger than the game. He didn't want them thinking they were bigger than the coach, either.

"Butch had a big ego," says Hot Rod Hundley, now, as then, a Jazz broadcaster.

Hot Rod and VBK, as he was called, could often be found at Pat O'Brien's, the legendary New Orleans drinking establishment, where they liked to hold court. Pat O'Brien's was famous for the Hurricane, a potent crimson concoction. But Butch preferred beer—a lot of it.

"Butch was *everybody's* drinking buddy," says Barry Mendelson, hired as the team's vice president of business operations.

Certainly, he reveled in the attention and adoration of the fans. *His* fans; one gets the impression that's how he thought of them. Intramural battle lines were being drawn. On one side was the coach, a self-styled basketball purist who treasured above all else movement without the ball. On the other, was a fledgling franchise's "marketing imperative"—Pete—a performer who needed the ball to perform.

"They didn't like each other," says Hundley.

"In Butch's mind, it was a popularity contest," says Mendelson, whom Van Breda Kolff derided as an interloper in basketball matters. "He couldn't stand Pete's popularity being greater than his. He just couldn't deal with it."

On the other hand, Pete couldn't deal with Butch, either. "One time I took him to a New Orleans health club and beat him in a racquetball game," the coach would recall. "He was furious. I mean, he wouldn't speak to me. He got in his car and drove home at 75 m.p.h. The next day, he demanded another game"—Pete paid the club's annual dues just to get on the court—"and beat me."

They might as well have been playing to answer the question: *Whose team is it anyway?* As there was no immediate answer, an odd stalemate evolved between the two caricatures: Bombastic Butch and Petulant Pete. "I play the way I'm told to play," said Maravich. ". . . My job is to slow things down and set up our so-called offense. Then if the shot goes in, well, that's leadership."

It was a trying season. One coach had already been fired. Team president Fred Rosenfeld was next. Bill Bertka, the general manager who hired Van Breda Kolff, could be found most of the time in Santa Barbara, California, where he still lived. The coach and the vice president of business operations had no use for each other. The star couldn't stand the "so-called offense." The roster was at best an ephemeral concept, with twenty-two guys playing for the Jazz that season. To make matters worse, the team had to evacuate Memorial Auditorium for the Mardi Gras balls, causing the team to play eleven consecutive games (all losses) on the road. Least encouraging of all were the telecasts on Channel 6. "Watching the first game I saw something that terrified me," says Bud Johnson, who recalls the station running public service announcements in place of ads. "All the diseases were represented: the Cancer Society, American Heart Association, leukemia. But there was not one commercial minute in that telecast. That's how much interest there was in pro basketball."

And yet, the team had the affections of its fans. New Orleans wasn't a normal city; nobody expected the Jazz to be a normal team. Even Pete's sense of persecution—"everything is negative, negative, negative" he'd complain to Bud Johnson—might as well have been part of the show, the highest moment of which came after a basket, as PA announcer Bob Longmire rolled his syllables loud and long: "Pist-uuuhhhlll Pete!"

"You went to see Pete. He was the team," says Guy Smith, a local attorney who had known Pete since the LSU years. "You didn't ask people, 'Are you going to the game tonight?' You said, 'You going to see Pete?' It was a ritual. The Jazz became a faith. They didn't win much, but they were a lot of fun."

In fact, the most surprising element of the entire season was the team's evolution toward a state of basketball competence. Despite all the obstacles, the Jazz won 6 straight in February. A *Sporting News* columnist went so far as to urge Coach of the Year honors for Van Breda Kolff. After a disastrous beginning, the Jazz closed out the season by going 18–17, an extraordinary feat for a first-year expansion team. Then again, in New Orleans the notion of victory was a relative one. It was during that first season that Hot Rod Hundley coined a team slogan: "Win or lose, everyone to Pat O'Brien's."

As a kid growing up in Rochester, Barry Mendelson became a dedicated fan of the Rochester Royals, often attending their games at Edgerton Park Arena. Configured like a giant auditorium, Edgerton Park seemed less of an arena than a stage, with rows of wooden seats that sloped gently to the floor level and those big old Parcans lights hanging like bats from the low-slung ceiling.

The lights cut through the cigarette haze and riveted your attention to the court, illuminating the players, adding a sheen to their satin uniforms, identifying the emotional content of their expressions, rendering them both magical and accessible. "I learned right there that the lights should always be on the performers," he says. "Broadway is that way. Basketball should be, too."

The line separating sport from amusement was an artificial one. The game *was* entertainment. That's what Mendelson had in mind as he prepared for the Jazz's debut season in the Superdome. There would be a second-line Mardi Gras band led by the parasol-wielding Elena Tatum, who liked to put the "gris gris" voodoo curse on opposing players. (Golden State's Rick Barry found her particularly unnerving and asked that she be removed from the premises.) There would be countless promotions. The lucky number in your game program got you a Rolex. Sinking a halfcourt shot got you a Subaru. Giveaways included T-shirts, sneakers, and, most famously, French fries. Those with ticket stubs were entitled to free fries at a hamburger chain if the Jazz scored 110 or more. The promo inspired thunderous chants—"Free fries! Free fries!"—even when the team was hopelessly behind. "We could be losing by 20, but guys would call time-out to argue over who was going to take the 'free fries' shot," says Mendelson, who recalls the Burger King on St. Charles Avenue being regularly overrun with gleeful fans.

On a given night, there could be an awful lot of them. The Superdome had 19,203 reserve seats for basketball, ranging in price from $3.50 to $7.50. But Mendelson decided to open the Terrace level for general admission at $1.50 a seat. For management, the buck-fifty seats were all-you-can-eat, as many as 20,000. The Superdome was so vast, occupying fifty-two acres, that thousands upon thousands of extras were needed to provide the feel of a good live crowd.

It didn't hurt that the Jazz got off to a great start. The team followed a loss in the opener—a bad knee forced Pete to sit out—with 6 straight wins in the Dome, the last of which, a 113–110 victory over the Lakers and their new center, Kareem Abdul-Jabbar, came amid torrential rains. Pete and Jackie had spent the day bailing and mopping (a task requiring thirty-seven towels) as their home took on nine inches of water. With the flood approaching biblical proportions, a question rose with the water level: How to get to the Superdome for the game?

Mendelson called the cops, but the Sheriff's Department Jeeps couldn't get through. Soon, a neighbor came by in a boat and offered Pete a lift.

"No thanks, Milton," said Pete. "I don't think I can get all the way downtown in that thing."

Eventually, Pete hustled a ride from a friend with a seaworthy vehicle. Traffic came to a standstill in New Orleans. Tip-off was delayed thirty minutes. But people kept streaming in, sopping wet. The final count was 26,511, a new NBA record, easily eclipsing the previous mark of 20,239 set the previous season when the Knicks and the Cavaliers met in Cleveland to battle for the final playoff spot.

"It might have been 30,000 if we hadn't had the greatest rain since Noah's Ark," said Pete, who had 30 points, 7 assists, and 5 rebounds on the night.

After the game, a pennant of the NFL's New Orleans Saints was removed from its lofty display behind the bar at Pat O'Brien's. In its place: the Mardi Gras colors and logo of the Jazz. Not bad for football country.

The $1.50 ticket, proclaimed the *New York Times*, "has proved to be a bonanza."

"The most fun I've ever had was putting asses in seats at basketball games," says Mendelson.

Pete went so far as to predict, in all seriousness, that this good feeling emanating from the Superdome would manifest itself in a drop in New Orleans's notoriously high murder rate. A week and a half later, he suffered a second-degree shoulder separation chasing down a loose ball in practice. "It seems like this has been the history of my career," he said.

Pete had prepared for the season with a new kind of diligence. Though he had given up red meat almost entirely, he managed to actually gain muscle. He was running along the Lake Pontchartrain levee, knocking off hundreds of situps at a time, and adhering to a grueling weightlifting regimen.

Pete's were not the average basketball player's workouts. He often joined members of the Saints during their training camp, squatting more than even the powerful, fireplug linemen. Unlike his teammates, who couldn't compete with the football players in the weight room, "Pete went through the whole training camp and came back 10 pounds heavier," Van Breda Kolff would recall. "Pete was a masochist. He didn't mind working, working, working."

And with his new physique came a new look. Finally, he had given up the floppy socks and the number 44, too. He now wore number 7 and took the floor clean-shaven. But in his forced absence—17 games with the separated shoulder—Pete had to wonder why all the preparation had failed to protect him. Giving up red meat didn't mean much if he still lived as fast as he drove his Porsche. He continued to play with what Richie Guerin called "a reckless abandon."

"Every time he went down, you held your breath." says Guy Smith, who never missed a home game. "But Pete seemed indestructible. People attributed supernatural powers to him." .

The idea of Pete as a superhero did not diminish in his absence. Including the opener he missed with a bad knee, the Jazz were 5–13 without him. A first-place team when he was injured was a last-place team by the time he returned to the lineup.

The Jazz finished 38–44 that season, better than any second-year expansion team, and 9 games better than the Hawks, but still not good enough to qualify for the playoffs. A healthy Pete—a first team All-NBA selection for the first time in his career—might have made all the difference. There was talk about the Jazz drawing 40,000 for the playoffs.

It was during that season, amid a bout of unaccustomed sanity, that Pete finally married Jackie. The date was January 11, 1976. The Jazz, on a five-game win streak, had won in Detroit the night before and Pete was all smiles when Jackie picked him up at the airport.

"What'd you do this weekend?" he asked coyly.

"I'll show you when we get home."

He knew, as Jackie had issued the ultimatum before his departure: *We're getting married when you get back, or I'm out of here.* Pete went through his phases, or, as one friend called them, his "isms"—from vegetarianism to Hinduism. But Jackie remained constant. It was all but impossible to disabuse Pete of certain notions; Jackie was the only one who had a chance. "Well, okay, *Pistol*," she'd say. That was often enough to bring him back to earth.

Of all his devotions to that point, Jackie-ism was the only one that brought him any lasting comfort. He wasn't going to live without Jackie. She was the only stabilizing force in his life.

She wasn't hard on the eyes, either, especially as she appeared in high hippie chic on the day of her wedding. Her hair remained long, as Pete preferred. She wore blue jeans and a blouse tied around her midriff. There were flowers in her hair.

The cake was waiting on the table when they arrived. The preacher was there, too, as were Ronnie, Jackie's sister and parents, even her grandmother, who had come all the way from France. Conspicuous in their absence, however, were Press and Diana.

After Appalachian State, Press had taken a job in Sweden, where, he liked to point out, he coached the only all-white team in that country's professional league. Halsingborg, as it was called, went 27–10 and finished in second place. He learned to live with just four hours of sunlight, not too difficult an acclimation for someone who grew up under Aliquippa's orange sky. Meanwhile, Diana learned Swedish. Together they traveled a good portion of Europe, with Press showing her everything from the Berlin Wall to Elsinor, Hamlet's legendary castle. Press also enrolled at Lund University, founded in 1666, where he studied Swedish and government. He did not take kindly to his professor's leftist worldview. "I told him to shove it up his butt," he said.

As for his fellow students, the crewcut American informed them that they were all slaves.

"You lie!" they would yell. "You lie."

"Typical," Press would say, "of brainwashed individuals."

Father and daughter returned stateside in the spring, settling in a new home alongside the seventh green of a golf club in Mandeville, Louisiana. To get to Mandeville, one had to cross the Lake Pontchartrain Bridge, which, at twenty-four miles, was the world's longest overwater span. There, Press and Diana fell into familiar rhythms, as he cooked, cleaned, and cared for a girl on the precipice of adolescence. Diana was tall—already five-seven before her 13th birthday. But unlike the Maravich sons, she was also an excellent student, a fixture on the honor roll.

Poppa Press, as he was often called, had accepted an offer to become a scout for the Jazz. Barry Mendelson respected his basketball acumen, of course, but more important, he thought that bringing Press into the organization would bolster his star's "support system." By now, Mendelson represented the power in the organization. With player personnel VP Bill Bertka away most of the time, the owners had seen fit to make Mendelson—formerly a personal manager to Laker stars like Jerry West—the general manager. Mendelson made other moves that summer. He acquired power forward Sidney Wicks, who would have shored up the team's glaring frontline weaknesses. He also acquired Laker guard Gail Goodrich, who had been a client in Los Angeles. Wicks refused to report to camp. But Goodrich, whom Mendelson and Bertka agreed to acquire for yet more first-round draft picks, was given a healthy raise to join the Jazz. It was supposed that Goodrich, a prolific if aging scorer who had been so effective paired with Jerry West, would take a good bit of the offensive pressure off Pete.

The theory was sound; what worked with the Lakers should work in New Orleans. Pete might lose faith in scrubs, but teamed with good offensive players, he was unselfish. He and Goodrich combined to score 53 in the season opener, a victory over Phoenix. Next, the 76ers came to town, a game that went into the books as a new NBA attendance record, with 27,383 fans curious to see former ABA superstars Julius Erving and George McGinniss, now playing for Philadelphia. Despite a Jazz loss, the highlight of the evening was a two-on-one fast break in which Pete and Goodrich passed the ball back and forth four times, a bit that earned a rousing ovation with the layup.

"That's the sort of thing Pete and I can do well together," said Goodrich. "We're conscious of each other out there."

However, the coach—who had recently celebrated his fifty-fourth birthday with what *Sports Illustrated* called "a nine-hour pub crawl"—was less than impressed by his guards' higher state of consciousness. "It's not enough for Pete and Gail to make each other better," said Van Breda Kolff. "They've got to make the rest of the team better, too."

The remark was directed at the thirty-three-year-old Mendelson as much as Pete. Van Breda Kolff resented the ambitious young promoter who had risen at the expense of his patron, Bertka, a *basketball man*. The coach wasn't shy about belittling his boss's promotional efforts, either. Mendelson, for his part, considered the coach a blowhard and a drunk who'd pass out and have to be carried off the team plane every once in a while.

As usual, the sides in this intramural conflict were drawn around Pete. Free fries were nice, but Mendelson—"pro-Peter all the way," he acknowledges—understood who and what put asses in seats. Butch, on the other hand, wanted Pete to become what he considered a better player, aspiring to Bill Bradleyesque virtues.

Of course, the people of New Orleans, never known as exponents of temperance, didn't want Bill Bradley. "Pete was paid to score points and draw," says Hundley, who ranks Maravich as the best ball handler he's ever seen. "I don't think we would have won many more games if Pete had played another way. We weren't going anywhere, regardless."

The situation, a stalemate the season before, reached crisis proportions with the return of Press, who sat by the basket at the Superdome's south end with Diana, Jackie, and Ronnie. If Pete came out of the game, Press would try to make eye contact with him on his way to the bench. Pete would avert his glance.

By halftime, Press would be stewing, incensed that Butch had yanked Pete out of the game or upbraided him on the sideline. Even if Pete were having a lousy game, Press wouldn't acknowledge as much. Rather, it was always the coach's fault. "Did you see that, Barry?" he would say. "Do you see what he's doing to my kid?"

Now Pete, who had always parroted his father, began to voice his displeasure to the new general manager. He didn't like how Butch played him (only 38 minutes a game the season before). He didn't like how Butch talked to him. He didn't like Butch. Once again, Pete was threatening to quit. He had already turned in some great games, including 35 points and 15 rebounds in a win over that season's eventual champions, Portland, a game in which he punched Dave Twardzik, cracking two of the aggressive defender's teeth. Pete was fed up, tired of the injuries, the coach, and the game. "Why am I here?" he wondered.

Whether Butch had become a pretext—for both Maravich and Mendelson—is open to debate. Still, in the longer term, Butch and Pete were mutually exclusive propositions. Sam Battistone, the team's majority owner, asked Mendelson for his recommendation on Butch. "I recommend that we terminate him," said Mendelson. "He's killing our star player. He's killing our franchise. We are going to lose Pete Maravich."

Van Breda Kolff had guided a third-year expansion team to a record of 16–14, despite Pete and Goodrich having missed substantial time due to injury. Still, he was summarily dismissed. And now Mendelson was about to find out that everybody's drinking buddy was much loved in New Orleans. The headline above Peter Finney's column in the *States-Item* summarized the town's reaction:

So long, Butch
The amateurs have taken over the Jazz

That night, occasioned by the Kansas City Kings' visit to the Superdome, established a new pattern in Mendelson's routine. "My life was threatened," he says. "I had to have a security guy with me for six months. People were coming up to me at the games and the cops had to step in front of them. The cops thought they were going to shoot me."

Pete had an easier time of it. Playing all but 30 seconds in the win over the Kings, he scored 51, a new career high.

•   •   •

The new Jazz coach, formerly Van Breda Kolff's assistant, was Elgin Baylor. After fourteen seasons with the Lakers, Baylor retired with career averages of 27.4 points and 13.5 rebounds. His prowess as a scorer had become part of the game's lore. In 1960, he scored 71 against the Knicks. In 1962, against the Boston Celtics, he scored 61 in the NBA Finals, still a record. The Lakers won the game but lost the series, as they would in each of Baylor's eight appearances in the championship round. Not until 1972, just after Baylor's retirement, would the Lakers win again—an odd fact contributing to the odder notion that Baylor's career was somehow unfulfilled.

Though he lacked a championship ring, Baylor was the progenitor in a line of revolutionary talents who would find their ultimate expression decades later, in a man named Michael Jordan. He understood how to use his formidable strength at either end of the court. He had a fine midrange jump shot and the ability to improvise while airborne. This amalgam of power, finesse, and much overlooked desire—Baylor came back after his kneecap had been literally split—became something never before seen. Known as "the man with a thousand moves," Baylor had been keenly observed and admired by Press and young Pete.

Now, as a pro, Pete's respect remained intact. He was always trying to get Elgin to come out of retirement. "How you think you'd do against EC?" Pete once asked him, referring to Jazz forward E. C. Coleman.

Baylor would be giving away three inches and sixteen years to Coleman, who would make the NBA's all-defensive team. But with Pete the instigator, the suggestion became a game: make it, take it, ten baskets wins. Baylor, despite the ruination of his knee and his Achilles' tendon, made the first basket and took it from there. Coleman never scored. He never even got the ball.

Here was a coach Pete could actually relate to, his brother in a very select fraternity, geniuses of the game. After six straight years of feuding with his coaches, Pete would never have so much as a harsh word for Baylor.

What's more, the admiration was mutual. "I had great communication with Pete," says Baylor, who calls him "as talented as anyone who ever played."

"Stars know stars," says Mendelson.

"Elgin was fairly passive as a coach," says Rich Kelley. "But he probably understood a lot of what Pete went through. There was a bond there."

Unfortunately, this bond didn't do much for more pedestrian players—of which the Jazz had plenty—nor did it translate into wins. Worse still was Goodrich's Achilles' tendon, which limited the team's second scoring option to only 27 games and required season-ending surgery in January. By then, the season seemed a lost cause. The Jazz's lease with the Superdome required them to go on extended road trips during Louisiana's annual boat show. They lost six consecutive away games to start the new year, and another five straight road dates in February. The team was 24–33 now, 8–19 since Van Breda Kolff's dismissal.

Then again, no one really cared. In the Jazz's promotional paradigm, wins and losses were almost beside the point. The only number that seemed to matter was Pete's scoring average.

He was, perhaps for the first time in his professional career, entirely sure of himself. Pete, now the team captain, didn't have to play anyone's game but his own. Given the Jazz's severe limitation in frontline talent, there was no other way for the team to entertain, much less win.

"When I'm on, nobody can stop me," he said. "I can do anything on the court I want."

Any debate as to that point was squelched the night of February 25, 1977. The Jazz weren't going anywhere; the season had reached a dead spot. Les Zittrain and Art Herskovitz had arrived in New Orleans to lay the groundwork for a new contract, as Pete's three-year $1.2 million deal was nearing its end. The lawyers sat with Press, three of the 11,033 fans on hand to see the Jazz and the Knicks. At 27–33, the Knicks were four seasons removed from their last championship. Still, their roster would make an interesting assemblage for any basketball museum. It included five future Hall-of-Famers: Walt

Frazier and Earl Monroe, maybe the greatest and certainly the most publicized backcourt in history; Bill Bradley, looking paunchy, in his final season; Bob McAdoo, a jump-shooting center who led the league in scoring the past three seasons; and Red Holzman, the coach who made "dee-fense" the hippest chant in basketball. Then there was Phil Jackson, a Holzman disciple who'd go on to win nine NBA championships as coach, and Dean Meminger, the star of the Marquette team that tormented Maravich in the NIT.

The Knick guards took turns checking him, beginning with Clyde Frazier, who had made the NBA's all-defensive team for seven consecutive years. One wonders if Pete recalled Clyde teasing him as an LSU senior seven years before. *Pistol Pete, I got something for you.*

Dee-fense? Not tonight. Pete had 17 at the end of the first quarter, 31 at the half. He was scoring on an assortment of long-range bombs, more than a few of which would have been 3-pointers after the rules were changed two years hence. But he also had his way inside, driving to the hoop and posting up with his back to the basket. At twenty-nine, with the benefit of all those hours in the weight room, he wasn't a skinny kid anymore. He had always been quicker, faster, and funkier. But now he was bigger and stronger than the other guards. This performance was the basketball equivalent of kicking sand in their faces.

At one point, Frazier proposed a change in assignments, with Monroe guarding Pete. The switch was declined, as Monroe shot back, "You're the defensive expert."

Another defensive ace, Dean Meminger—he who had once claimed there were plenty of guys in the schoolyards just as good as Pete—got his chance. But again, to no avail. Then Holzman sent in Butch Beard and, finally, Ticky Burden.

"Seemed like all of them got a shot with Pete," recalls Aaron James.

As it ended, Pete had 68 points, more than any guard had ever scored in an NBA game. Only Wilt Chamberlain and Elgin Baylor had ever scored more. The line in the box score read: 26 of 43 from the field, 16 of 19 from the line. With a 3-point line, he would have finished the game well over 70. But as was often the case with Pete, the evening incited an assortment of "what ifs," and "should have beens."

With 1:18 left in the fourth quarter, Pete was called for an offensive foul driving to the basket on Knicks' center Tom McMillen. Instead of going to the line for a possible 2 points, he had fouled out of the game. As it happened, this was Pete's second offensive foul in the closing minutes. The previous one was logged as he hit a driving layup over the six-eleven McMillen. That should have given Maravich a chance at a 3-point play. In the case of both calls, game film clearly shows that McMillen never established the position required to draw the charge. Viewed through the prism of the contemporary NBA, however, it is strange to see a superstar not getting superstar calls, particularly at the end of a game that would be celebrated as basketball history.

Pete left the court without protest. Toward the end of the game, his teammates had become ebullient, celebrating their leader's accomplishment and their lopsided victory with palm slaps and pats on the ass. The Pistol had served a kind of notice on the mandarins of the basketball world. It was true: no one could stop him. But even amid the ovation, as the fans stood to cheer him at the Superdome, he never allowed himself so much as a smile.

"His performance was the best I've ever seen by a guard," said Red Holzman.

"I'm glad he was one short of his best effort at LSU," said Press, referring to Pete's 69-point night against Alabama. "It gives him something to shoot for."

Later, Press would be quoted as saying that Pete could have scored 88, what with all the easy shots he had missed. Pete harped on all the easy misses as well. Even as newspaper articles promulgated the idea that the 68 points entitled him to consideration as the game's greatest offensive player, Pete felt a familiar vise tightening.

"As morning rolled around the next day, I wanted nothing more than to stay in bed and hope the world would somehow disappear," he wrote in his autobiography. "All I could think of were the expectations of the New Orleans fans, the club owners, the coach, the players, my dad, and worst of all, myself. Something in me was still demanding that I surpass anything I had ever done. I figured the only way I would continue to be accepted by the public would be to score sixty-eight points again and again."

There wouldn't be any more 68-point nights, but there were still some memorable performances. Three weeks later, an automobile accident temporarily left the Jazz with only seven players—two of them rookie guards—capable of playing that evening against the Suns in Phoenix. Before the game could begin, Baylor had to petition the commissioner for an exemption from a rule requiring that each team have at least eight players in uniform. But with Pete scoring 51 (along with 6 rebounds, 5 steals, 4 assists, and a couple of blocked shots) and playing all 48 minutes, the severely undermanned Jazz would win by 3. Not only did the Phoenix crowd cheer for him that night, but so did the opposition. Dave Fredman, who had succeeded Bud Johnson as the Jazz's publicity man, would recall the Suns' bench, the expressions of awe and admiration on the player's faces. "In the end," said Fredman, "everybody was rooting for Maravich."

A couple of nights later, in Los Angeles, Pete torched the Lakers for 46. "Damn near beat LA by himself," Press would brag to old friends. Press seemed particularly pleased that Jack Nicholson, who starred as an insane asylum inmate in *One Flew Over the Cuckoo's Nest*, fawned over Pete.

"No one will ever be able to carry your jock," said Nicholson, just one crazy guy to another.

Pete led the NBA in scoring that season, averaging 31.1, almost 5 points more than anyone else in the league. For this, he was rewarded with a five-year contract estimated to be worth $3 million. The deal came as yet another affirmation that Pete—unlike any other player in the league—was bigger than his team.

Like the French Quarter, Pistol Pete was regarded as something that had to be experienced. Still, despite his status as a Crescent City attraction and the economic leverage it conferred, the scoring and salary numbers afforded him little satisfaction. Outside of Jackie, only the movies seemed to provide Pete with any relief. Among his

favorites, recalls Guy Smith, was *The Wind and the Lion*, starring
Sean Connery and Candice Bergen, the saga of an American woman
abducted in Morocco by Berbers. On the road, he had become a
recluse, preferring to stay in his room and watch reruns and classics.
He was partial to comedies, with a particular affinity for the Marx
Brothers.

Meanwhile, his search for meaning, peace, and diversion had
become more frenetic, desperate, and bizarre. Even his isms begat
isms. His vegetarianism, for instance, went through a bean phase.
And within the bean phase, there were snap beans, red beans, white
beans, and green beans.

He still drank beer, lots of it, but had given up white bread, white
sugar, and salt. If it weren't for all the junk food he had eaten as a kid,
Pete was convinced he'd be a six-eight guard instead of a six-five
guard.

For a time, he was an absurdly dedicated practitioner of Pong, one
of the early video games. Pete would play for four, five hours straight,
completely fixated. Then, soon enough, no more Pong.

Looking back on all the compulsive behavior, the highs and the
unreachably sullen lows, Rich Kelley can't help but wonder if Pete
was an undiagnosed manic-depressive: "He would take us all down a
dark alley when he was in one of his moods."

Press attributed his son's ill humors to the cumulative effect of losing. Pete had experienced just one winning season in seven years of
pro ball. "He still can't take a loss well," Press told *Sport* magazine.
"He replays the game again and again and he falls into very dark
moods . . . You can't talk to him at all."

And yet, even Press knew there was more to it than that. What
plagued Pete had traveled across generations — just like those basketball genes. Two years after Helen's death, Press finally spoke of what
had been passed through the blood. "We are Serbian and we have
very violent emotions . . . which are hard, very hard, to contain."

By now, Press's own emotions seem to have had their way with
him. His letters hit all the familiar notes. He kept his old friends
apprised of Diana's grades — five A's and a B on her eighth-grade
report card — and Pete's scoring exploits. Press had developed a fixa-

tion about his son joining the NBA's 20,000 point club, an exclusive fraternity to which only eight former players then belonged. Aside from a championship, he wrote, it was "the only thing left for Pete."

But just as defeat had darkened Pete, so had the losses wounded his father: his firing at LSU, Helen's suicide, his resignation from Appalachian State. They had fractured his sense of optimism, his very American, egalitarian ideals. Press had always been foul-mouthed, with a taste for ethnic humor—poking fun at Poles, Jews, blacks, and Serbs like himself. But by the late 1970s, the tone of his letters had degenerated. The man who had taken such obvious comfort in Negro spirituals, who had tried to integrate LSU basketball way back in '65, had begun complaining about "the damn niggers." His character seems to have been corroded by years of disappointment. Typical was his take on Diana's junior high school basketball career. As the team's center, she played good defense and rebounded well, but didn't do much scoring. Press attributed this to the four other starters being black and not passing her the ball.

Meanwhile, Pete wasn't getting any saner, either. There was an afternoon Mendelson would never forget, as he was summoned to Pete's house in Metairie. Pete wanted to talk, though not about basketball. "You couldn't laugh at him, not the way he looked you in the eye," says Mendelson. "He was so sincere, so serious, *deadly* serious. He was concerned about the world coming to an end, something catastrophic happening. There was a voice of doom in him."

Pete directed the executive's attentions to his gabled roof. "He felt," recalls Mendelson, "that since flying saucers are essentially flat, they couldn't possibly land on his house."

And yet, despite all the turmoil and the hours spent in anticipation of an apocalypse, Pete was finally able to reach a higher ground within the game. This state of harmony went against every expectation, as the Jazz endured a period of tumult leading up to the 1977–78 season. Citing dissatisfaction with the Goodrich trade, ownership fired Mendelson in March, only to rehire him before the summer. The new general manager for the basketball side was Lew Schaffel. A former player agent, Schaffel acquired free agent Leonard "Truck"

Robinson, who had proven himself an exceptionally rugged rebounder and 20-point-a-game scorer in Atlanta.

An adjustment period was to be expected. Truck was new, and Goodrich was back from Achilles' tendon surgery. There were a lot of elements to assimilate, not the least of which were Pete's infamous moods. For the first time since he came to New Orleans, Pete, also suffering from intense lower back pain, had begun to hear real criticism at home. He went so far as to call out a season ticket holder who had said, with some justification, that Pete was more interested in hoisting up shots than leading a team. The fan, Henry Rosenblat, whose two courtside seats cost $630 a year, wasn't alone, either.

Early in the season, Truck Robinson remarked that the Jazz "didn't have enough ball movement." Not only was Truck eager to establish himself as a star in his own right, he was Schaffel's guy. Schaffel, who had little use for Maravich, had already begun to wonder, quite publicly, if the team wouldn't be better off without its biggest star. Of course, this did nothing to mollify Pete's already full-blown sense that people were out to get him. "A lying backstabbing son of a bitch who's been out to get me from the start," he called Schaffel, who in fact had been shopping him almost since getting the job.

Pete responded to the ball movement critique on a November night in New York. The score remained close, despite the fact that he declined to put up a single shot in the fourth quarter. After the game, a fifth consecutive loss, an anonymous teammate took him to task in the press for "not making sacrifices."

"If they want me to sacrifice, I'll sacrifice," said Pete, who went 4 of 5 while handing out 15 assists in the next game, a win over Seattle. Then, a couple of nights later, he was back to his old self, scoring 39, including the game-winning basket with fifteen seconds left on the clock.

To pass or to shoot? Given Pete's excessive nature, these pendulum swings can be seen as his attempt to find some balance in his game, and his life. As ever, Pete was a creature of contradictions. On one hand, as if bent on proving his critics right, he had taken to wearing a pendant with the emblem "ME 1st." On the other, his reputation for generosity among teammates was unrivaled.

The problem, at least as it manifested itself on the court, was that ever since high school, the best way for Pete's team to win had been for Pete to shoot. He took all the shots, just as he took the pressure. He had been on his own for so long he had to learn how to play well with others. "I don't think it was ever a question of Pete being selfish," says Baylor. "He just felt more confidence in his own ability to get the job done than [in] the others'. But I kept talking to him and talking to him and talking to him, and finally I got him to play in a way that was beneficial to the team. He was getting his teammates involved, not taking the burden so much on himself, not trying to win games on his own."

He didn't have to. His supporting cast was in fact better. Five players on the 1977–78 Jazz would post double-digit scoring averages, including Goodrich, Aaron James, and Rich Kelley, who also added almost 10 rebounds a night. But the big difference was Truck, who could be counted on for about 23 points and 16 boards a night, best in the league.

"He is exactly what this team has never had," Pete said in December. ". . . We need rebounds to run, and we need to run to win."

The Jazz would never be a great team. But despite all their internal turmoil, they were often great to watch, especially with the ball in Pete's hands. The crowds, bolstered by Mendelson's $1.50 cheap seats, reached absurd proportions. Four times that season, the Jazz would fill the Superdome with more than 31,000 fans, including a count of 35,077 for the 76ers. Crazy as it might have sounded, people had begun to speak of a great party rolling into town when the Jazz actually made the playoffs, something the New Orleans Saints had never come close to doing. When asked about possible seating configurations in the Superdome, Mendelson spoke of his intention to print 40,000 tickets.

By late January, the idea didn't seem so crazy after all. In fact, the playoffs seemed a likely proposition. Despite his conflict with the general manager—or perhaps because of it—Pete was playing the best basketball of his career. It was no accident that this elevation in his game coincided with the best stretch in Jazz history. Even as he led the league in scoring, he enabled the team to find something in itself.

"Quite honestly, he was the best player in the league," says Rich Kelley, who had also expressed his dissatisfaction with Pete earlier in the season. "He had become less showy and so much stronger." Mentally stronger, too. "He realized he didn't have to do every-thing. He just *got* it. He had reached that balance."

On January 27, New Orleans beat the Kings with four Jazz players scoring 20 or more. In their four years, the Jazz had never been above .500 after mid-December. But two nights later, Pete tallied 35 points, 11 assists, and 5 steals as they beat the Indiana Pacers to even their record at 24–24. It was their eighth win in a row.

Next up was Buffalo, now coached by Cotton Fitzsimmons, who was thrown out of the game in the fourth quarter with his second technical. By then, the game had ceased to exist as a competitive proposition. With a little over four minutes left in the game, the Jazz were up 103–82.

In that moment, Pete Maravich inhabited a kind of promised land. He was the best player in basketball, in a state of high harmony with the game. His team was about to win its ninth in a row. The Jazz were more than a lock for the playoffs; they had a future.

Pete had already scored 26 when he received the ball on the break—"three on none," recalls Baylor—and prepared to throw his 15th assist. That would be everybody's favorite pass: behind the back, between his legs, airborne as he whipped the ball upcourt to Aaron James for the easy basket.

"The fans loved it," says Baylor.

"I caught it and made the layup," says James, who didn't know anything was wrong until he turned to run back on defense. Pete was already curled on the floor, clutching his right knee, moaning. Team trainer Don Sparks wheeled him off in a stretcher.

"I didn't touch him," said Buffalo's Marvin Barnes. "I didn't touch him."

Nobody touched him. It was the manner of his fall, accompanied by a "snapping sound" audible to those with courtside seats. Some-thing in that magnificent pass had left him unbalanced.

20. The Loser

Pete's brief stay in basketball paradise was followed by a prolonged stint on the injured list, as the Jazz lost their next 8 games. Attendance began to plummet. Once again, New Orleans proved it wasn't basketball country. Truck Robinson became especially frustrated: "I'd come in . . . play 45 minutes, we'd get our tails kicked, nobody'd give a damn. Then I'd go home and come back again for the same routine."

The theory that the team would do better without Pete—a school of thought propagated by Schaffel—was soon thoroughly discredited. But, then, so were the Jazz's playoff hopes.

When the swelling in his knee began to subside, Pete worked feverishly on the stationary bike, hoping to be back jogging by early March. But it soon became clear that the initial diagnosis—twisted knee, strained ligament—was unreasonably optimistic. Unfortunately, Pete felt about doctors the way he felt about sugar and salt, a distrust that complicated the prospect of additional diagnostic work. He didn't even want to sit for X-rays, as he feared they would riddle him with cancer. Eventually, he agreed to two procedures. The team doctor drained his knee, the fluid from which was saturated with blood—a sign that it would require surgery to repair a ruptured ligament. A subsequent arthroscopic exam, however, found the ligament to be intact.

Buoyed by the results of the arthroscope, Pete continued to supervise his own rehabilitation. It would be March 21 before he returned to the lineup. With a cumbersome brace on his knee and shot full of cortisone, he managed to play 12 scoreless minutes against the New

259

Jersey Nets. Then his knee again became bloated with fluid. "Just a shadow of himself," Ron Brocato wrote in the *States-Item*. ". . . The mind was willing, the body was not."

Pete's comeback was motivated by the extant possibility of a play-off berth. Despite his absence, all the Jazz had to do to qualify was beat out the Hawks, whom they played a couple of nights later. Pete hobbled around, scoring 17 points—"Kept us in the game with one good leg," Mendelson recalls—as the Jazz lost by 2 in overtime. That's not all they lost, though. "The pain reached a point I couldn't bear," recalled Pete, who was unable to play any more that season. The Jazz lost their next four games, and with them, their chance at the postseason. That failure, it is said, would change the history of the franchise.

Meanwhile, finally acknowledging the inevitable, Pete reported to the hospital for the removal of the torn lateral meniscus cartilage. The hospital stay proved horrific beyond his imagination, as he saw recovering patients being fed sugar, salt, white bread, and coffee. "You'll never change the eating habits of 98 percent of Americans," Pete said, "because there's too much money, and too many jobs involved."

If not for this nutritional-industrial complex—the purveyors of Frosted Flakes and colas, the very diet he held dear as a kid—American life expectancy would range somewhere between 100 and 150 years, he postulated. Pete himself—now partial to fertile eggs, freshly squeezed vegetable juices, unpasteurized milk, and organic chickens—planned on living to be 100.

The summer of '78 proved a curious off-season, even for Pete. Sometime after his discharge from the hospital, he retired to his condominium in Clearwater, Florida, where Jackie prepared his favorite raw and organic delicacies as they basked in their anonymity. Pete liked to be alone. From there, though, he traveled to Cedar Rapids, Iowa, to act (a term used advisedly) in a movie about a randy women's basketball team. The highlight of the filming seems to have been the entertainment he provided for the extras, one of whom mistakenly wagered $50 that Pete couldn't lob the ball on a single bounce into the basket from halfcourt. The shot aroused mur-

murs of awe from the crowd of maybe 500. Pete feigned no surprise, of course, even as he performed his encore: throwing the ball off a support beam above the basket and watching it drop through the net.

Now he turned to address his audience. "Don't you ever doubt me," he said.

Shot for $1.3 million, the movie was called *Dribble* and later repackaged with the title *Scoring*. By now it should have come as no surprise that, even in the movies, Pete's team loses. He had, in some perverse sense, perfected the role.

In November of the following season, Curry Kirkpatrick traveled to New Orleans to write again about Maravich. A decade had now passed since Kirkpatrick first codified the Pistol Pete myth in the pages of *Sports Illustrated*. The new piece, taking stock of his years in the pros, lacked the celebratory tone. Rather, it read like an obituary for his career.

Even the epigraph, a quote from Lou Hudson, had the feel of an epitaph:

This man has been quicker and faster than Jerry West or Oscar Robertson. He gets the ball up the floor better. He shoots as well. Raw-talent-wise, he's the greatest who ever played. The difference comes down to style. He will be a loser, always, no matter what he does. That's his legacy. It never looked easy being Pete Maravich.

In fact, in a physically diminished state, it was looking harder than ever. Sure, Pete retained the capacity to inspire awe. Kirkpatrick liked to cite the example of Marv Roberts, who caught on with the Lakers after a stint in the ABA. At his first glimpse of Showtime, Roberts was moved to leap from his seat on the bench and utter praise more fitting for a revival meeting. "I sees ya, Pete," he shouted. "I sees ya."

But these impromptu testimonies would become infrequent. The nearly perfect player who had been leading the league in scoring at the time of his injury now seemed a distant memory. Pete showed up for the 1978–79 season wearing a two-pound steel brace made famous by the famously gimpy Joe Namath but never before worn by a basketball player. The unwieldy contraption further compromised his already limited mobility. Then there were the back spasms, which forced him to miss a handful of exhibition games. And tendonitis, which required rest (just the opposite of what he needed to condition the muscles atrophied by the surgery). Finally, he suffered a typically mysterious bacterial infection that robbed him of ten pounds and two regular season games.

Even with all that, Pete's physical self appeared to be in better shape than his psyche. Ten years after finding a big-eyed boy who was every coed's crush, Kirkpatrick found a man perilously close to the breaking point. Pete's concern with security spoke of his paranoia. The family home featured burglar alarms at every turn and electronic sensor pads under all the doors and windows. Elvis might have understood.

Pete would often go sleepless for a week at a time and expressed a desire to be invisible. That way, he said, "I could kill the heads of all the rich banking families, redistribute the wealth and make the world a better place."

And, of course, he was still waiting on those spaceships to take him away. By now, Pete had a Talmudic understanding of the collected works of Erich von Däniken, a convicted Swiss embezzler who argued that extraterrestrials had been influencing human civilization since prehistoric times. They had already been here, and one fine day they'd come back to make everything better. "I'm going," he said. "I've made a commitment to myself and Jackie that I'm going."

Those aliens couldn't come soon enough to suit Lew Schaffel and Truck Robinson. Though he would average more points playing with Pete than at any other time in his career, Truck never liked him. As he later told *Sports Illustrated*, "I came into a situation where Maravich was all the people knew. Pete. Pete. Pete . . . All of a sudden I come in—a black player in the South—and it's Pete *and* Truck. A lot of people didn't care for that."

Perhaps. Then again, a lot of people didn't care for Truck holding out during training camp in an unsuccessful attempt to renegotiate a contract that still had five years to go. "The Jazz has two sets of rules," Robinson's agent announced: "One for Pete and one for the rest of the players."

What developed during the holdout was a full-blown locker-room feud. "It was more Truck than Peter," says Aaron James. "Truck had resentment. But he signed that contract—didn't nobody force him."

With Robinson's unhappiness out in the open, Pete was not to be outdone. If nothing else, he had acquired an intimate understanding of the politics of blame: "I'm the white boy making the most money, so it's my fault."

He asked to be traded. Now someone had to go. It was a mess, one that made for what Baylor aptly called "disgusting basketball." Of course, the biggest single factor in the team's deterioration was the deterioration in its biggest star. Pete was logging about 37 minutes and 23 points a night. Though still considerably short of his father's goal for him, Pete would become the twenty-seventh player in league history to reach the 15,000-point mark that season. But Showtime seemed to be making only sporadic revivals. "He wasn't the same player," says Baylor. "I guess the knee was more severe than anybody thought."

With the empathy of one genius toward another, Baylor understood Pete's perfectionism. As a player, he had it himself. But Baylor had only his own knee with which to compare. In 1965, the kneecap split and the patella tendon ruptured. The doctor told him he would never play again. But he did, eight more years. Baylor was never quite the same, either. But his love for the game enabled him to will his body to a state in which pain became mere discomfort.

One wonders, however, if Pete's love for basketball hadn't atrophied with the muscles in his right leg, the circumference of which was now an inch and a half less than the left. Pete had always spoken of his desire to play a perfect game. But in his present condition, lacking the possibility of perfection, the capacity for his fabulously flawed form of art, what was the point? With a body unable to perform in ways that had been both stunning and routine, Pete couldn't cope with his own imperfections. This is what he had feared after he had first been injured, when he drove out over the causeway, to the other side of Lake Pontchartrain, where he watched the waves lap against the land. "It would hurt me too much," he wrote at the time. "My insides would turn knowing I could not do the things on the court I've always done."

In late February, after playing in 49 of 61 games, Pete Maravich announced that he would sit out the rest of the 1979 season.

By then, Jackie was not only pregnant, but in her third trimester. Unfortunately, the prospect of fatherhood did nothing to alter Pete's depression or his self-pity or improve his manner of coping. When not contemplating life in another world, he could often be found drinking with his brother, Ronnie. Still, even Jackie had her limits. She recalled "the only time I really got upset," beginning with Pete calling her from the French Quarter, telling her he was out with his big brother.

"I want you home," said Jackie. "I don't want you staying there all night."

Hearing a response other than the one she wanted, Jackie jumped in the Porsche, her belly just about touching the steering wheel, and headed for the bar. Once there, she proceeded to admonish them both, reserving an especially vituperative scolding for Ronnie. "I let him have it," says Jackie. As brothers went, Ronnie was not a good influence. She was tired of them hanging out at the bar. She was tired of Pete drinking. She knew too well that when he drank, he could get silly. And therein was her real fear. "People might laugh at him, and that really, really upset me," says Jackie. "I was like his protector."

Jaeson Peter Maravich was born April 1, 1979, amid a spell of great turmoil for his father and the Jazz. Elgin Baylor, who went 26–56 in his final campaign as a coach, was fired after the season. The Jazz, he learned, would be moving to Salt Lake City, where their name and logo would rank among the most gloriously incongruous in professional sports.

In retrospect, Baylor sees the history of the franchise turning on the moment of Pete's ill-fated, between-the-legs pass, a moment that subjected him to great criticism for still having Pete in the game.

"Just make the simple basic pass—the guy's wide open," says Baylor. "But it cost him. And it cost us. No doubt we would have made the playoffs . . . The playoffs might have been the beginning of something . . . I don't think we would have moved."

Baylor is not alone in seeing Pete's knee injury as the beginning of the end for New Orleans's pro franchise. Instead of getting 40,000 fans for playoff games at the Superdome, they got feuds and bad basketball. The 1978–79 Jazz finished 30 games below .500. Attendance dropped by a third. The team had always depended on big crowds. But without Pete as the bait to lure them in, it became apparent that the Crescent City—with its prohibitive 11 percent amusement tax, its date-stealing boat show, and an insufficient corporate base—was no place for an NBA team. With fans knowing that cheap seats were always available, the rolls of season ticket holders never rose above 2,600.

Circumstances only became more dire as Sambo's fast-food restaurants—majority owner Sam Battistone's primary business—fell on tough times. Battistone, a devout Mormon from California, had never been an overly involved owner. But now he found a better venue and a more favorable deal in Salt Lake City, which also placed his team at the center of Mormon life.

With the exception of the name—"Sam didn't want to order new uniforms," says Mendelson—the move to Salt Lake City was intended as a clear break with the past. Just two players from the previous year's roster would see any action for the Utah Jazz: six-eight forward James Hardy and Pete. In fact, Pete was all that remained of the franchise's original roster, a fact that the new regime, including General Manager Frank Layden and Coach Tom Nissalke, seemed eager to correct.

After taking the job, Nissalke, who had devised the famously ineffective "make Pete go left" strategy back at Tulane in 1966, contacted each of his players—except for Pete. "He was unreachable," says the coach.

Worse still, recalled trainer Don Sparks, "he couldn't go through a full practice." Not only was his knee a mess, but the effects of drinking (alcohol being conspicuously absent from Pete's ever-expanding list of dietary taboos), depression, and inactivity were becoming plain to see. For the first time in his life—a life marked by an almost nonstop tolerance for aerobic activity—he had fallen out of shape. "He hadn't taken care of himself in the summer," says Nissalke. "I don't think he made a strong effort to rehabilitate the knee."

Now thirty-one, Pete lived in a condo in Bountiful, Utah, with Jackie and the baby. Two or three times a week, he would make the trip to a goat farm in Sandy, twenty-four miles away. No mere cow's milk would pass his son's lips. Who knows? Perhaps, with an early diet that included goat's milk, things would've turned out better for Pete. As it was, his playing time had been drastically reduced.

"It just killed his spirit," says Baylor, who recalls watching the reconstituted Jazz on television. "I could see it in his face."

Pete didn't confide in the other players. Or the assistant coaches. Nissalke never saw him smile. He didn't want to be in Utah, and management didn't want him there, either. Through the first twenty games of the season, three of which Pete missed due to a pinched nerve, the Jazz were 2–18. Before the last of those games, Nissalke told him that he would play only the first and third quarters in Detroit. The Jazz then lost their thirteenth in a row, 98–93. Next up, on November 27, they hosted the Lakers at the Salt Palace. The game was billed as a meeting of two basketball magicians separated by a generation: Pete and super-rookie Earvin "Magic" Johnson, a six-eight point guard (the kind of player who might once have been consigned to Press's imagination) the Lakers had acquired with one of the first-round draft picks they received in exchange for Gail Goodrich. The Jazz, still willing to exploit Pete's power at the box office, had gone so far as to print souvenir posters for the occasion. The crowd of 11,673 was among the biggest that season in Salt Lake. But the matchup never came off, as Pete was benched. Management's idea was to be rid of him and his salary by any means necessary. If they couldn't make a trade, they would try to humiliate him into quitting. "When a team wants to discard a player, he usually doesn't play," Nissalke told the press. "That is what we are doing, except the player happens to be Pete Maravich."

As this was playing out against the Iranian hostage crisis, placards began to appear in the Salt Palace urging Nissalke to "Free the hostage." The coach was unmoved. In Seattle, eight days after the Lakers game, Nissalke received a call from a fellow hotel guest in the middle of the night.

"I've got one of your players here. He's passed out."

Drunk, Pete had stumbled into the wrong room before collapsing. He was taken to the hospital. Pete survived the drunk. But doctors were unable to do anything for a career that remained on life support.

There were no trades to be had, no takers for a high-priced, temperamental, gimpy superstar. Finally, on January 17, after the parties negotiated a settlement as to payments on the remaining $1.8 million on Pete's contract, he was waived. As no team moved to pick up his contract, he became a free agent forty-eight hours later.

But suddenly, Maravich became a prize in the battle between the 76ers and the Celtics, both of whom had legitimate championship aspirations. On January 21, 1980, he arrived in Philadelphia, where he was greeted by the general manager, Pat Williams, the same guy who had traded him from Atlanta almost six years before. If Pete still had hard feelings, he kept them to himself as he prepared to take a physical at Temple University Hospital.

"The only real issue," says Williams, "was his knee."

To that point, the Sixers were considered front-runners to secure Pete's services. Not only was their need more acute, having already lost shooting guard Doug Collins to season-ending foot surgery: the deal seemed inspired. In playing for Philadelphia, Pete would be teamed with Julius Erving, another aesthetically revolutionary player. Whereas Pete's talents were most apparent as he handled the ball, Dr. J, as he was still known, was a leaper whose aptitude and improvisational ability became manifest at higher altitudes. Williams had already taken the liberty of having a Sixer jersey embroidered with Maravich's name. No less an authority than the *New York Times* reported in a headline that Pete was "Likely to Sign with 76ers."

By the time the paper hit the stands, however, Pete had signed with Boston. Philadelphia owner Fritz Dixon was irate and called to upbraid his general manager: "How did you screw it up?"

Williams didn't have an answer. In time, though, he would attribute the loss of Maravich to an overzealous physician, who insisted on administering a rectal examination as part of Pete's physical. "Pete was really put out by that," says Williams.

His meeting with the Celtics included no invasive procedures. Red Auerbach, Boston's legendary general manager, and his coach, Bill Fitch, had long been big Maravich fans. It was Auerbach who once said of Pete, "Some guys break the laws of gravity. This guy breaks the laws of physics." Now, just hours after the physical at Temple, Auerbach dangled the prospect of a multiyear deal. He didn't want a hired gun so much as a member of what he liked to call the Celtics Family. That was the real sell: the Celtics themselves, or rather, the *idea* of the Celtics. Pete understood too well how he was perceived: "If you score points on a losing team, you're a loser . . . Pete Maravich was always a loser." But the Celtics offered a cure for this regret. With thirteen championship banners hanging from the rafters at Boston Garden, the Celtics were winners. What's more, this notion of the Celtics was tethered to Press himself. From the way he referred to the team's "tradition," Pete might as well have been talking about the *Original* Celtics, the band of barnstormers enshrined in his father's memory. Then as now, the shamrock logo signified a franchise that believed in the sanctity of fast-break basketball.

As Pete would confess in the press conference to announce his signing, "I've always wanted to be a Celtic."

As coach of the Cleveland Cavaliers, Bill Fitch once said he would trade his entire team for Maravich. But now, on proper inspection, he became quickly appalled at the condition of the new acquisition. Pete's latest malady was called a groin pull, but that didn't begin to describe a body that had fallen into a state of decrepitude during seven weeks of inactivity. "Never seen an athlete in poorer shape," said Fitch, who thought it a wonder Pete could even pull his socks on.

Sporting a new shaggy perm, Pete went about his rehabilitation, refurbishing his physique with the help of Nautilus weight and pulley machines before eventually joining the team. The 1980 Boston Celtics were a skilled and intriguing assortment of players, including center Dave Cowens, a friend since their days as counselors at Lefty Driesell's camp; point guard Nate Archibald, a nine-year veteran who'd rank as perhaps the best little man ever to play the pro game; swingman M. L. Carr, who had idolized Pete as a camper back at Campbell College; and Larry Bird, voted Rookie of the Year, single-handedly responsible for the Celtics' resurgence as contenders. At six-nine, from French Lick, Indiana, Bird was the best passing big man Auerbach had ever seen. He averaged better than 10 rebounds and 21 points, with a soft, long-range jumper that enabled him to take advantage of the NBA's new 3-point shot. A decade after Pete had been drafted, Bird was what the basketball business had never stopped lusting for: a great white hope.

The pairing of Bird and Pete made for some spectacular postpractice games of horse, but their commonality engendered no special bond. Arriving when he did, Pete remained an outsider. Not only did Pete still need the ball—for a while, it seemed as if he still needed to catch his breath. It was almost mid-February before he played his first game for the Celtics. By then, however, he had become Fitch's favorite whipping boy.

"We all had our issues with him," says Carr, who remembers Fitch as being better at driving young players than dealing with veterans. But the coach, who liked to describe himself as "a carrier" of ulcers, took a special glee in riding Pete. "I was a bigger fan of his before I coached him," said Fitch. Even in his conversations with reporters, he never passed up a shot at his five-time All-Star, calling him undisciplined ("He was always allowed to do as he damn well pleased"), lazy ("His practice habits are lousy"), and stupid ("He still can't run and think at the same time").

By late February, Fitch had finally begun using him as a substitute, though at 17 minutes a game, it was less than half what Pete was accustomed to playing. Though Pete had spoken of subjugating his ego and ambition for the greater Celtic good, the reality was a blow to his pride. "To just bring him off the bench like a spot player," says Elgin Baylor, who again noticed the unmistakably forlorn look, "that had to be a tremendous blow to him."

Still, within a month, Pete's talent had begun to show flashes.

Starting in place of the injured Chris Ford, he made the most of his time. Against the Nets, he hit five shots in a row and starting playing give-and-go with Bird. A spectacular inbound lob that Pete converted for a basket drew a huge cheer from the New Jersey crowd. The next night, with the team short-handed and Bird enduring an off-night, Pete went off for 31 against Indiana, a performance featuring what the *Boston Globe*'s Bob Ryan called "a burst that would have been very recognizable to the folks in Raleigh, Baton Rouge and New Orleans." A couple of nights later in Detroit, Pete scored 20 in the Celtics' fourth consecutive win.

Even after Ford returned to the starting lineup, Pete had become impossible to ignore. He could play either guard position, with or without the ball. On March 25, he scored 17 fourth-quarter points, including a fade-away 3-pointer to beat Washington in the final minute. "That's what we got him for," said Fitch, whose team was still locked in a fight with Philly to secure home court advantage through the playoffs.

As it happened, Boston would finish with the league's best record, their 61 victories being two more than the 76ers. This margin might as well have been due to Pete, whose acquisition was merely the latest affirmation of Auerbach's genius. After sweeping Houston in the first round of the playoffs, the Celtics were poised to reclaim the championship, and with it, their rightful place in the game. As for Pete, at long last, the ring would set him free. By gaining custody of that talisman, he would never again be called a loser.

But the best regular season record granted nothing but an advantage. The Celtics still had to get by Philly. In anticipation of the Sixers, a more experienced team, Fitch shortened his rotation and increased the burden on his rookie, Larry Bird. The effect transformed the Celtics into "a one-man show," as *Globe* columnist Leigh Montville wrote. "If Bird was covered, the offense seemed desperate."

As for Bird, he looked to be worn down by the series end. "Maybe the Celtics relied on him too much," said Bobby Jones, the Sixers' forward.

Still, with the star fatigued and the offense stifled, Pete's playing time only decreased. The mystery was compounded by the fact that

Chris Ford was having a terrible series, scoring just 4 points in the last two games. Averaging just over 13 minutes for the series, Pete had difficulty establishing any kind of rhythm, though there was a game that saw him shoot 4 for 5. The Celtics won, 96–90. It was the only game they took from the Sixers, who won the series 4 games to 1.

That ring would have to wait another year. Pete returned to Louisiana, devoting himself to his son, a newfound obsession with gardening, and his conditioning. He was determined to return to the Celtics—who had voted him only a half-share of their playoff earnings—as a starter on a championship team. Pete's daily regimen included two hours on the Nautilus machines, followed by forty-five minutes with free weights. Then he ran wind sprints. His weight was up to 210, which he attributed to additional grain in his diet.

The training seemed to have paid off on his return to camp. In the final intrasquad scrimmage, Pete made a statement with 38 points. It was the kind of performance that made M. L. Carr feel like a kid again. Though entering his sixth pro season, Carr's adolescent awe remained undiminished. Even his teammates would tease him as Pete entered a room: "Here comes your idol."

If only the coach shared these sentiments. No matter what Pete did, however, starting was not an option. Despite Archibald holding out in camp, Pete still found himself playing behind Ford and second-year pro Gerald Henderson. The way Carr recalls it, the day after Pete's 38-point scrimmage saw Fitch in a particularly foul mood, ripping everyone, but most of all, Pistol. Finally, with Fitch's back turned, Carr punted the basketball across the gym.

Now the coach wheeled around with a vengeance and began to lace into Pete, who had been standing next to Carr, thinking that he was the one responsible for such a teenage show of disrespect. "We don't need that kind of stuff from veterans," he screamed. "We need leadership."

Just as Carr stepped forward to take responsibility for booting the ball, Pete waved him off. Pete remained still until Fitch had finished his diatribe. Finally, practice resumed as Pete was heard to utter, "I don't need this."

The following morning, Carr and the guys were already stretching when the conversation turned to Pistol's arrival at practice. How far would he push the coach's patience? For every minute you were late, Fitch would add another $5 to the fine. The guys were laughing as they started counting Pete's debt: $15, $25, then $50. Practice was already in full swing.

"Pete never showed," says Carr. "I was so upset."

That afternoon, Pete called Bob Sandford. He told his friend pretty much what he had told Fitch: "I think I've shot one basket too many," he said.

Pete was tired. He wanted to spend time with his boy. He wanted to plant his garden. He wanted to heal. Truth was, though, his pride was more damaged than his knee; he didn't want a championship ring if it meant being a benchwarmer.

Sandford had been listening to his friend talk about spaceships and goat's milk for years now. But because Pete was his buddy, he had never once questioned him—until now.

"Pete," he asked, "are you crazy?"

21. Take Me, Part 2

As far as Pete's sanity was concerned, it didn't help that the Celtics won the championship in his first season away from the game. Apparently, basketball didn't miss the Pistol, especially now that it had Larry Bird. The game might as well have assumed a human voice and spoken to Pete, rendering the cruelest judgment: *So long, sucker. We have a real white hope now, thank you very much.* Boston's off-season moves made Bird part of the greatest front line in NBA history, as the Celtics acquired Robert Parish, a 7-footer Press had tried to recruit at LSU, and Kevin McHale, who was all but unstoppable around the basket. When the playoffs finally arrived, the Celtics would avenge their playoff loss to Philadelphia. Next, they vanquished the Houston Rockets in six games.

Pete made it a point not to watch the finals. He had better things to do, tending to his garden, for instance. He would prepare the harvests—zucchini, bell peppers, and tomatoes stand out in Jackie's recollection—as elaborate feasts for his wife and child. Pete himself would not always partake in these repasts, as he made a habit of fasting. It was during this period that he went without food for twenty-five days, subsisting only on freshly squeezed juices. His weight dropped to 170.

"I was testing myself," he said.

Testing for what? Jackie thought. Without basketball, her husband's search for meaning became even more frenetic, but still lacked any sense of destination. It got to where he was driving *her* nuts.

Pete asked Jackie to teach him French. Not long after that, he began playing French cassette tapes in Jaeson's crib at night, figuring that the child would wake up bilingual one morning. It was all part of Pete's plan to become "Father of the Year," as he once called it, by raising an *über* son. There would be no basketball in Jaeson's crib. Instead, he guided the toddler's fingers over puzzles intended for grade school children, hoping that this would unleash his son's conceptual genius.

When Pete wasn't gardening, fasting, or conducting experiments in behavioral engineering, he spent good amounts of time reading up on reincarnation, betting the stock market, or megadosing on vitamins. He arranged for the purchase and transportation of drugs from East Germany said to have life-extending properties, "stuff from Europe that was going to help me live to be 150," he would recall.

Meanwhile, he began planning for an apocalypse, albeit one of an unspecified nature. Spurred on by dedicated reading of the latest survivalist magazines, he bought thirty acres in Folsom, a secluded spread almost fifty miles away. He envisioned a solar-powered home with an underground bomb shelter.

When that urge passed, he would lie around the house in Metairie. For all his searching, he seemed to do a lot of that.

"Pete," Jackie would ask, "when are you going to get out of the house?"

"I get out," he'd mumble, unaware that she'd only asked because he hadn't stepped foot outside for two weeks.

On March 25, 1982, Jackie gave birth to another son, Joshua. The blessed event didn't change Pete's life much, though. He remained in the house, from which he had banished the artifacts of his basketball life: memorabilia, awards, even his sneakers. He changed his phone numbers so nobody would call. Pete didn't need anyone or anything to remind him of who he used be. It was a whole lot easier to drink his beer and pickle his regret.

At night, he'd venture out in the Porsche, flooring it on the Lake Pontchartrain bridge. The speedometer would hit 135, 140, maybe more.

"So many times," Pete would recall, "suicide came into my

thoughts. All I had to do was turn the wheel just ten degrees, and it would be history. Everybody would say, 'What an accident. Isn't it terrible what happened to Pistol Pete?' "

This went on for about two years, until November 1982. On a night he recalls as being entirely ordinary, Pete watched TV and moped before finally turning in around midnight. Jackie had been asleep for some time. Pete couldn't sleep. Nothing unusual there. But then came these flashes of memory, a merciless reel in his mind. Perhaps they should have been introduced by Bob Longmire, the Jazz's P.A. man: *Here he is, ladies and gentlemen, at guard, from LSU, Pistttuu-uhhhlll Pete!* And what of that reel? What might it have been, the sequence of images? Pete as a blindfolded boy, dribbling in the basement for his father. Pete taking his first sip of beer on the steps of the Methodist Church back in Clemson. Pete gurgling in the parking lot as the girl from the bar put the barrel of a gun in his mouth. Pete getting shitfaced the night before playing Marquette in the NIT. Pete on the phone in the airport, not knowing his mother had already blown her brains out. Pete as a father himself, still blindfolded, still dribbling in the basement.

The recollections of these abuses, those committed and those endured, were as vivid as they were relentless.

"It was driving me nuts," he'd remember. "I couldn't get away."

By 5:40 A.M., the sheets were soaked with sweat.

He didn't know how to pray, but he began just the same.

He asked God to forgive him. "Please, save me, please."

Take me.

He began to weep.

Deliver me.

Finally, he heard an audible voice: *Be strong and lift thine own heart.*

It was the voice of God. He woke Jackie, asking if she had heard it. She told him to go back to sleep.

Jackie had been with him long enough to think that this was just another of his phases: vegetarianism, Hinduism, extraterrestrialism, survivalism, and now, Christianity. So she waited for all this Jesus business to pass. But Pete instantly became as devotional about religion as he had once been about basketball. He prayed three times a day, minimum, with the morning hours reserved for Bible study. He learned to be *in Christ*, as he would call it. In Pete's estimation, salvation required only faith. "You either believe it or you don't," he said. "You're either in Christ or you're out of Christ. You either have life, or you have death."

One is tempted to argue that this idea of being born again was another kind of reincarnation. The Pistol had died, only to return as Pete Maravich, a blind man now able to see. *I sees you, Pete. I sees you, too, Jesus.*

After his progression through the isms, he seemed especially well suited for fundamentalist Christianity. What more could Pete, of all people, want than a system of belief derived from Father and Son? The son of God died for his sins. By accepting that much as fact, he was expiated from his guilt. His life began anew.

He bought a dilapidated old Victorian house in Covington, thirty-five miles north of Metairie on the other side of the Lake. Among the first acts in its restoration was the construction of two-inch-thick mahogany doors inscribed with biblical verses. The front door, from Thessalonians: "In everything give thanks." The back door, from Proverbs: "Commit thy works unto the Lord."

Among Pete's works was a basketball camp at Clearwater Christian College. Begun in the summer of 1983, with the price of a two-week session set at $185 per camper, Pete had no expectation of turning a profit. Rather, he had gone back on the basketball circuit to incite belief and save souls, melding the uniquely Maravichian views on nutrition, God, and the game.

"Everything that went into that camp," said Pete, "was hand-picked by me and my dad."

Unlike Press, however, Pete wasn't much interested in producing star ballplayers. Rather, he found himself drawn to the fat kid or the angry kid (many of whom he would write to or call after the session was over). In addition to nine and a half hours of daily basketball instruction, campers received a dose of religious-themed discussion.

On most nights, they were given a chance to declare Jesus Christ their lord and savior. Logstown's Reverend Anderton would have wholeheartedly approved, though he might have found the menu curious. It included a twenty-two-item salad bar, fresh fish, and organic chicken, but observed strict prohibitions on red meat and tap water. "I tape the faucets shut," Pete said.

Leaving aside the question of his excessive nature, the camp represented his return to the game, a considerable feat for a man who often compared his basketball jones to a heroin addiction. Then again, maybe he hadn't much choice, as the game never left him. A friend would recall how Pete, who hadn't shot a ball in quite some time, suddenly picked one up and bet him he could shoot from a distance of thirty feet for a full half hour without missing two in a row. They had two balls. The friend would rebound and pass to Pete as soon as he shot. Sure enough, he never missed consecutive shots.

Pete played an exhibition at halftime of a Mavericks-Lakers game to benefit sickle cell and cystic fibrosis research. He agreed to join a team of former NBA players, including Earl Monroe and Rick Barry, on a tour of the Far East. He even broke his vow and returned to LSU, appearing at a clinic at the request of Collis Temple, his father's first black recruit.

At thirty-five, Pete became the youngest ex-star in the NBA's annual Old Timers' Game. Playing for a team coached by Red Auerbach, he saw to it that Showtime had a proper encore. As George Vecsey wrote in the *New York Times*, "With the older old-timers circling around him, Pistol Pete Maravich went to his knees, toyed with the ball like a child making mud pies in a vacant lot. He patted it, stopped its forward roll, made it quiver, made it obey."

"I'd like to play in the game when I'm 100," he said. "I'd like to be the oldest human being still playing . . . Still filling the lanes."

There was joy in his game, maybe for the first time in his life.

It took a while for Jackie to overcome her skepticism. But she knew what she saw, and with whom she lived, both before and after God spoke to her husband: "He was like a different person. I saw how happy he was, how he was at peace with everything. I kind of envied him. I wanted what he had."

Jackie, raised Catholic, resisted Pete's entreaties to attend Baptist services. But in 1984, at the First Baptist Church in Kenner, she was baptized. It came as a surprise to Pete, who began to weep uncontrollably as she rose and made her way to the water.

However one might describe Pete's transformation—in terms theological or psychiatric—there was yet another name for what had taken hold of him. It was love. Anyone doubting that proposition need only see him with his sons.

He put them to bed every night. He hugged them and kissed them. He pushed them on the swings, but never pushed basketball. When Jaeson was six, he told his father he wanted to be a mailman. That was fine with Pete, as the game was just a game now. There were other things to do. Jaeson recalls trips to the zoo and the bowling alley. He played a lot of air hockey with his dad.

Jaeson often traveled with Pete as he gave his testimony, regaling audiences with the story of his religious conversion. And when Pete went for his runs with Reverend Alfred Young, pastor of the Faith Bible Church in Covington, Jaeson would follow on his bicycle. "Whatever my dad was doing," he says, "I wanted to be around him."

As for Joshua, his earliest memories are of being in his father's grasp: "I remember Disney World. I remember him holding me on his shoulders the whole time.

"Sea World. I remember seeing Shamu. I was on my dad's shoulders again. He brought us real close to the glass and we got splashed. We all laughed. Whenever I was with him, he was always holding on to me: He never let go. He was just filled with"—all these years later, a young man searches for the right word—"filled with love."

Once, Pete held Joshua for thirty-six hours, most of that time in a hospital bed. He was two, and while roaming though what was still a renovation site in Covington, had fallen down a sixteen-foot air vent. Pete heard the thump, and within seconds found the boy limp in a pool of blood on the hardwood floor. The right side of Josh's face, Pete recalled, was "grossly misshapen" and his eye swollen shut. In the emergency room, a specialist figured the best-case scenario had Josh losing sight in the right eye, but only after extensive surgery. A diagnosis on possible brain damage would have to wait.

So began Pete's vigil. In short order, he was informed that the boy would live. Sometime after that, the doctors reversed their initial finding; surgery would not be necessary. In a matter of hours, it became clear that Joshua would be just fine. Pete declared it a miracle. He held Josh and prayed through the next day. "I had to believe," he said, "God was in total control."

What Pete saw in God, Joshua saw in his father. He has no recollection of falling down the vent. Rather, what stands out in his memory is the time he managed to get his head caught between the wrought iron bars of a banister. Unable to move his head, he began to wail. Again, Pete came running. "He pried the metal bars apart and pulled my head out real gently," says Josh. "Like Superman."

That Pete was a good father might have had something to do with the example Press set in raising Diana, the most valiantly successful mission of his life. Hers was not an adolescence marked by the typical rebellions. In response to Press's occasional exaggerations, she might nudge him and say, "Now, *Daddy*." But that was the most severe rebuke she would offer. They were inseparable.

Doubling as a mother had no doubt helped him become a better father. He had brushed her hair and put it in barrettes. With his salary as a scout for the Jazz, a job that lasted until she was through high school, he took her to his ancestral home, now Yugoslavia, and paid for the braces that finally came off in the tenth grade. In 1982, Diana graduated from Mandeville High School, an honor student who played three sports: basketball, volleyball, and track.

Following graduation, father and daughter went to Campbell University in Buies Creek, North Carolina, where Press had spent so many summers. She went as a student; he signed on, at the age of sixty-eight, as the associate basketball coach. "A package deal," Press called it. He was happy. "I'd like be around coaching until I'm 100," he said.

In the spring of 1985, Press traveled to Israel for two weeks. Accompanying him were Pete and Notch Petkovich, an old and dear friend from Aliquippa. The first week was a tour of the Holy Land that gratified Pete, who sobbed with joy as he waded from the Jordan River. The second week was a basketball clinic, with Press lecturing about various offensive and defensive schemes. Hundreds of coaches attended, a resounding success except for Press's physical condition. He had begun to urinate blood. By the end of the week, the pain had become too excruciating for him to carry on, and Pete brought him to an emergency room.

"There's no way he should be alive," said the doctor.

"A problem," Pete wrote in his autobiography, "had developed in his prostate gland." Friends and family learned another name for this problem: prostate cancer. The disease only intensified the connection between father and son, eliciting a confessional nerve in Pete. He now felt the need to tell Press that his untimely desertion of the Celtics—and their unfulfilled dream of a championship—was a result of his hubris. Even worse, in Pete's estimation, was his drinking the night before playing Marquette, an act of recklessness that cost Press a chance to win the NIT. Pete asked for forgiveness. Press laughed him off. But Pete insisted on formalizing a ritual of contrition and clemency. "I'm serious," he said. "I will not leave this room until this is right between us."

"Okay," Press said, finally. ". . . I forgive you."

Soon, Press would be forgiven, too. "I became a Born Again Christian at the First Baptist Church," he informed old friends Bob and Louise Bradley. "Even got immersed in water. I don't want any part of Satan. No way."

There were any number of reasons for Press's conversion, beginning, obviously, with the prospect of his own mortality. "I think he was scared," says Jackie. That's not to say Press's reformation lacked sincerity. He had seen what it had done for his son. Moreover, as faiths go, this wasn't much of a leap for Press, who had been reading the Bible since Reverend Anderton made it a requirement to play at the Logstown Mission. Still, his oldest friends noticed another factor. The father had become the follower. If Pete was with Jesus, then Press had to be there, too.

This reversal of their long-standing roles had begun some years before. In the early 1980s, Charlie Bryant ran into his former boss in the dining room at Campbell College. Press was drawing up plays on a steno pad when he looked up and saw his former assistant, who was wearing an ace bandage for his tennis elbow. Though they hadn't seen each other in years, Press didn't bother with hellos.

"I know a doctor in Alabama who can cure that," he said, nodding at the elbow.

"I've already seen a doctor," said Charlie, who meant *a real* doctor.

"You dumb son of a bitch," said Press. "How long have I been telling you: You got to quit eating that damn red meat."

"But my doctor says what I need is *more* hamburger."

Charlie should've known what he was in for: the full speech on the virtues of vegetarianism and the evils of modern medicine. Upon its conclusion, Charlie put out his hand. "By the way," he said, "it's good to see you, Press."

Press melted, and gave him a fierce hug.

It *was* good to see him, thought Bryant. Still, he couldn't help but notice how things had come full circle. Press was starting to sound just like Pete.

They had danced and dueled through decades, the patriarch and his progeny. As sons imitate fathers, so do fathers come to echo their sons. By now, Press and Pete had been chasing each other for so long, it had become all but impossible to determine where one ended and the other began.

Once again, the odd man out was Ronnie. "Ronnie still lives on Bourbon St.," Press told the Bradleys. "He is a lost soul and we (Pete and I) are trying to save him. We pray nightly and I'm sure the Lord will answer us."

We.

Even when it came to proselytizing, they were an indivisible proposition.

"He started accepting everything Pistol would tell him," says Wally Zernich, now a physician back in Aliquippa, who still thought of Press as his idol.

Such blind acceptance was not without complications. Neither father nor son was given to casual beliefs. What's more, their thinking was not just extreme, but often flakey. On Pete's recommendation, they decided to treat the cancer holistically, through a combination of diet and herbal medicines.

"I didn't agree with that," says Jackie. "And I told them."

Good luck. "Whatever Pete did, Press did, too," says Joe Pukach. "Pete had the idea that if you have surgery, you're only going to live a couple of years. If you don't have surgery, you'll live at least five. Five is better than two."

Finally, after a week or so of brow-beating, Pukach prevailed on Press to speak with Zernich, who made an appointment for him at Memorial Sloan-Kettering Cancer Center in New York. When another couple of weeks passed without any word from Press, Zernich called him.

"I cancelled out, doc," said Press.

"You what?"

"It's all the way in New York. It's hard to get there."

"Press, you've been all over the world, and you can't get to New York?"

Apparently not.

In time, however, it became evident that no amount of whole grains, organic broth, or vitamins would cure his cancer, which in due course invaded his bones. Radiation treatments were unable to stop either the malignancy or the ancillary insults to his body. He contracted pneumonia.

On February 11, 1987, Pete and Press flew to Hanover, Germany, for an experimental protocol. They were there eleven days and spent many of their hours together reading the Bible. Press's cough subsided, but the cancer did not. The flight home was a nightmare, as the only available seats were in the smoking section. Meanwhile, the phlebitis in Press's right leg had gotten so bad he had to wear one of Pete's size 15 shoes. Managing the pain was more difficult, as there was always more pain than morphine.

The cancer's course was inexorable. John Wooden called his old friend. They would read verses of scripture to each other over the phone.

"He was skin and bones, totally eaten up with cancer," recalls Russ Bergman, who found Press's physical appearance the least remarkable aspect of his transformation. "How many times had I heard him say, 'I want to be buried with a basketball in my coffin'? But he no longer felt that way. Basketball was just a game to him now. He had even stopped cussing."

Joe Pukach recalls Press telling him, "To go to heaven, you've got to be sanctified."

The problem was, Pukach wasn't ready for heaven. "How about I stay down here a few more years and I'll meet you? You get a team up there. I'll bring my team. Then we'll play each other."

It was only a matter of time now. Press understood. His regrets, he told Pukach, numbered just one: "Wish I had a good steak."

All told, he spent more than three months at Pete's house in Covington. "Pete was basically a nurse," said John Lotz, the assistant athletic director at the University of North Carolina and formerly the coach at Florida. "A lot of times, he stayed with Press twenty-four hours a day. He did everything he could."

Unfortunately, nothing from the health food store in Mandeville made dying any easier. Every so often, Press would call on Jackie. She'd arrive as an angel of minor, if surreptitious, mercies, bearing Baby Ruths and Nestlé Crunch bars. "The man was dying," she says. "He wanted candy."

God would understand. Pete would not.

By then, preparing Press for his eternal life had become an orthodox rite, though not lacking in tenderness or grace. What Pete didn't know about the candy bars wouldn't hurt him. More important, there was a poem in the manner of Press's submission, a writ of forgiveness. Sins of the father may be visited upon the son, but Press would heal his own boy as he lay dying.

As he let Pete bathe him.

As Pete carried him up the stairs, his father draped across his arms like a swathe of silk.

As Pete informed him of his selection as a member of the Basketball Hall of Fame.

As Pete read to him from the Bible, the murmur of his voice reaching Jackie like an incantation.

Sometimes, Jackie would peek into the room. Press might have fallen asleep, the Bible on his chest. But Pete would still be there, rubbing his father's hands.

Pete imagined they were barnstormers, traveling the country testifying to the glories of Jesus Christ. He was praying for a miracle. "Then I realized," he wrote, "the real miracle already happened."

One day, Josh saw the paramedics flying up the stairs with the stretcher. As they took Press away, the boy could not help but consider the idea that this man with "his slick silver hair" was related to him. *Related.* What did that mean?

Press lived his last days in Highland Park Hospital in Covington. Pete and Jackie watched as he took his last breath, shortly before 6:30 P.M., April 15, 1987. Jackie ran crying into the hallway, then let herself back in the room. Pete was still at his father's side, talking into his ear.

"I'll see you soon," he said.

Pete remained there—hugging, holding, whispering—until hospital workers zipped the body bag closed. When the earthly remains had been removed, Jackie turned to her husband. "Pete," she asked, "what did you mean, 'I'll see you soon'?"

From across the street, neighbors would watch Pete with rapt curiosity. Neither Jimbo McLachlan nor his father had ever seen a guy mow his lawn like Pete. He didn't miss a spot. Even more striking was the way he hunched over the lawnmower with the same intensely contorted expression he once wore on the court.

"What's he doing?" asked Jimbo.

"Trying to be normal, I think," said his father.

Normal? Pete should have known better. He had no better chance at being normal than he had at being anonymous. Pistol Pete might be dead to him, but he remained alive to the public, a pleasing ghost. Jaeson was in the first grade when he heard his teacher speaking of all the great ballplayers he had seen. It came as something of an epiphany to the boy that there had been basketball stars before Larry Bird, Magic Johnson, and this new one, Michael Jordan.

"Daddy," he asked later that day, "did you used to be Pistol Pete?"

In an effort to answer the question, and perhaps to satisfy any vestige of his vanity, Pete called Leah Wilcox in the league's new entertainment division. She collected and dubbed his highlights on a video, finding the process to be an unexpected treat. Wilcox, then in her early twenties, had grown up in the Bronx at the dawn of the hip-hop age. But the video had something—a lot of somethings, actually—that cut across all the demography that might ordinarily have made a middle-aged white man from the South less than accessible to her. "I had no idea," says Wilcox, who then played the tape for her brothers. They had never seen him before. Suddenly, they couldn't get enough.

Neither could Jaeson. He was intoxicated with the sight of his father, or rather, this man his father had been. "I just knew him as Dad," he says.

To that point, Jaeson's interest in basketball had been a casual one, which is to say that he was not untalented with a nerfball. Pete had mounted two rims (eight feet for Jaeson, six feet for Josh) on beams in the playroom. The boys would horse around, though not much more. But that video changed everything. Jaeson now demanded that his father teach him the drills that Press had taught him. As Pete performed them for his son, they were mesmerizing at first, then addicting.

Jaeson, whose rec league team was called the Little Pistols, would always remember the day he finally mastered the spider drill, a rapid dribbling exercise. "There was no better feeling," he says.

In 1987, after Pete's election to the Basketball Hall of Fame, he brought Jaeson to the NBA's All-Star weekend in Seattle, where the bellman approached to thank him as he checked in. "All that fancy stuff you used to do," he said. "It made basketball more . . . more fun."

By now, the reassessment of Pete's professional career had begun in earnest. The *Detroit News*' Shelby Strother, who watched this exchange, was taken by the appearance of a middle-aged man he remembered as a teenager. Men of a certain age could now mark time by the wrinkles and creases around Pete's eyes. More remarkable, though, was the idea that basketball had finally caught up to him. "Pistol Pete was branded a hot dog and today's players are anointed as creative artists for the same stuff," wrote Strother, who called Maravich "the bridge" in the game's evolution between Bob Cousy and Magic Johnson.

Jaeson was more impressed that his dad could get him an audience with Michael Jordan. That was in the locker room before the dunking contest, a fan favorite in a league now known for its production values. Even better than getting the superstar's autograph was the way Jordan, who'd win his first dunking title that night, acknowledged his father. "It seemed like they were pretty good friends," says Jaeson, who recalls the weekend as the best of his life, despite the trauma of a single incident that marred it.

Pete was scheduled to be introduced at halftime of the All-Star game. He gave Jaeson firm instructions to remain in his seat. After a while, though, the boy lost track of his father. Unable to see him on the court, Jaeson got up to look for himself. Not long after, Pete returned to the seats and panicked when he could not find his boy. Later that night, he put a belt to Jaeson's backside.

"The only time I ever got spanked," says Jaeson.

Basketball's erstwhile rebel had come to detest rebellion. But that's not why he put a whupping on his boy. Rather, Jaeson's temporary disappearance had aroused Pete's own worst fear, that which still defined him as Helen's son: the dread of being lost, abandoned, separated from those of his own blood.

That weekend Pete delivered the prayer at the All-Star Chapel, citing Psalms (149:10) and Matthew (16:26). He had become, basically, a full-time evangelist, dedicated to "the winning of souls to the kingdom." What Press had when he spoke of the game, Pete had when he spoke of Jesus. As it turned out, the gift he had for preaching would've made him a good coach, too. He could make people believe.

He did some touring with the Shooting Stars, whose founding star, former Globetrotter Meadowlark Lemon (a k a the "Clown Prince of Basketball"), had become an ordained minister. He raised money for the Leukemia Society. He praised God on Larry King's syndicated radio show. It was now his habit to carry religious pamphlets on his person, handing them to complete strangers and old friends. The loud, tipsy fool who once gave a shoeshine boy $300 and told him to keep the change now lifted loads from the trunk of his Chevy Impala to distribute free Thanksgiving turkeys through black churches.

With the help of people like John Lotz, prominent in evangelical circles, and Frank Schroeder, a television producer for a Christian-themed sports show, he fashioned his story into a multimedia message. There would be a cassette tape of his testimony of faith; a biography, *Heir to a Dream*, published in October 1987; even a movie, *The Pistol: Birth of a Legend*, a father and son saga based on Pete and Press back in Clemson. What's more, his testimony became an event. He bore witness at prisons, psychiatric hospitals, high schools, and churches. He spoke before tens of thousands at Billy Graham's crusades.

"I almost fell out of my chair," says Wally Zernich, who was channel surfing on his TV when he came upon the sight of Pistol Pete at a church podium. "At first I thought: What the heck is *he* doing up there? But I couldn't turn it off. He gave one of the most inspiring speeches I ever heard. He was as good as Billy Graham."

Bud Johnson was similarly stunned on seeing him live at a church in Covington: "I'd known him since he was a freshman at LSU. The kid I knew was shy, sullen, moody, given to temper tantrums. But he went for forty-five minutes without stammering or stuttering. He was in complete control. For the first time since I'd known him, I thought he was happy."

Neal Walk, who attended his testimony in Phoenix, noticed that the sadness in Pete's eyes was gone. Who'd have thought, after all the isms they had tried as young men, that Pete would find peace in Christianity? "I was thrilled for him," says Walk. "Whatever gets you through to the other side."

Pete's religious beliefs were no less extreme than his secular ones had been. He linked a rise in teen suicide to the abolishment of school prayer. He was firmly against the teaching of evolution: "When you're told you're a monkey, you're going to start acting like one."

Jackie would watch him as he sat at the desk in his study, furiously jotting notes to himself and memos to God. He prayed "to serve with joy Jackie, Jaeson and Joshua." He prayed for Ronnie: "Open the dead ears of my brother Ronnie before it is too late." His personal stationery bore a line from Psalm 37:23: *The steps of a good man are ordered by the Lord; and he delighteth in his way.* At the core of his experience and his religion was the idea of the father, both heavenly and earthly:

> *We have a weak nation*
> *because of weak churches*
> *because of weak families*
> *because of weak fathers*

Jackie wouldn't quarrel with this line of thinking. But she did have a problem with the way Pete had recast his story as a religious parable. By his own account, he had had difficulty kicking booze. "My instincts to drink were still there," he said. Pete would speak of the time he sat down for a beer with an old friend. Before he knew it, he'd had ten.

But that didn't certify him, in Jackie's estimation, as an alcoholic. She saw him as a man who drank to relieve immense pressure, a man who, truth be told, couldn't hold his liquor. Certainly, Pete didn't drink as Helen had, hiding bottles, sneaking sips to get through the day. Jackie didn't like it when Pete spoke of himself as a drunk. She was protecting him, again.

But Pete was less interested in the nature of alcoholism than in saving souls. Hank Kalb would always recall the day Pete came to visit him in Georgia. Hank was having a tough time, his own drinking having gotten out of control. They spent the day talking. It was difficult to reconcile this new Pete Maravich with the man who had reminded him of Elvis. "I had never seen him at peace," says Kalb. "Too bad Elvis died before he got to be like Pete."

Some days later, Pete sent him a study Bible. Kalb took it with him into rehab and has read from it every morning since February 3, 1987, the day he became sober.

There were limits, however, to Christ's earthly healing power. "When I think about my dad," said Pete, "I really can't handle it too well." He'd be driving down the highway, then all of a sudden, as Press popped into his head, he'd burst out crying. He'd weep for ten minutes straight.

In Jackie's mind, this pain over Press's death was linked to an overall physical decline. Even as Pete's spirit rose, his body looked like it was going to hell. "Horrible," says Jackie. "He looked gray."

"I ran into him a few times," recalls Elgin Baylor. "He had that glow in his face and his eyes, like the burden was off him. But his *body*. I was shocked. He didn't look well at all. He had lost so much weight."

Bob Sandford was shocked, too, when he saw Pete in Raleigh around Christmas 1987. He didn't look much like Pete anymore, arriving in a baggy overcoat for the retiring of his number at Needham-Broughton High School. When the festivities were concluded, Bob and Pete talked all night, making plans. That summer, Jaeson and Bob's son, Gray, would room together at the camp.

Finally, unable to ignore his friend's drawn appearance, Bob asked if Pete was okay.

"Having some trouble with my shoulder," he said, referring to the pain that periodically shot down through his arm. "It's an old injury."

Weren't they all?

Nine days later, early on the morning of January 5, 1988, a Chevy Blazer driven by a man named Gary Lydic arrived at a hotel in San Dimas, California. Lydic was the director of Ministry Services for Focus on the Family, on whose syndicated radio show Pete would be a guest. The interview, conducted by Dr. James Dobson, would be taped later that day. But first, there was a more urgent matter. Dobson, who had founded Focus on the Family to combine his psychiatric training and his evangelical belief, was also an avid ballplayer, playing pickup games three times a week at the First Church of the Nazarene in Pasadena. It was with a sense of unmistakable pride and expectation that he informed his fellow regulars that Pistol Pete had agreed to play with them.

Dobson called Ralph Drollinger, a fellow evangelist who had played on John Wooden's last championship team at UCLA. "Would you come down to Pasadena-Nazarene and be on my team?" The 7-foot Drollinger agreed, though he wasn't particularly looking forward to it. He had had his share of big-time basketball. He wasn't in shape. He didn't feel like being anyone's ringer. Nor did he feel that need to prove, an urge that possesses players on the court, transforming men back into boys.

Then again, most men would call themselves lucky for another chance, however fleeting, to be boys. In anticipation of the game, Norman Moline, an accountant with a practice in nearby Arcadia, foraged through a crawlspace in his parents' basement and found his 1970 Pistol Pete Topps bubblegum card. He wanted Pete to sign it. As he wanted a record of the event, he also set aside his video camera before going to bed. He didn't sleep much, though.

Neither did Lydic. As per Dobson's instructions, he arrived at the hotel before 7 A.M. to pick up Pete and Frank Schoeder. The freeway traffic was already heavy, so he decided to take local streets. But as Lydic steered into the right lane, an oncoming car almost plowed into the Blazer. *Maybe we're not supposed to be there today*, he thought.

By then, he had become engrossed in what Pete had to say, especially as it concerned the events leading up to Press's death. "There were times when I was carrying him that I didn't know if he was dead or alive," said Pete.

The game of four-on-four was already in progress as they finally arrived at the church gymnasium. Only after Pete began to warm up did Lydic tell him that his own father was dying of bone cancer in Dayton, Ohio. Pete put down the ball and embraced him.

"I've been there," he said. "I want to help you."

Then it was time to play. Pete hadn't been on a court in a long time, the longest such stretch of his life. At least, that's what he told Drollinger, who couldn't help but notice Pete's anemic appearance. He was not what Drollinger would have expected, the blasphemously talented player his high school coach had warned him about.

Though Pete acclimated to the beat of the game very slowly, the others were juiced from the start—and none more so than Dobson. "Dr. Dobson was not screwing around," says Drollinger. "He was almost angered with me as a teammate because I had such a lighthearted, almost flippant attitude. Dr. Dobson was intense, like this was the NCAA Final Four . . . Dobson wanted to tell all of his cronies how he schooled Pete."

But Pete proved impossible to perturb, much less offend. Pete was in his own wonderful place, "enjoying the game for the game," says Lydic.

During a break, as guys went off to get water, Dobson and Pete found themselves near the 3-point line, shooting as Lydic retrieved the ball.

"Two weeks ago, I couldn't even get my arm up this high," said Pete, raising a hand over his head.

"How do you feel now?" asked Dobson.

"I feel great."

In the next moment, Lydic could see Pete begin to sway. Was he kidding around? Then the eyes rolled back in his head. The sound of his head hitting the floor would haunt those who heard it, the full revulsion of the thwacking sound being impossible to adequately describe or forget. Pete had begun to foam at the mouth. Dobson held his head, trying to keep Pete from swallowing his tongue. He and Drollinger administered CPR. Next, the EMS crew took its turn. As they worked, shooting fierce jolts of electricity through his torso, the players knelt in prayer.

God's will be done, they said.

Why now? they asked.

Finally, what remained of Pete Maravich was taken away in a slow-moving ambulance. No siren, as Lydic recalls.

Joshua didn't have to be told. Though only five years old, he attained his understanding in a way that was beyond language.

He looked in the mirror, seeing himself through his father's eyes.

Eyes of mine, guard that which is thine.

"My daddy's dead."

Jaeson knew something was up when a teacher found him in the school cafeteria. "You need to go home now," she said.

The living room was already crowded with grown-ups by the time Jaeson arrived. His mother, who had been crying in the corner, got up as he came through the door. She hugged him tight.

"I knew it was going to be real bad," he says.

She told him, then he went to his room. He felt nothing. He pulled up the blinds and stared out the window. Five minutes passed. Or was it ten? He does not know. "When I finally figured out that he wasn't coming back I started to cry," he says.

The next day, in an act that stretched the limits of an eight-year-old's capacity for bravery and observance, Jaeson Maravich practiced with his rec league team, the Little Pistols.

A strange natural heart defect—so rare no statistics exist on how often it occurs—took the life of basketball star Pete Maravich last week, a coroner's report concluded Monday.

Maravich, 40, died of deterioration of the tissues in his heart because he was born without one of the two artery systems that supply the heart with blood.

The finding stunned cardiologists and other experts in sudden death in young athletes since the nearly unheard of condition is usually assumed to preclude strenuous activities. It usually kills its victims before they are 20.

> Allan Parachini, "Maravich Victim of
> Very Rare Heart Defect,"
> Los Angeles Times, *January 12, 1988*

22. AMAZING GRACE

The autopsy found that Maravich had been born without a left artery complex, what the *Times'* medical writer Allan Parachini described as "one of two systems of pencil-thick arteries that nourish the heart muscle." Even more improbable than this congenital abnormality, however, was Pete having lived to the age of forty.

As one expert put it, "How could a guy like that run up and down the court for 20 years?"

More like thirty-five. But, then, who was counting? Besides, as far as Jackie was concerned, there was a measure of time even more significant. It had been less than nine months since Press had died.

Jackie kept playing back a line in her head: *I'll see you soon.*

When she had asked what Pete meant by that, he became defensive. "Well," he said, "we're all going to die one day."

He knew better, though. Looking back, one can see the signs: the weight loss, the pain emanating from his shoulder, the pallor. It all seemed to start with Press's death. "Once that happened," says Jackie, "it was all downhill. Did Pete know something? I think so. I really think he did. He didn't want to upset me."

The doctors were entitled to their diagnosis; the autopsy yielded an incontrovertible, scientific truth. But Jackie's analysis was no less accurate. "I believe that, when people say that someone died of a broken heart," she says.

It happened to Pete.

"I know he didn't want to leave," she says. "It wasn't intentional or anything. I know he wouldn't want to leave his sons."

By the same token, it was impossible to consider Pete without his father. There was that fact, too: without Press, Pete withered.

Whatever doubts still lingered about Pete's standing in the game or even his place in popular culture ended with his death. His image would be eternally consigned—along with the likes of James Dean, Elvis, and at least a couple of Kennedys—to a celebrity purgatory reserved for the young dead. In a generation's collective memory, Pete would remain much like the sad-eyed wizard of his rookie card.

Those eyes—never so haunting as they appeared with the news of his death, in a tight, grainy photograph on the front page of *USA Today*—were much remarked upon. Scott Ostler, writing in the *Los Angeles Times*, recalled Pete as he used to warm up in New Orleans: "Unsmiling, he gazed all around the Superdome with, as J. D. Salinger wrote in 'For Esme—With Love and Squalor,' 'blasé eyes that, I thought, might have very possibly counted the house.' "

Pete's death came as an unexpected boon for obituary writers and columnists, inspiring deeply personal tributes from those who had known him just a little or not at all. Andy Nuzzo, of the *Beaver County* (Pennsylvania) *Times*, wrote of their interview back in '74, when Pete told him, "I don't want to play ten years in the NBA and die of a heart attack at 40."

In New York, the *Daily News*' Harvey Araton remembered going to the NIT as a kid and hearing fans complain that Pete had scored only 37 against Oklahoma. "I don't even remember if LSU won the game," wrote Araton. "I remember the next day, though, rolling socks down to my ankles, dribbling on the concrete and looking for a shadow to see if my hair flopped around like his."

The *New York Post* devoted its entire back page to the news, white type set off against a black background: *"Pistol dies playing the game he loved."* Peter Vecsey, who had cultivated a reputation as basketball's cruelest critic, became misty with the recollection of playing against a teenage Maravich while in the army at Fort Bragg: "He performed tricks our imaginations couldn't comprehend, threw blind bounce passes that spun like a cue ball off a pool shark's stick . . .

"He was a man I had great difficulty writing about objectively. I liked him an awful lot and never quite got over being in awe of his presence and immense talent."

In Chicago, Maravich's death occasioned an editorial in the *Tribune*, a warning against the dangers of parental pressure and ambition, "the crushing weight of a peculiarly American nightmare." But where this editorialist saw tragedy, evangelicals saw opportunity. The circumstances of Pete's death were ripe for the saving of souls.

"In retrospect, I can see the hand of God in the whole day," says Drollinger, whose grief was tempered by an "overwhelming joy" commensurate with the possibilities for proselytizing. "Dr. Dobson has an ace PR staff. I believe the holy spirit entrusted Dr. Dobson to Pete's testimony . . . If Pete had died anywhere else, there would not have been the Christian spin—for lack of the right word—on his life story."

Dobson delivered the eulogy for Peter Press Maravich on a cold, wet day at the First Baptist Church of Baton Rouge. "Basketball at one time was his greatest love," he said. "But his greatest passion was the love of the Lord he served."

"None of the guys were there," recalls Elgin Baylor, noting the absence of Pete's teammates from the Jazz. "That bothered me."

Baylor wept with the organ's melody, mourning his fellow genius of the game.

Amazing Grace! how sweet the sound.

Even more unforgettable was an image that appeared on the front page of the next day's *Times-Picayune*: a sandy-haired boy in an LSU jacket staring bravely at Pete's casket. Carl Vondembussche, from Clearwater, Florida, first attended Pete's camp three summers before, when he was eight years old. Carl wasn't so crazy about basketball. It was his dad's idea; his father was a big fan. And as soon as his parents dropped him off, Carl became weepy and frightened. He had never been away from home.

Pete told him it would be all right, assured him he would have fun. He even told Carl he could sleep in the same dorm room where he stayed with Jaeson and Josh. The next morning, Pete carried Carl on his shoulders to breakfast.

Pete was right. It wasn't so bad being carried around by the guy whose name was on your T-shirt. But more than that, remembers Carl, "it felt good not to feel alone."

That's what Carl Vondembussche, now eleven, was thinking as he gazed at the casket.

"I'll always remember that kid," says Rich Hickman, Pete's backcourt mate at LSU. "I remember thinking that, not too many years before, he could've been Pete."

That saved a wretch like me.

After the service, the LSU guys gathered at Randy Lamont's home in Baton Rouge. The night grew late. They drank beer and told stories, all of them avoiding the obvious.

"Everybody was kind of shook up," says Hickman. "You're a kid until that first guy you knew dies."

Pete was that guy.

I once was lost, but now am found.

As it happened, Hickman had known him longer than anyone else at Lamont's. They had played biddy ball as seven-year-olds at New Sheffield Elementary back in Aliquippa. That would've been 1954.

And now it occurred to Hickman that the older they got, the more alike they had become.

That kid staring at the casket could've been any of them.

Was blind, but now I see.

By an act of the Louisiana State Legislature, the spaceship-like arena on LSU's campus, the House That Pete Built, was officially renamed the Pete Maravich Assembly Center. House Bill No. 443 acknowledged the Old War Skule's great debt, especially now that its basketball program, all but unknown before Pete's arrival in Baton Rouge, had become a perennial powerhouse.

An accounting of Pete's earthly debts and credits is not a simple matter. His last will and testament contained instructions for Jackie to assume the titles of trustee and executor. With no mention of his brother, Ronnie, it provided for the creation of equal trusts in the names of Jaeson Peter and Joshua Simon Maravich. Pete's assets at the time of his death included houses in Covington and Metairie and 28.964 acres in Folsom. The Jazz still owed him $223,691 in deferred compensation. His NBA pension was worth $79,722. His business agreements with Frank Schroeder's company, LA Production Group, included $50,000 for the right to use his likeness and image in a highlight video of his college years. He was also entitled to 33 percent of the net profits from *Homework Basketball*, four soon-to-be released instructional videos based on the drills Press had taught him as a kid. His 1974 Porsche Carrera was estimated at $13,000, and his collection of silver coins valued at $95,500.

Pete had left it all to Jackie and the kids. That's not all he left, of course, just the minor, quantifiable items. There was no way to measure his effect on a boy like Carl Vondembussche or all the boys who came before him. They were now men of a certain age, having grown up to be accountants or coaches or even troubadours. Bob Dylan grieved the morning he heard of Maravich's death on the radio. He recalled seeing Pete—"the holy terror of the basketball world"—perform in New Orleans with the Jazz. "He could have played blind," Dylan would recall in his memoirs. "Pistol Pete hadn't played professionally for a while, and he was thought of as forgotten.

I hadn't forgotten about him, though. Some people seem to fade away but when they are truly gone, it's like they didn't fade away at all."

After hearing the news, Dylan was moved to write a song, "Dignity," that began with the line: "Sick man lookin' for the doctor's cure . . ."

What Press bequeathed to Pete had now been willed to other people's sons. It cut across generations. Boys would still recall it as they became men, but none more than Pete's own boys.

23. PATRIMONY

On Tuesday, January 5, 1988, the morning Pete died, this column item appeared under Bruce Smith's byline in the *Raleigh News and Observer*:

Son of a gun,
Look at Jaeson

Tuesday Turns: There just might be another Pistol smokin' down in Covington, La. Already, Pete Maravich's 8-year-old son, Jaeson, is brandishing derringer-caliber skills in midget league basketball.

"He has great talent," proud papa Pete said in Raleigh last week. "It just depends on what he will do with that God-given talent and how far he will take it."

Jaeson started at age 6, three years later than when Press Maravich handed Pete a basketball and said, "Play."

"Jaeson is just like I was," Maravich said. "He took basketball up two years ago, and it was like a baby duck taking to water. I taught him how to shoot—and he can really shoot. He made 27 of 30 free throws at camp when he had turned just 8.

"He is built like me. Big hands. Big feet. Long arms. He can do what he wants to in basketball. It will depend on how much commitment he has to the game."

Pete's other son, Joshua, 5, is into soccer. But just in case his interest should change, Dad erected a 6-foot basketball goal in the backyard for Joshua to use, at his convenience, of course.

Like his father and his father's father, Jaeson was already tethered to the game, though not as a result of any paternal pressure. Kids his age wanted to Be Like Mike. But Jaeson wanted to be like his dad.

Jaeson had been there at the gym in Hammond just eight months before, as Pete and Frank Schroeder put in six consecutive twelve-hour days filming the *Homework Basketball* videos. As Pete performed, his son remained just out of the camera's view, dribbling and keeping the beats in time with his dad.

To see Jaeson do that spider drill was a treat. The kids at school could not contain their awe.

"How did you do that?" they would ask.

Some of them figured Jaeson's magic was a birthright. After all, he was Pistol Pete's son.

But Jaeson already knew better. There was more to magic than blood. "Practice," he says. "That's all I did."

When his dad was alive, the drills had been a way for Jaeson to keep him close. After he died, they became a way for Jaeson to keep him around, a ritual to summon his spirit. Now it was Jaeson who learned to live with a ghost, one who made frequent, if unannounced, appearances. He might show up at school, whenever kids started talking basketball. He might appear on a highlight clip on ESPN. In the autumn, he appeared at the Superdome, where Jaeson and Josh attended an exhibition between the Jazz and the Washington Bullets. A Barry Mendelson production, "The Pistol Pete Shootout," saw Pete's number 7 retired and raised to the rafters at the Superdome. The evening's program devoted an entire page to the LA Production Group's "Pistol Pete Collection." These included *Heir to a Dream*, the *Homework Basketball* tapes, and a forty-minute highlight video, *Maravich Memories: The LSU Years*. In addition, production was moving forward on a feature directed by Schroeder and written by Darrel Campbell, *The Pistol: The Birth of a Legend*. "Not so much a movie as it is a sermon," noted *Christianity Today*, it was based (very loosely) on Pete's eighth-grade season at Daniel High.

By the time Jaeson was an eighth-grader, he was already averaging 30 points a game. That number, along with his name, conspired to transform him, an extremely shy kid, into a kind of celebrity. It was an unwanted fame, but inevitable. Everybody wanted Jaeson's autograph. Hordes would approach with paper and pen, asking which one was the Maravich boy. Recognizing Jaeson's discomfort, his friends started answering for him. "That's me," they'd say, and sign his name.

Requests for interviews were no less relentless. It wasn't just the newspaper reporters, either. Billy Packer, now CBS's basketball analyst, wanted to do a piece on Jaeson. Then it was ABC News. And so on.

"Every day after practice there'd be somebody different wanting to do an interview," he recalls. "We'd have to stop in the middle of practice because a camera crew came in and wanted to film me. So the rest of the team would go to the other end of the gym to finish the scrimmage, and I'd be off by myself doing drills for the camera. It was too much, too soon, playing with that name."

He had begun to think his life might be easier if he were Jaeson Smith. There would be no comparisons, no ghosts, and, maybe best of all, no autographs. Jaeson Maravich started hiding under the bleachers, sheltered from the autograph seekers.

He made the varsity as a ninth-grader at St. Paul's, a private school in Covington. It was about the last thing he wanted. Playing varsity as a freshman, just like his daddy? That's all anyone would say. No thanks. Jaeson opted to play on the freshman team instead. Still, the requests for autographs and interviews didn't let up.

He was averaging about 35 points, 8 assists, but he wasn't having even a little fun. "Why am I playing?" he asked himself.

Only in retrospect does he understand why: "I played because I liked basketball, but I also wanted to do it for my dad. I felt it was a good way to honor him and be close with him spiritually. I felt like I had to carry on that tradition, like that was part of my being, part of the reason I was here."

The problem was, as Pistol Pete's kid, Jaeson couldn't average a mere 35. He might as well have cursed the family name. "He thought he was supposed to go out and score 50 points a game," Josh told a reporter.

So before the start of his sophomore season, he quit. Jaeson wouldn't even touch a basketball. He lifted weights. He ate prodigious amounts of food. But mostly, he lay around the house and watched TV. Every day after school, he watched three, four, five hours of television. Then he slept. He slept a lot. Looking back, he says, "It was a way of not thinking about anything."

What his daddy went through after ten NBA seasons, Jaeson endured as a tenth-grader at St. Paul's. The depression would last through his junior year.

By then, 1996, his father had been dead eight years. But Jaeson's grief remained fresh. "I was still having a lot of problems with it," he says. "It was still sitting inside of me—I didn't tell anybody—and it was just killing me . . . I was trying to figure out what was missing. Why I was so unhappy?"

Then one day a friend of Jaeson's named Eric King dropped by the house. "Let's go shoot around," he said.

It wasn't as if Jaeson had anything better to do.

There was a run-down park with chain nets a few blocks from the house, right behind the Budweiser plant. Budweiser park, they called it. Mostly, it was black kids who played there.

They shot around for a while, Jaeson and Eric. They played horse. Jaeson was rusty, but a couple of moves—the crossover dribble and the step-back jumper—came back to him instantly.

"Thought you hadn't been playing," said Eric.

The next day Jaeson went back to the park by himself and shot around some more.

It felt good. Real good.

Now Jaeson started to wonder: "Is this what I've been missing?"

By the fall of his senior year, he had grown to six-four. And if his shot had an unorthodox release—generating as much sidespin as backspin—it also had uncanny range. More uncanny, though, was what could be discerned from Jaeson's body language. Aaron James, a Louisianan who had played five seasons with the Jazz, saw Pete's mannerisms replicated with exactitude as he watched Jaeson: "the way he flicks at his nose, the way he stands, the way he puts his hands on his hips, the way he won't look at you if he don't know you."

Though it felt as if he were learning the game all over again, Jaeson had a fine season, scoring 18 points a game and leading St. Paul's as they upset the state's top-ranked team in the opening round of the playoffs. He wore his father's old number, 44, but unlike his father, he was seen cracking a smile on the court.

It happened on a fast break against Central. Jaeson had already begun his ascent when the coach blurted out, "Dunk it."

So he did. Dunking was something else his father had never done in a game. In Jaeson's adrenalized memory, the moment remains as rapturous as it was unexpected. The fans went wild. He had nourished the crowd, and now the crowd nourished him. As Jaeson turned to run back on defense, he could not contain his glee, thinking: *Damn, I gotta start dunking more often.*

The game had changed. It wasn't just the dunking, or even the expectation that white high school players had the capacity for a kind of showtime. Rather, it had been a *coach* who implored him to dunk. Back when Pete was coming up, coaches acted as if they were the appointed guardians of the game's Protestant pieties. As it turned out, though, the game wanted players who could not only play, but who could perform. Press's vision had been correct.

A half century had passed since Press played for the Pittsburgh Ironmen. The NBA, under the aegis of Commissioner David Stern, was now held up as the ideal among professional sports enterprises. Stern's oft-stated model wasn't another league, but the savagely synergistic Disney Corporation. Instead of selling Mickey, Minnie, and Snow White, the NBA was marketing the greatest athletes in team sports, most of them being Americans of African descent.

It was Pete Maravich, however, who had anticipated what the game would become: a hip-hop ballet, a rapper's delight, a cause for great celebration in the corporate suite. Pistol Pete was a harbinger of the high-concept ballplayer. These were the stars identifiable merely as Magic or Charles or, most of all, Michael, athletes who could be reconstituted in a variety of media, guys who could play as easily with animated characters as they could on the street.

In 1997, to celebrate its first fifty years, the NBA enlisted a panel to name the fifty greatest players in its history. Of those fifty, Pete was the only one who would have fared better in the contemporary game than when he had actually played. This much was now accepted as gospel: Pete had been well ahead of his time. "If he was playing today," said Walt Frazier, one of the chosen fifty, "he'd be the most popular player in the league."

He was also the only one of the fifty not still alive. In his place, Jaeson and Josh attended the 1997 All-Star game in Cleveland, where they would accept the honor on their father's behalf. As they awaited their introductions in the tunnel at Gund Arena, the game's greatest fawned over the brothers Maravich. Isiah Thomas told them how much he had learned from watching their father. Magic Johnson, whose championship Lakers teams had appropriated use of the term "Showtime," felt a need to correct the record. "Your pops," he gushed, "he was the original. He was the *real* showtime."

Finally, the P.A. announcer called their names: *Representing Pete Maravich, his sons, Jaeson and Josh.* Theirs was among the loudest ovations, as the boys, now ages seventeen and fourteen, stepped forward into a harsh light, their likenesses appearing simultaneously on the Jumbotron scoreboard. At first, Jaeson feared he would cry.

But then that instinct to well up, that clutch at the back of his throat, gave way to anger. *Why us?* he asked himself. *Why are we the only ones?*

Josh felt it, too: *This is all wrong. He should be here.*

As they left the floor, Charles Barkley pulled them aside. In the last years of Pete's life, Barkley had been his favorite player. Pete wasn't much of a fan by then, but he could still appreciate the unlikely combination of girth and touch, strength and skill. Barkley's game didn't look like anyone else's.

"Y'alls' father," said Barkley, "he'd be real proud."

Jaeson was a gifted scorer and hard worker, with his father's unnatural endurance for practicing alone. But these assets were still not enough to offset the two formative years he had missed as a player. He decided, therefore, to enroll in a prep school. The New Hampton School, all the way up in New Hampshire, might have seemed a curious choice for a boy who, except for a couple of NBA All-Star games, had never been north of Georgia. Then again, New Hampton's program had had its share of basketball scions, including the sons of Indiana coach Bobby Knight, former USC coach George Raveling, and longtime NBA guard Gerald Henderson. It might be good, Jaeson reasoned, to go far away, where the Maravich name held less sway.

"Maybe I can just come up here and just forget about all that," he told a reporter from the *Boston Globe*. "In Louisiana, there was so much pressure."

In preparation for the season, he submitted himself to a grueling weight-lifting regimen. Figuring he could increase a vertical leap that was already about thirty-eight inches, he did a lot of squats—at least one too many. The weighted bar was resting behind his neck when he heard the pop in his lower back.

The next morning Jaeson couldn't get out of bed. The doctor told him there was nothing much he could do but rest. By the time he arrived in New Hampton, he was so well-rested he could barely tie his shoes. A cortisone shot helped—for about a week. The second and third shots, all within a couple of months, brought less relief.

Even in his diminished state, one couldn't help but notice his talent as he worked on his skills, hitting 87 of 100 from behind the 3-point line. The question was, When would he be able to play? After Christmas break, he tried going full-speed. There was a full-court drill that ended with him laying the ball into the basket. He froze in pain, then collapsed. "I couldn't even get up," he says. "Two of the players had to help carry me off the court."

Jaeson went home and spent the better part of six months rehabbing his back. It was during this period that he seized on the brilliant idea to walk on—to try making the team without a scholarship—at Alabama. "Don't even ask me how I came up with that one," he says.

In fact, Jaeson went to Alabama because it was considered big-time SEC basketball, almost an oxymoron in his father's time. He didn't figure to make much of an immediate impact, as he played the same position as an all-conference senior. Then again, just making the team should have qualified as an accomplishment. His back was still far from healed, not to mention the effects of all that time he had missed. Now nineteen, Jaeson had played just one season of organized ball since he was a freshman in high school.

"Basically," he says, "I was starting over."

Big-time SEC schools were not good places for kids looking to start over.

He logged three minutes of playing time that season. "Alabama," he says, "wasn't the right place for me."

Not knowing what else to do, he went back to Covington.

It is a wonder that Jaeson's troubles did not dissuade Josh from pursuing his own fate in the game. For a time, it seemed as if Josh would be spared the comparisons with his father, or the heartbreak that basketball visited upon the Maraviches before him. He played soccer. He rode BMX bikes. He even rode a unicycle. Josh was always in motion, unable to sit still. He got in his share of scrapes at school, too.

"I was a wild child," he says.

Suspecting he had some kind of attention deficit disorder, Jackie had him tested. This was just two or three years after Pete had died. Josh was seven, maybe eight. As the evaluation neared its conclusion, he was given a pencil and paper. "Draw something," said a person he now takes to be a psychiatrist. "Whatever comes to mind."

"Draw anything I want?"

"Anything."

Josh drew a heart. It was a nice enough heart, at least the psychiatrist said so. But without any warning, he began to scribble over it furiously, as if to cover any traces of what he had drawn. Then he began to mutilate the heart, slamming down on it with the pencil point.

"Until it was ripped to bits," he recalls.

That might as well have been the diagnosis: ripped-up heart.

Josh managed to avoid basketball until junior high school. By then, however, its pull on him seemed inexorable. It didn't have much to do with his father, at least not consciously. He remained willfully ignorant of Pistol Pete, refusing even to watch the *Homework Basketball* videos. "I hated seeing my dad," he says. "It would just mess me up mentally." He preferred to recall the man who had carried him on his shoulders at Sea World, not the ballplayer.

Rather, it was the ballplaying itself—the rhythms and language of the game—that spoke to him, that had quite suddenly staked a claim on his heart.

It just happened. One day, he's messing around on that damn unicycle. The next day, Jimbo McLachlan, who used to watch quizzically from across the street as Pete tried to mow his lawn, sees him spinning a ball on his finger. Jimbo figured the kid was going through another of his phases.

Basketball wasn't a phase, though. "It was a very deep love, that I really can't explain," says Josh. "All I know is, when the game was good, it was my life. Everywhere I went I wanted to hold the ball. I thought: 'This is what I'm going to do for the rest of my life.' "

He asked his mom where she kept all the tapes. He would watch them in the den—but only if Jackie and Jaeson were not around. He didn't want them to see him weeping.

LSU Memories was his favorite. Josh could watch it for hours. *I want to be like him*, he thought.

He watched with great care as his dad went behind his back on the run, faked the pass, then laid it up, as if he controlled the ball with a jai alai cesta. *Impossible*, thought Josh. Then he went out to the basket in his driveway, and in four or five hours, he had the move down pat. He even managed to do it in a game. That was eighth grade.

About the only one of his dad's moves that Josh couldn't seem to master was the cue ball pass, in which the ball was thrown in one direction, only to have it spin off in another. It was the move that had led Red Auerbach to note that Pete was alone among players in his capacity to violate of the laws of physics.

Still, as he practiced in the driveway or in the gym at St. Paul's, Josh made believe he possessed superpowers inherent in his bloodline. He imagined he was his father. "I'd start doing some crazy shit and I'd always narrate," he recalls. *Pistol goes left. Pistol goes right. Pistol—behind the back. Pistol with the hook. Pistol shoots—scores!*

He even did his own breathy approximation of crowd noise. *HAAAA-HHHHH!!!!*

And when Josh wasn't imagining that he was his father, he imagined—or maybe, *knew*—that his father could see him. *Eyes of mine.* "I always wanted him to be proud of me," says Josh. "I wanted him to see."

He wasn't the player Jaeson was. He didn't have quite the range, or the height (he'd be six-three by the time he finished high school, two inches shorter than his brother). On the other hand, he was quick and completely at ease on the court. Kids were more than willing to give him the ball. Some of them, he recalls, before they even knew his last name.

Josh enjoyed the attention that came with leading St. Paul's in scoring. The game was his joy. Being the second son had its advantages, first among them being the easing of expectations. It afforded Josh an opportunity that had eluded his brother, his father, even his grandfather. "The game came to me," he says.

But this high harmony gave way to the most fierce and primal urges as soon as he squared off to go one-on-one with his brother. Their battles in an otherwise idyllic driveway setting would end violently—the only rule, however implicit, being a prohibition against blows to the face. "It was all body shots," says Josh. "Even if we went to the ground."

Jaeson was victorious in every contest but one, the outcome of which remains in dispute. As Josh scored what he thought to be his first winning basket—finally!—Jaeson shook his head, his mouth creasing into a thin smile.

"Nah, bring it back," he said. "That don't count."

"What?" said Josh, recognizing his brother's expression to be a smirk.

"You walked."

"I did not walk." That smirk signaled a lack of respect—and that set Josh off.

"Yeah, you did," said Jaeson, as if he were trying to be patient with a little kid. "You walked."

The first accessible object in Josh's view was an old broom handle. He wasted little time bringing it down, Samurai style, over his brother's head. The broom handle broke. Jaeson did not. Instead, he smirked again.

For a moment, Josh thought his heart had stopped. Then he ran off, not to return until long after dark.

Curiously enough, there was an equal and opposite feeling to the one that possessed these brothers in the driveway. "When we played each other, it was gruesome," says Josh, "but when we played on the same team, everything flowed—smooth, just perfect."

Faced with a common opponent, Josh had no problem deferring to his older brother. As soon as he got the ball, he'd be looking for Jaeson. If he drove, he knew exactly—without having to look—where Jaeson would be positioned for the 3-pointer. When Jaeson went to the basket, Josh knew to get his man out of the lane. And when Jaeson took the rebound on the break, Josh knew to start sprinting.

Wingman, middle man, go . . .

The brothers knew all this without ever having been told. Such was the instinct that had traveled across generations through their blood.

By the summer of 1999, Jimbo McLachlan, now dating Jackie, had grown concerned about Jaeson. The boy was despondent, feeling that his basketball options had run out since returning home from Alabama. But Jimbo knew a guy who knew the coach at Gulf Coast Community College in Perkinston, Mississippi. His name was Bob Weathers, and Jimbo gave him a call.

"I got this kid," he explained.

"Sorry, we already signed all our players," said Weathers, then entering his fortieth season at Gulf Coast.

"Past, present, or future," said Jimbo, "you don't have anyone good as this kid. You get the best sonofabitch you can find, and I'm telling you right now, he can't guard this boy."

Weathers agreed, reluctantly, to watch the boy play. "Can't promise you anything," he said.

The tryout, such as it was, took place in Perkinston, a three-on-three game pitting Jaeson, Josh, and another guy against three Gulf Coast players. They went hard for about half an hour.

"I might have missed one shot," Jaeson recalls.

Finally, Coach Weathers called over to Jimbo. "Can we sign him right now?"

It turned out to be a great season for Jaeson, who shot 90 percent from the line, 52 percent from the field, and 44 percent from behind the 3-point line. He averaged better than 28 points, but toward the end of the season was regularly putting up 40-point games for the Bulldogs. "Offensively," says Weathers, "nobody could stop him."

More than that, though, Jaeson recovered a sense of himself, and what he might yet be. Not long after arriving in Perkinston, he abandoned his habit of wearing dark sunglasses and staring at the ground. Over the Christmas break, he had the word "PISTOL" tattooed in gothic letters across his left shoulder.

The needle etched an acknowledgment in ink and blood: Jaeson could be his own man and yet remain his father's son. In fact, he had no choice. He was who he was; there was no sense hiding from it, especially now that Gulf Coast Community College had become a hot ticket.

Weathers had had plenty of good players over the years, and nobody much cared. But the Maravich name was still money, especially deep in the South. As word spread about Pete's son, the Bulldogs found themselves playing before packed houses on the road. People were being turned away at the door, as many as 500 at a time.

They never stopped asking Weathers if the boy was as good as his daddy.

And Weathers never stopped telling them: "There hasn't been *anybody* good as his daddy."

While at Gulf Coast, Jaeson got another tattoo, now the height of basketball chic. This one was stenciled over his heart: the numbers 23, 44, and 7—his father's numbers—inside an NBA basketball. Jaeson left a space for the number he hoped a pro team would one day assign him. This was his goal: the pros. He felt more comfortable inscribing it on his chest, where it would remain hidden under his jersey, than proclaiming it aloud.

Before he left Perkinston, Jaeson turned down offers from Ole

Miss and Mississippi State, both SEC schools, to sign with McNeese State in Lake Charles, Louisiana. It was close to home, and he liked the coach. Ron Everhart was from West Virginia. He had a foul mouth, a big heart, and he knew the game. There was always a dip of tobacco in his mouth.

"He's Poppa Press reincarnated," Jaeson told his mother.

Jaeson worked hard getting ready for the season and started maxing out on squats again. And once again, he tore up his back. He was done for the season before there even was a season. The following year, Coach Everhart took a job up at Northeastern University in Boston. And as much as Jaeson liked Everhart, he wasn't going back up north.

"Coach," he said, "I don't want to go that far away again."

He went back to Covington and took some classes at Southeastern Louisiana State. The seemingly endless cycle of despair and rapture, disappointment and hope—all that the game had brought the Maraviches—had finally run its course. He was done with basketball.

Still, Jaeson felt no relief, as basketball wasn't done with him. His disposition remained incurably sullen. He missed his dad, maybe worse than ever.

And in due course, he started missing the game. After all, basketball was a way of keeping his daddy alive.

Then one day he got a call from a guy he had played with at Gulf Coast. "Where you at?" asked Jaeson.

"William Carey."

"Who the hell is William Carey?"

As it happened, William Carey was an English cobbler-cum-missionary who published *An Enquiry into the Obligations of Christians to Use Means for the Conversion of the Heathens.* That was 1792, the year before Carey left for India, where he spent the rest of his natural life. More relevant to Jaeson, Carey would also become the namesake of a small Baptist college in Hattiesburg, Mississippi, an hour and forty-five minutes from Covington.

The Crusaders, as they were called, competed under the auspices of the National Association of Intercollegiate Athletics and were not bound by NCAA eligibility requirements. Better yet, their basketball team played a run-and-gun style—"like streetball," says

Jaeson—bound to please anyone with a Pistol Pete pedigree. Jaeson transferred early in 2002. In little more than a year, he would be selected as an NAIA third-team All-American, with a burgeoning reputation as a long-distance bomber.

Of course, not everyone had been easily convinced. Loyola coach Jerry Hernandez had instructed his players to let the Maravich kid fire away. Not a good decision, as Jaeson went 9 for 14 from behind the 3-point line, finishing with 41 points.

"Kind of freaky," Hernandez said later, noting the similarities between Jaeson and his father.

Jaeson, for his part, wasn't buying any of it. "Forty-one," he said, "would have been an average game for my dad."

Below average, actually.

Jaeson was playing point guard now. Having the ball in his hands suited him, as he was actually timed to be faster with the ball than without. ("Guess that's something I got from my dad," he says.) What's more, the position allowed him to create, and nowhere was that creativity held in higher esteem than at the predominantly black schools like Xavier University in New Orleans.

Xavier's home court was called the Barn. It wasn't much more than an old high school gym. But Jaeson would think of the Barn as the best place he ever played. "They appreciate good ball down there," he says.

The sequence Jaeson would always recall began with him hitting a long 3. In Carey's next possession, he came downcourt looking as if he were going to shoot the 3 again, but instead, froze his man, blew past him with a crossover dribble and drove for a basket, which he scored despite a foul. The crowd erupted. Finally, he soared into the lane as if to dunk, only to be fouled again. This time, though, he gathered himself in midair, absorbing and redirecting the force of the blow, flipping the ball behind him, over his shoulder. It hit the backboard, then dropped through the net.

"It was like a Pistol Pete shot," Jaeson explains.

Fans had to be restrained from coming onto the court. For the rest of the game, they would cheer and chant whenever he had the ball.

Cross him over, Jay!

Bust another 3 in his eye!

He had never felt that kind of love from a crowd. "I play more black than I play white," he says.

Still, Jaeson's most memorable game might have been against Alabama's Athens State. It was January 5, 2003, the sixteenth anniversary of his father's death. The trauma Jaeson associated with the date had never dissipated. He could still see his dad in his dreams. Pete would be sitting up in the stands.

Jaeson scored 34 that night, much to his own relief. "I wanted to have a good game for him," he explained.

Him. The way Jaeson spoke of his father struck William Neikirk, a *Chicago Tribune* correspondent, who wrote, "It was as if 'Pistol' Pete was in the stands, watching."

After concluding his high school career as co-MVP of the district, Josh made a momentous decision, one that went squarely against the urgings of his mother and his brother. In fact, everyone but Josh seemed to realize that trying to walk on at his father's alma mater would be an excruciating way to prove that he was his own man. Even LSU's coach, John Brady, had grave misgivings about Josh playing in the P-Mac, as the Assembly Center was called.

Brady paid a visit to Jackie and her sons, presenting all the arguments why Josh should not attend LSU. Walk-ons were practice fodder; the best of them usually didn't last long. Brady would not extend himself to make the kid comfortable. He made it clear that he already had plenty of guards on scholarship. He didn't need a celebrity bench warmer—especially not one with that last name. By the same token, the political implications were clear for a man whose team played in the Pete Maravich Assembly Center. As Brady himself would explain, "I certainly wasn't going to be the coach not to let the son of Pistol Pete walk on at LSU."

But Josh remained resolute. "I wanted to do it for my dad," he says. "Even if I didn't play, I wanted him to be proud of me. I saw what my brother went through. I didn't want to hide from my name. The only way I felt I could do that was to go to LSU and show everybody that I wasn't afraid, that I could step out of the shadow."

Step away from the ghost.

By his own admission, Josh wasn't ready as a freshman. Brady declared him a red-shirt, meaning that he practiced with the team, but couldn't dress out for games. Most nights, Josh stayed late at the P-Mac with Antonio Hudson and Xavier Whipple, black teammates who soon became the best of friends. They could often be found having impromptu dunking contests in the Dungeon, a practice gym in the bowels of the Assembly Center, or tooling around campus in Hudson's Expedition, its fifteen-inch speakers blaring T.I. and Lil John, the latest hip-hop sensations from Atlanta.

"Josh was friendly with a couple of the white guys," says Whipple, from McIntyre, Georgia. "But he just fit in more with us."

By the time he returned for his sophomore season, Josh had put on twenty pounds of muscle without losing any quickness. He had begun to make a good account of himself in practice; even one of the assistant coaches took note, suggesting that he might be ready to run with the second team. That never happened, though. Brady wouldn't hear of it.

At one point during a slump in his sophomore year, Antonio Hudson even went to the coach, suggesting that he give some of the other guys a chance to play. Some of the other guys included Josh.

"Brady looked right through me," says Hudson.

"Coach took him because he was Josh *Maravich*," says Whipple, a guard who broke into the starting lineup that season. "He never had any intentions of playing him at all."

Josh would appear in seven games that season, a total of ten minutes. He hit both his shots from the field, each of which drew a standing ovation. He had become a fan favorite at an arena that doubled as a shrine to his father's memory. A banner representing Pete's number 23 jersey hung over the seats. Then there was the "Pete Maravich Pass," a section of the concourse that included video and photographic tributes and the 1970 Naismith Trophy behind protective glass. Teenagers attended games in replica Maravich jerseys. But even as they wore Pete's number, they called for Josh.

Put Pete's kid in the game!

Occasionally, they struck up a chant: *We want Josh! We want Josh!*

Josh put on his best face, but the chanting came to hurt him. He hadn't gone to LSU to be some kind of a mascot. "He didn't think of himself as a novelty," says Brian Green, also a walk-on. "He wanted to show he was a good player."

"Every game he just sat on the bench and looked at his daddy's jersey," says Antonio Hudson. "No way for him to hide from that."

In practice, his finest moments became his most humiliating. As per Josh's recollection, it would happen just about every time he scored in a scrimmage. He might beat his man and pull up for a baseline jumper. But he'd recall Brady blowing the whistle even before the ball went through the net. A disdainful wince would come across the coach's face as he began to excoriate the guy who just got beat, reminding him that he wasn't guarding an All-American from Kentucky or Florida. "C'mon," Brady would say. "This is Josh Maravich . . . *Josh*."

"As a player," says Xavier Whipple, "that's the stuff that just kills you."

Josh would look up, snatching a glance at the banner hanging from the rafters.

Xavier could see what was happening.

Josh just hoped that his daddy could not.

In 1999, the *Times-Picayune* published a list, voted on by the Louisiana Sports Writers Association and the Louisiana Sports Hall of Fame, naming Pete Maravich as the state's top athlete of the century. The roster included ever sacred football heroes like Billy Cannon and Jim Taylor; quarterbacks Terry Bradshaw, Y. A. Tittle, and Archie Manning; Hall of Fame big men like Elvin Hayes and Karl Malone and Bob Pettit; even a couple of baseball players who had been enshrined in Cooperstown, Mel Ott and Lou Brock.

At the dawn of a new millennium, the idea of Pistol Pete was more potent than ever. In March 2001, on the eve of the NCAA championship game, CBS aired a ninety-minute documentary devoted to his life and times. It wasn't just kids at the LSU games who were wearing his jersey. He resonated in ways that cut across the usual social and racial divides. A generation of aspiring players had now grown up on the *Homework Basketball* videos. Duke coach Mike Krzyzewski, operating at the very apex of the basketball establishment, recommended the tapes to recruits who needed to work on their ballhandling skills.

But, then, so were they endorsed by Rafer Alston. "I still watch tapes of Pistol Pete, always," said Alston, then heading into his seventh NBA season.

Though he had just signed a $29 million contract with the Toronto Raptors, Alston was best known as a playground legend, Skip to My Lou. He had acquired the handle while still a teenager in Harlem's Rucker Park, where the P.A. announcer used the lyric from a children's song to celebrate Alston's outrageously high, taunting dribble. Skip was in many ways the prototypical schoolyard fable: a fatherless truant more at home on an asphalt court than in a classroom. But as he grew up in the age of the handheld camera, footage of his exploits became, like bootleg DJ tapes, an underground sensation. In time, And1, a company that made basketball sneakers for the hip-hop generation, would offer a mix tape starring Alston just for trying on its shoes at FootAction. The retail chain sold 200,000 And1's in just three weeks. The success of the mix tape featuring Skip to My Lou led to more mix tapes and eventually an ESPN reality show, *Streetball*. An amalgam of hip-hop vernacular and Showtime, the formerly titled City Game had achieved new legitimacy. Nothing on the And1 tour could approach what Pete had done in college or professional competition, but with better camera angles and voluble MC's, *Streetball* might have had better production values. Kids all over the country were imitating Skip.

What they didn't know, however, was that Skip was imitating Pistol. "He was so deceptive," said Alston. ". . . That's what I wanted to be: the guy that could fool you with the basketball."

The business of basketball owed an ever-increasing debt to the Pistol; his was a legacy reflected in the tally at malls across America, wherever sneakers and retro jerseys were available for purchase. By 2005, Adidas would come out with a new line of Pistol Pete merchandise and shoes. The world had changed, but Pistol Pete was still what everybody wanted. As one black NBA executive said admiringly, "A white boy with flavor."

None of this incessant fascination with Pistol Pete made life any easier for Jaeson or Josh. In early November 2003, as he prepared for his senior season at William Carey, Jaeson suddenly stopped sleeping. Instead, he watched informercials and thought about basketball. He would play back games in his head, like the time he scored 47 at Gulf Coast. Now it occurred to him that three free throws would have given him an even 50. "I was never satisfied," he says. "It was never enough."

After four nights, he could barely walk up stairs, much less go to practice. Doctors told him the problem was anxiety-related. They gave him a pill, Ambien.

"I slept about an hour," he says.

Ambien was the first of about eight or nine sleep and anxiety medications he would try. Nothing really worked. Perhaps he felt less anxious, but no less obsessed or sleep-deprived. "Jaeson isn't real interested in anything but basketball," one of his teammates told the *New York Times*. "It isn't really healthy."

The days were even worse than his sleepless nights. He often felt as if he were about to pass out.

And yet, by season's end he had been selected as an NAIA first-team All-American. In April, a month before graduating with a degree in psychology, he attended the Portsmouth Invitational Camp in Virginia, where front-office types assessed prospective NBA rookies. Jerry West, Larry Bird, and Kevin McHale were sitting in the front row as he came out for his first scrimmage game.

"It helped that I hit my first shot," he says.

He hit a bunch more, going 4 for 4 from behind the 3-point line. The next game, though, saw him shoot 1 for 5.

Maybe it would have been different if he had been running the point, he thought. Or maybe if his dad and grandpa had been around to teach him. "No telling how good I would've been then," he'd say.

Or maybe it was just that he was going on two or three hours of sleep.

As it happened, Jaeson wasn't drafted, but he did get a four-day try-out with the Dallas Mavericks. They liked what they saw, which was a lot of potential. They wanted him to play on their summer league team, then maybe a year or so in Europe.

But the closer he got to the pros, the less he could sleep. Josh told the Mavericks he needed to get the problem fixed once and for all. Again, he went back to Covington. He saw all kinds of doctors. They gave him a new assortment of meds.

The bulk of his days were spent at a local health club. He'd push weights for a couple of hours. Then it was another two hours on the court, as he drilled himself without mercy. Next, he'd go forty-five minutes to an hour on an elliptical machine or treadmill. He'd finish by working his abdominal muscles and doing some yoga. Six days a week he worked himself to the point of exhaustion. But it didn't help him sleep. Nor did it grant him any peace.

"Part of me wants to be in the NBA, and part of me doesn't," he says. "I pray about it every day. I don't know whether he wants me to be an NBA player or somebody who's going to be doing camps and helping kids."

He. Did he mean God, or his father? Did he make the distinction?

And what of that *helping kids?* Was it a damaged child who illuminated the destination for Jaeson Maravich? A couple of years before, at the camp in Clearwater that still bore his father's name, he saw a runty kid with a buzz cut get off the bus crying. The boy was eight years old, and he wanted to go home.

The other kids teased him. He couldn't shoot. Then he'd get all nervous, which only made it worse. He'd start throwing up airballs.

So Jaeson took him to the gym every morning at 10:30 when everybody else was in the snack bar. They worked on mechanics and form, and by the end of the week the kid hit three foul shots in a row. He was never going to be a ballplayer. But three in a row was something he'd always remember.

And so would Jaeson.

Without warning, the kid put the ball down and gave him a hug. It was better than a 40-point game.

• • •

As for Josh, the two baskets he tallied in his second season turned out to be the highlights of a college career that degenerated into a series of humiliating rituals. After playing only ten minutes in 2002–2003, he would play a single minute the following season.

He was persona non grata in practice. The coach would mention his name only to admonish another player. *You just let Josh Maravich go by you, son.*

Josh would look up at his father's banner and mumble to himself. *What am I doing here? Please help me.* "I dropped a couple tears on that court," he says.

"Brady would tell everybody how he admired Pete Maravich, but then he goes and treats his son like crap," says Jackie. "People who were there called me and told me how Brady humiliated him a couple of times in practice. I told Josh, 'I would've quit a long time ago.' "

The thought had crossed his mind, but he wasn't quitting. "I had to prove I wasn't scared of my own name," he says.

By the 2004–2005 season, Josh had stopped working hard. A depression set in. Perhaps at some level he knew he was desecrating the game. He attended practice in body, but not in spirit.

"Almost like I was a ghost," he says.

"Coach didn't even notice if he was there or not," says Xavier Whipple. "That's how bad it got."

Josh might slip out with a ball and go to the Dungeon. There, he would shoot around, trying to remember how good the game could feel, pretending once again that he was Pistol Pete Maravich.

The low point came on January 29, 2005, at home against Mississippi State. The fans had begun to chant: *We want Josh.* Finally, with just a couple of seconds left on the clock, Brady motioned for him to go in the game. But the ref wouldn't allow him in, as the T-shirt under his uniform was not regulation color.

So he stripped down to the waist, frozen as the fans giggled at him. He tossed the T-shirt aside, put his jersey back on, and reported to the scorer's table. As soon as he got in the game, the buzzer sounded.

I didn't come here to be no giggle-ass, he thought.

● ● ●

The fans might be laughing, but he had earned a reverence he had always sought. Jaeson sat for a year at Alabama and it almost killed him. But Josh had now served four years on the bench.

"I could never have done what my brother did," says Jaeson.

How many times had the Maravich boys come to blows under the basket in their driveway? All Josh wanted was his big brother's respect.

But only now, having proven himself brave enough to stick it out as a giggle-ass, did he have it.

Fraternal histories are fraught with peril.

Harry's Corner, 900 Chartres Street, is located in the French Quarter of New Orleans. The high-back bar stools are upholstered in Naugahyde. The video poker machine holds patrons in a trance. A sign on the wall reads: "Drunk is not an excuse."

Here at Harry's, even the tourists are regulars. It is 8 A.M., and the bartender came on two hours ago. This is a good shift for him, as there are fewer fights in the late morning hours. Lord knows, he's seen enough of that.

There's a rim of scar tissue along the bridge of his nose. His teeth are rotting. A baseball cap identifies him as a member of a Marine recon team. He doesn't want to talk.

The deep scars you can't see. His brother has been dead seventeen years. He's estranged from his sister-in-law. The girl who was born his daughter lives in North Carolina now. Diana is a research scientist, working for one of the big drug companies.

"She changed his life totally," he says.

Changed Press's life, he means.

He is told that Josh would like to see him.

"I'm easy to find," he says.

Then Ronnie Maravich puts on his dark glasses, the ones that shield his eyes. Now he asks about his nephews. He hasn't seen them since they were children. "From what I know, they're good guys," he says. "They must have heard I'm some kind of monster."

● ● ●

March 5, 2005.

It is Senior Day, and LSU is playing Vanderbilt at the P-Mac. This is the last time Josh will dress out in the arena named for his father. He has decided to be considered an outgoing senior. The coaches, he believes, don't want him around. He doesn't want to be around, either. He wants to go out with his boys, Xavier and Antonio. Still, that's not the real reason either.

His photograph appears with the other seniors on the cover of the game program. He issues a perfunctory thank you to the boosters at the pregame brunch. Soon, he'll be introduced before the big home crowd. His name commands a standing ovation. His mother and brother hug him at center court. But Josh seems stiff, almost frozen. He wants to point up at his father's banner, but can't. "I had so many emotions running through me," he would recall. "I felt like I was paralyzed."

At halftime, there are more introductions as the fans are asked to "welcome players from the Press Maravich Era." A procession of old guys—all of them white, except for Collis Temple—trudge onto the court. It is an awkward moment, as they find themselves suddenly on display. Their bodies are destined to lose this war of attrition, a physical state just beyond middle age. Drinking light beer can do only so much. The years have wrapped themselves around their bellies. It is difficult to imagine them as the boys they once were.

Someone in the stands is heard to ask, "Who are they?"

"They're the ones played with Maravich."

Ralph Jukkola still gets calls at home at odd hours: "Are you the Ralph Jukkola who played with Pete?"

The game resumes. LSU plays the kind of fast-paced, athletic basketball that Press had envisioned as the norm—everything but the baggy shorts. LSU beats Vanderbilt, 81–69, the Tigers concluding their season undefeated at home. On Senior Day, the only senior not to play is Josh Maravich.

He looks up at the banner and holds it all in, the tears and the anger. In a few moments he'll be sitting at his locker, hiding his face in his hands.

Xavier Whipple taps him on the shoulder. "Your daddy'd be proud of you, dog."

It's over, the affliction encoded in his basketball genes. The game has no claim on him anymore. He's broken through, made his peace with his holy ghost.

"I couldn't have put up with the stuff he put up with," says Antonio. "I'd have walked."

And now, at last, so does Josh, walking from the Pete Maravich Assembly Center with his brother, as yet unsaved, but still unbowed. Jimbo, now married to Jackie, takes their p icture as they leave the building.

Eyes of mine.

What is it that they see?

Dexter Bott, student-manager for their grandfather, is walking toward them on the concourse. He's wearing a rumpled seersucker jacket, his shirttail half-tucked. His hair is long, unruly, and gray, giving him the appearance of an odd wizard. The too-big, old-school sneakers add a clownish effect. That's how Jaeson will recall him, as "that crazy dude with the Chuck Taylors."

These would be black, low-cut Converse, one of which he now removes and hands to Josh. "These were your father's," he says. "Freshman year."

Josh inspects the canvas upper: size 12, just like he wears. Inside, written in indelible pen, is an identifying mark: "F-24."

"I don't know if you knew it," says Bott, "but your dad wore number 24 as a freshman."

LSU didn't have a 23 freshman jersey. Jaeson knew; Josh does not. Josh is still examining the sneaker. He's tempted to try it on, but then thinks better of it. He hands the shoe back. "Cool," he says. "You can put 'em on eBay."

The conversation trips through time. The famous *going down shot* at Georgia, remember that? Each of Pete's teammates has his own version: Pete flipping the ball into the basket, the cheerleaders carrying him off.

How did he do it?

And why?

It is impossible to distinguish what is remembered from what actually happened. Memory becomes its own fact.

Still, Jaeson and Josh are curious. They have never seen the shot, as no film exists. Did he bank it in? Was his back turned to the basket? How could he even see the rim?

It's the crazy dude with the Chuck Taylors who knows the secret. He was there, looking right in Pete's eyes as he put the ball up.

Pete didn't need to see the basket.

It wasn't something to see.

It was something to feel.

Still is.

"Joy," says the crazy dude. "It was pure joy."

PETE MARAVICH
THE NUMBERS

Collegiate Totals

FRESHMAN 1966–67

TOTALS	FG	FGA	PCT.	FT	FTA	PCT.	RB	A	FP	TP
Season 17 games	273	604	.452	195	234	.833	176	124	48	741
SEC 7 games	111	239	.464	86	103	.835	56	45	22	308

REBOUNDING AVERAGE: 10.4
SEC 8.0

POINT AVERAGE: 43.6
SEC 44.0

ASSIST AVERAGE: 6.9
SEC 6.4

SEASON RECORD
Won 17
Lost 2

SEC RECORD
Won 6
Lost 1

PETE MARAVICH: THE NUMBERS

SOPHOMORE 1967–68

GAME	FG	FGA	PCT.	FT	FTA	PCT.	RB	A	PF	TP
LSU 97 Tampa 81	20	50	.400	8	9	.889	16	4	1	48
LSU 87 Texas 74	15	34	.441	12	16	.750	5	5	2	42
LSU 90 Loyola 56	22	43	.512	7	11	.636	9	4	2	51
LSU 94 Wisconsin 96	16	40	.400	10	13	.769	9	6	5	42
LSU 100 Fl. State 130	17	41	.415	8	10	.800	5	9	3	42
LSU 81 Mississippi 68	17	34	.500	12	13	.923	11	3	4	46
LSU 111 Miss. State 87	22	40	.550	14	16	.875	8	3	2	58
LSU 81 Alabama 70	10	30	.333	10	11	.909	6	5	3	30
LSU 76 Auburn 72	20	38	.526	15	17	.882	9	1	2	55
LSU 90 Florida 97	9	22	.409	14	17	.824	10	8	5	32
LSU 79 Georgia 76	14	37	.378	14	17	.824	11	5	3	42
LSU 100 Tulane 91	20	42	.476	12	15	.800	5	8	4	52
LSU 104 Clemson 81	14	29	.483	5	6	.833	6	2	5	33
LSU 95 Kentucky 121	19	51	.373	14	17	.824	11	2	3	52
LSU 91 Vanderbilt 99	22	57	.386	10	15	.667	6	3	4	54

PETE MARAVICH: THE NUMBERS

GAME	FG	FGA	PCT.	FT	FTA	PCT.	RB	A	PF	TP
LSU 96 Kentucky 109	16	38	.421	12	15	.800	8	3	4	44
LSU 67 Tennessee 87	9	34	.265	3	3	1.000	6	0	5	21
LSU 69 Auburn 74	18	47	.383	13	13	1.000	6	1	1	49
LSU 93 Florida 92(OT)	17	48	.354	13	15	.867	7	3	4	47
LSU 73 Georgia 78	20	47	.426	11	18	.611	4	2	4	51
LSU 99 Alabama 89	24	52	.462	11	13	.846	12	3	2	59
LSU 94 Miss. State 83	13	38	.342	8	12	.667	7	7	4	34
LSU 99 Tulane 92	21	47	.447	13	15	.867	5	0	3	55
LSU 85 Mississippi 87	13	26	.500	14	16	.875	4	8	2	40
LSU 71 Tennessee 74	7	18	.389	3	4	.750	3	1	5	17
LSU 86 Vanderbilt 115	17	39	.436	8	11	.727	6	9	3	42
Season Totals 26 Games	432	1022	.422	274	338	.810	195	105	85	1138
SEC Totals 18 Games	274	696	.394	199	243	.819	135	67	60	773

REBOUNDING AVERAGE: 7.5
SEC   7.5

POINT AVERAGE: 43.8
SEC   42.9

ASSIST AVERAGE: 4.0
SEC   3.7

LSU SEASON RECORD
Won   14
Lost   12

LSU SEC RECORD
Won   8
Lost   10

JUNIOR 1968–69

GAME	FG	FGA	PCT.	FT	FTA	PCT.	RB	A	PF	TP
LSU 109 Loyola 82	22	34	.647	8	9	.889	7	11	1	52
LSU 86 Clemson 85	10	32	.313	18	22	.818	4	4	3	38
LSU 99 Tulane 101	20	48	.417	15	20	.750	7	2	4	55
LSU 93 Florida 89	17	32	.531	11	15	.733	8	5	3	45
LSU 98 Georgia 89	18	33	.545	11	16	.688	10	5	3	47
LSU 84 Wyoming 78	14	34	.412	17	24	.708	6	2	2	45
LSU 101 OK City 85	19	36	.528	2	5	.400	8	7	2	40
LSU 94 Duquesne 91	18	36	.500	17	21	.810	2	6	3	53
LSU 82 Alabama 85	19	49	.388	4	4	1.000	10	5	4	42
LSU 92 Vanderbilt 94	15	30	.500	8	13	.615	4	3	3	38
LSU 71 Auburn 90	16	41	.390	14	18	.778	5	5	3	46

PETE MARAVICH: THE NUMBERS

GAME	FG	FGA	PCT.	FT	FTA	PCT.	RB	A	PF	TP
LSU 96 Kentucky 108	20	48	.417	12	14	.857	11	2	3	52
LSU 68 Tennessee 81	8	18	.444	5	8	.625	4	2	5	21
LSU 120 Pittsburgh 79	13	34	.382	14	18	.778	8	11	3	40
LSU 81 Mississippi 84	11	33	.333	9	13	.692	11	5	4	31
LSU 95 Miss. State 71	14	32	.438	5	6	.833	11	10	3	33
LSU 81 Alabama 75	15	30	.500	8	12	.667	5	6	1	38
LSU 94 Tulane 110	25	51	.490	16	20	.800	10	1	4	66
LSU 79 Florida 95	14	41	.341	22	27	.815	6	2	2	50
LSU 93 Auburn 81	20	44	.455	14	15	.933	3	5	3	54
LSU 83 Vanderbilt 85	14	33	.424	7	8	.875	8	8	3	35
LSU 89 Kentucky 103	21	53	.396	3	7	.429	5	2	4	45
LSU 63 Tennessee 87	8	18	.444	4	8	.500	3	7	3	20
LSU 76 Mississippi 78	21	39	.538	7	11	.636	3	1	2	49
LSU 99 Miss. State 89	20	49	.408	15	19	.789	4	5	2	55
LSU 90 Georgia 80	21	48	.438	16	25	.640	6	4	4	58
Season Totals 26 Games	433	976	.444	282	378	.746	169	128	77	1148

PETE MARAVICH: THE NUMBERS

GAME	FG	FGA	PCT.	FT	FTA	PCT.	RB	A	PF	TP
SEC Totals										
18 Games	292	671	.435	175	239	.732	117	82	55	759

REBOUNDING AVERAGE:	6.5
SEC	6.5

POINT AVERAGE:	44.2
SEC	42.2

ASSIST AVERAGE:	4.9
SEC	4.6

LSU SEASON RECORD
Won   13
Lost   13

LSU SEC RECORD
Won   7
Lost   11

SENIOR 1969–70

GAME	FG	FGA	PCT.	FT	FTA	PCT.	RB	A	PF	TP
LSU 94										
Oregon St. 72	14	32	.438	15	19	.789	5	7	1	43
LSU 100										
Loyola 87	18	36	.500	9	10	.900	6	6	4	45
LSU 109										
Vanderbilt 86	26	54	.481	9	10	.900	10	5	1	61
LSU 97										
Tulane 91	17	42	.405	12	19	.632	4	5	3	46
LSU 98										
Sthrn. Cal. 101	18	43	.419	14	16	.875	6	4	3	50
LSU 111										
Clemson 103	22	30	.733	5	8	.625	6	9	3	49
LSU 76										
Oregon St. 68	8	23	.349	30	31	.968	1	8	3	46

PETE MARAVICH: THE NUMBERS

GAME	FG	FGA	PCT.	FT	FTA	PCT.	RB	A	PF	TP
LSU 84 UCLA 133	14	42	.333	10	12	.833	4	7	4	38
LSU 80 St. John's 70	20	44	.455	13	16	.813	8	1	2	53
LSU 94 Yale 97	13	28	.464	8	11	.727	5	8	4	34
LSU 90 Alabama 83	22	42	.524	11	18	.611	7	2	4	55
LSU 70 Auburn 79	18	46	.391	8	11	.727	6	2	4	44
LSU 96 Kentucky 109	21	44	.477	13	15	.867	5	4	4	55
LSU 71 Tennessee 59	12	23	.522	5	7	.714	4	9	3	29
LSU 109 Mississippi 86	21	46	.457	11	15	.733	5	12	3	53
LSU 109 Miss. State 91	21	40	.525	7	9	.778	3	6	4	49
LSU 97 Florida 75	20	38	.526	12	16	.750	9	7	1	52
LSU 104 Alabama 106	26	57	.456	17	21	.810	5	4	3	69
LSU 127 Tulane 114	18	45	.400	13	15	.867	4	6	3	49
LSU 94 Florida 85	16	35	.457	6	10	.600	6	8	2	38
LSU 99 Vanderbilt 89	14	46	.304	10	13	.769	5	3	2	38
LSU 70 Auburn 64	18	46	.391	10	15	.667	8	4	4	46

GAME	FG	FGA	PCT.	FT	FTA	PCT.	RB	A	PF	TP
LSU 88 Georgia 86	17	34	.500	3	6	.500	2	6	3	37
LSU 105 Kentucky 121	23	42	.548	18	22	.818	4	7	4	64
LSU 87 Tennessee 88	10	24	.417	10	13	.769	7	6	2	30
LSU 103 Mississippi 90	13	43	.302	9	14	.643	9	4	3	35
LSU 97 Miss State 87	22	44	.500	11	13	.846	2	8	4	55
LSU 99 Georgia 88	16	37	.432	9	10	.900	3	11	2	41
Season Totals 28 games	498	1106	.450	308	395	.780	149	169	82	1304
SEC Totals 18 games	336	741	.453	179	238	.752	97	108	53	851

REBOUNDING AVERAGE: 5.3
SEC 5.4

POINT AVERAGE: 46.6
SEC 47.3

ASSIST AVERAGE: 6.0
SEC 6.0

LSU SEASON RECORD
Won   20
Lost   8

LSU SEC RECORD
Won   13
Lost   5

PETE MARAVICH: THE NUMBERS

NCAA CAREER TOTALS

Games	FG	FGA	PCT.	FT	FTA	PCT.	RB	AVG.	A	PF
83	1387	3166	.438	893	1152	.775	528	6.4	425	251

Total Points	AVG.
3667	44.2

(Source: Louisiana State University)

COLLEGE CAREER HIGHLIGHTS

- All-Time NCAA Career Scoring Leader with 3,667 points, an average of 44.2 points for 83 games.
- Ranks first, fourth, and fifth for most points in a single season in NCAA history. Averaged 44.5 points in 1970, 44.2 points in 1969, and 43.8 points in 1968.
- Scored 69 points vs. Alabama, February 7, 1970.
- Led LSU to the NIT Final Four in 1970, its first postseason appearance in 16 years.
- Unanimous first team All-American in 1968, 1969, 1970.
- Naismith Award winner in 1970.

(Source: NCAA)

PRO STATS

Totals

Season	Team	G	MP	FG	FGA	3P	3PA	FT	FTA
1970–71	ATL	81	2926	738	1613			404	505
1971–72	ATL	66	2302	460	1077			355	438
1972–73	ATL	79	3089	789	1788			485	606
1973–74	ATL	76	2903	819	1791			469	568
1974–75	NOJ	79	2853	655	1562			390	481
1975–76	NOJ	62	2373	604	1316			396	488
1976–77	NOJ	73	3041	886	2047			501	600
1977–78	NOJ	50	2041	556	1253			240	276
1978–79	NOJ	49	1824	436	1035			233	277
1979–80	UTA	17	522	121	294	7	11	41	50
	BOS	26	442	123	249	3	4	50	55
10 Seasons		658	24316	6187	14025	10	15	3564	4344
Averages		82	3030	771	1748	19	29	444	541
Career High		81	3089	886	2047	10	15	501	606

Average Per Game

Season	Team	G	MP	FG	FGA	3P	3PA	FT	FTA
1970–71	ATL	81	36.1	9.1	19.9			5.0	6.2
1971–72	ATL	66	34.9	7.0	16.3			5.4	6.6
1972–73	ATL	79	39.1	10.0	22.6			6.1	7.7
1973–74	ATL	76	38.2	10.8	23.6			6.2	7.5
1974–75	NOJ	79	36.1	8.3	19.8			4.9	6.1
1975–76	NOJ	62	38.3	9.7	21.2			6.4	7.9
1976–77	NOJ	73	41.7	12.1	28.0			6.9	8.2
1977–78	NOJ	50	40.8	11.1	25.1			4.8	5.5
1978–79	NOJ	49	37.2	8.9	21.1			4.8	5.7
1979–80	UTA	17	30.7	7.1	17.3	0.4	0.6	2.4	2.9
	BOS	26	17.0	4.7	9.6	0.1	0.2	1.9	2.1
10 Seasons		658	37.0	9.4	21.3	0.2	0.3	5.4	6.6

Playoffs

Year	Team	G	MP	FG	FGA	3P	3PA	FT	FTA
1971	ATL	5	199	46	122			18	26
1972	ATL	6	219	54	121			58	71
1973	ATL	6	234	65	155			27	34
1980	BOS	9	104	25	51	2	6	2	3
4 Seasons		26	756	190	449	2	6	105	134

All-Star Games

Year	Team	MP	FG	FGA	3P	3PA	FT	FTA
1973	East	22	4	8			0	0
1974	East	22	4	15			7	9
1977	East	21	5	13			0	0
1978	East	*Selected but did not play due to injury.*						
1979	East	14	5	8			0	0
4 Games		79	18	44			7	9

Appearances on Leader Boards, Awards, and Honors

All-Star

1972–73
1973–74
1976–77
1977–78
1978–79

Honors

1970–71   All-Rookie
1972–73   All-NBA (2nd)

1975–76   All-NBA (1st)
1976–77   All-NBA (1st)
1977–78   All-NBA (2nd)

Assists (Rank)
1972–73   546 (7)
1974–75   488 (7)

Assists Per Game
1972–73   6.9 (6)
1974–75   6.2 (5)
Career   5.4 (69)

Points
1970–71   880 (8)
1972–73   2,063 (4)
1973–74   2,107 (3)
1974–75   1,700 (8)
1976–77   2,273 (1)
Career   15,948 (86)

Average Points Per Game
1970–71   23.2 (8)
1972–73   26.1 (5)
1973–74   27.2 (2)
1975–76   25.9 (3)
1976–77   31.1 (1)
Career   24.2 (17)

NOTES

PROLOGUE

Details from this opening scene are based primarily on interviews with three participants in Pete's final game at First Church of the Nazarene of Pasadena: Norman Moline, interviewed August 23, 2005; Ralph Drollinger, interviewed July 11, 2005; and Gary Lydic, interviewed September 28, 2005. Moline, identified in these passages as the accountant, was also kind enough to provide me with a videotape shot that morning. At 9 minutes and 32 seconds, I had it converted onto a CD and watched it frequently while writing the prologue.

The five-year-old boy is Josh Maravich, interviewed April 6, 2005.

2   a father addressing his son: This Serbian folk melody was brought to my attention by Boris Daich, an aficionado of traditional Serbian folk songs and lore. He also translated the verses into English for me.

3   "The space will open up,": Robert Ward, "Pete Maravich Is Still Magic," *Sport*, December 1976.

3   "I feel great,": Mark Di Ionno, "Pistol Dies Playing the Game He Loved," *New York Post*, January 6, 1988.

1. SPECIAL OPPORTUNITY

Interviews: Lazo Maravich, February 7, 2005; Jenny Zakovich and Milo Kosanovich, February 11, 2005; Sharon Danovich, October 24, 2005; Mary Cribbs, née Yovich, February 10, 2006; Helen Kosanovich, February 14, 2005; Sarah Kostal, February 16, 2005.

5   Yearbook of the Aliquippa, Pennsylvania, school district: *Condor*, 1929, on file at the B. F. Jones Memorial Library, Aliquippa, Pennsylvania (hereafter, BF Jones).

6   February 28, 1909: Birth and death records from St. George Serbian Orthodox Church, provided and translated from Cyrillic by Father Rajko Kosic of Holy Trinity Serbian Cathedral, Pittsburgh.

6   "the soundest material measure: Tom M. Girdler, in collaboration with Boyden

NOTES

Sparks, *Boot Straps* (New York: Charles Scribner's Sons, 1943). From the dust-jacket.

6   "hell with the lid: James Parton, "Pittsburgh," *Atlantic Monthly*, January, 1868.

6   "Six months residence: Burton Jesse Hendrick, *The Life of Andrew Carnegie*, (Garden City, NY: Doubleday, Doran & Company, 1932) vol. 1, 240.

6   "shock and hemorrhage: The coroner case file for Alex Marovich includes several documents: "Press Report," "Proof of Identity," and inquest order are all dated March 11, 1918. "Testimony before Coroner and Jury" is undated. The coroner's jury verdict was entered seventeen days later, on March 28. The documents were made available upon request by the University of Pittsburgh, Archives Service Center.

6   December 4, 1913: Djuro Kosanovich, Declaration of Intention, May 23, 1939, No. 152486, National Archives and Records Administration; 900 Market Street, Philadelphia, PA 19107.

7   "We want to make it: Girdler and Sparks, 166.

7   they had a system of spying: Bob Bauder, "Joseph Perriello Was J&L Steel Union Organizer," *Beaver County Times*, October 21, 2005.

7   The town was laid out: Michael Nicklanovich, "Aliquippa: Of Serbs and Steel," *Serb World USA*, November–December 1996; also "Steel Company Planned Ahead to Create Aliquippa's Neighborhoods," *Beaver County Times*, July 13, 1998.

8   The company was beneficent: Girdler and Sparks, 175.

8   "When I recall how well: Ibid., 166.

8   a state supreme court justice wrote: Bob Bauder, "The Death of a Steel Union: Rise and Fall," *Beaver County Times*, December 21, 2003.

8   "the most loathsome towns: H. L. Mencken, "The Libido for the Ugly," in *Prejudices: Sixth Series*, 1927, http://www.bizbag.com/mencklibid.htm.

8   117 Iron Street: *Beaver Valley Directory* (1925), Beaver County Research Center at the Carnegie Free Library, Beaver Falls, Pennsylvania.

10 When he filed his petition: Djuro Kosanovich, Declaration of Intention, No. 152486.

11 That same year: "Logstown Mission Re-Dedicated after Decade of Service," *Aliquippa Gazette*, December 3, 1929; "A Dream of Aliquippa Church Comes True," *Beaver County Times*, March 6, 1959.

11 was a lay worker: Anderton was ordained in 1944.

12 J&L Family's largesse: "Logstown Mission Re-Dedicated."

12 "Real baskets: Phil Berger, *Forever Showtime: The Checkered Life of Pistol Pete Maravich* (Dallas: Taylor Publishing, 1999), 9.

13 Confession of Faith: "List of the Members of Logstown Presbyterian Mission Church, 1943–44," from the personal papers of Mary Cribbs.

2. MR. BASKETBALL

Interviews: Lazo Maravich; Cribbs; Dr. Richard Lippe, February 17, 2005; Chuck Belas, November 5, 2005; Gino Piroli, November 8, 2005; Paul Piccirilli, February 16,

2005; Pecky Suder, February 10, 2005; Wallace Zernich, February 10, 2005; Danovich; Les Robinson, June 22, 2005; Joe Ceravolo, February 22, 2005.

15 "Those boys simply would not play: Quoted in Alexander Wolff, *100 Years of Hoops* (Birmingham, AL: Oxmoor House, 1991), 8.

15 "The game grew astonishingly quickly: Ibid., 9.

17 his secret intact: Berger, 10.

17 as a senior: "Nate Lippe, Ex-High School Coach, Called by Death," *Beaver Falls News-Tribune*, June 26, 1967. According to the 1926 *Genevan*, the Geneva College yearbook on file at the Beaver County Research Center, the varsity averaged 29.72 points a game.

18 East Liverpool Elks: "Resume of Applicant Nathan M. Lippe" and a six-page typewritten bio, from the personal papers of Dr. Richard Lippe.

18 Aliquippa High School: Until 1929 it was called Harding High School.

18 "a world of basketball science: 1928 *Condor*, on file at BF Jones.

18 detested each other: Gino Piroli, "Coaches' Rivalry Began in College Days," *Beaver County Times*, January 15, 2001. Lippe and Rubenstein were filing protests against each other through the 1940s.

19 In the last week of February: "Ambridge Wins Section," *Aliquippa Gazette*, undated, from the personal papers of Sharon Danovich.

19 Lippe promptly filed a protest: "Will Act on Lippe Protest," *News-Tribune* (Beaver Falls, PA), February 23, 1933; "Moguls Reject Lippe Protest," *News-Tribune* (Beaver Falls, PA), February 24, 1933.

19 pipe threader: Berger, 10.

20 "Peter Munnell": Pete Maravich and Darrel Campbell, with Frank Schroeder, *Heir to a Dream* (Nashville: Thomas Nelson Publishers, 1987), 31.

21 fewer injuries: "Aliquippa High Quintet Puts Away Uniforms: Won 14 of Season's 22 Games," *Aliquippa Gazette*, March 9, 1934.

21 "completely outclassed the other contestants: Ted Aschman, "Beaver High Cagers Bow to Aliquippa in Exciting Game," *Daily Times* (Beaver County, PA), February 3, 1934.

21 held Freedom to 13 points: "Maravich Again Proved Unstoppable: Steelers Bump Freedom, 39–13," *News-Tribune* (Beaver Falls, PA), February 7, 1934.

21 "Maravich again proved unstoppable: "18th Win for Ambridge Hi," *News-Tribune* (Beaver Falls, PA), February 10, 1934.

21 "the stupendous total: "Marovich Heads County and All-Season Games Individual Score List," *Aliquippa Gazette*, March 2, 1934.

21 "Press Maravich, Eger Jeweler ace: "Capacity Crowd Attracted to Aliquippa High School for Floor Eliminations," *Aliquippa Gazette*, April 10, 1934.

22 "The biggest cause: Ralph Hobbs, "Butler Quintet Trounces Aliquippa Hi Cagers in Section III Upset, 36–19," *Aliquippa Gazette*, January 22, 1935.

22 "The worst defeat: Hobbs, "Lippemen Trounce Bitter Rivals under Blistering 30–10 Score Friday Night," *Aliquippa Gazette*, January 29, 1935.

22 "with Captain 'Press' Maravich: Hobbs, "Aliquippa High Passers Down Ambridge Floormen Second Time This Season," *Aliquippa Gazette*, February 26, 1935.

NOTES

22 "the nearest approach to Paul Birch: Hobbs, "Aliquippa High Floormen Turned in Banner Season 1934–1935 Review Shows," *Aliquippa Gazette*, April 5, 1935.

23 His room was adorned: Berger, 27.

23 "Pop 'Em In Paul.": Claire Burcky, "In Need, They Pass to Paul," *Pittsburgh Post-Gazette*, March 9, 1934.

23 a high school sophomore: Peter Maravich, secondary school record, Aliquippa High School, Aliquippa, Pennsylvania. Obtained for the author by Lazo Maravich.

23 Social Security application: Application for Account Number, December 1, 1936, Social Security Administration, Baltimore, Maryland.

23 "The Celtics have done more: John "Dink" Ulm, "Curby's Scrapbook," *McKeesport Daily News*, March 25, 1949.

24 11,000 fans: *http://www.hoophall.com/halloffamers/celtics%20Original.htm*.

24 guests of Calvin Coolidge: *The Official NBA Encyclopedia*, 3rd ed., edited by Jan Hubbard (New York: Doubleday, 2000), 46–47.

24 "the game's first: *http://www.hoophall.com/halloffamers/Lapchick.htm*.

24 "He dribbled like a demon: Ralph Hobbs, "Celtics, High School and Drinkmor Girl Quintets Win Bank Benefit Games," *Aliquippa Gazette*, March 12, 1935.

24 the paper would herald: *Aliquippa Gazette*, February 23, 1937.

24 "what every player would: "Crowd Greets N.Y. Celtics in Fast Exhibition Contest: Defeat Collegians 62–49," *Aliquippa Gazette*, February 21, 1937.

25 attending Geneva: *Aliquippa Gazette*, February 26, 1935.

25 Duke University offered him: Maravich and Campbell, 33.

25 still needed more than two years. Press Maravich, secondary school record.

25 He took algebra: Ibid.

26 letter sweaters and varsity jackets.: *Senatus '39*, the Davis and Elkins yearbook, on file at Booth Library, Davis and Elkins College, Elkins, West Virginia.

26 "Who's Who: "Maravich, Ristick Will Be Listed in 1940–41 'Whos Who,'" *Beaver County Times*, December 2, 1940.

26 "honorable mention.": "Davis-Elkins Students Show Higher Average," *Elkins (West Virginia) Inter-Mountain*, February 27, 1940.

26 a "flashy" player: *The Senator* (Elkins, WV), February 7, 1939.

26 "the fast break style." *Senatus*, 1939.

27 the story went: From interviews with Danovich, Les Robinson (a West Virginian steeped in Cam Henderson lore), and Joe Ceravolo, an Aliquippan who would play for Press at D & E. Woody Woodrum, regarded as a sports historian at Marshall, adds that Henderson would likely have been very familiar with Press.

27 In January 1941: According to Stacey Brann, media relations director for LIU, the game took place at the Brooklyn College of Pharmacy, LIU's usual home court. The score was 54–42. LIU finished 25–2 that year and won the National Invitational Tournament.

27 more than anyone had ever scored: "Maravich Sets Court Record against L.I.U.," *The Senator* (Elkins, WV), January 24, 1941.

27 In one stretch: "Peter 'Press' Maravich Makes All-State Team," *The Senator* (Elkins, WV), March 14, 1941.

27 "He left the court: "Maravich sets Court Record against L.I.U."

27 A few nights later: "Peter 'Press' Maravich Makes All-State Team."

27 1,635: From the speech inducting Press Maravich into the D & E Athletic Hall of Fame, May 9, 1978.

27 The college paper predicted: "Maravich Sets Court Record."

28 those barnstorming weekends: Pat Gurney, "Maravich Says Basketball Is Now a Lonely Business," *Watauga Democrat* (Boone, NC), December 26, 1974.

28 his official debut: "Press Maravich Signs with Clarksburg Oilers," *Elkins Inter-Mountain*, March 6, 1941.

3. PRO BALL

Interviews: Peter Lalich, November 11, 2005; Lazo Maravich; Lucy Biega, April 30, 2005; Veda Milanovich, April 29, 2005; Piccirilli; Coulby Gunther, January 22, 2005; Jerry Fleishman, January 19, 2005; Chuck Mrazovich, February 24, 2005.

29 promptly invited Press: Maravich and Campbell, 35.

29 a four-day event: *http://members.aol.com/bradleyrd/tourney.html.*

29 neighborhood of $3,000." Berger, 16.

29 Press had enlisted: He enlisted September 30, 1941. Enlistment papers for Peter Maravich, National Personnel Records Center (hereafter, NPRC), Military Personnel Records, 9700 Page Ave., St. Louis, Missouri 63132-5100.

29 third in a group of eighteen: Order issued March 27, 1942, NPRC.

30 "outstanding aptitude": Maravich Peter, "Report on the Fitness of Officers," 15 July 1944, NPRC.

30 Black Cat patrol bomber: *http://www.daveswarbirds.com/blackcat/catalina.htm.*

30 awarded the Air Medal: "Citation" for combat missions between 24 September 1944 and 15 December 1945, D. E. Barbey, Vice Admiral, U.S. Navy, Commander Seventh Fleet, NPRC.

30 "On the night of 28 October: Maravich Peter, "Report on the Fitness of Officers," 15 May 1945, NPRC.

30 "A Hero Comes Home: *Srbobran*, undated from 1945, from the papers of Sharon Danovich.

30 when he heard from the man: Maravich and Campbell, 49.

30 a new NBL team: The NBL then consisted of eight franchises: Indianapolis, Fort Wayne, Sheboygan, Oshkosh, Youngstown, Cleveland, Rochester, and Chicago.

30 Dick Dead-Eye: "Gentlemen May Prefer Blonds—But Youngstown Bears Run to Brunets," *Youngstown Vindicator*, November 11, 1945.

31 Youngstown's inaugural effort: "2,700 See Sheboygan Down Youngstown, 45–39, in National Pro Loop Opener Here," *Youngstown Vindicator*, November 27, 1945.

32 locker-room tirades: Berger, 25.

32 "He always took it out on me,": Ibid, 27.

32 "He always had a smile.: Jim Davidson, "DOA in the NBA: The Short Inglorious Life of the Pittsburgh Ironmen," *Pittsburgh Press*, April 1, 1990.

32 The impact, Berger, 25.

32 hastily conceived: Frank B. Ward, "Youngstown Granted Pro Cage League Franchise," *Youngstown Vindicator*, September 11, 1945.

32 lost their first nine: "Youngstown Bears Snap Losing Streak, Topple Indianapolis Cagers, 44–35," *Youngstown Vindicator*, December 24, 1945.

32 finishing sixth: *http://members.aol.com/apbrhoops/nblstand.html*.

33 "He looked terrible,": Meredith Council, "Introducing Mrs. Press Maravich," *News and Observer* (Raleigh, NC), February 28, 1965.

33 "We should be married,": Maravich and Campbell, 51.

33 almost nine years his junior: Marriage license, Helen Gravor–Elvidio Montini, October 19, 1942, Register of Wills, Beaver County Courthouse (hereafter BCC). A subsequent marriage license, issued for her marriage to Press, lists her date of birth as February 23, 1925.

33 a fruit packer: Marriage license, Helen Gravor–Elvidio Montini, BCC.

33 joined the army: "Helen Montini Is Bride of Former Naval Pilot," *Evening Times* (Beaver County) June 24, 1946. Describes Helen's father as Sergeant Nicholas Gravor, "stationed with the U.S. Army at Long Beach, Cal."

33 church records: "List of Members of Logstown Presbyterian Mission Church," from the papers of Mary Cribbs.

34 "he-man.": 1942 *Quippan*, on file BF Jones.

34 October 11, 1942: Marriage license, Helen Gravor–Elvidio Montini, BCC.

34 Then came the bulletin: *Evening Times*, January 2, 1945.

35 "frock of aqua crepe: *Evening Times*, June 24, 1946.

35 his occupation: Marriage license, Helen Gravor–Peter Maravich, June 15, 1946, Register of Wills, BCC.

35 the Arena Managers Association: See Leonard Koppett, "The NBA 1946: A New League," in *The Official NBA Encyclopedia*, 38–41.

36 Arena Basketball League.: "Shannon Signs as Manager of Youngstown Bears," *Youngstown Vindicator*, September 1, 1946.

36 "In whose office: Koppett, *The Official NBA Encyclopedia*, 39.

36 "It won't be long: Bob Drum, "Paul Birch Hopes His Ironmen Will Keep Him in 'Victory Rut,' " *Pittsburgh Post-Gazette*, October 7, 1946.

37 Birch wasted little time: "Press Maravich with Pgh. Ironmen," *Evening Tribune*, September 26, 1946.

37 "The idea,": Jack Sell, "Floor Plans Recall Days of Ironmen," *Pittsburgh Post-Gazette and Sun-Telegraph*, May 15, 1960.

37 already considered a dump: Davidson, "DOA in the NBA."

37 even 300 fans: Ibid.

38 a $100 fine: Berger, 27.

38 keep Press on the bench: Davidson, "DOA in the NBA."

39 "If it's a girl: Maravich and Campbell, 55.

39 St. Elijah the Prophet: Excerpt from the Parish Record of Births and Baptisms, Serbian Orthodox Church in the United States of America and Canada, from Lazo Maravich's personal papers.

4. THE CULT OF PRESS

Interviews: Lazo Maravich; Zernich; Ceravolo, Mrazovich; Ted Chizmar, provided as a written response to author's questions, March 5, 2005; Joe Pukach, February 9, 2005; Gloria Marquette Payne, February 23, 2005; Bob Kent, June 19, 2005; Harold Forbes, March 16, 2005; Danovich; Hank Ellis, February 22, 2005; Mike Linkovich, February 23, 2005; Nick Lackovich, February 17, 2005; Pete Suder, June 18, 2005; Joe Lee, May 17, 2006; Mark Battalini, grade school friend of Ronnie Maravich from Aliquippa, May 11, 2005; Chuck Elkins, March 3, 2005; Woody Sauldsberry, August 4, 2005.

41   a commercial pilot: Maravich and Campbell, 52; Berger, 32.

41   championships in '47, '48, and '50: Program from the American-Serbian Basketball Tournament, March 23–25, 1951, from the papers of Sharon Danovich.

42   a Serbian charity game: Gino Piroli, "Coaches' Rivalry Began in College Days," *Beaver County Times*, January 15, 2001.

43   "racehorse basketball.": Phillip D. Hart, "The Press Maravich Story," *Serb World USA*, May–June 1997.

43   they went 21–8: *Senatus*, 1948, Booth Library at Davis and Elkins College.

44   the fall of 1948: West Virginia University Registrar's grade cards, Reel No. 14, Morgantown, West Virginia.

44   "Basketball Scouting,": Press Maravich and James C. Steel, "Basketball Scouting," Clarks Letter Service, 1949. From Lazo Maravich's personal papers.

44   he started four freshmen.: *Murmurontis* 1950, West Virginia Wesleyan College, Buckhannon.

44   best in the conference.: Ibid.

44   graduate school transcript: West Virginia University Registrar's grade cards, Reel No. 14, McGlynn-Mertes.

44   Dr. Georgianna Stary: Davis and Elkins Catalogue, 1948. Thanks to Dr. David Turner, professor of history, Davis and Elkins College.

45   potential and mental fitness: Maravich and Campbell, 57–58.

45   a stone's throw: E-mail from Tom Sakal, who grew up next door to George Danovich, to Sharon Danovich, December 1, 2005.

45   a powerful incentive: Maravich and Campbell, 58–59.

46   the team improved: "Maravich Opens Basketball Drill with 30 Prospects," *Buckhannon Record*, November 10, 1949.

46   "Little George Danovich,": "Bobcats Edge W. Liberty 60–57," *Wesleyan Pharos*, March 10, 1950.

46   hoisted their coach: Ibid.

46   "Press Maravich Day,": "Wesleyan Is Winner in 'Maravich Day,' " *Buckhannon Record*, March 17, 1950.

46   about $2,800: Also see Sandy Grady, "Press: 'I'm Here to Stay,' " *Charlotte News*, June 26, 1956.

46   "The only worries: "D-E Takes Tourney Final 77–56," *Wesleyan Pharos*, March 10, 1950.

47   solicited to raise $400: Ed Conley, "Time Out," *Wesleyan Pharos*, March 24, 1950.

47   neglecting Brown's warning: Maravich and Campbell, 59.

47   "We couldn't go on: Berger, 34.

47   "Ground Cleared for Gymnasium: Peter Finney, "Press and Pete Maravich." The Maravich files at Louisiana State University include a draft of an eight-page, double-spaced typewritten manuscript written by Finney, then columnist for the *States-Item*, when Pete and Press came to Baton Rouge in 1966. Bud Johnson, the University's sports information director at the time, allows that he would have been the one to put it in the file, especially as Finney was way out in front of the Maravich story. Finney recalls the details of the piece—written in October or November 1967, on the eve of Pete's varsity debut—but not where it ran. Unlike most of Finney's longer free-lance work, it was not published in *The Sporting News*. Hereafter, Finney's Manuscript.

47   "It wasn't much,": Ibid.

47   Over the next two seasons: "Maravich to Coach Baldwin Cagers," *Pittsburgh Post-Gazette*, August 13, 1952.

47   he'd be great: Bill Ballenger, "Love Was Not Enough," *Charlotte News*, March 7, 1972.

48   With some summer hours: Maravich and Campbell, 61.

48   The Quips were 9–13: *Quippan* 1955, *Quippan* 1956. BF Jones.

48   "hated the rebellion: Maravich and Campbell, 60.

48   "big shot Navy man,": Ibid., 62.

48   "and the dead-end world: Ibid., 60.

49   "Press would run us: *Pistol Pete: The Life and Times of Pete Maravich*, directed by George Roy, written by Steven Stern, Black Canyon Films, aired on CBS, 2001.

50   "I was so impressed: Maravich and Campbell, 56–57.

50   Press brought him and Ronnie: Ibid., 57.

51   humiliated by Marques Haynes: Ben Green, *Spinning the Globe: The Rise, Fall, and Return to Greatness of the Harlem Globetrotters* (New York: Amistad, 2005), 211–215.

5. COUNTRY GENTLEMEN

Interviews: Louise Bradley, May 17, 2005; Joyce Bagwell, June 23, 2005; George Krajack, June 9, 1965; Bill Hensley, May 8, 2005; John Wooden, May 10, 2005.

53   Clemson was 1–39 in conference: To that point, their sole ACC victory had been a 2-point win over Virginia during the 1955–56 season.

53   "You've got to face it: Red Canup, "Like It or Not," *The Independent (Anderson, SC)*, December 1, 1959.

53   "I do think that being: Jim Anderson, "Tigs Consider Full-Time Cage Coach; Relieve McFadden," *Greenville News (SC)*, March 6, 1956.

54   "the dark house,": Jim Foster, "Paint and Bulbs Needed at Clemson," *Spartanburg Herald (SC)*, April 7, 1960.

54   "A man who could sell anyone: Bill Ballenger, "Maravich: From Rags to Riches," *Charlotte News*, March 8, 1965. North Carolina State Sports Information Office Archive hereafter, (NCS).

54 apparently miffed: Wilton Garrison, "New Clemson Cage Coach to Have Same Starting Five Back Again," *Charlotte Observer*, May 23, 1956.

54 "the referees had to use flashlights.": Bones McKinney with Garland Atkins, *Bones* (Garland Publications, 1988), 84.

54 "He's sent me a mess: Sandy Grady, *Charlotte News*, May 21, 1956.

54 His references included: "Tiger Basketball Facts 1956–57," Clemson University Sports Information Office archive, hereafter, Clemson.

54 "All of 'em talked: Grady.

55 "Some fine high school players,": Sandy Grady, "Press: 'I'm Here to Stay,'" *Charlotte News*, June 26, 1956.

55 "Maravich took over,": "Tiger Basketball Facts 1956–57," Clemson.

57 The Wonderworker: *http://www.geocities.com/Athens/7175/stnich-lk.html?200513*, St. Nicholas the Wonderworker page.

58 always tried to avoid: Jim Foster, "Paint and Bulbs Needed at Clemson," *Spartanburg Herald*, April 7, 1960.

58 "Many of them stood: Jerry McLeese, "Maravich—Man on the Way Up," *Winston-Salem Journal*, August 17, 1962.

59 an overtime triumph against North Carolina State: "Clemson College Tigers, 1957–58 Basketball," Clemson.

59 "This has been an exceptional year: Red Canup, "Here We Go Again," *The Independent*, February 25, 1959.

59 only its third victory over Duke: "Tips on the Tigers, 1959–60," Clemson.

59 he called *junto*: Phil Grose, "Clemson Destroys N.C. State, 67–46," *Charlotte Observer*, March 2, 1962.

59 allowed 64.2: Ibid.

59 "I'm a fast break man,": Jim Anderson, "Maravich Expects Tigers to Play Interesting Ball," *Greenville News*, June 25, 1956.

59 concave backboards: Ernie Salvatore, "Looking Ahead with Mr. Press Maravich," *Herald Advertiser*, January 14, 1962.

59 "I'll try anything: Johnny Martin, "On the Spot," *The Independent*, January 10, 1962.

59 "This West is: Jake Penland, "In the Press Box," *The State* (Columbia, S.C.), February 26, 1960.

59 "so colorful, so resplendent: Martin, "On the Spot," January 10, 1962.

60 "It's crazy,": Davis Merritt, "Outlaw Jump Shot, Proposes Maravich," *Charlotte Observer*, February 15, 1961.

60 "He would blindfold Pete: See also Joe Menzer, *Four Corners: How UNC, N.C. State, Duke and Wake Forest Made North Carolina the Center of the Basketball Universe* (New York: Simon & Schuster, 1999), 37–38.

6. THE BASKETBALL GENE

Interviews: Ben Wagener, May 12, 2005; Charlie Bryant, May 3, 2005; Lou Pucillo, May 4, 2005; Paul Phillips, May 6, 2004; Mrazovich; Pukach; Ah Chew Goo, March 10, 2005; Jim Sutherland, May 18, 2005; Rob Hubbard, May 17, 2005; Herbert Cooper, May 17, 2005; Jimmy Howard, May 17, 2005; Leonard Keller, May 17, 2005; Ed

Coakley, May 21, 2005; Krajack; Len Chappell, May 13, 2005; Tommy Hess, March 24, 2005; Charles "Lefty" Driesell, May 13, 2005; Ed McLean, May 4, 2005.

63 "The sun was bright: Bill Gutman, *Pistol Pete Maravich: The Making of a Basketball Superstar* (New York: Grosset & Dunlap, 1972), 10.
63 "He had the eighth grade coach: Maravich and Campbell, 73.
64 making his "muscles twitch: Jerry McLeese, "Maravich—Man on the Way Up," *Winston-Salem Journal*, August 17, 1962.
64 flat-footed and dumbfounded: Although "flat-footed and dumbfounded" are the author's words, Goo is not given to false modesty in recounting his abilities. "I'm 86," he says. "I'm entitled to blow my own horn."
64 "Homework Basketball,": See Gutman, 14–15; Maravich and Campbell, 70, 75.
65 Christmas tree in 1956: Photographs of the bicycles under the tree are from Louise Bradley.
66 Pete balked.: *"Pistol" Pete Maravich*, Life Story Foundation, a cassette tape recording of Maravich's testimony (hereafter, Testimony tape). Available by calling 1-800-661-1141.
66 learning to control the ball: Maravich and Campbell, 75.
66 "several kids gathered: Ibid., 76.
66 He would repeat the words: Ibid., 70.
66 "Lightning illuminated the puddles: Ibid., 71.
68 "Out in front of a crowd: Pete Maravich with Curry Kirkpatrick, "I Want to Put On a Show," *Sports Illustrated*, December 1, 1969.
69 Pete would sneak out of bed: Maravich and Campbell, 67.
69 time-lapse photographs: Photos by Bennie J. Granger appeared under the cutline "For Clemson's Maravich, Two Hours Can Be a Long Work Day," *Greenville Piedmont* (South Carolina), January 8, 1960.
69 "I tried every defense: Dan Foster, "Maravich: 'I Tried Every Defense but Nothing Worked,' " *Greenville Piedmont*, January 8, 1960.
70 9 of 25 shooting: Jim Anderson, "Sharp-Shooting Furman Rips in 80–69 Win off Clemson," *Greenville News*, January 8, 1960.
70 The dummy was outfitted: Jim Noyes, "Maravich: 'Glad to See a Little Basketball Interest,' " *The Independent* (Anderson, SC), January 9, 1960.
70 a thankless job: Red Canup, *The Independent*, January 12, 1960.
70 "This effigy business: Jim Noyes, "Clemson's Edwards 'for' Maravich," *The Independent*, January 12, 1960.

7. THE DEVIL IN RONNIE MONTINI

Interviews: Wooden; Bradley; Jim Brennan, May 27, 2005; Gail Benke (nee Garrison), May 31, 2005; Wagener; Dick Singleton, May 23, 2005; Jimmy Lever, May 25, 2005; Pete Carlisle, May 26, 2005; Tommy McNeill, May 26, 2005.

71 "He has all the weapons: Jake Penland, "In the Press Box," *The State* (Columbia, SC), March 2, 1960.

71 voted "best dressed": *Summit* 1961, on file in the library at D. W. Daniel High School, Clemson, S.C.

72 Ronnie set a Daniel scoring record: "Maravich Gets It from All Directions," *Columbia Record*, January 12, 1960.

72 stole an Edsel: Maravich and Campbell, 79.

72 "It was just too much: Ballenger, "Maravich: From Rags to Riches."

72 It was the same name: *Summit*, 1959, D. W. Daniel High School.

73 "Just you wait,": "Maravich Gets It from All Directions," *Columbia Record*.

73 stole the ball from his kid brother: Maravich and Campbell, 79.

73 "Ronnie and Pete used to fuss: Robert L. Bradley, "Clemson Shocked by Death of 'Pistol Pete,' " *The Messenger*, (Clemson, S.C.), January 6, 1988.

73 memorable performances: "Maravich Gets 30 Points, 31 Rebounds, in Team Win," *The Independent*, February 21, 1961.

73 33 points and 26 rebounds: "Maravich Upsets Palmetto, 63–58," *The Independent*, February 23, 1961.

74 "When I threw a behind-the-back: Maravich and Campbell, 78.

74 averaging 11 points: Johnny Martin, "On the Spot," *The Independent* (Anderson, SC), December 28, 1960.

74 Pete would recall: Maravich and Campbell, 80. This recollection escapes Jimmy Lever, Jim Sutherland, Tommy McNeill, and Pete Carlisle.

74 "Wine, women and song: *Summit* 1961, D. W. Daniel High School.

8. "PISTOL PETE"

Interviews: Jerry McLeese, May 27, 2005: Lazo Maravich; Brennan; Wooden; Dr. Billy Hunter, May 16, 2005; Coakley; Rudy Antoncic, February 12, 2005; Wooden; Coakley; Frank Weedon, May 2, 2005; Vic Bubas, May 12, 2005; Robinson; Jimmy Howard, May 17, 2005.

78 The only returning regulars: "Daniel Plays BHS Tuesday," *The Independent* (Anderson, SC), December 10, 1961.

78 "I threw a behind-the-back: Maravich, "I Want to Put On a Show."

79 "Sometimes I'm playing ball: *Pistol Pete: The Life and Times of Pete Maravich*.

79 "Pete is his first love,": Jerry McLeese, "Maravich—Man on the Way Up."

79 two before each game: Johnny Martin, "Tranquilizers for Coaches?," *The Independent*, December 11, 1961.

79 "How can I do that?": Herman Hickman, "Basketball Is Pill for Maravich," *Winston-Salem Journal*, January 7, 1962.

83 never won a tournament game: Clemson's previous tournament win was a 44–43 victory over North Carolina in 1939 in the defunct Southern Conference.

83 "This one you'll never believe.": Phil Grose, "Clemson Destroys N.C. State, 67–46," *Charlotte Observer*, March 2, 1962.

83 "I'm ashamed: Bob Hampton, "Clemson 'Soph Touches' Put Wolfpack to Shame," *Winston-Salem Journal*, March 2, 1962.

84 "We can go: UPI, "Maravich: 'We Can Go All the Way' to ACC Title," *Greenville Piedmont* (South Carolina) March 3, 1962.

NOTES

84 "I put up signs: Steve Guback, "Maravich Recalls Youth Experiment," *Washington Star*, undated, c. March 1964, NCS.

84 Syracuse was interested: Dick Herbert, "The Sports Observer," *News and Observer* (Raleigh, NC), March 4, 1962; Johnny Martin, "Syracuse Eyes Tigs' Maravich," *The Independent*, March 5, 1962.

84 Over the next twenty-three years: "Meet the Wolfpack," 1962–63, NCS.

84 "Too small,": Menzer, 32.

85 "The basketball capital: Smith Barrier of the *Greensboro News and Record*, in ibid., 33.

85 State won more basketball games: "Meet the Wolfpack," 1962–63.

85 Case called Press: Johnny Martin, "Case Asks Maravich to Be Aide at N.C. State College," *The Independent*, August 9, 1962.

85 The understanding, though not written: George Cunningham, "State to Announce Next Week Hiring of Clemson's Maravich," *Charlotte Observer*, August 10, 1962.

86 about $3,000 better: Gutman, 25.

86 "I believe it is a step: "Coach Press Maravich's Statement upon His Resignation at Clemson," NCS.

86 an ancillary motive: Menzer, 38.

9. CHANGING THE GAME

Interviews: Jimmy Broadway, June 16, 2005; Olin Broadway, June 16, 2005; Paul Phillips, May 6, 2005; McLean; Hal Blondeau, May 4, 2005; Robinson; Ken Rohloff, May 23, 2005; Ed Biedenbach, June 12, 2005; Bryant; Weedon; Pucillo; Pete Coker, July 9, 2005; Bubas.

87 Duke's "scoring machine": Johnny Martin, "At Duke, It's Heyman and Mullins; At Daniel, It's Maravich-Sutherland," *The Independent* (Anderson, SC), February 7, 1963.

87 a mere 44: "Daniel Edged, Palmetto in Semi-finals," *The Independent*, February 23, 1963.

89 the Y's summer basketball: Raleigh YMCA Men's Summer Basketball League statistics, 1963 season, from Jimmy Broadway's scrapbook.

89 "Tournament Highlights": Broadway's scrapbook.

90 the Caps' leading scorer: Paul V. Phillips Jr., "Caps Have Big Hooping Hopes," *Raleigh Times*, October 24, 1963.

91 Burlington coach Twig Wiggins: Paul V. Phillips Jr., "Thirteen Is Lucky on 13th for Caps," *Raleigh Times*, December 14, 1963.

91 They survived a scare: Grady Elmore, "Broughton Nips Wildcats, 59–55," *News and Observer* (Raleigh, NC), February 29, 1964.

91 Pete scored 29: Gene Cherry, "Caps Edge Fayetteville for Title by 63 to 60," *News and Observer* (Raleigh, NC), March 1, 1964.

91 "With the way basketball: Grady Elmore, Best Ever' Caps Launch Bid," *News and Observer* (Raleigh, NC), March 5, 1964.

348

92 He missed from 15: "Reynolds Nips Caps by 64 to 63," *News and Observer* (Raleigh, NC), March 6, 1964.

93 "I need 20 pounds: Bob Myers, "Charlotte Teams Are Glad Young Maravich Is Gone," *Charlotte News*, December 24, 1964.

93 a severely sprained ankle: "Fayetteville, Durham Victorious," *News and Observer* (Raleigh, NC), February 27, 1965.

93 Against Rocky Mount: Jack Stephens, "Blackbirds Top Caps, 73–61," *News and Observer* (Raleigh, NC), February 6, 1965.

93 headline fodder: *News and Observer* (Raleigh, NC), December 24, 1964; February 3; February 20.

93 one enthralled opponent: Myers, "Charlotte Teams Are Glad Young Maravich Is Gone."

93 a never-to-be-broken record: Dustin Long, "50 & Counting," *News and Record* (Greensboro, NC), July 19, 1998.

93 took their first vacation: Meredith Council, "Introducing Mrs. Press Maravich: The Woman Behind the Wolfpack Coach," *News and Observer* (Raleigh, NC), February 28, 1965.

93 "The pretty blue water: "They Said It," *Sports Illustrated*, February 17, 1969.

94 "The motliest gang: Bill Ballenger, "Love Was Not Enough," *Charlotte News*, March 7, 1972.

95 "Pete Maravich's father": *Meet the Wolfpack, 1964–65*, NCS.

95 had them watch film: Steve Guback, "The 'Black Cat' Leads N.C. State," *Evening Star* (Washington, D.C.), December 9, 1964.

96 Hawley's Snack Shoppe: Program for the Eighth Annual Sportsman Club, Inc. Basketball Tournament, March 27–April 1, 1950, from Les Robinson's personal papers.

98 down 14 in the second half: Mary Garber, "N.C. State's Cagers Go Back to Work," *Winston-Salem Journal Sentinel*, c. January 1965, NCS.

99 combined for only three: Guback, "ACC Titlists Find Bits and Pieces Fit," *Evening Star* (Washington, D.C.), March 8, 1965.

99 Press ran out: Dan Foster, " 'Greatest Thrill,' " *Greenville* (S.C.) *News*, March 8, 1965.

99 "ancestral form,": Reprinted as John McPhee, *A Sense of Where You Are: A Profile of Bill Bradley at Princeton* (New York: Farrar, Strauss and Giroux; 1999), 20–21.

100 khakis and white shirts: Ibid., 43.

100 Even Bradley was astonished: Ibid., 121.

100 By halftime: Gordon S. White Jr., "Tiger Five Points N.C. State, 66–48," *New York Times*, March 13, 1965.

100 "Seldom has there ever: Bill Ballenger, "Maravich Coach of Year," *Charlotte News*, March 9, 1965.

101 "We loved to play against Pete,": Tim Peeler, "One of the Game's Great Players Cut Teeth at Reynolds," *News and Record* (Greensboro, NC), February 25, 1999.

101 pool hustler's cue stick: Peter Vecsey, "Pistol: The Real Magic," *New York Post*, January 8, 1988.

NOTES

10. THE DEEP END

Interviews: Wooden; Robinson; Coakley; Sutherland; Bryant; Blondeau; Biedenbach; McLean; Pucillo; Jimmy Broadway; Bradley; Weedon, Hunter; Robinson; Bob Sandford, May 3, 2005; Bud Johnson, March 20, 2005; Bucky Waters, May 24, 2005; Bob Roesler, June 1, 2005.

104 "got every ounce: Ronald Green, "State Has Big Shoes to Fill," *Charlotte News,* May 3, 1966.

104 one of three players: "Final 1965–66 North Carolina State Basketball Statistics," NCS.

104 send a message: Green, "State Has Big Shoes to Fill."

105 "I was real sick,": Dan Foster, "Thousand Times," *Greenville* (S.C.) *News,* December 29, 1966.

105 "She's his good luck: Foster, " 'Greatest Thrill.' "

105 "one of America's most beautiful: Ibid.

105 "I'm a very sensitive: Council, "Introducing Mrs. Press Maravich."

106 "Basketball has just been our life: Barbara McAden, "N.C. State's Head Coach Has Basketball Family," *Charlotte Observer,* December 19, 1964.

106 "The lonesomeness: Council, "Introducing Mrs. Press Maravich."

107 "Mrs. Ronald Maravich,": Ibid.

107 couldn't so much as change a diaper: McAden, "N.C. State's Head Coach Has Basketball Family."

109 "entire evenings of strategy sessions: Maravich and Campbell, 92.

109 "It wouldn't be fair,": Jake Penland, "In the Press Box," *The State* (Columbia, SC), March 2, 1960.

109 "I can't afford to let him play: UPI, "Press Maravich Has a 'Problem,' " *Fayetteville Observer,* August 27, 1965.

110 By December of Pete's senior year: Myers, "Charlotte Teams Are Glad Young Maravich Is Gone."

110 "When you're in high school: *Pistol Pete: The Life and Times of Pete Maravich,* Black Canyon Films. Recalling the ill-fated recruitment of Charlie Scott, Les Robinson says, "That was about the worst thing he could have said: Come here and be Pete's caddy for four years. But that was the way Press recruited."

111 In fact, he scored only 26: Gutman, 42–43.

112 a pretty brown-haired girl: Maravich and Campbell, 85.

115 Founded in 1860: "Welcome to LSU," c. 1969, East Baton Rouge Parish Library.

115 nineteen students and four professors: "The Inauguration of John Anderson Hunter as President of Louisiana State University," April 6–7, 1962, program on file at the East Baton Rouge Parish Library.

115 approximately 17,000: *LSU Basketball 1966–1967,* on file at the LSU Sports Information Office (hereafter, LSU).

115 two years of Reserve Officers Training: Dick Wright, "LSU Faculty Council Votes for Abolition of Required ROTC," *Morning Advocate* (Baton Rouge), October 11, 1968.

115 "because I doubted: *LSU Basketball 2004–05 Media Guide,* 200, LSU.

115 "A good start,": Bud Montet, "Random Shots," *Morning Advocate*, April 6, 1966.

115 chairman of the NCAA Television Committee: *LSU Basketball 1966–1967*, LSU.

116 negotiating with the NBA's Baltimore Bullets: Dick Herbert, "The Sports Observer," *Raleigh News and Observer*, May 2, 1966.

116 shook hands with Press: Maravich and Campbell, 95.

116 Reporters estimated: AP, "Maravich Reportedly Getting $5,000 Hike as New LSU Coach," *Rocky Mount Telegram* (NC), May 2, 1966; Whitey Kelley, "Case Helped Maravich Make Up His Mind on LSU Offer," *Charlotte Observer*, May 2, 1966.

116 "one I just couldn't afford: Herbert, "The Sports Observer."

117 *Don't ever come home*: Maravich and Campbell, 96.

11. KING OF THE COW PALACE

Interviews: Russ Bergman, June 24, 2005; Billy Simmons, March 21, 2005; Johnson; Dexter Bott, March 24, 2005; Randy Lamont, March 23, 2005; Ralph Jukkola, March 23, 2005; Rich Hickman, April 20, 2005; Boots Garland, March 23, 2005; Harold Sylvester, March 26, 2005; Herb White, June 18, 2005; Paul Milanovich, April 27, 2005; Jeff Tribbett, April 28, 2005.

119 "Don't expect miracles: Letter from Press Maravich (Press) to Les Robinson (LR), September 13, 1966. Like all Press's dated letters in this chapter, they are from Robinson's personal papers.

120 "the roughest year: Paul V. Phillips, " 'Roughest Year in Basketball,' " *Raleigh Times*, undated, c. July 1967, LSU.

122 press release drafted: Draft of untitled press release, LSU.

122 "From this day hence,": Joe Planas, "For Pete's Sake—Frosh Win," *The Advocate* (Baton Rouge), December 2, 1966.

123 "schedule classes just to make sure: Cheryl Talbot Macaluso, "Maravich Changed the Lifestyle of LSU's Freshman Class of '66," *State-Times* (Baton Rouge), January 6, 1988.

123 "As soon as he touched: *SportsCentury: Pete Maravich*, ESPN Classic, aired March 23, 2001.

123 McKeithen became a fixture: Sandy Padwe, "Maraviches Press for LSU Revival," Newspaper Enterprise Association, January 14, 1966.

123 "A great basketball fan,": Letter from Press to LR, February 21, 1967.

124 an autographed publicity photo: White was kind enough to bring it to his interview for the author's perusal.

125 averaged 43.6 points: "LSU Freshman Basketball Records," press release, March 10, 1967, LSU.

126 Pete had an off game: "Baby Bengals Drop 75–74 Cliffhanger," *Sunday Advocate* (Baton Rouge), March 5, 1967.

126 the time he lost in Rochester: Gutman, 53.

126 thirty-nine LSU freshman records: "LSU Freshman Basketball Records," LSU.

126 capacity for 8,000: *LSU Basketball 1966–1967*, LSU.

126 packed with 9,200: AP, "Maraviches Have Fans Anxious," October 19, 1967, NCS.

126 Pete was a weekly guest: Letter from Press to LR, January 17, 1967.

126 sporting goods stores: Untitled press release, c. March 1967, LSU.

127 suspended for a game: It was January 8, 1967. Though the reasons for Pete's absence were kept vague, both Dexter Bott and Billy Simmons recall it as a suspension.

12. SHOWTIME

Interviews: Johnson; Bergman; M. L. Carr, July 11, 2005; Tribbett; Jukkola; Charlie McCarthy, June 7, 2005; Charlie Bloodworth, June 8, 2005; Simmons; Bott; Johnny Arthurs, March 26, 2005; Rich Lupcho, April 21, 2005; Robinson; Hickman; Wooden; Sylvester; Dan Issel, August 10, 2005; Blondeau; Ray Mears, July 18, 2005; Sandford; Howard; Ronnie Maravich (phone conversation), April 5, 2005; Driesell; Bradley; Steve Shumaker, April 22, 2005; Dan Hester, April 29, 2005; Jackie Maravich, March 25, 2005; White.

129 Dolph Schayes: In 1970, on the eve of the NBA draft, Dolph Schayes said of Pete, "He's the greatest ballhandler in the history of the game." Larry Merchant, "Headed Off at the Pass," *New York Post*, March 20, 1970.

130 "a bleached Globetrotter.": Finney Manuscript.

130 "He's as good: Peter Finney, "LSU's Pistol Pete Top Gun in Nation," *New Orleans States-Item*, December 6, 1967.

131 "I'm in a slump,": Paul Atkinson, "Showman Maravich: LSU's Soph Cage Flash," *Sporting News*, January 20, 1968.

131 "elevator shoes": Press release; special to the *Beaver County Times*, November 19, 1968, LSU.

131 Pete would have to shoot 40 times: Jim Martz, "Wesleyan Cager Gave Up Supporting Role at L.S.U.," *Des Moines Register*, December 22, 1969.

131 "He's got more pressure on him: Joe Tiede, "LSU Coach's Son Nation's Top Scorer," *Christian Science Monitor*, January 22, 1968.

132 biggest basketball crowd: Ibid.

132 15,014 turned out for LSU: Ted Castillo, "Pistol Pete Guns Down Tide, 99–89," *Sunday Advocate*, February 18, 1968.

133 His shot charts indicated: Peter Finney, "A Shooting Magician," *States-Item*, January 12, 1968.

133 "I've never seen: Ibid.

133 It had a revival atmosphere: George Sweeney, "Greenies Are Believers," *Times-Picayune*, January 12, 1968.

134 "I get to the point: "A Guy Named Pete," *Time*, January 19, 1968.

135 reported in the *Advocate*: "Florida Too Tall for Tigers; Maravich 'Held' to 32 Points," *Morning Advocate*, undated, LSU.

135 "I wish he'd shoot a thousand: Atkinson, "Showman Maravich,"

136 "Just another fish: Paul V. Phillips Jr., " 'I'll Be Just Another Fish in the Pond,' " *Raleigh Times*, c. June 1967, LSU.

137 named to five different All-America teams: "Pistol Pete Maravich—All American," press release, c. November 1968, LSU.

137 104-degree fever: Joe Planas, "Fever Weakened Pistol Still Fired 54 Slugs," *Morning Advocate*, January 30, 1968.

137 "The Globetrotters do it: Atkinson, "Showman Maravich: LSU's Soph Cage Flash."

138 "The Ballad of Pistol Pete": Lyrics printed with illustration to Sam Goldaper, "The Maravich Shows Moves in Friday," *New York Times*, March 8, 1970.

138 a cover story in *Sports Illustrated*: Curry Kirkpatrick, "The Coed Boppers' Top Cat," *Sports Illustrated*, March 4, 1968.

138 methodical and low-scoring: *http://www.hoophall.com/halloffamers/Iba.htm*.

138 the Pistol act.: Peter Finney, "Tantrums Lessen Maravich's Talent," *Sporting News*, c. 1969, LSU; also Berger, 102–103.

139 "A big joke": letter from Press to LR, April 29, 1968.

139 "$35 a week": Berger, 91.

141 fist through a cheap bathroom wall: Maravich and Campbell, 114.

142 plowing into a stalled automobile: UPI Dispatch, c. July 1968.

142 charged with driving while intoxicated: Peter Finney, memo to *Sports Illustrated*, July 5, 1968, SI Library.

143 "Suddenly, the girl: Maravich and Campbell, 116–117.

143 "a beautiful woman: Ibid., 112.

144 "the center of our life,": Letter from Press to Nick Lalich, August 16, 1968, Sharon Danovich's papers.

145 "You shoot it,": Charles Coe, "Life with Father on the Court," *Life*, February 7, 1969.

145 "all in the past,": Bill Neikirk, "Pete Not Aiming for Repeat of His Scoring Title," *Alexandria Daily Town Talk*, December 1, 1968.

145 a 40-foot behind-the-back toss: *http://www.pistolpete23.com/pete_maravich_top-college.htm*.

145 Duquesne's vaunted defense: Maravich and Campbell, 122.

146 a slew of new records: These included twenty-three LSU records, eighteen SEC records, and NCAA marks. "Records Fall," press release, March 16, 1969, LSU.

146 "This year I think: Bill Neikirk, "Pistol Pete SEC Player of Year," *Times Picayune*, March 4, 1969.

146 torn cartilage would require surgery: Ibid.

147 thrown out of a game: Dan Hardesty, "Vandy Trims Tigs Again," *State-Times*, February 18, 1969.

147 "I'm the coach,": Maravich and Campbell, 112.

148 "I saw her laugh: Ibid., 120.

148 drank a little too much: Ibid., 121.

149 the Quarter Horse phase: "Area Horsewomen Capture Top Honors at LSU Show," *State-Times*, March 8, 1969.

149 "seldom matched in SEC basketball,": "Pete Scores 58 as Tigers Win," *State-Times*, March 10, 1969.

149 24 of his team's last 29 points: AP "LSU Cagers Win in 2 Overtimes, 90–80," *Sunday Advocate*, March 9, 1969.

150 With twelve seconds remaining: "Pete Scores 58 as Tigers Win."

150   "They had fire in their eyes,": Maravich with Kirkpatrick, "I Want to Put On a Show."

150   "A 30-foot hook shot: "Pete Scores 58 as Tigers Win."

13. ONE OF US

Interviews: Billy Packer, June 5, 2005; Cleo Hill, July 24, 2005; McLeese; Marvin Turner, April 18, 2005; Fred Hilton, March 23, 2005; Johnson; Sylvester; White; Hess; Bill Newton, April 26, 2005; Wooden; Red Rocha, May 10, 2005; Tribbett; Hickman; Bergman.

153   "Billy didn't say much: Clarence E. Gaines with Clint Johnson, *They Call Me Big House* (Winston-Salem, N.C.: John F. Blair, 2004), 147.

154   "I watched for a few seconds: Ibid., 149.

154   confused even ACC refs: McKinney and Atkins, *Bones*, 113.

154   "a mild passing game: Gaines and Johnson, *They Call Me Big House*, 89.

155   The boy was captivated: Jerry McLeese, "Inscrutable Auerbach Mum on Earl Monroe," *Winston-Salem Journal*, February 5, 1967.

155   much alike as prodigious scorers: Jerry McLeese, "An Ex-Shipping Clerk Puts Old Point Marks in the Suspense File," *Sporting News*, February 4, 1967.

155   The answer depended on: Billy Packer theorizes that Pete's game developed, in part, because of television. "Pete was one of the first kids who grew up on television," he says, meaning that he saw a variety of styles—Jerry West, Oscar Robertson, Elgin Baylor—and could pick and choose moves that worked for him.

156   "They were going crazy,": Sam King, "Maravich Stories Will Live Forever," *State-Times*, January 9, 1988.

156   First among these players: See Robin Fambrough, "Ex-McKinley Player Scott Remembered as "One of a Kind,' " *Sunday Advocate*, June 6, 1999.

158   "Why No Black Athletes?": Don Howze, "Sutter's Goal Ices Double-Overtime Win," *Alexandria Daily Town Talk*, December 15, 1968.

159   cover of *Sports Illustrated: Sports Illustrated*, December 1, 1969.

159   "The most amazing scorer: Marvin West, "SEC Teams Have No Place to Hide from Pistol Pete," *Sporting News*, December 6, 1969.

159   "Shoot the ball, Freddie,": Maravich and Campbell, 128.

160   "this gangly kid: Jeff Prugh, "Maravich: Hair Flops, Socks Sag—but What Moves," *Los Angeles Times*, December 23, 1969.

160   "What I want to do: Ibid.

160   "A definite advantage,": Dwight Chapin, "Bruins, Not Pete, Set Scoring Record," *Los Angeles Times*, December 24, 1969.

160   each of his five starters: Sidney Wicks, Curtis Rowe, Steve Patterson, John Vallely, Henry Bibby.

161   "You didn't see the real Pete: Chapin, "Bruins, Not Pete, Set Scoring Record."

161   "the best 15 minute performance: Maury Allen, "Louie's Impossible Dream . . . Maravich & Co. for Nets," *New York Post*, January 6, 1970.

161   "You talk of Jerry West: Gordon S. White, "Maravich Is Hailed as Basketball Artist," *New York Times*, January 6, 1970.

162   "It was obvious,": Letter from T. Steven Bland, Judge, Ninth Judicial Circuit, Divi-

sion I, Hardin County Courthouse, Elizabeth, Kentucky, to Joe Dean, Athletic Director, LSU, March 10, 1997, LSU.

162 at least five minutes: Ibid.
163 broadcast on closed-circuit television: Gutman, 94.
163 He failed to connect: Ibid.
164 "Please," he told the newsmen: Ibid., 95.
164 "I think I'm very fortunate,": *Pistol Pete: The Life and Times of Pete Maravich*, Black Canyon Films.
164 "The Nixons: Text of letter in Press Release, February 19, 1970, LSU.
165 She seemed to be in a trance: Maravich and Campbell, 129.
165 discover the bottles: Ibid., 132.
165 "With all the strength: Ibid., 130.

14. MARKED MAN

Interviews: Hester; Eddie Einhorn, August 4, 2005; Johnson; Hickman; Hess; Simmons.

167 206 stations: "Tiger Tracks," Press Release, February 19, 1970, LSU.
168 with 9:17 left: Dick Fenlon, "UK Spoils Pete's Home Finale," *Louisville Courier Journal*, February 22, 1970 from *http:/www.ukfans.net/jps/uk/Statistics/Games/19700221LouisianaState.html*.
168 Season tickets sales: Sam Goldaper, "The Maravich Show Moves in Friday," *New York Times*, March 8, 1970.
169 "The House That Pete Built.": In Gutman, 85, it is referred to as "the House That Maravich Built."
169 "Our growth,": "NBA Signs $17 Million TV Contract," *Cleveland Plain Dealer*, February 18, 1970.
169 "I don't want a penny: Larry Merchant, "Maravich U.," *New York Post*, March 13, 1970.
170 "It has always been a dream: Dave Anderson, "Pistol Pete Is Drawing a Bead on College Basketball's Career Scoring Record," *New York Times*, January 25, 1970.
170 "Pete Maravich and the Garden: Merchant. "Maravich U."
170 staggeringly over-publicized: Leonard Koppett, "Georgetown Five Beaten by 83–82," *New York Times*, March 16, 1970.
170 "the city's full publicity paraphernalia: Lynn Hudson, "Pete Holds Court—Broadway Joe Style," *New York Daily News*, March 4, 1970.
171 "Did anyone ever tell you,": Ibid.
171 The Garden concession stands: Goldaper, "The Maravich Show Moves in Friday."
171 favorable comparisons of Pete: Phil Pepe, "For Pistol Pete . . . A New Audience," *Daily News*, March 15, 1970.
171 "the best damned basketball player: Milton Gross, "That's His Boy," *New York Post*, January 28, 1970.
171 "He'd make it as big: Ibid.
171 "The coach maintains: Leonard Cohen, "Press on Pete: Avant Guard," *New York Post*, March 14, 1970.

171 "He's given his life to basketball: Ed Tunstall, "NIT Title Last Big Target for Maravich," *State-Times*, March 11, 1970.

172 "never met a kid: Phil Pepe, "Pistol Pete Blasts Plan; Joe Is Lavish in Praise," *New York Daily News*, March 16, 1970.

172 "His worst game: Larry Merchant, "Merely Brilliant," *New York Post*, March 16, 1970.

172 "He was emotionally wiped: Ibid.

172 "Pete has made a fan: Sam Goldaper, "Maravich's Off-Game Turns Scouts On," *New York Times*, March 16, 1970.

172 "Tremendous talent,": Ibid.

172 "I had a slap pass: Merchant, "Merely Brilliant."

173 "I told the little bastards: Paul Zimmerman, "Pete's Still Firing," *New York Post*, March 18, 1970.

173 a pair of free throws to clinch: Gene Ward, "Ward to the Wise," *Daily News*, March 19, 1970.

173 "Felt like I made 35,": Zimmerman, "Pete's Still Firing."

173 "A perfectionist who: Ward, "Ward to the Wise."

174 "I can tell: Zimmerman, "Pete's Still Firing."

174 "We're staying: Ibid.

174 "watching grass grow." Pete Axthelm, *The City Game* (Lincoln, NE: Bison Books, 1999) 27; originally published New York: Harper's Magazine Press, 1970, 27.

174 rooted in a vendetta: Ibid., 22–23.

175 "The party continued: Maravich and Campbell, 134.

175 "We mowed his lawn:": quoted in Axthelm, 27.

175 "He's good,": Ibid.

176 "My stupidity: Maravich and Campbell, 135.

176 a hip pointer: Gene Roswell, "Pete Hurt May Not Play," *New York Post*, March 20, 1970.

177 concussed with blurred vision: Jimmy Davy, "Loaded Pistol Rubs Out VU," *Nashville Tennessean*, February 15, 1970.

177 the last team: Goldaper, "Maravich's Off-Game Turns Scouts On."

177 a Carolina Cougars deal: Dick Young, "Young Ideas," *New York Daily News*, March 20, 1970.

177 "His presence would guarantee: Larry Merchant, "Headed Off at the Pass," *New York Post*, March 29, 1970.

15. THE BLACKHAWKS

Interviews: Kent; Tom Cousins, July 14, 2005; John Wilcox, July 14, 2005; Packer; Hill; Sauldsberry; Gene Tormohlen, June 18, 2005; Marty Blake, April 24, 2005; Bill Bridges, August 8, 2005; Joe Caldwell, July 15, 2005; Hank Kalb, July 18, 2005; White.

179 twenty-nine hours shy: "Newsmakers," *Newsweek*, April 13, 1970.

179 courting both father and son: UPI, "ABA Cougars Seek Maravich," *New York Daily News*, April 2, 1969.

180   the initial contact with Press: Frank Deford, "Merger, Madness and Maravich," *Sports Illustrated*, April 6, 1969.

180   even a movie deal: Phil Pepe, "Through the Press Gate," *New York Daily News*, March 31, 1970.

180   a Maravich hamburger franchise: Smith Barrier, memo to *Sports Illustrated*, March 27, 1970, SI Library.

180   its "most wanted" list: Sam Goldaper, "3 Stars Placed on A.B.A. Wanted List," *New York Times*, July 16, 1969.

180   over 52 points: Berger, 128. Said Sam King of the *State-Times*, "I went through the score sheets of all his varsity games and figured out that he would have averaged 7.8 points a game more if there'd been the three-point shot."

181   the Tri-Cities Blackhawks: *The Official NBA Encyclopedia*, 94.

182   "generally acknowledged as the best: Deford, "Merger, Madness and Maravich."

182   This bit of good fortune: After the 1968–69 season, Beaty left the Hawks to join the Los Angeles Stars of the ABA. But the Stars, it turned out, were not viable in LA, and Beaty ended up sitting out the season. In the meantime, the Warriors—who had lost their own All-Star center, Nate Thurmond, to injury—decided to make a run at Beaty. But first, they had to compensate the Hawks. The price was their first pick in the draft.

183   "Drafting Pete Maravich: UPI, "Hawks 'Sure' of Pete: Cougars to Retaliate," *New York Daily News*, March 25, 1970.

183   "Tom Cousins will think: quoted in Deford, "Merger, Madness and Maravich."

183   "With everything else equal,": UPI, "Hawks 'Sure' of Pete."

183   "You won't find them: Maravich and Campbell, 139.

184   "Pete will do: Milton Gross, "That's His Boy," *New York Post*, January 28, 1970.

184   class of '42: *Quippan* 1942, BF Jones.

184   "Pete Maravich will play: Lynn Hudson, "NBA Hawks Swoop Up Pistol Pete for $1.9 Million," *New York Daily News*, March 27, 1970.

184   "one that compensates: AP, "Atlanta Packs the Pistol," *New York Post*, March 27, 1970.

184   $1.5 million over five years: Pete's contract with the Hawks, dated March 23, 1970, from Jackie Maravich's papers, summarized and sent in an e-mail, April 8, 2006.

184   $400,000 more: Hudson, "NBA Hawks Swoop Up Pistol Pete for $1.9 Million."

184   "I can't understand: Smith Barrier, memo to *Sports Illustrated*, received March 27, 1970, SI Library.

184   "I think time: Ibid.

185   increased its roll: Pepe, "Through the Press Gate."

185   "Cleo," said Seymour: Clipping from Hill's scrapbook.

185   "The most complete player": "Cleo Hill: Gaines' Most Complete Player," clipping from Hill's scrapbook, dated January 15, 1973.

186   exhibitions with the Philadelphia Warriors: "Pettit Hits 30, Hill 21 for Hawks," *St. Louis Post Dispatch*, October 1, 1961, from Hill's scrapbook.

186   "Can't you give up: Bob Cole, "Cleo Hill: Old Nest vs. New Hawk," *Winston Salem Journal-Sentinel*, c. November 1961.

186   After hearing of the boycott: "7 Negroes Are Denied Service in Lexington," *St. Louis Post-Dispatch*, October 19, 1961.

186   "I'm not saying: Cole, "Cleo Hill: Old Nest vs. New Hawk."

187 "I wouldn't treat a dog: Bud Thies, "Seymour Blasts Players, Says Some Veteran Hawks Treated Hill 'Worse Than Dog,' " *St. Louis Post-Dispatch*, c. November 18, 1961, from Hill's papers.

187 the coach was willfully disobeying: Ibid.

187 "Paul is entitled: AP, "Hawks Drop Seymour as Coach After Dispute with Top Players," *New York Times*, November 17, 1961.

189 inscribed on the trophy: Frank Deford, "Beware of the Hawks," *Sports Illustrated*, April 13, 1970.

189 "began fouling us: Berger, 142.

190 "a couple of pops: Frank Hyland, "Hawks Fans Won't Forget Guerin's Feat," *Atlanta Journal*, April 17, 1979.

190 Jumping Joe cleared: When asked about jumping over the Mercury, Caldwell claims that his approach consisted of no more than "three or four steps."

190 $11,500 as a rookie: George Cunningham, "Hawks Caldwell Man with a Plan," *Atlanta Constitution*, June 5, 1970.

190 "That guy jumps so well: George Cunningham, "Pogo Picks Up an Admirer," *Atlanta Constitution*, March 27, 1970.

191 "Caldwell is the best: George Cunningham, "Caldwell Can't Score on Defensive Team," *Atlanta Constitution*, April 22, 1970.

191 "Let's face it,": George Cunningham, "Hawk Players Hoping Pete Will Make Good," *Atlanta Constitution*, March 24, 1970.

16. THE UNBEARABLE WHITENESS OF BEING PETE

Interviews: Richie Guerin, April 26, 2005; Bridges; Kent; Caldwell; Cousins; Kalb; White; Blondeau; Coker; Sylvester; Jackie Maravich.

193 "This damn Yankee: Press to LR, May 25, 1970, from LR personal papers.

194 "An exorbitant amount: *Pistol Pete: The Life and Times of Pete Maravich*, Black Canyon Films.

194 "Maravich has to prove himself: Al Thomy, "Richie Forsees 'No Letdown,' " *Atlanta Constitution*, March 26, 1970.

195 leaving the old Hawks to wonder: George Cunningham, "Pistol Pete Piling Up Mistakes Which Is What Hawks Expected," *Sporting News*, October 24, 1970.

195 "I'm not asking: George Cunningham, "Bridges Rap Hits Hawks," *Atlanta Constitution*, June 13, 1970.

195 his request for a raise: Ibid.

196 had to tell the all-white band: Bill Bradley, *Life on the Run* (New York: Quadrangle/New York Times Book Co., 1976), 38.

196 between $40,000 and $50,000: George Cunningham, "Caldwell Reportedly Seeking a Million," *Atlanta Constitution*, September 28, 1970.

197 began his holdout: George Cunningham, "It's Official Now: Caldwell a Holdout," *Atlanta Constitution*, September 18, 1970.

197 "Joe Caldwell has just received: George Cunningham, "Caldwell Goes to ABA," *Atlanta Constitution*, October 31, 1970.

197 At $175,000 a year: Lewis Grizzard, memo to *Sports Illustrated*, September 17, 1971, SI Library.

199 "a white boy who played: Scott Ostler, "The Leaping Legends of Basketball," *Los Angeles Times*, February 12, 1989.

199 the most underrated dunker: "The Rating Game," *Sports Illustrated*, August 27, 2001.

199 *Wide World of Sports:* Tom Herman, "A Long-Haired Rookie Makes Losing Season a Box-Office Victory," *Wall Street Journal*, March 25, 1971.

199 "The loudest cheer: Peter Carry, "We Have a Slight Delay in Show Time," *Sports Illustrated*, October 10, 1970.

200 "I felt," said Pete: Ibid.

200 "It was going to be: Noah Sanders, "Pistol Pete Now Is Up against the Pros," *New York Times Magazine*, October 11, 1970.

200 started out 7–21: *http://www.basketball-reference.com/teams/ATL/1971/_games .html.*

200 "I was so frustrated: Milton Gross, "A Member," *New York Post*, November 27, 1970.

200 13 turnovers: UPI, "Pete Maravich: Problems of Adjustment Over, He Would Like to Make Hawks Soar—Instead of Sore," *New York Times*, February 28, 1971.

200 "You try to get him angry: Walt Frazier and Ira Berkow, *Rockin' Steady* (New York: Warner Paperback, 1974), 66.

200 "What's wrong: Gross, "A Member."

201 "As welcome as George Wallace: Jesse Outlar, "A Year to Forget," *Atlanta Constitution*, September 8, 1971.

201 the crowds kept urging: Paul Hemphill, "Viewpoint South," *Sport*, December 1970.

201 Maravich would quip bitterly: Grizzard, memo to *Sports Illustrated*, September 17, 1971, SI Library.

201 "the rookie is: George Cunningham, "Pistol Pete Hot, But . . . ," *Atlanta Journal*, November 16, 1970.

202 why do hot dogs: Tom Dial, "Here's Why 'Hot Dogs' Cost More," *Atlanta Constitution*, March 19, 1971.

202 "made a close game: Leonard Lewin, "The Pistol Steal . . . ," *New York Post*, November 25, 1970.

202 36 points and 11 assists: Frank Hyland, "Maravich Bets Wests's 36 Won't Happen Again," *Atlanta Journal*, December 21, 1970.

202 "probably more pressure: George Cunningham, " 'Pressure Hurt Maravich,' " *Atlanta Constitution*, April 21, 1971.

202 "The incident: Furman Bisher, "The High Price of Genius," *Atlanta Journal*, November 5, 1970.

202 "Atlanta's most eligible bachelor,": George Cunningham, "The 'Pistol,' " *Atlanta Constitution*, December 26, 1970.

203 "looked like a decorator's showroom: *Pistol Pete: The Life and Times of Pete Maravich*, Black Canyon Films.

203 "Maravich-style hairdos: Cunningham, "The 'Pistol.' "

203 He refused to talk about Jackie: UPI, "Pete Maravich: Problems of Adjustment

Over, He Would Like to Make Hawks Soar—Instead of Sore," *New York Times*, February 28, 1971.

204   a secret back exit: Berger, 148.

204   "Before long I'm so nervous: Ron Hudspeth, "Pistol's Gun-Shy of Loving Public," *Atlanta Journal*, March 11, 1971.

204   Finally, the cops were called: Frank Hyland, "Hairy Escape for Pete," *Atlanta Journal*, March 17, 1971.

204   "We didn't have any choice,": *SportsCentury: Pete Maravich*, ESPN Classic.

208   the morning of February 16, 1971: Herb White is the main source for this scene, but some details are provided in Lewis Grizzard, memo to *Sports Illustrated*, September 17, 1971, SI Library.

208   Atlanta lost to the Bulls: *http://www.basketball-reference.com/teams/ATL/ 1971_games.html*.

209   He even played a little defense: Tom Dial, "Pistol Pete's Showtime Here," *Atlanta Constitution*, March 11, 1971.

209   Over the last seventeen games: Grizzard memo, September 17, 1971.

209   "the new Jerry West.": George Cunningham, " 'Pistol' Reaches Basketball Maturity Just in Time," *Journal and Constitution* (Atlanta), March 7, 1971.

209   "Some of the shots,": Larry Merchant, "Champion Calibre," *New York Post*, April 2, 1971.

209   "He can make: Frazier and Berkow, 66.

209   "He can beat: Merchant, "Champion Calibre."

209   "He's proved himself: Ibid.

209   "If I make that one,": Ibid.

210   "I'd be satisfied: AP, "Came through Year as Good as I Could—Maravich," *Atlanta Constitution*, April 3, 1971.

210   "You don't know: Ibid.

210   "a substantial profit,": Herman, "A Long-Haired Rookie Makes Losing Season a Box-Office Victory."

210   gross revenues jump: Ibid.

210   Atlanta even outdrew: George Cunningham, "Only Ali Draws Better Than 'Pistol,' " *Atlanta Constitution*, August 20, 1971.

210   $17 million arena: "Alderman Approve Plan for New Home of Hawks," *Sporting News*, January 30, 1971; see also AP, "Came through Year as Good as I Could—Maravich."

210   "the house that Pete built.": UPI, "Pete Maravich: Problems of Adjustment Over."

1 7 . TAKE ME

Interviews: Kent; Guerin; Tormohlen; Bergman; Greg Bernbrock, June 21, 2005; Hess; Newton; Johnson; Garland; Sandford; Greg Smith, July 19, 2005; Biedenbach; Robinson; Pat Williams, April 22, 2005.

211   four of 192 votes: Jim Huber, "Contemporary Maravich Redecorated in Old Ideas and Brand New Tricks," *Atlanta Journal*, August 22, 1971.

211 "I want to forget it,": *Sports Illustrated*, October 25, 1971.

211 "You can forget about alcohol,": Lewis Grizzard, memo to *Sports Illustrated*, July 1, 1971, SI Library.

212 wire service briefs: UPI, "Maravich Fined, Warned by Judge," *Atlanta Journal*, June 28, 1971; AP, "Maravich Fined $150 by Judge," *Atlanta Constitution*, June 29, 1971.

212 $125 tuition: Brochure and application to the Pete Maravich Basketball Camp, from Lazo Maravich's papers.

212 The Hawks would adopt: Lewis Grizzard, memo to *Sports Illustrated*, October 29, 1971, SI Library.

212 "Wait'll he sees: Huber, "Contemporary Maravich Redecorated in Old Ideas and Brand New Tricks."

212 picked the reconstituted Hawks: *Sports Illustrated*, October 25, 1971.

213 "established himself: George Cunningham, " 'Mono' Hits Pistol Pete," *Atlanta Constitution*, October 5, 1971.

213 "shaking uncontrollably,": Jim Huber, "Pete May Miss Hawks' Florida Series," *Atlanta Journal*, September 23, 1971.

213 The first diagnosis: George Cunningham, "Virus Stops 'Pistol Pete,' " *Atlanta Constitution*, September 27, 1971.

213 write messages on a clipboard: George Cunningham, "Recovery Aim of Pistol Pete May Be Off-Target by a Month," *Atlanta Constitution*, October 15, 1971.

213 "I feel like I'm in cold storage: Jim Huber, "Fan Letters Please Pete," *Atlanta Journal*, October 19, 1971.

213 "You know you die: Jim Huber, "Pete Blames Jax Doctors," *Atlanta Journal*, October 15, 1971.

213 "If I am going to die,": Cunningham, "Recovery Aim of Pistol Pete May Be Off-Target by a Month."

213 the Hawks' team physician: Cunningham, " 'Mono' Hits Pistol Pete."

213 "every test for mono: Jim Huber, "Hawks Keep the Physicians Hopping," *Atlanta Journal*, November 19, 1971.

213 crackpots and would-be sweethearts: Huber, "Fan Letters Please Pete."

213 eat any solid food: Cunningham, "Recovery Aim of Pistol Pete May Be Off-Target by a Month."

213 205 to 168: Maravich and Campbell, 151.

214 "I thought I was going: Jesse Outlar, "Never Tilt Wilt," *Atlanta Constitution*, October 21, 1971.

214 12 turnovers: George Cunningham, "Hawk Followers Need Patience," *Atlanta Constitution*, November 19, 1971.

214 "He tried to keep us: Steve Clark, "Pistol Cooled," *Atlanta Constitution*, November 18, 1971.

214 "I was dead: George Cunningham, "Pistol's Recovery Hits Big Roadblock," *Atlanta Constitution*, November 24, 1971.

214 "My heart, man: Jim Huber, "Maravich May Be Lost for the Year," *Atlanta Journal*, November 30, 1971.

214 the first of two: On February 5, 1972, he scored 50 in a 120–117 win over Cleveland. *http://sports.yahoo.com/nba/news?slug=50pointsinagame&prov=st&type=lgns*.

215 "Pete has lots more: George Cunningham, "Maravich Hawks' Best Ever?," *Atlanta Constitution*, January 20, 1972.

215 "There wasn't a player: Chuck Culpepper, "Pistol Pete, 1947–1988," *Los Angeles Herald-Examiner*, January 6, 1988.

215 "Thrill me,": George Cunningham, "Maravich Answers Gilliam's 'Thrill Me' Plea," *Atlanta Constitution*, January 24, 1972.

215 "As the Pistol Goes: George Cunningham, "As the Pistol Goes, So Goes the Hawks," *Atlanta Constitution*, December 25, 1971.

215 four meals a day: Leonard Lewin, "Pete's Always Feeding," *New York Post*, March 15, 1972.

215 he went scoreless: Frank Hyland, "The Pistol Fires a Blank," *Atlanta Journal*, March 16, 1971.

217 "Nobody knows the game: Bill Ballenger, "Love Was Not Enough," *Charlotte News*, March 2, 1972.

217 "It's got a big hole: Mike McKenzie, "LSU's No Longer Home to Pete—'They Fired My Father,'" *Atlanta Journal*, October 2, 1972.

218 "knock him down: *SportsCentury: Pete Maravich*, ESPN Classic.

218 "He needs constant reassurance,": Jim Huber, "'Look Up, Pete . . . Please Look Up,'" *Sunday Journal Constitution*, October 1, 1972.

219 "How'd you like: Ibid.

219 "He loves the damn stuff,": Letter from Press to Bob and Louise Bradley, August 24, 1972, from Louise Bradley.

220 a giant waffle iron: *http://basketball.ballparks.com/NBA/AtlantaHawks/oldindex.htm*.

220 "Easily his best: Memo to *Sports Illustrated*, December 26, 1972.

220 "The New Pete,": Mike McKenzie, "The New Pete," *Atlanta Journal*, September 12, 1972.

220 he'd be perfectly content: Huber, "'Look Up, Pete'"

220 "I don't feel anything,": McKenzie, "The New Pete."

220 "He knows that: George Cunningham, "Pete Trades a Frown for Cool New Look," *Atlanta Constitution*, September 19, 1972.

220 "excruciating head pain": George Cunningham, "Pistol Guns 44; Hawks Win by 8," *Sunday Journal Constitution*, November 5, 1972.

221 Despite assurances: Mike McKenzie, "Maravich Is a Pain Only to Baltimore," *Atlanta Journal*, November 7, 1972.

221 "I can't blink: Leonard Lewin, "Pete Maravich's Nightmare," *New York Post*, December 12, 1972.

221 tape his right eye shut: AP, "Bell's Palsy Putting Question Mark on Pistol Pete," *New York Post*, November 17, 1972.

221 "the same embarrassment,": Mike McKenzie, "Pete Will Rejoin Hawks Thursday," *Atlanta Journal*, November 15, 1972.

221 "Pete's got it in the: George Cunningham, "There's Just Not Much Improvement," *Atlanta Journal*, November 14, 1972.

221 "A witch doctor: McKenzie, "Pete Will Rejoin Hawks Thursday."

222 vitamin C and protein: Press's letter to family and friends, November 17, 1972, from Louise Bradley.

222   the doormat: AP, "Press Maravich: Happy in the Hills," December 17, 1972.

222   Mountaineer season ticket holders: Joe Tiede, "Press Maravich Returns for Impossible Task," *Raleigh Observer*, November 26, 1972.

222   "small, thin and inexperienced.": Ibid.

222   He could see it in the kids: AP, "Press Maravich: Happy in the Hills."

223   "Eighty points,": Ken Alyta, "Two Long Rides," *Winston-Salem Journal*, c. December 1972, NCS.

223   "If you ever get fired: AP, "Press Maravich: Happy in the Hills."

223   12–4 that month: *http://www.basketball-reference.com/teams/ATL/1973_games.html*.

223   fourth leading scorer: Memo to *Sports Illustrated*, December 26, 1972.

223   "As hard as he tries: Jesse Outlar, "Hawk Talk," *Sunday Journal-Constitution*, December 10, 1972.

223   "I've always been a target,": Mike McKenzie, memo to *Sports Illustrated*, January 14, 1973.

223   his planned escape: Dave Anderson, "One for the Show," *New York Times*, December 8, 1973.

224   "He never learned: Al Thomy, " 'Never Learned to Lose,' " *Atlanta Constitution*, April 5, 1973.

224   His seasons with Pete: In the four years they played together, Hudson averaged exactly 26 points a game. See *http://www.basketball-reference.com/players/h/hudsolo01.html*.

224   "the white darling": Bradley, 38.

224   "There was no reason: Peter Carry, "He's Shooting the Works," *Sports Illustrated*, November 12, 1973.

224   almost 30 a game: 29.2 as of December 8, 1973.

224   "He's playing basketball as nobody ever: Dave Anderson, "One for the Show; Acts of Deception His Obsession," *New York Times*, December 8, 1973.

225   "a promotional wizard: Carry, "He's Shooting the Works."

225   He often seemed absent: Jesse Outlar, "Can Anyone Discipline Pistol Pete?," *Atlanta Constitution*, February 6, 1974.

226   Fitzsimmons sent him to the bench: Darrell Simmons, "Maravich Suspended; Fitzsimmons Is Mum," *Atlanta Journal*, February 5, 1974.

226   seven technicals: Sam Goldaper, "Hawks Maravich Suspended 'Indefinitely' by His Coach," *New York Times*, February 6, 1974.

226   getting drunk on beer: Williams interview; Berger, 165.

226   babbling without pause: Darrell Simmons, "Pete Fined, Reinstated," *Atlanta Journal*, February 7, 1974.

226   "When we lose,": Leonard Lewin, "Cotton's Crisis," *New York Post*, February 6, 1974.

226   "You could tell,": Berger 165.

226   "I went against: Furman Bisher, "A Tarnished White Hope," *Atlanta Journal*, February 8, 1974.

227   "I can play: Alan Richman, "76ers Smash Hawks," *Philadelphia Bulletin*, in *Atlanta Constitution*, February 9, 1974.

227   There would be injuries: Darrell Simmons, "An Angry Pistol," *Atlanta Journal*, February 27, 1974.

227 "When I shoot: Al Thomy, "Maravich Fed Up with Scapegoat Role," *Atlanta Constitution*, February 27, 1974.
227 "I don't want to play: Andy Nuzzo, "Friends Remember a Legend," *Beaver County* (Pennsylvania) *Times*, January 6, 1988.
227 "Everyone thinks: Peter Vecsey, "Pistol Pete—Smokin' & Burnin'," *New York Post*, February 25, 1974.
227 "Take me": Berger, 153.

18. SMOTHERED

Interviews: Guy Smith, March 21, 2005; Barry Mendelson, March 4, 2005; Aaron James, July 24, 2005; Rich Kelley, July 12, 2005; Neal Walk, July 14, 2005; Russ Bergman; Jackie Maravich; Ann Bergman, June 24, 2005; Robinson.

229 "We'd like to trade you: Jim Hunter, "Pete's Move," *Atlanta Journal*, April 26, 1974.
229 four first-round picks: Darrell Simmons, "New Orleans Pays Dearly for Maravich," *Atlanta Journal*, May 3, 1974.
229 "I really can't tolerate: Ibid.
230 "If imitation: Al Thomy, "Who Did It? Pete Did It, That's Who," *Atlanta Constitution*, May 4, 1974.
230 "The trading of Maravich,": Ron Hudspeth, "Perspective: Trade Maravich? Why Add Dullness atop Mediocrity?," *Atlanta Journal*, April 30, 1974.
230 "Without a doubt: Darrell Simmons, "Cotton Feels Swap Gives Hawks 'Chance,'" *Sunday Journal-Constitution*, May 5, 1974.
230 "That incredible pass: Keith Coulbourn, "Trade of Hawks' Superstar Stirs Fond Memories in One of His Ardent Fans," *Sunday Journal-Constitution*, September 15, 1974.
230 average only 2,599 fans: *http://www.remembertheaba.com/MemphisMaterial/BuccaneersMemphisYearly.html*.
230 leaky roof: Marty Mule, "In the Beginning," *New Orleans Times-Picayune*, July 6, 1997.
231 fewer than 7,000: Ibid
231 169,000 cubic yards: *http://www.superdome.com/site75.php*.
234 Catawba Memorial Hospital: AP, "Pete Maravich's Mother Dies of Gunshot Wounds," *New York Post*, October 10, 1974.
235 "I went out of bounds: Les East, "Pete Made Every Jazz Game Mardi Gras," *Times-Picayune*, October 16, 1988 (a condensed version of a story that originally ran in the paper on December 13, 1985).
235 last-second shot: AP, "Maravich Resigns as Coach at ASU," January 14, 1974 (NCS).

19. ALL THAT JAZZ

Interviews: Johnson; Mendelson; Guerin; Smith; Jackie Maravich; Kalb; Hot Rod Hundley, July 28, 2005; Elgin Baylor, July 26, 2005; James; Walk; Kelley.

237 off 10 points: "Jazz Getting Hot as Maravich Goes Back to Old Scoring Style," *New York Times*, January 21, 1975.

237 severe case of tendonitis: Pat Putnam, "Maravich and All Those Jazz," *Sports Illustrated*, February 17, 1975.

237 "I'm not like Muhammad Ali: Ted Green, Los Angeles Times Syndicate, "Maravich Has to Live with His Double Image," *New York Post*, January 30, 1975.

237 first consecutive wins: Putnam, "Maravich and All Those Jazz."

237 shrunk twenty pounds: Ibid.

238 "Hey coach: Wayne Minshew and Chris Cobbs, "Do Not Disturb," *Atlanta Constitution*, January 22, 1975.

238 "If there were five fast breaks: Darrell Williams, "Maravich's Teammates Dish off Praise," *Times-Picayune*, October 16, 1988.

238 "Doesn't shoot: Letter from Press to Bob and Louise Bradley, December 26, 1974, from Louise Bradley.

239 "One time I took him: Earl Gustkey, "Maravich Dies at 40 of Heart Attack," *Los Angeles Times*, January 6, 1988.

239 "I play the way: Putnam, "Maravich and All Those Jazz."

240 Coach of the Year: Steve Hershey, "VBK Deserves Coach of Year Nod for Jazz Job," *Sporting News*, April 19, 1975.

240 "Win or lose: Ibid.

241 19,203 reserve seats: Sam Goldaper, "Jazz, $1.50 Seats Hit in Superdome," *New York Times*, November 7, 1975.

242 bailing and mopping: David Snyder, Memo to *Time*, sports desk, November 6, 1975, SI Library.

242 Sheriff's Department Jeeps: Goldaper, "Jazz, $1.50 Seats Hit in Superdome."

242 "No thanks, Milton,": Peter Finney, "New Jazz Age Sweeping Over New Orleans," *Sporting News*, November 22, 1975.

242 previous mark of 20,239: Bob Roesler, "26511 Undaunted," *Times-Picayune*, November 6, 1975.

242 NFL's New Orleans Saints: Peter Finney, Memo to *Sports Illustrated*, November 6, 1975.

242 Pete went so far as to predict: Finney, "New Jazz Age."

242 "It seems like: "Maravich Injured," *New York Times*, November 18, 1975.

242 given up red meat: Maravich and Campbell, 166.

243 "Pete went through: Berger, 184.

243 a last-place team: Sam Goldaper, "Cavs No Longer a Butt of Jokers," *New York Times*, December 23, 1975.

244 the only all-white team: Letter from Press to Bob and Louise Bradley, March 22, 1977, from Louise Bradley.

244 27–10: Joe Planas, "The Serb Is Stateside," *Morning Advocate* (Baton Rouge), November 1, 1976.

244 "I told him to shove it: Press to the Bradleys, March 22, 1977.

245 Diana was tall: Ibid.

245 Mendelson and Bertka agreed to acquire: Jerry Kirshenbaum, "New Guard for the Old Guard," *Sports Illustrated*, November 8, 1976.

246 "That's the sort of thing Pete and I can do: Ibid.

246 "It's not enough: Ibid.

246   The coach wasn't shy: Berger, 190.

247   punched Dave Twardzik: UPI, "Maravich Fighting Mad," *Pittsburgh Press*, November 17, 1976.

247   "Why am I here?": *New York Times*, November 25, 1976.

247   **So long, Butch:** *States-Item*, December 15, 1976.

248   "the man with a thousand moves,": *http://www.hoophall.com/halloffamers/Baylor.htm*.

249   "When I'm on: Kirshenbaum, "New Guard for the Old Guard."

249   night of February 25: Brian McIntyre of the National Basketball Association was kind enough to provide the author with a tape of the game. Also used was a documentary of that game on DVD, *The Night of Pistol Pete*, Mendelson Entertainment, 2004.

250   "You're the defensive expert.": Berger, 193.

251   "His performance was the best: Marty Mule, "Pistol Power!," *Times-Picayune*, February 26, 1977.

251   "I'm glad he was one short: Jim O'Brien, "Pistol Shoots Down Knicks," *New York Post*, February 26, 1977.

251   could have scored 88: A. J. Carr, "Press Seeks Pizzazz for Jazz," *Raleigh News and Observer*, March 13, 1977.

251   the game's greatest: Will Peneguy, "Does 68 Prove 'Pete's Greatest'?," *Times-Picayune*, February 27, 1977.

251   "As morning rolled around: Maravich and Campbell, 169.

252   Baylor had to petition: "Cracked Up Jazz May Walk to Forum," *Times-Picayune*, March 20, 1977.

252   "In the end,": Berger, 195.

252   "Damn near beat LA: Letter from Press to the Bradleys, March 22, 1977.

252   almost 5 points more: Billy Knight of the Indiana Pacers was second, with an average of 26.6.

252   a five-year contract: AP, "Maravich Signs: 5 Years, $3 Million," *New York Times*, August 12, 1977. Mendelson, who initiated the negotiations over coffee in Art Herskovitz's kitchen back in Aliquippa, recalls the deal as being slightly richer than that, with a starting salary of $675,000. "Whatever the price," says Mendelson, "it was a bargain."

253   the Marx Brothers: Peter Finney, Memo to *Sports Illustrated*, April 1, 1978, SI Library.

253   all the junk food: Peter Finney, Memo to *Sports Illustrated*, May 31, 1978, SI Library.

253   "He still can't take: Robert Ward, "Pete Maravich Is Still Magic," *Sport*, December 1976.

253   "We are Serbian: Ibid.

253   five A's and a B: Letter from Press to LR, November 8, 1977, from Les Robinson.

254   "the only thing left: Letter from Press to the Bradleys, March 22, 1977, from Louise Bradley.

254   "the damn niggers.": Letter from Press to the Bradleys, February 24, 1978.

254   Press attributed this to: Letter from Press to LR, February 8, 1978.

254   the Goodrich trade: "Citing Trade for Goodrich, Jazz Drop General Manager," *New York Times*, March 24, 1977.

255   call out a season ticket holder: Peter Finney and Ron Brocato, Memo to *Sports Illustrated*, January 4, 1978, SI Library.

255   "didn't have enough ball movement.": Curry Kirkpatrick, "No One Can Cap the Pistol," *Sports Illustrated*, December 4, 1978.

255   "A lying backstabbing: Ibid.

255   "If they want me to sacrifice: John Papanek, "Heavy Truckin' on Bourbon Street," *Sports Illustrated*, December 5, 1977.

256   "He is exactly: Ibid.

256   Four times that season: *http://www.superdome.com/uploads/SuperdomeAttendanceRecords.doc.*

257   scoring 20 or more: Austin Wilson, "Only One Difference in Jazz," *Times-Picayune*, January 31, 1978.

257   35 points, 11 assists, and 5 steals: Dick Mittman, "Jazz Captures Eighth Straight," *Times-Picayune*, January 30, 1978.

257   "I didn't touch him,": Fred Robinson, "Maravich Hurt," *Times-Picayune*, February 1, 1978.

257   "snapping sound": Berger, 211.

20. THE LOSER

Interviews: James; Baylor; Jackie Maravich; Mendelson; Tom Nissalke, July 19, 2005; Williams: Carr; Sandford.

259   "I'd come in: John Papanek, "The Truck Stops Here," *Sports Illustrated*, January 29, 1979.

259   hoping to be back jogging: Letter from Press to the Bradleys, February 24, 1978, from Louise Bradley.

259   twisted knee: AP, "Pistol May Be Lost for Week," *New York Post*, February 1, 1978.

259   riddle him with cancer: AP, "Pistol May Need Surgery on Knee," *New York Post*, February 14, 1978.

260   "Just a shadow: Quoted in "It's Time of Decision," *Sporting News*, April 8, 1978.

260   "The pain reached a point: Maravich and Campbell, 175.

260   "You'll never change: Peter Finney, Memo to *Sports Illustrated*, May 31, 1978, SI Library.

260   living to be 100: Ibid.

260   randy women's basketball team: *Scoring*, directed by Michael De Gaetano, 1979. From the box of the video, released in 1982: "The movie *Scoring* may well turn the sport of basketball into the nation's number one pastime. Here's a battle (a ball, really) between an all-girl's basketball team and a men's team, combining fun, sex and a lot of honest to gosh athletic prowess (on and off the court) into one of the wildest movie experiences ever to hit the screen. It's guaranteed to leave you dribbling for more."

260   highlight of the filming: Patrick K. Lackey, Memo to *Sports Illustrated*, September 14, 1978.

261   the epigraph: Kirkpatrick, "No One Can Cap the Pistol."

262   "I could kill: Ibid.

262 Erich von Däniken: Testimony tape.

262 "I'm going,": Kirkpatrick, "No One Can Cap the Pistol."

262 "I came into a situation: Papanek, "The Truck Stops Here."

262 "The Jazz has two sets: Ibid.

263 "I'm the white boy: Kirkpatrick, "No One Can Cap the Pistol."

263 "disgusting basketball,": Sam Goldaper, "Haywood Practices amid Feuding Jazz," New York Times, January 9, 1979.

263 an inch and a half less: AP, "Ailing Knee Ends Season for Pistol," New York Post, February 22, 1978.

264 "It would hurt me: Maravich and Campbell, 174.

264 49 of 61 games: AP, "Ailing Knee Ends Season for Pistol," New York Post, February 22, 1978.

265 dropped by a third: Home attendance dropped from 527,351, an average crowd of 12,862, in 1977–78 to 364,205, an average of 8,883, in 1978–79. Statistics from the Utah Jazz Public Relations Office.

265 season ticket holders never rose: Marty Mule, "Cards Were Stacked Against Team Staying," Times-Picayune, July 9, 1997.

265 "he couldn't go through: Berger, 218.

266 trip to a goat farm: Peter Vecsey, "Pistol: The Real Magic," New York Post, January 8, 1988.

266 the first and third quarters: Dave Blackwell, "Maravich a Spectator," Atlanta Constitution, December 12, 1979.

266 souvenir posters: Peter Vecsey, "Jazz to Waive Maravich," New York Post, November 28, 1979.

266 "When a team wants: Ibid.

267 the parties negotiated a settlement: AP, "Maravich Is Waived by Jazz," Atlanta Constitution, January 18, 1980.

267 reported in a headline: Sam Goldaper, "Maravich Becomes Free Agent; Likely to Sign with 76ers," New York Times, January 22, 1980.

268 "If you score points: Jack Wilkinson, "Pistol's New Act," New York Daily News, April 13, 1980.

268 "I've always wanted: UPI, "Maravich Signs Pact to Play with Celtics," New York Times, January 23, 1980.

268 "Never seen an athlete: Carrie Seidman, "Maravich Is Trying to Go Out a Winner," New York Times, March 19, 1980.

268 refurbishing his physique: Leigh Montville, "It's Fun Time for Maravich," Boston Globe, January 25, 1980.

269 "a carrier": Leo Monahan, Memo to Sports Illustrated, January 27, 1980.

269 "I was a bigger fan: Wilkinson, "Pistol's New Act."

269 "He was always allowed: George Cunningham, "Maravich," Atlanta Constitution, February 26, 1980.

269 "His practice habits: Wilkinson, "Pistol's New Act."

269 "He still can't run: Ibid.

270 A spectacular inbound lob: Bob Ryan, "Celtics Explode—Nets Expire, 117–92," Boston Globe, March 18, 1980.

270 "a burst: Bob Ryan, "Pistol Riddles Pacers," Boston Globe, March 19, 1980.

270 "That's what we got him for,": David Dupree, "Celtics Drop Bullets, 96–95," *Washington Post*, March 26, 1980.

270 "a one-man show,": Leigh Montville, "Celtics We Saw All Season Didn't Show Up," *Boston Globe*, April 28, 1980.

270 "Maybe the Celtics: Ray Fitzgerald, "A Sour End to a Super Debut," *Boston Globe*, April 28, 1980.

271 just over 13 minutes: From *Boston Globe* box scores, April 19, 21, 24, 26, 28, 1980.

271 only a half-share: Joe D' Adamo, Memo to *Sports Illustrated*, May 13, 1980.

271 Pete's daily regimen: *Sporting News*, c. summer 1980.

271 Pete made a statement: Maravich and Campbell, 185.

272 "I think I've shot: George Sullivan, "Maravich Quits, Fed Up with Basketball," *Boston Globe*, September 21, 1980.

272 he didn't want a championship ring: Maravich and Campbell, 17.

21. TAKE ME, PART 2

Interviews: Jackie Maravich; Johnson; Jaeson Maravich, April 3, 2005; Joshua Maravich; Russ Bergman; Zernich; Bryant; Pukach; Wooden; James McLachlan, April 5, 2005; Leah Wilcox, January 19, 2005; Walk; Kalb; Baylor; Drollinger; Moline; Lydic.

273 "I was testing: Lisa Twyman, "On the Scene: Pete Maravich Used to Be a Hot Dog, but Nowadays He Won't Even Eat One," *Sports Illustrated*, October 29, 1984.

274 guided the toddler's fingers: Testimony tape.

274 "stuff from Europe: Barry Cooper, "Maravich Is Giving Religion His Best Shot," *Orlando Sentinel*, July 28, 1985.

274 hadn't stepped foot outside: Cassette tape of *The Larry King Show*, recorded February 27, 1986. From George Roy's research materials for *Pistol Pete: The Life and Times of Pete Maravich*.

274 Pete didn't need anyone: Testimony tape.

274 "So many times,": Ibid.

275 "It was driving me nuts": Ibid.

275 "Please, save me: Maravich and Campbell, 192.

276 "You either believe it: Testimony tape.

276 "Everything that went: John Adams, "Maravich Still on Target with New Goals," *Sunday Advocate* (Baton Rouge), July 10, 1983.

277 "I tape the faucets: Stan Hochman, "Maravich Finally Content with Life after Basketball," Knight-Ridder Newspapers, Baton Rouge *State-Times*, February 1, 1984.

277 a heroin addiction: Shelby Strother, "A Curtain Call for Pistol Pete: Before the Magic, There Was Maravich," *Detroit News*, February 7, 1987.

277 he never missed: Scott Ostler, "We Should Be Grateful for Gift of Pete Maravich's Time," *Los Angeles Times*, January 13, 1988.

277 an exhibition at halftime: Dan Bareiro, "Born-again Maravich Develops New Outlook," *Dallas Morning News*, January 13, 1985.

277 request of Collis Temple: Adams, "Maravich Still on Target with New Goals."
277 "With the older: George Vecsey, "Pistol Pete's Brief Show," *New York Times*, February 6, 1984.
277 "I'd like to play: Hochman, "Maravich Finally Content with Life after Basketball."
278 wanted to be a mailman: Ed Hinton, "Show Time's over for Pistol Pete Maravich," *Atlanta Journal-Constitution*, December 15, 1985.
278 for thirty-six hours: Twyman, "On the Scene: Pete Maravich Used to Be a Hot Dog, but Nowadays He Won't Even Eat One."
278 possible brain damage: Maravich and Campbell, 197.
279 "I had to believe,": Ibid., 198.
279 braces that finally came off: Letter from Press to the Bradleys, July 9, 1980.
279 an honor student: A. J. Carr, "Maravich Recalls Years at State," *Raleigh News and Observer*, June 14, 1981.
279 "A package deal,": Campbell University Basketball Yearbook, 1987–88, dedicated to Press Maravich.
279 sobbed with joy: Maravich and Campbell, 203.
280 "There's no way: Ibid., 205.
280 "I'm serious,": Ibid., 206–207.
280 "I became: Letter from Press to the Bradleys, February 26, 1986.
281 "Ronnie still lives: Ibid.
282 He contracted pneumonia: Maravich and Campbell, 217–218.
283 "Pete was basically: Kevin Thomas, " 'I Learned a Great Deal from Dad': Pete Maravich Credits His Father for Teaching Him about Basketball, Life," *St. Petersburg Times*, June 21, 1987.
284 "Then I realized,": Maravich and Campbell, 222.
284 Highland Park Hospital: AP, "Press Made Impact on Deep South," *Raleigh Times*, April 16, 1987.
284 "Daddy," he asked: Maravich and Campbell, 215.
285 "All that fancy stuff: Strother, "A Curtain Call for Pistol Pete."
286 "the winning of souls: Pete Maravich, prayer, NBA All-Star Chapel, from Pete Maravich funeral program, Jackie Maravich's papers.
287 "When you're told: Hinton, "Show Time's over for Pistol Pete Maravich."
288 *We have a weak nation:* "From the desk of Pete Maravich," Jackie Maravich personal papers.
288 "My instincts to drink: Quoted in Peter Finney Jr., "Pistol Pete's Death Shocks Hometown," *New York Post*, January 6, 1988.
288 "When I think": Thomas, " 'I Learned a Great Deal from Dad.' "
291 swallowing his tongue: Mark Di Ionno, "Pistol Died Playing the Game He Loved," *New York Post*, January 6, 1988.

Interviews: Jackie Maravich; Drollinger; Baylor; Carl Vondembussche, June 5, 2006; Hickman.

293   "How could a guy: Allan Parachini, "Maravich Victim of Very Rare Heart Defect," *Los Angeles Times*, January 12, 1988.

294   "Unsmiling, he gazed: Scott Ostler, "Pete Was Intense to the Very End," *Los Angeles Times*, January 6, 1988.

295   "I don't want to play: Andy Nuzzo, "Friends Remember a Legend," *Beaver County* (Pennsylvania) *Times*, January 6, 1988.

295   "I don't even remember: Harvey Araton, "The Pistol Was the Pied Piper of Hoop," *Daily News*, January 6, 1988.

295   "He performed tricks: Peter Vecsey, "Pistol: The Real Magic," *New York Post*, January 8, 1988.

295   "the crushing weight: "Pistol Pete and Somebody's Dream," *Chicago Tribune*, January 8, 1988.

295   "Basketball at one time: Marty Mule, " 'Pistol Pete' Laid to Rest as 'Amazing Grace' Plays," *Times-Picayune*, January 10, 1988.

297   Louisiana State Legislature: House Bill No. 443, Regular Session, 1988, on file at LSU.

297   His last will and testament: Succession of Peter Press Maravich, 22nd Judicial District, Parish of St. Tammany, Louisiana, Docket # 8830077.

297   "He could have played blind,": Bob Dylan, *Chronicles* (New York: Simon & Schuster, 2004), 168.

23. PATRIMONY

Interviews: Jaeson Maravich; James; Josh Maravich; McLachlan; Bob Weathers, June 14, 2006; Xavier Whipple, June 7, 2006; Antonio Hudson, June 14, 2006; Brian Green, June 5, 2006; Ed Singler (father of Kyle Singler, who was being recruited by Duke in the spring of 2006), June 9, 2006; Ron Naclerio (Rafer Alston's high school coach, who introduced him to the Maravich videos), August 8, 2005; Ed Tapscott (then President and CEO of the Charlotte Bobcats), June 16, 2005; Ronnie Maravich; Jukkola; Bott.

299   **Son of a gun:** Bruce Phillips, "Son of a Gun, Look at Jaeson," *Raleigh News and Observer*, January 5, 1988.

300   six consecutive twelve-hour days: Scott Ostler, "We Should Be Grateful for Gift of Pete Maravich's Time," *Los Angeles Times*, January 13, 1988.

300   devoted an entire page: "Pistol Pete Shootout," Louisiana Superdome, game program, October 17, 1988.

300   "Not so much a movie: David Neff, "Preaching Pete's American Dream," *Christianity Today*, March 11, 1991.

301   "That's me,": Tammy Leigh Cook, "No Comparisons," *Times-Picayune*, February 2, 1997.

301   "He thought he was supposed: Pete Thamel, "In the Name of His Father," *New York Times*, February 17, 2004.

303   "Dunk it.": Cook, "No Comparisons."

304 "If he was playing: Bud Shaw, "Maravich's Sons Fill Dad's 'Greatest' Role," *Cleveland Plain Dealer*, February 9, 1997.

304 endurance for practicing alone: Mike Christensen, "Jaeson Maravich: The Next Generation," *Clarion-Ledger* (Jackson, MS), January 30, 2000.

305 New Hampton's program: Bob Reinart, "He Has the Drive to Be as Hot as 'Pistol,' " *Boston Globe*, November 9, 1997.

310 turned away at the door: Bernard Fernandez, "Sitting Ducks," *Philadelphia Daily News*, March 19, 2001.

310 "There hasn't been *anybody*: Christensen, "Jaeson Maravich: The Next Generation."

310 turned down offers: Gary Laney, "Cowboys Draw Pistol's Son to Lake Charles," *American Press* (Lake Charles, LA) June 30, 2000.

311 He missed his dad: Quoted in Tom Weir, "Pistol Pete's Sons Find Their Own Comfort Zone," *USA Today*, February 13, 2003. Jaeson said, "A lot of people ask me why I'm quiet. I just miss my dad."

311 English cobbler-cum-missionary: *http://www.wmcarey.edu/carey/description.htm*.

312 "Kind of freaky,": Weir, "Pistol Pete's Sons Find Their Own Comfort Zone."

312 "Forty-one," he said: Ibid.

313 "It was as if: William Neikirk, "Sons of a Gunner," *Chicago Tribune*, January 21, 2004.

313 co-MVP: Fernandez, "Sitting Ducks."

313 the best of them: AP, "Youngest Maravich Son to Walk On at LSU," *The Advocate* (Baton Rouge), June 20, 2001.

313 "I certainly wasn't: Steve Wiseman, "Son of Pistol Pete Unfazed by Pressure," *The State* (Columbia, S.C.), March 15, 2003.

314 seven games that season: LSU Basketball Media Guide, 2004–05 (LSU).

314 standing ovation: Glenn Guilbeau, "Living Out a Dream—Pistol's Son Enjoys Playing in 'Dad's House,' " *The Advocate*, March 12, 2003.

315 the state's top athlete: Ted Lewis, "Maravich Tops State's Century List," *Times-Picayune*, July 18, 1999.

316 200,000 And1's: Alexander Wolff, "The Other Basketball," *Sports Illustrated*, June 13, 2005.

316 "He was so deceptive,": "Frame by Frame," *Inside Stuff*, June–July 2005.

317 "Jaeson isn't real interested: Thamel, "In the Name of His Father."

ACKNOWLEDGMENTS

An accounting of the many debts incurred in the writing of this book must begin with Jackie Maravich. I've seen photographs of her about the time Pete first caught a glimpse of her in a mirror behind the bar at Southdowns. With that image in mind, I find it something of a wonder that Pete didn't recognize the hand of God earlier in his life. Still, apart from Jackie's obvious charms and her capacity to instigate a belly laugh, her virtues exceed the usual if well-earned praise for Southern womanhood. When it comes to her family and the Maravich name, she is a ferocious protector. She trusted me not only with her story but with stories of the boys she raised so well.

Those boys are men now, and being men, their candor constitutes an act of courage. It is difficult enough to follow an outsized father, but living with the ghost of Pistol Pete has proven a relentlessly unforgiving task. I should mention that Jaeson let me win a game of horse. As for Josh, he kept calling, usually in the early morning hours. At first he had questions about his father and his grandfather. Then the questions gave way to something else, born of a compassionate instinct. He began calling just to make me laugh.

Barry Mendelson, representing the Maravich family, understood that a biography might advance the family's interests. But his motives were not mercenary so much as memorial. Pete's memory is dear to him, as he has become dear to me—for his generosity, his insight, and his good company, not to mention the extraordinary crawfish boils prepared by his wife, Sandi.

Sharon Danovich has cooperated on Maravich projects before

and was not at all eager to do so again. But I talked her into it, and have talked to her just about every day since. She speaks with great authority on the Serbian experience in Aliquippa, and led me to places I could not otherwise have gone, many of them intimate, personal histories in and around the J & L mill. What's more, she is the expert on all things Press. It was Press, she likes to say, who emancipated her father, George "Sudie" Danovich. I didn't meet her father, as he died 1982. But I know he would be immensely proud of Sharon.

Lazo Maravich allowed me to excavate the early parts of Press's life, the foundation of the Maravich myth. He is many things, all of them good. He is also the youngest nonagenarian I will ever have the pleasure of meeting.

That does not include his fellow ninety-something John Wooden, probably the greatest coach basketball has ever known. Our conversation—invaluable for its insight into Press's contradictions and conceptual brilliance—took place over the phone.

Just as Lazo helped me with Press as a young man, Les Robinson enabled me to comprehend Press as a coach—his love for the game and for his players. Their relationship was almost like father and son, though unencumbered by talent and ambition. Their bond wasn't blood, but the basketball gene.

That goes for Russ Bergman, too.

Bud Johnson helped me to grasp the peculiarly perilous family dynamic that made Pistol at such a price to Press and Helen.

As for Helen, despite all the pain she endured, I know it was her good fortune to have a friend like Louise Bradley, who spoke so well of her and misses her still.

Sam Allen, research librarian at the Carnegie Free Library in Beaver Falls, Pennsylvania, provided the same extraordinary service for this book as he did for my last. Keen and impossibly kind, he is an indefatigable investigator, able to make magic from brittle bits of aging microfilm.

I am beholden to more than a few librarians, libraries, and newspapers: Mary Elizabeth Colombo, Gloria Wanchock, Cindy Murphy, and Rebecca Fetzner at B. F. Jones Memorial Library; Dr. William Irion and Betty Conner of the Beaver County Research Center; Ronnie Cianci, a volunteer at the center who tracked down the 1929 photograph of Press in the Special Opportunity Group; Laura Harris, the extraordinarily bighearted director of information services at the *New York Post*; the staff of the East Baton Rouge Parish Library, who maintain excellent files on Pete Maravich and LSU; Ronnie Ramos, sports editor of the *Atlanta Journal Constitution*, and his assistant, Kim Cooper; Dr. David Turner and Wendy Cuningham at Davis & Elkins; Ellis Hodgin and Cathy Doig at D&E's Booth Library; Harold Forbes, associate curator at the West Virginia University Libraries; Tim Channel at West Virginia Wesleyan; the Humanities and Social Sciences Library of the New York Public Library; the Central Library of the Brooklyn Public Library; the Santa Monica Public Library; Faigi Rosenthal at the New York *Daily News*; Ruth Miles at the *Detroit Free Press*; the *Detroit News*; the *Pittsburgh Post-Gazette*; Theresa Guillen at the *Times-Picayune*; Gail Waite of the Carnegie Library of McKeesport; the McKeesport Historical Society; the John C. Heinz Pittsburgh Regional Historical Center; the Carnegie Library of Pittsburgh; Paul Jagnow, managing editor at the Youngstown *Vindicator*.

Through all of Pete's phases, there was one constant: his friendship with Bob Sandford. I was honored to have him share it with me.

Herb White is not merely "the dunkingest son of a bitch," as Dave DeBusschere once called him. He might also be the most solid.

The families of two old friends, both transplanted North Carolinians—Dr. John Perry of Greensboro and Chris Weiller of Charlotte—provided me with deluxe accommodations, moral support, and more than a few memorable evenings.

As this project began, George Roy provided me with two substantial boxes of research materials from the superb documentary he directed and produced, *Pistol Pete: The Life and Times of Pete Maravich*. Later, he granted me full run of his office and access to all the footage he had. This wasn't mere professional courtesy. These were acts of extraordinary generosity and friendship.

Thanks to all the guys who showed up when Billy Simmons organized a reunion for Press's LSU players, especially Dexter Bott, Tommy Hess, Danny Hester, Rich Hickman, Ralph Jukkola, Randy

Lamont, Paul Milanovich, Bill "Fig" Newton, Steve Shumaker, and Jeff Tribbett.

At Press's funeral, Pete pulled Les Robinson aside and told him that the Wolfpack team that won the 1965 ACC Champions was his father's favorite. It's easy to understand why. I thank those who worked with and played for Press at N.C. State: Eddie Biedenbach, Hal Blondeau, Charlie Bryant, Pete Coker, Lou Pucillo, and Frank Weedon.

The Sports Information Offices at Clemson, North Carolina State, and Louisiana State University (especially the sainted Miss Pat) provided unfettered access to their archives and files.

As it pertains to the Maravich myth, the writers who went before me left a lot to work with. I am particularly indebted to Curry Kirkpatrick, whose *Sports Illustrated* pieces informed America of the Pistol Pete phenomenon long before there was an ESPN; Phil Berger, author of *Forever Showtime*, whom I was fortunate to know from the boxing beat; Darrel Campbell, who co-wrote Pete's autobiography. Don't forget the newspapermen, either: Peter Finney, a gentleman and a columnist, who understood this story as soon as Press opened his mouth at his first press conference as coach of LSU; Paul Phillips; Jerry McLeese; Bill Ballenger; Dan Foster; Marty Mule; George Cunningham; Frank Hyland; Jim Huber; and the *Winston-Salem Journal*'s Joe Menzer, author of *Four Corners*. On this book, as with my last, I am taken with how well Larry Merchant's columns from the *New York Post* have aged.

Much appreciated are Brothers Broadway, Jimmy and Olin, not just for their memories, but for use of the scrapbooks, yearbooks, and photographs.

Boris Daich, a musician and devotee of Serbian song, found the melody with the "eyes of mine" lyric.

Father Rasko Kosich, pastor of Holy Trinity Church in Pittsburgh, located and translated the cemetery records of Press's siblings.

Ralph Drollinger, Gary Lydic, and Norman Moline were kind enough to share with me their remembrances of Pete's final game.

What I miss most about smoking is hanging out with the NBA's Brian McIntyre, a gifted conversationalist and one of the great gentlemen in the sports business.

ACKNOWLEDGMENTS

Shelly Schneider couldn't do much for my game, but he sure helped with this book, beginning with an introduction to John Guthrie, former associate commissioner of the Southeastern Conference.

Bill Bridges, Cleo Hill, Fred Hilton, Billy Packer, Woody Sauldsberry, and Harold Sylvester granted me an understanding of basketball's racial calculus in the 1960s.

In the autumn of 2005, as I began to write, I got a call from Adrian Wojnarowski, fresh from the success of *The Miracle of St. Anthony*. He was beginning to research a book on former North Carolina State coach Jim Valvano, and said he wanted a little guidance with his first foray into biography. As the months passed, however, it became clear that he was helping me a lot more than I was helping him.

Harvey Araton, whose fierce intelligence and good heart I have long admired, was kind enough to provide me with notes on the manuscript. Nobody knows more about the NBA, and how it became what it is, than Harvey.

For one night, before Katrina cursed New Orleans, I held the highest honor that city could bestow upon a visitor: Eddie Sapir had me as his guest.

Rob Fleder of *Sports Illustrated* was a source of expert advice and boundless encouragement.

Always there: Wallace Matthews and Joe Sexton.

Gratitude alphabetized: Dr. Rudy Antoncic; Joyce Bagwell; Gary Baronofsky; Basketball-reference.com; Elgin Baylor; Ann Bergman; Lucy Biega; Drew Breittholz; Jim Brennan; Joe Caldwell; Pete Carlisle; M. L. Carr; Joe Ceravolo; Ted Chizmar; Ed Coakley; Blossom Colley; Bobby Colomby; Scott Cooper; Tom Cousins; Mary Cribbs; Tad Dowd; Lefty Driesell; Bob Drury; Eddie Einhorn; Caryn Espo; Joe Favorito; Boots Garland; Gail Garrison; Joe Goldstein; Richie Guerin; Bill Hensley; Judith Hoover; Jimmy Howard and his regulars at the Sloane Street Tap Room; Antonio Hudson; Hot Rod Hundley; Dr. Billy Hunter; Dan Issel; Hank Kalb; Leonard Keller; Rich Kelley; Bob Kent; Helen Kosanovich; Sarah Kostal; Rick Kot; George Krajack; Bruce Kriegel; Nick Lackovich; Peter Lalich; Joe Lee; Dr. Richard Lippe; Sam Marchiano; Dvorah Markman; Lance Mayer; James "Jimbo" McLachlan; Ed McLean; Veda Milanovich;

Ken Moran; Chuck Mrazovich; Dusty Oates, athletic director at Daniel High School; Billy Packer; Peter Parcher; Paul Piccirilli; Joanna Port; Joe Pukach; Bob Raissman; Anita Siegman; Dick Single-ton; Guy Smith; Alec and Leslie Sokolow; Zelda Spoelstra; Jerry Steinberg; Pete and Pecky Suder; Peter Sullivan; Jim and Mary Sutherland (who filled my notebook *and* my belly); Ed Tapscott; Michael Thorsland, then the principal at Daniel High School; John Vassallo; Carl Vondembussche; Neal Walk; Bucky Waters; Xavier Whipple; Mary Williams; Pat Williams; Jennie Zakovich; Dr. Wallace Zernich.

David Vigliano, my agent and friend, came through bigger than ever.

At Free Press, I am deeply indebted to Martha Levin and Dominick Anfuso for the commitment they made. Also, thanks to Kirsa Rein, assistant to Martin Beiser. Marty did more than just edit this book. He possesses great faith, fine judgment, and intellectual rigor. But for meritorious service to this author alone, he deserves a medal for valor.

I don't know how I could have begun writing without extraordinary aid and comfort from Dan Klores, Alice McAlary, and Roger Tully.

Completion of the project would have been impossible but for my daughter, Holiday—more understanding than a kindergartener should have to be—and my parents, Leonard and Harriet Kriegel.

Across the years, Barry Weiss and I have maintained an undimin-ished ability to delight ourselves (and occasionally irritate others) with oddly hilarious basketball memories: the drafty gym at Gompers High School, E-Bird on angel dust, the legend of the White Jesus, and a kid called Chap on the tiled court at Our Lady of Pompeii, howling "Take me!"

At least now we know what he meant by that.

And now Bo should know how much his friendship has meant to me, and how much he gave to this book.

Finally, there is Jessica Queller, exquisitely feminine, as brave as she is beautiful, a writer and a muse. The inspiration she provided was abundant, her mercies tenderly applied. But what she gave had less to do with language than with love.

INDEX

ABOUT THE AUTHOR

Mark Kriegel, a former sports columnist for the *New York Daily News*, is the author of the critically acclaimed bestseller *Namath: A Biography*. He lives in Santa Monica, California, with his daughter, Holiday.